Coup d'État!

ALSO BY STANLEY J. MARKS

Nonfiction:

The Bear That Walks Like a Man. A Diplomatic and Military Analysis of Soviet Russia

Murder Most Foul! The Conspiracy That Murdered President Kennedy

Two Days of Infamy: November 22, 1963; September 28, 1964

Yes, Americans, A Conspiracy Murdered JFK!

Dramatic Works:

A Murder Most Foul; or, A Time to Die, A Time to Cry. ("A three-act play that reveals how a chief of state was assassinated.")

Coup d'État!

Three Murders That Changed the Course of History

President Kennedy, Reverend King, Senator R. F. Kennedy

With comments on the trials of Clay Shaw, Sirhan B. Sirhan, and James Earl Ray.

A true detective story with photographs, charts, and affidavits from the files of the FBI and U.S. Secret Service in the National Archives which reveal the prostitution of the "basic principles of American justice" as practiced by the Warren Commission.

"Since the dead cannot speak, should not the living?"

Stanley J. Marks

Edited with an Introduction
by Rob Couteau

DOMINANTSTAR

Dominantstar LLC, New York.

Coup d'État! Three Murders That Changed the Course of History. President Kennedy, Reverend King, Senator R. F. Kennedy Copyright © 1969 by Stanley J. Marks.

"Politics as (Un)usual: Stanley J. Marks and *Coup d'État!*" Copyright © 2021 by Rob Couteau.

All Rights Reserved. No part of this book may be reproduced or utilized in any form without written permission from the editor.

ISBN: 978-1-7360049-2-0

1 2 3 4 5 6 7 8 9 10 01

(Library Of Congress Catalog Card Number for the original, February 1969 edition: 75-111118.)

Special thanks to James DiEugenio, Jim Lampos, Bobbie Marks, Al Rossi, and Yongzhen Zhang for their help, support, and encouragement. And to Stanley Marks, for his enduring and unflagging courage.

Cover photo: President John F. Kennedy's Funeral Procession to St. Matthew's Cathedral. Abbie Rowe, November 25, 1963. John F. Kennedy Presidential Library and Museum, Boston.

TO

ETHEL (Butch)

and

ROBERTA (Corky)

Contents

Politics as (Un)usual: Stanley J. Marks and *Coup d'État!*
by Rob Couteau xi

Author's Preface: *J'Accuse* xli

PART ONE

The Ananias Club 12

The Fraudulent Autopsy or How to Lie in a Military Manner 24

Nonexisting Evidence: The Rifles, Palm Prints, and Photographs 44

The Nonexisting Paper Bag or How to Manufacture Evidence 63

"LSD"—Hallucinations and Charades 72

Whose Body? Tippit's? 88

PART TWO

The Guts of the Conspiracy 122

The Two Conspiracies in Operation 158

More Pieces of the Conspiracy 190

Three Trials: Clay Shaw, Sirhan B. Sirhan, James Earl Ray 209

A Short Reprise of the Evidence 243

Epilogue: Lt. Col. Finck Admitting Fraudulent Autopsy 254

Photographs and Affidavits 258

Bibliography 297

Index 305

Cover of the first paperback edition (1970)

POLITICS AS (UN)USUAL:
STANLEY J. MARKS AND *COUP D'ÉTAT!*

> "It is true that time cannot be reversed—that John F. Kennedy cannot be returned to life—but it is also true that no nation can continue to live a lie." Stanley Marks, *Coup d'État!*

In September 1967 Stanley Marks published his first book about the JFK assassination, *Murder Most Foul! The Conspiracy That Murdered President Kennedy: 975 Questions & Answers.* One of the things that makes it such an exceptional text for its time is that the author's political views regarding the events of November 22, 1963 remain far in advance of other contemporaneous authors. At the end of the book, in a chapter titled "The Rape of the American Conscience," Marks writes: "It can now be said that the American people do not believe anything stated in the 'Report.' Due to this lack of belief, a cynicism has now gathered among the citizenry that bodes ill for the nation. A nation whose moral fiber has been torn and shattered cannot long live; for when the nation's spirit is destroyed, no nation will live." Reflecting on this passage, author Jim DiEugenio adds that Marks sounded "a note that no other critic of that time voiced."[1]

"People, in all nations," Marks continues, "must stand for an ideal. The United States of America was not born on the idea that its President could be shot like a dog in the street and his murderers be 'shielded from this day on' because it would be 'against the national interests.' The Spirit has in this year of 1967 been replaced by cynicism of everything 'American.' […] How long, o how long, Americans, will we permit our silence to perpetuate the evil in the Warren Report?" (And in *Coup d'État!*, Marks plays with a variation on this theme by stating: "Not only did they deliberately conceal the conspiracy but they committed a rape of the American conscience. There can be no forgiving when that rape destroyed the soul of the nation.")

---

[1] "The Dylan / Kennedy Sensation," March 30, 2020, Kennedys and King web site.

The author adds that "many of the inactive and active participants of the conspiracy will be found in the ranks of the government and the economic strata of our nation." Thus, as early as 1967, Marks did not neglect to discuss the role of the ruling economic elite, which exists one level above the intelligence agencies and that utilizes the mass media to suit its ends, sell its products, and guarantee its remunerative investments in the war machine. This concept was rarely broached by assassination researchers other than Jim Garrison until Fletcher Prouty (the Pentagon's liaison officer to the CIA) published *The Secret Team* in 1972. In going that extra step of recognizing the deeper currents that remained invisible to so many other authors fifty-four years ago, Marks also lays much of the blame on the media, pointing to both their culpability and their infiltration by the CIA, as well as their subservience to the economic forces that rule the nation: "That the CIA controls many of the news columns in both the press and magazines is now known. What is not known, and what will never be known, is how many agents of the CIA now work for various organs in the mass communication media." How many people thinking about this in 1967?

In March 1969 Marks published his second assassination-related work of nonfiction: *Two Days of Infamy: November 22, 1963; September 28, 1964*. The second date refers to the day the Warren Commission (WC) released its report, a document Marks regards as "an out-and-out whitewash"[2] that "would wilt in the noonday sun."[3] Although *Two Days* is focused on the JFK case it does include some remarks about the deaths of Martin Luther King and Senator Robert Kennedy. In the opening paragraphs of the author's Introduction, he states: "All three were murdered as the end result of three interrelated conspiracies." Thus, Marks was one of the first American researchers to reach such a conclusion. And he adds: "The citizen's failure to understand law, in theory and practice, has permitted the mass communication media to thoroughly confuse the citizen's knowledge regarding the application of the

---

[2] *Two Days of Infamy* (New York: Dominantstar, 2020), p. xliii.
[3] *Murder Most Foul!* (New York: Dominantstar, 2020), p. 352.

law to those three murders."

Since Marks was himself a lawyer, his work on the assassinations is endowed with a special perspective. This is especially the case with *Coup d'État!*, much of which is devoted to unveiling the faulty evidence that would have made a successful prosecution in the case against Lee Oswald impossible in any court that adhered to the "basic principles of American justice." As Jim DiEugenio has pointed out, among the early notable researchers there were only two others who shared Marks' profession: Vincent Salandria and Mark Lane. In DiEugenio's essay, "Sylvia Meagher and Clay Shaw vs. Jim Garrison,"[4] he writes: "Salandria was one of the few early critics who was also a lawyer. In fact, in the early critical period of 1964-66, aside from Mark Lane, he may have been the only one. (They would later be joined by attorney Stanley Marks of Los Angeles.) This placed him in a position to not only understand more precisely what the Warren Commission had done with the evidence, but also to understand what Jim Garrison was up against when he began his criminal investigation in New Orleans." I believe we can look upon the work of Stanley Marks from a similar point of view, both as regards the special juridical insights he provides and the manner in which he presents his "case."

Along with Salandria, Lane, and Paris Flammonde, Marks was also one of the few who defended the work of District Attorney Garrison right from the beginning. Compare this to the record of Sylvia Meagher, who not only publically criticized Garrison; she also contributed financially to Clay Shaw's defense fund![5] Another prominent Warren Commission critic at the time, Harold Weisberg, claimed that Garrison didn't conduct any "real" investigating in New Orleans. Anthony Summers, author of *Conspiracy*, called the Garrison investigation "grotesque." Other well-known critics of the Commission such as Josiah Thompson and Peter Dale Scott

---

[4] See James DiEugenio, "Sylvia Meagher and Clay Shaw vs. Jim Garrison," Kennedys and King website, October 9, 2020.
[5] See also Meagher, *Accessories After the Fact* (Indianapolis: Bobbs-Merrill, 1967), pp. 456–457.

regarded Garrison as something of a clown, yet soon enough the joke would be on them. But as early as 1967, in *Murder Most Foul!* Marks compares Garrison to St. George fighting the latest incarnation of the dragon: The Establishment hiding behind the excuse of protecting the "national interest." This was precisely the sort of thing that would later lead DiEugenio to declare: "Marks was way ahead of the field. While people like Weisberg and Thompson were still counting bullets, he was calling JFK's death a coup d'état. That is the perspective he wrote from way back in the late Sixties." That Marks would, at this early date, unfashionably side with Garrison instead of joining with the likes of Paul Hoch, David Lifton, Sylvia Meagher, Peter Dale Scott, Anthony Summers, Josiah Thompson, Harold Weisberg, and other Warren Commission critics who turned against the D.A. and ridiculed his investigation speaks well of him and of his critical thinking. (And despite all that we've learned about the CIA's covert assistance to Clay Shaw during the Garrison investigation, and the documentation that proves Shaw was an Agency asset, Thompson's assessment of Garrison still hasn't changed much after all these years. In his 2021 publication, *Last Second in Dallas*, he continues to regard Garrison's investigation as a "circus," and he says that his case against Shaw "seemed preposterous.")

In *Coup d'État!*, which is subtitled *Three Murders That Changed the Course of History*, Marks broadens his focus to include an investigation into the deaths of Dr. King and Robert Kennedy. As the book's subtitle implies, the author was not a member of that neoliberal clan that regarded the deaths of these legendary leaders as merely passing events that had nothing to do with any larger systemic shift. Instead, he was always aware that the Sixties assassinations represented a macrocosmic, systemic change. In *Murder Most Foul!*, he writes:

> A conspiracy has been proven beyond a reasonable doubt. But what was the purpose of the conspiracy?
>
> History has shown that an invisible *coup d'état* occurred when President Kennedy was murdered. It is the belief of the author that more than the murder of a head of state was

involved. [...] The life of President Kennedy was only an incident to bring into operation the main purpose of the conspiracy. The conspiracy was a 4-pronged affair: (1) the murder of President Kennedy; (2) the invasion and overthrow of the Castro regime in Cuba with the installation of a right-wing dictatorship under the direct control of the CIA, which, in turn, is controlled by the fascist forces in the United States; (3) involvement with a war with the Soviet Union, but if that not be possible, a complete diplomatic break with the Soviet Union isolating that nation by the new government in the United States by exerting economic pressure upon NATO and nations receiving our foreign aid; and (4) a "coup d'état."

Marks exhibited an early and prescient awareness of what we now refer to as a macroanalysis of the case by linking the assassination to JFK's radical foreign policy initiatives and goals, which the business interests of The Establishment would not condone. In one of his later publications, *A Year in the Lives of the Damned!* (1988), he even calls Kennedy "a twentieth century radical."

His four nonfiction works on the assassination, coupled with two plays[6] that he authored on the same subject, can be read as

---

[6] In February 1968 Marks copyrighted his first play about the assassination: an eighty-one page manuscript titled "A Murder Most Foul; or, A Time to Die, A Time to Cry," which he describes as "a three-act play that reveals how a chief of state was assassinated." This was the first of several dramatic works penned by the author, all of them political in nature. As various copyright registrations attest to, he continued to fiddle with this particular play, revising and expanding it. By 1970 it was described as "A three-act play concerning the three murders that changed the course of history: President Kennedy, Martin Luther King, and Senator Robert F. Kennedy." In the spring of 2021 I was able to retrieve copies of the original 1968 play about the JFK assassination and the expanded 1979 version, the latter titled "A Time to Die, A Time to Cry, or, Murders Most Foul!". (A final version of the same play, since lost, was deposited in the Copyright Office in 1988.)

an interweaving sextet that chronicles the evolution and development of his thought. Sometimes the author tweaks certain elements of his analysis, especially when new evidence has emerged. But at other times the same view is extended, broadened, and further fleshed out in the manner of a musician rendering a variation on a theme. For example, in *Coup d'État!*, Marks again elaborates on how the assassination heralded a marked sea change that would alter the direction of the nation for decades:

> When the CIA accomplished its objective, that organization knew that the new power in Washington, President Johnson, would reverse the attempt of a detente between Cuba and the United States. To say that the murder of President Kennedy did not change the course of history is to deny the truth. Five days after the Dallas murder, President Johnson's favorite news columnist, William S. White, was to write that the new President would definitely increase this nation's war efforts—including the increment of many GIs—to militarily defeat the North Vietnamese. Mr. White, knowing his subject well, also wrote that the "conservatives [...] have less to fear, domestically, from Johnson than from any of the other Democratic candidates." The events from the day President Johnson took the oath of office until he retired to his Texas ranch bore out Mr. White's column which was published on November 27, 1963.

Marks concludes that "The conspiracy deliberately changed the course of world history."

In *Coup d'État!* the author continues his excoriation of the press and its role in the cover-up, which he first highlighted back in 1967:

> Many persons cannot understand the reason why the powerful newspapers and the ABC, CBS, and NBC television and radio chains have kept a constant drumbeat

against the critics of the Warren Commission. The reason is quite simple—when the president was murdered the power structure shifted both economically and politically. It would take a little time, but, since the Kennedy—Johnson philosophies were in basic conflict, the murder of the president gave power to the Johnson philosophy. A reading of history throughout the ages reveals the shifting sands of power. President Johnson and the martyred president were as far apart as today's "generation gap." Although history has shown that the old was disposed of by the young, the assassination proved the exception. Thus, the magnates of the mass communication system simply got on the bandwagon.

In the Preface to *Coup d'État!* Marks notes that although the Warren Commission Report was "unsupported by the evidence" its authors "knew, in their hearts, that it was in the 'interests of national security' to prove no conspiracy existed." Therefore, the purpose of the Commission was not to uncover the truth.[7] Such remarks led author Joachim Joesten to write in the May 1, 1972 edition of his mimeographed "Truth Letter" broadsheet: "To my knowledge, nobody but Jim Garrison (and an obscure West Coast writer named Stanley J. Marks) has ever endorsed before my unswerving contention that the murder of John F. Kennedy was nothing short of a camouflaged *coup d'état*."

As Marks points out in *Murder Most Foul!*, the lies of the Warren Commission would result in poisoning the collective national psyche with a toxic brew of cynicism and despair that lingers on to the present day. One may wonder how, in the years to come, Marks looked back upon his prophetic vision after this

---

[7] As author John Newman has it: "What is Dealey Plaza if not a psychological warfare operation against the American people, and the Warren Commission and all that?" Marks would have endorsed this view wholeheartedly. As quoted in Alan Dale and Malcolm Blunt, *The Devil is in the Details: Alan Dale with Malcolm Blunt on the Assassination of President Kennedy* (Independently published, 2020), chapter five (e-book version).

cynicism continued to spread and infect the body politic. In *Two Days of Infamy* he returns to this subject when he writes: "Perhaps it was the cynicism, inherent in citizens of all nations, that convinced the American citizenry that the 'Report' issued by the Warren Commission was supported by rotten timbers incapable of supporting the truth. The suspicion increased in the same ratio and in the same speed as smog increased with the density of automobiles on a Los Angeles freeway." And in *Coup d'État!* he adds that the Commission's misdeeds led to the public's "erosion of faith" in government institutions.

But the answer to this question may also be found in a document composed about a dozen years after *Murder Most Foul!*, in the October 1979 version of his play about the assassinations: "A Time to Die, A Time to Cry, or, Murders Most Foul!" In a scene that involves a trio of fictional assassins—"Ramal," his brother "Noslen," and their father, "King"—Ramal remarks: "The country is out of kilter. Nobody trusts anyone. Something's cooking. I can't see what's in the pot." After some back and forth between Ramal and his father, King asks: "Have you already forgotten why we had the Kennedys killed?" He goes on to say that the Kennedys, Malcolm X, and Martin Luther King were "killed for the sole purpose of putting our kind of people in power. People who are exercising that power on our behalf." To this Ramal replies, "But was it worth it? Look at our country today. Faith has been destroyed in the governing process. Look at the price, Father." The other brother, Noslen, concludes: "I guess this lack of trust started when the Warren Commission whitewashed the whole thing."

In this same play, Marks is unequivocal in his assessment of Allen Dulles' role in the conspiracy:

> KING: Our late, to me, unlamented president failed to have his own men, the king's men if you please, control the police power of the state. The leaders and middle management executives of the FBI, the CIA, hated him personally. A leader who permits his enemies to control that police power is not a leader, but a fool.

RAMEL: Kennedy was a fool. After the Bay of Pigs, a leader would have known he was betrayed. He would have dismissed every one of these leaders, from top to bottom. Dulles marked him for death when he resigned.

NOSLEN: What will Johnson do?

KING: Nothing. Mark my words, he will appoint Hoover to investigate an agency that was itself involved. He knows the CIA was involved, so the CIA and the FBI will protect each other. The committee appointed by the new president will blame Lee.

While Marks was composing *Coup d'État!* in the late Sixties, a wave of government-sponsored disinformation on the assassination was cresting. Marks fell prey to a few of these red herrings along the way, as did many of the early researchers; although he seems to have dropped most of these fruitless detours by the time he published his fourth and final JFK assassination title, *Yes, Americans, A Conspiracy Murdered JFK!* (1992). Nonetheless, an examination of these missteps helps us to understand how research was unfolding during this period and how various authors attempted to grapple with the missing pieces of a vast and enigmatic puzzle that was rendered even more confusing by the production of such clever lies. In the annotated footnotes that I've included in the new edition of *Coup d'État*, I've attempted to provide some additional context for such false leads, chief among them being the idea that Jack Ruby was somehow involved in a plot to kill Governor Connally. But the ability to exercise the wisdom of hindsight comes only as a result of almost sixty years of additional work conducted by so many devoted, indefatigable scholars who followed in the footsteps of the first generation of assassination researchers.

Besides being versed in the history of military science and warfare,[8] Marks received a broad cultural education that

---

[8] Marks was the author of a 1943 bestseller, *The Bear That Walks Like a Man: A Diplomatic and Military Analysis of Soviet Russia*. The

included an exposure to classical literature and philosophy (the latter developing into a lifelong study). His work is often peppered with quotations from a wide variety of sources that reflect an eclectic, voracious reading habit. For example, in *Coup d'État!*, he writes:

> When the French people were under the heel of the Nazis—who were also great believers in "law and order"—a famous French poet of the Resistance, Jean Tardieu, wrote for an underground newspaper:
>
> > Puisque les morts ne peuvent plus se taire,
> > est-ce aux vivants à garder leur silence?
>
> "Since the dead can no longer be silenced, Are the living entitled to keep their mouths shut?"

At first glance Marks appears to be taking certain liberties with the translation of this phrase, borrowed from Jean Tardieu's poem "Vacances." The verse is also reproduced on the title pages of *Coup d'État!* and *Two Days of Infamy*, where it's rendered as: "Since the dead cannot speak, should not the living?" With variations on the translation, it appears on several pages in the main body of text in both these works. However, the identity of the poet is not revealed until the publication of *Coup d'État!*

U.S. Army also commissioned him to write a 750-page tome, "History of the U.S. Army and Military Science." Both of these works were completed thanks to the assistance of FDR's Secretary of State, Cordell Hull, who granted the young author access to State Department files. Marks' book on Russia received positive reviews in over thirty mainstream publications, including one penned by John Cudahy for the *Chicago Tribune*. Cudahy had served as FDR's ambassador to Poland and Belgium, and as minister to Luxembourg and the Irish Free State. Because Marks expressed positive views about Russia—our ally during World War Two—in 1944 he was blacklisted by the House Un-American Activities Committee.

Literally translated, the verse would read: "Since the dead can no longer be silent, is it up to the living to keep their silence?" This appears to be a somewhat paradoxical line until we realize that Tardieu is referring to French Resistance prisoners who courageously maintained their silence and refused to denounce their comrades or surrender information even while suffering horrendous torture at the hands of the Nazis. After they are executed they "can no longer be silent." But for those of us who haven't been imprisoned and have always enjoyed our freedom, maintaining silence in the face of such atrocities would be both immoral and cowardly. Hence, we have an obligation to speak out on behalf of those who have perished: to give to voice to and to preserve their ideals. Thus, Tardieu poses the question: "Is it up to the living to keep their silence?"

The title of Tardieu's poem might best be translated as "Vacancies," which refers to the vacant posts of the executed Resistance members that can only be filled by those willing to struggle for freedom. Given this broader context, Marks' translation remains faithful to the spirit of the poem. But more importantly, by invoking Tardieu, he places the assassination researchers in the role of Resistance fighters who must continue to battle for the emergence of truth. Marks reminds us that we have a moral obligation to speak for those—such as John Kennedy—who lost their lives in a clandestine global war waged against the left during the decades following World War II.

* * *

Marks begins his Preface to *Coup d'État!* by noting that seventy-five years have passed since the Dreyfus Affair first rocked the French Republic. "The upholders of the Warren Commission's conclusion that 'Oswald was the sole assassin of President Kennedy' rely one hundred percent upon the 'prestige' of the commissioners. So did many Frenchmen in the Dreyfus Affaire!" Thus, in the opening salvo of this text, Marks is positioning himself right beside Bertrand Russell: one of the first Warren Commission (WC) critics to note this parallel. In his September 1964 essay, "16 Questions on the

Assassination," Russell writes: "In the name of national security ... the Commission's hearings were held in secret, thereby continuing the policy which has marked the entire course of the case. This prompts my second question: If, as we are told, Oswald was the lone assassin, where is the issue of national security? Indeed, precisely the same question must be put here as was posed in France during the Dreyfus case: If the Government is so certain of its case, why has it conducted all its inquiries in the strictest secrecy?"

Mark Lane also spoke about the Dreyfus Affair in a debate on the Kennedy assassination held at Beverly Hills High School on December 4, 1964. Located less than four and a half miles from Stanley's apartment on Laurel Avenue, it's quite likely that Stanley was seated in the audience. And author Joachim Joesten, in a book that also appeared in 1964, wrote that "If no more than half of the facts, testimony, and speculations in this book [*Oswald: Assassin or Fall Guy?*] are true, the Oswald Case is America's Dreyfus Case. The Dreyfus Case changed French history.... The consequences for the American society of the breaking open of the Oswald Case would also change American history, and since the United States is one of the two superpowers, it would change world history." (Stanley Marks was well acquainted with the work of Joesten and cites his book in *Murder Most Foul!*)

But Marks mentions Dreyfus for another reason as well: By establishing this historical context, it allows him to end many of his chapters with the exclamatory phrase: "J'accuse!"—echoing Émile Zola's letter to the president of the French Republic in defense of Alfred Dreyfus.

He follows this with a passage that underscores the connection between the assassination and JFK's foreign policy: "The reasons for his murder can be traced to his conduct of his internal and external program. His ideas for a Test Ban on the use of atomic weapons, his groping and initial steps toward Red China, his attempt to secure a détente with the Soviet Union, and even his seemingly slight step to bring some small normalization between Cuba and the United States met with tremendous opposition. Opposition came not from the great majority of the people but from the military, economic, and fascist groups."

How many researchers during this period even *thought* about JFK's China policy? But the author was not making this up out of whole cloth. In a 1969 interview, Roger Hilsman, an adviser to President Kennedy, confirmed that as far back as 1961 the president had informed him that he wanted to move toward a diplomatic recognition of Red China.[9]

By opening *Coup d'État!* on such a note, Marks is again signaling his focus on a "bigger picture" perspective. He goes on to say the "prime function of the Warren Commission was to protect the transfer of power from President Kennedy's philosophy to those diametrically opposed. The Commission was to 'cover-up' the conspiracy, and the Commission was to succeed beyond its fondest hope." The result, he says, was nothing less than "a falsification of history." Once again displaying an acute political awareness of the case, he adds: "The primary reason why the Warren Commission must be exposed is due to the political axioms they enunciated. A future president of the United States may be assassinated where friends of the vice president believe the president does not favor their philosophy and the assassinators believe the vice president may be amenable to their philosophy."

As I mentioned earlier, *Coup d'État!* enables us to envision the case through the eyes of an attorney. With this in mind, the author highlights how the evidence submitted to the WC clearly revealed that the president was murdered as the result of a conspiracy. "Whether Oswald was a part of the conspiracy cannot be ascertained," he says, but "under the 'basic principles of American justice' if a person enters into a conspiracy to commit murder, and the murder is committed, then the degree of the participation is of no consequence—that person is guilty of the full penalty. If, however, a person takes some action of which he has no knowledge that his action is part of a conspiracy, he cannot be guilty of any crime. There is evidence

---

[9] See Hilsman's interview with Paige E. Mulhollan on May 15, 1969. Their talk is archived courtesy of the National Archives and Records Service.

that Oswald was used as a 'patsy'; that he executed a part of the conspiracy but he had no knowledge of what was to occur. Since the Commission unequivocally stated that no conspiracy existed, and since the evidence proved beyond a reasonable doubt that Oswald was not involved in the murder, he was not guilty of any murder." But instead of serving to uncover the truth in a fair and unbiased fashion, the actual purpose of the Commission was to "fabricate a 'Report' by selecting words from affidavits or documents which would enable the Commission to say that 'Oswald was the sole and only assassin of President Kennedy.'"

Note the phrase: "by selecting words." Time and again, Attorney Marks shows us that it was never solid evidence that was used to build a case against Oswald. Instead, it was the careful selection of words—often pried out of context, or obtained illegally by threatening and intimidating witnesses—that cemented the case against him. Crucial testimony that flew in the face of the Commission's official story was simply ignored—whether it originated in witness affidavits or in reports issued by the FBI or Secret Service. In a later chapter he adds: "An analysis of the 'Hearings' always revealed that where the testimony of the police, the FBI, or the Secret Service conflicted, the Commission always published that testimony which supported its theory." Through his diligent reading of the WC Hearings, Marks was aware that numerous "'off the record' hearings were made by the aides, and many of those 'off the record' hearings permitted the aides to conceal the actual evidence that proved a conspiracy."

At the end of the Preface he reminds us that the crime committed by the seven commissioners and by their numerous aides was also a "moral crime"; for "by their concealment of the conspiracy the conspirators were permitted to erode the public's faith in their government, for it is now permissible to assassinate elected leaders to obtain a change in the policies of the murdered leader." Therefore, it's fitting that Marks titles chapter one of this work, "The Ananias Club."

Ananias is a New Testament figure who instantly perishes

(from divine retribution) after he tells a lie to the apostle Peter.[10] At the turn of the century, "The Ananias Club" was a euphemism created by journalists to refer to figures that President Theodore Roosevelt accused of dishonesty. "Thus," says Marks, now employing the same polemical skills that endow *Murder Most Foul!* with such a unique tone, "the question arises whether seven men can give authorship of a single lie. That lie, in history, is known as the 'Warren Report.' However, although Ananias was one, the Commission comprised seven men that concocted a single lie that 'Oswald was the sole assassin of President Kennedy.'" Again returning to the attorney's legal framework, Marks concludes that "the failure of the American people to understand the principles of law governing the nation permitted the Warren Commission to practice deceit, deception, and duplicity."

In a chapter titled "The Nonexisting Paper Bag, or How to Manufacture Evidence," the author examines the principal "conclusions" of the WC Report, comprised of "eight specific accusations which, in turn, were supported by nineteen additional allegations." Marks then proceeds to demolish the basis for each of these eight points, which are quoted from the Report in full. For example, the Commission reports that "Lee Harvey Oswald (1) owned and possessed the rifle used to kill President Kennedy and wound Governor Connally; (2) brought this rifle into the Book Depository building on the morning of the assassination; (3) was present at the time of the assassination, at the window from which the shots were fired." By way of a reply, Marks focuses on an issue first raised by Leo Sauvage in his 1966 publication, *The Oswald Affair*; namely, the distinction between *owning* a weapon and *using* it to kill someone.

Marks regards this passage as "the most fascinating [one]

---

[10] As Marks' later publications reveal, throughout his life he was deeply immersed in biblical studies and the history of religion. His 1972 text *Through Distorted Mirrors! The Impact of Monotheism—One God–Upon Modern World Civilization* received an endorsement from the German-American philosopher Herbert Marcuse and the British historian Arnold Toynbee.

written by the Commission. Nowhere in that paragraph does the Commission categorically state that Lee Harvey Oswald was the assassin! In (1) Oswald only 'owned and possessed' the rifle but the Commission refused to say that Oswald used that rifle. In (2) and (3) the Commission alleged Oswald brought the rifle into the building and was present at the window from where they alleged the bullets were discharged. Again, the Commission refused to state that Oswald used the rifle, or that he was the rifleman when the shots rang out." In a later chapter, "Nonexisting Evidence: The Rifles, Palm Prints, and Photographs," he adds: "The palm print also denotes no crime, for any man may disassemble a rifle without using it for a crime."

Marks is convinced that by portraying Oswald as a psychotic killer the Commission helped to absolve the Dallas police of "being implicated in the Tippit murder and the Kennedy conspiracy itself." He tracks the involvement of the police before, during, and after the assassination, and he shows how the Commission continued to accept "deliberate perjury committed by members of that department." One of the key pieces of such perjury was, as Mark Lane first discovered, the "overwhelming evidence that the Dallas police 'switched' rifles from the 7.65 German Mauser found on the 6th floor to a 6.5 nonlethal, nonoperating Italian Mannlicher-Carcano rifle." While Josiah Thompson accepted police officer Weitzman's word that the initial identification of the Mauser was simply an "honest mistake" (*Six Seconds*, pp. 220-21), Marks examines the photos of police displaying several different types of rifles that were offered as initial evidence, and he comes to a markedly different conclusion: "The Warren Commission deliberately and willfully lied, for they knew that the evidence proved the Dallas police had substituted several rifles for the 7.65mm German Mauser rifle found on the 6th floor. To protect whom?" Marks reminds us that it wasn't just Weitzman who initially identified the rifle as a Mauser; the German Mauser was also seen by Deputies Boone and Mooney, Lieutenant Day, and Captain Fritz. The photos also reveal two completely different Mannlicher-Carcano rifles, each bearing clearly identifiable details that prove they were not the same weapon.

that turned up each had different characteristics. (Hence, chapter three of *Murder Most Foul!* is titled, "Rifles, Rifles Everywhere.") Marks concludes *Coup d'État!*'s "Nonexisting Evidence" chapter by stating: "Manufactured evidence and perjury cannot be used 'under the basic principles of American justice' to convict a man accused of murder."

Resorting to his piquant polemical wit, he then titles the next chapter "LSD"—Hallucinations and Charades," for "the Commission's imagination, based on Oswald's fingerprints being found on two cartons, must have been induced by the Commission's use of 'LSD'—figuratively speaking." And he again reminds us that the use of words "cannot substitute for that of evidence secured under oath in a law court." For the researcher exercising his due diligence, this false narrative penned by the Commission was effectively "swept away by the testimony of its own witnesses. And even worse, by invoking phrases such as 'national security' and 'in the national interest,' the Commission deluded and deceived the people from whom they had accepted an 'obligation of honor.'"

From the very inception of his interest in the JFK affair, Marks remained highly suspicious of the Commission's conclusion that Oswald had murdered Tippit. For example, in *Murder Most Foul!* he asks: "Why do police departments all over the world consider the Tippit murder case a 'mystery within a mystery'? For the exciting reason that the number of shots do not match the number of bullets in the body; and the number of shells found beside the body; and the fact that there are *either more bullet holes than bullets extracted from the body or more bullets and less holes!*" In a later series of Q&As featured in *Murder Most Foul!* he resorts to rhetorical device as he wonders how many Tippits there really are:

> 923. Is Officer Tippit legally dead? In view of the testimony, who knows? From a legal standpoint, the Warren Commission has yet to prove he is dead; someone in the Dallas Police Department had some explaining to do. Three bodies are involved: (1) One body has three bullets in the chest, and one in the head. (2) One body had a .38 caliber bullet hole in its stomach. (3) One body has

two holes in his chest and one in the head.
    924. Is there a fourth "Tippit" body? There is! Way, way, down deep in the "Hearings" is a statement by Detective J. Leavelle that Tippit "was shot three times: one time each in the hand, chest, and stomach." Now, a hand wound appears. [...] This is the fourth "body."
    925. Who is perjuring himself? Who knows? The Commission made sure it did not find out.

He further develops this rhetorical device in *Coup d'État!*'s chapter VI, which is titled: "Whose Body? Tippit's?" where he writes: "Everyone knows that where a person is accused of murdering one person, then the body of that person is sufficient. However, in the Tippit murder, the Warren Commission calmly used five different bodies to prove that there existed one Tippit body. Under the 'basic principles of American justice' no court would permit the prosecution to simply go to the police morgue and select any body waiting for identification and burial. As the testimony showed, that is exactly what the Dallas police and the Warren Commission did." All this leads Marks to conclude: "True, officer Tippit is dead—but how he died, legally, no one knows." He adds that the Commission "would 'pin' Tippit's murder upon Lee Harvey Oswald if they had to use every body in the Dallas police morgue." When remarking upon the Commission's attempt to fudge Tippit's actual time of death, Marks again approaches this with the eye of an attorney by observing that just as hardened criminals are known to utilize the same modus operandi, the Commission "was no exception, since it adopted the identical pattern when the Commission determined the time of the president's murder by moving the clock ahead, from 12:25 p.m. to 12:30 p.m. In that murder they used five minutes, in the Tippit murder 10 minutes."

In Part Two of *Coup d'État!* the author increasingly shifts his focus to the bigger picture perspective of the case, and he does so by setting it within a proper historical framework:

Many persons believe that only the so-called criminal elements would commit murder through a conspiracy. But history has revealed that it is not the criminal elements that do the conspiring to eliminate the leaders of a nation. The mainspring of any conspiracy, as shown throughout the ages, has always been the "honorable" men. The men who threw the knife, the bomb, or pulled the trigger have always been backed by "honorable" men. The five attempts on the life of General De Gaulle have been the result of conspiracies organized by "honorable men," but the men who did the actual "dirty" work were not from the ranks of those persons of "honor." Caesar was not murdered by the "criminal class."

"Honorable" men planned, organized, and paid for the murder President Kennedy.

One of the most prominent of these "men of honor" was Allen Dulles, and Marks doesn't hesitate to lambaste the former CIA director with a scathing cross-examination riddled with scorn. In 1966 Dulles had the temerity to state that the WC critics should "name names and produce their evidence." Marks responds to this by saying "it was not the critics of the Commission that accepted perjury, manufactured evidence, and planted evidence. Nor did any citizen assist in writing the 'Report' that was contradicted by the testimony in the 'Hearings.' Nor did any citizen suppress affidavits, documents, and letters from the FBI that proved Oswald innocent and, with that proof, revealed a conspiracy."

Another seemingly "respectable" figure associated with yet another intelligence agency was Ruth Hyde Paine, the "helpful" Quaker lady who "kindly" assisted Lee Oswald in obtaining his Texas School Book Depository job, although she kept Lee in the dark about another employment opportunity that would have paid a much higher salary. In his earlier works Marks pegs Paine as an FBI informer; in the present volume he limns her portrait with an illuminating commentary: "If ever a person made a mockery of the words 'friend' and 'friendship,'" he says, "Mrs. Ruth Paine would head the list." (Here Marks is making a sly reference to the fact that Quakers, also known as "Friends," are part of a Protestant set of denominations known as the Religious Society of Friends.) "Her activities were carefully researched by the Commission so that her testimony would reveal as little as possible. Through dribs and drabs of testimony came a picture of Mrs. Paine that was a little nauseating to the soul. She set up Oswald to be the perfect 'patsy,' and she was as friendly to Oswald as another Judas who kissed his friend. Both kisses were to lead to death."[11]

Yet Ruth and her husband Michael (who, upon hearing of Oswald's arrest, cryptically declared to a fellow employee: "He is not even supposed to have a gun") were merely two figures among many that steered this young patsy to Hades. Marks regards Oswald as "A young man of 24 involved in a matter far over his head. A man selected to enact the role of a 'patsy,' but when he was engaged to play that role the producer failed to inform him that the final scene was to be enacted on a dirty, damp, oil-stained floor in a police station basement with the spotlight slowly being dimmed on his own red blood gushing out of a wound given to him by a fellow conspirator."

Marks also zeros in on Dulles' former employer, the CIA (which he regards as "the fourth arm of the federal government") and on its deeply strained relationship with President Kennedy. As he does in his play about the Sixties assassinations and in works such as *Yes, Americans, A Conspiracy Murdered JFK!*," here in *Coup d'État!* Marks expounds upon his view that Kennedy made a major blunder in allowing some of his staunchest enemies to remain in place. "President Kennedy's failure to remove the operating heads of that organization would be one of the causes of his assassination." In this context, he also cites George Washington's farewell address: 'Let there be no change by usurpation; for though this, in one instance, may be an instrument of good, it is the customary weapon by which free governments are destroyed.'" And in a chilling piece of prose that again reflects the author's awareness of the deeper political

---

[11] Ruth would later offer more of her generous "help" while working with Quakers in Nicaragua in the 1980s, during the reign of the left-wing Sandinista government. Once again, she fell under suspicion when she began to poke her nose into the affairs of American volunteers who had traveled to Nicaragua to offer their assistance to the impoverished citizens.

implications of the case, he concludes: "The gods that were the CIA were not going to permit any mere U.S. president to 'break the CIA into little pieces'—not if the gods could prevent it. And the gods did prevent the making of little pieces with the final result being enacted when pieces of the president's skull went hurtling to the dirty street […] The Bay of Pigs and President Kennedy's threat to break the CIA into small pieces was the initial starting point of a slow-burning fuse that led to a keg of dynamite blowing up in Dallas, Texas." And he concludes: "One should not forget that, in the modern world of politics, the phrase 'to protect the national security' has now been broadened to mean those persons whom the CIA interprets to be 'internal' as well as external enemies."

This was also the operating philosophy behind the clandestine global war on the left that commenced after the end of the Second World War. In support of this view, Marks cites Garrison's 1967 *Playboy* interview, which Marks says "should dispel any naive idea that the CIA is under the direct command of the president of the United States, or the National Security Council, or the Senate Committee that is supposed to oversee and control that agency's activities. The CIA does what it wants and controls the methods of accomplishing its objectives."

What Marks could not have been privy to at the time is certain information contained in recently declassified documents that illustrate the profound depth of hostility and rancor that had spread against Kennedy throughout the upper echelons of the entire military industrial complex. That is to say, the *depth* was matched the *breadth* of this movement against him. Therefore, it was indeed a *camouflaged* coup d'état that irrevocably altered the future course of American history. Thanks to the release of such documents and their analysis by researchers such as Malcolm Blunt, Alan Dale, and John Newman, we are only now seeing the tip of a vast iceberg that was headed directly toward the good ship Kennedy. And clearly, it was one that remained far too large for any one man to stop. And while a figure such as Charles de Gaulle had assembled a vast organization of support over the years—one that included military and intelligence personnel who did not hesitate to confront the terrorism aimed at De Gaulle with their own form of terrorism launched with equal ferocity at the opposition—the ranks of the New Frontiersman were, by comparison, merely a fledgling group that would soon be cast aside and exiled from government. Or, in the case of the president's brother, be summarily executed. (De Gaulle survived thirty-one documented assassination attempts.)[12]

The penultimate chapter of *Coup d'État!* is devoted to the Clay Shaw trial and the trials of Sirhan Sirhan and James Earl Ray. The author's acute awareness of the CIA's role in the JFK assassination allowed him to correctly assess the Agency's hand in propping up Shaw's defense against Jim Garrison. It also led to his immediate suspicion that the Agency was behind the other assassinations launched against Dr. King and Senator Kennedy. Though so much more has come to light regarding all these affairs since the February 1970 publication of *Coup d'État!*, it's rewarding to study how Marks viewed these cases and assessed the modus operandi that repeated itself from one

---

[12] As I mention in my essay "NATO's Secret Armies, Operation Gladio, and JFK" (see Kennedys and King web site, July 15, 2019), De Gaulle was targeted by members of the CIA-sponsored Gladio network: a fact acknowledged by the French chief of the secret services (DGSE), Admiral Pierre Lacoste, in 1990. But unlike President Kennedy, De Gaulle was protected by an extensive network of loyal military and secret service personnel that were willing to engage in "unorthodox" operations to avenge their president and war hero. This included former members of the Service d'Action Civique, a veritable Gaullist praetorian guard; and loyalists in the Service de Documentation Extérieure et de Contre-Espionnage (SDECE). After the failed Generals' Putsch of April 21-26, 1961, De Gaulle's SDECE operatives were said to have placed bombs in Algerian cafes frequented by the same Gladio/OAS members (Organisation Armée Secrète) who had tried to snuff De Gaulle—and blew them to smithereens. As David Talbot remarks in *The Devil's Chessboard*, "The old general was willing to fight with equal ferocity" (p. 423). And in his book *NATO's Secret Armies*, Danielle Ganser writes: "Like few others, Charles de Gaulle had been at the center of secret warfare in France for most of his lifetime" (p. 78). During the attempted coup, President de Gaulle called directly upon *les françaises*—the ordinary French citizens—to help rally against these seditious threats.

murder to the next.

The author sums up his view on what was happening behind the scenes of the Shaw trial when he notes that "Never has a defendant in any crime been so ably defended by the full power of the federal government—from the Attorney General of the United States, Mr. Ramsey Clark, to a half dozen governors of various states. Not only was the Department of Justice used to defend Shaw, but the Central Intelligence Agency was thrown into the battle on his behalf." Indeed, Garrison was unable to obtain the extradition of key witnesses who had flown the coop to seek refuge beyond the state boundary line of Louisiana; and the governors of those respective states were strong-armed into refusing to agree to their extradition. Marks adds that "After long and arduous research of available legal records, this author could find no proceeding for extradition being dismissed by the governor of the state where the wanted person had been indicted by a grand jury for a felony and the governor had refused to grant extradition." It was only in the decades following the trial and the publication of *Coup d'État!* that we have absolute confirmation that what Garrison and Marks had suspected was undeniably true: the Agency went full hog in its attempt to assist Shaw because he was one of their own.

Compared to what we know with certainty today, there was relatively little that was known for sure about the MLK and RFK assassinations in early 1970. Marks' chapter on these affairs offers no stunning new revelations but instead should be viewed as an historical document that illustrates how an attorney versed in all the current assassination literature came to grapple with an understanding of such interrelated affairs. One way he does so is to study the patterns that unfold and reoccur from one assassination to the next. And so, in the opening of this "Three Trials" chapter, the author remarks upon the fact that all three assassination patsies—Oswald, Sirhan, and Ray—although ostensibly living on subsistence wages, took it upon themselves to travel around like men born into a different class:

> The outstanding characteristic of Lee Harvey Oswald, Sirhan B. Sirhan, and James Earl Ray is the fact that all

three of them, although of very poor families and earning very poor wages, could travel around the country with no visible funds. Who gave Oswald the money to travel from New Orleans, to Dallas, to Los Angeles, to Mexico, and everywhere he wanted to go? How did James Earl Ray obtain the various sums of money to travel around the United States, secure a fake passport, go to London, then Portugal, and then back to London? He was supposed to have left a trail of robberies but, for some strange reason, the FBI was never able to catch up to that trail. Of course, there also seemed to be no witnesses who identified Ray as the robber. As to Sirhan B. Sirhan, he also seemed to travel.

The section devoted to the RFK murder is fittingly titled: "The Trial of Sirhan B. Sirhan, or .... How an 8-Bullet Gun Can Fire 10 to 14 Bullets without Reloading," thus highlighting what is still the most telling piece of evidence that Senator Kennedy was felled by a conspiracy and not by Sirhan Sirhan. LA County Chief Medical Examiner Thomas Noguchi's official autopsy report also supports this view, since it states that RFK's fatal head shot was fired from a gun held within three inches of Kennedy's right ear, and from behind him, even though Sirhan was standing several feet in front of Senator Kennedy. In Noguchi's memoir, *Coroner*, Noguchi boldly states: "Tracks of twelve bullets were found at the scene, and Sirhan's gun contained only eight."

Marks also discusses some of the glaring parallels between the JFK and MLK assassinations. To cite just a few: "(1) A rifle is conveniently dropped at the ambush site [of the MLK assassination] in spite of the fact that the killer had sufficient time to run out of the boarding house and drive away in an automobile after first opening the trunk of the car to throw in some clothes. (2) The rifle is quickly traced to the 'killer,' an alleged hardened killer who left his fingerprints all over the murder weapon. (3) The 'killer' conveniently leaves his clothes, which are traced to him; but, as in the Tippit murder, where the police 'found' a jacket belonging to Tippit's killer which they say belonged to Oswald although it contained a laundry mark that could not be traced to him, the clothes did not fit the King murderer. Nor did the jacket fit Oswald." Thus, besides utilizing an in-depth knowledge of the law and of legal procedures, Marks shows us that, often, a good lawyer's best friend is that rare commodity known as "common sense." He concludes that, as a result of the assassinations, "the United States of America has now taken the path of dictatorship."

In the final chapter of the book, "A Short Reprise of the Evidence," the author features a statement, or rather a prophecy, that came terribly close to fulfillment during the years of the Trump presidency:

> The responsibility for the "success" of the Warren Commission and its "Report" must rest solely upon the mass communication media, which went out of its way to protect the duplicity, deceit, and deception practiced by the Commission upon the American citizen. Why the "lords" of the press decided to uphold such fraud can only be answered by them…. Whatever the reason, the "lords" acquiesced in the "Report" and, in the long run, the "lords" and their "peasant" readers will pay the price with the gradual erosion of freedom of the press. The rise of fascism in the United States is proceeding on the same ground, and in the same manner, that the press lords of Germany paved the way for Hitler; those same "lords" in Italy for the Mussolini; those same "lords" who preferred Hitler to Blum; and the same "lords" who exalted at the demise of democracy in Greece in 1967-68.

And as we all know, the danger of such an endgame is far from over.

Sometimes a step backward enables us to take a proper step forward. At the end of *Two Days of Infamy* Marks informs us that he's recently come upon a newspaper article published five years earlier on November 28, 1963, in which a journalist named Martin J. Steadman interviews Dr. Shaw of the Parkland Memorial Hospital medical staff. (Robert Shaw was the surgeon who treated Governor Connally.) In the present volume, Marks discusses the Steadman article in greater depth and adds that he first obtained a copy thanks to a reader who was following his work. According to Steadman, Dr. Shaw said that the bullet that punctured the front of the president's throat and "coursed downward into his lung was removed in the Bethesda Naval Hospital, where the autopsy was performed."

Steadman was a respected journalist with the *New York Herald-Tribune*, and his story was transmitted on the news wires and reproduced that same day in various other mainstream outlets, including the *Boston Globe*. In the *Globe* article, headlined "Kennedy's Wounds Described," Steadman quotes Dr. Shaw as follows: "The first bullet entered President Kennedy's trachea, in the front of his neck, coursing downward into his right lung. The bullet was removed in the Bethesda Naval Hospital, in Maryland, where an autopsy was performed." Despite the gravity of this testimony and the obvious implications it has on the case, I cannot recall seeing this piece reproduced elsewhere in the assassination literature.

As I continued to research Steadman, I next came upon an even more startling article that he published on the fiftieth anniversary of JFK's assassination. In this 2013 piece, featured in small online journal that seemed to escape the attention of other assassination researchers, Steadman chronicles an encounter he had with Dr. Perry while he was a guest at Perry's home on the evening of December 2, 1963. During that occasion, Perry told Steadman and a couple of his journalist colleagues that he had received "a series of phone calls" during the middle of the night of November 22, 1963 from the military doctors at Bethesda Naval Hospital, who were in attendance at Kennedy's autopsy there. Just hours before, Perry had announced to television journalists that the wound in JFK's throat was one of entry (Perry had performed the tracheotomy that sliced across this wound). But now, the Bethesda doctors threatened to destroy his career if he failed to recant his story and testify that he was mistaken. Which he eventually did. Steadman reports: "They threatened his license to practice medicine" and adds: "I can't fault Dr. Perry for his testimony before the Warren Commission…. But I'll never forget what he said to three reporters that night in Dallas."

Shortly after I discovered Steadman's 2013 essay I forwarded it to my colleague Jim DiEugenio, who used it as a centerpiece for his article "The Ordeal of Malcolm Perry," featured on the Kennedys and King web site. I've also reproduced an excerpt from Steadman's essay in this new reissue of *Coup d'État!*, a book that is once again in print for the first time in over fifty years.

* * *

In this edition of *Coup D'État!*, minor changes in grammar and punctuation have been made; and, where necessary, the spelling of proper nouns has been corrected. Textual changes involving anything more complex, such as inserting missing phrases, are indicated by brackets.

A bibliography of works cited in the text has been added, along with annotated footnotes and a general index. Otherwise, the original *Coup D'État!* is reproduced here without any substantial changes.

In chapter XI, "A Short Reprise of the Evidence," Marks enumerates many of the clues, leads, contradictions, and outright lies that he mined throughout his years of research on the documents comprising the official Warren Commission Report and the twenty-six volumes of WC "Hearings and Testimony." Here, as well as in the main body of text, when citing the WC Report or the WC Hearings and Exhibits, he uses the abbreviation "R" for the Report and "H" for the Hearings and Exhibits (e.g., "R81, 235" refers to the WC Report, pp. 81, 235; while "3H294-95" refers to the third volume of the Hearings and Exhibits, pp. 294-95).

Volumes 16-26 of the WC Hearings and Exhibits contain photos of the Commission Exhibits, abbreviated as "CE" (e.g., CE 3031). "C.D." refers to the FBI's Commission Document. (E.g., "C.D. 1" is Commission Document 1, the Bureau's thirty-nine-page assassination report.)

Some of the witness statements quoted by Marks are not verbatim transcripts but instead represent a slightly condensed or abbreviated version of their remarks.

JAMES CURRY--AN ADMISSION!

EX-DALLAS CHIEF OF POLICE JESSE CURRY

ADMITS AND CONFESSES

That LEE HARVEY OSWALD WAS INNOCENT, UNDER the "basic Principles of AMERICAN JUSTICE, of murdering PRESIDENT JOHN F. KENNEDY, in Dallas, Texas.

At 11 p.m., of November 5, 1969, 5 years, 11 months, and 17 days, nearly to the hour, Jesse Curry, ex-Dallas Chief of Police, who directed the investigation of the murder of President Kennedy, and who has since November 22, 1963, proclaimed that Lee Harvey Oswald was the sole and only murderer of President Kennedy, admitted and confessed that the Dallas Police Department had no positive evidence that Lee Harvey Oswald was the killer. The former Police Chief admitted that at no time did the Dallas Police Department find proof that Oswald fired any rifle bullets into the President's body. Ex-Chief Curry also admitted that the Police found no evidence that Oswald was at the 6th floor window when the shots were fired.

5 Years, 11 Months, and 17 Days!

The above news was released under a "UPI" radio wire and was flashed to every television and radio station in the United States. On the West Coast only one station used that statement: TV-KCOP, Mr. Bill Johns, news commentator. No magazine, weekly or NATIONAL monthly, reported the former Chief's admission.

(Since 1966 the author has written to the former Chief requesting clarification of several points in issue. They were reported in his former books, "Two Days of Infamy," and "Murder Most Foul," but the letters remained unanswered. The ex-Chief's statement of November 5, 1969, clarifies the air; no more letters except one will be continued to be sent: "Mr. Curry, who selected the infamous 'double detour' route which led the President into a three-pronged ambush site?" If the ex-Chief will answer that question, then some of the non-shooting Conspirators will be revealed.)

Frontispiece from the original edition of *Coup D'État!*

J'ACCUSE

Nearly 75 years have passed since the Dreyfus Affaire shook foundations of the French government and divided its society into divisions that still exist today. The framed Captain Dreyfus was only a symbol, and the frame-up would have succeeded if the critics of the French investigating committee had not spoken up. That investigating committee used the identical reason why evidence was suppressed—"it was not in the national interests"—to prevent the French Army from being exposed as the culprit in the investigation, trial, and sentencing of an innocent man to life imprisonment on Devil's Island.

The murder of President Kennedy radically changed the course of history in the United States. The reasons for his murder can be traced to his conduct of his internal and external program. His ideas for a test ban on the use of atomic weapons, his groping and initial steps toward Red China, his attempt to secure a detente with the Soviet Union, and even his seemingly slight step to bring some small normalization between Cuba and the United States met with tremendous opposition. Opposition came not from the great majority of the people but from the military, economic, and fascist groups.

During the time when this book was being drafted and written the nation [was becoming] greatly divided over the Vietnam "War" —the word "war" is used advisedly, for Congress over the past ten years has never voted a Declaration of War—and race relations. The attacks on the press, ordered by President Nixon on November 13, 1969, was the orderly progression of equating dissent with treason. History has proved that every democracy that has passed away has had as the agent for death the elected leaders who proclaim their adherence to one set of principles but act to the contrary. Of course, if Vice President Agnew's logic of November 1969 is to be applied to the [Warren Commission] "Report," the only one who can legally dissent from any government pronouncement would permit only the government agency issuing that pronouncement to dissent![13]

The prime function of the Warren Commission was to protect the transfer of power from President Kennedy's philosophy to those diametrically opposed. The Commission was to "cover-up" the conspiracy, and the Commission was to succeed beyond its fondest hope. The men that activated the conspiracy were those a generation from John F. Kennedy. It was the "generation gap" that figuratively assassinated the president.[14]

The bizarre surrounds the Warren Commission and its fabricated 888-page book titled "Report."

The bizarre is the fact that in the National Archives is a memo from a Commission aide to the general counsel of the Warren Commission, revealing the fact that the 888-page "Report" was being written before major witnesses were being examined! Thus proving that the Commission had determined (or had been instructed) to produce "evidence" convicting Oswald.

If the reader has in his possession the "Report," [a] U.S. government publication, and turns to page 95, the Commission has adopted the sentence: "Where bullet entered the president's back." On page 105, the Commission stated: "the bullet hit President Kennedy in the back." Finally, on page 111: "the president has been shot in the back."

In spite of these three sentences on pages 95, 105, and 111, the Commission cynically stated that the president had no wound in the back, and the Commission was to spend several

---

[13] See Marks' critique of the Nixon administration, published the following year: *Watch What We Do ... Not What We Say!* (Los Angeles: Bureau of International Affairs, 1971). "An account of the present trend of the Nixon–Agnew–Mitchell–Southern strategy axis to the possibility of Orwell's '1984' being accomplished by 1972" (from the title page).

[14] Cf. Ken Kesey, in a satirical letter to fellow Merry Prankster Ken Babbs, claimed that "Big Nurse" killed JFK—referring to the character "Nurse Ratched" in his epoch defining anti-Establishment novel, *One Flew Over the Cuckoo's Nest* (1962). The letter is reproduced in Ken Kesey, *One Flew Over the Cuckoo's Nest: Text and Criticism*, ed. John C. Pratt (New York: Viking Press, 1973), pp. 335-38.

million dollars to prove what they originally said was untrue.[15] Since the Commission used those words not once, but several times, it cannot be considered a "Freudian" slip.

The Chief Justice of the United States Supreme Court, Earl Warren, proudly proclaimed that the conduct of the Commission would be guided by "the basic principles of American justice." If their conduct revealed the acceptance of those guidelines, then the interpretation of that ringing phrase raises doubt that the chief justice knew anything about the "basic principles of American justice." The Commission, in its unanimous opinion as expressed in its "Report," clearly stated that the president was hit in the back; thus a conspiracy, in fact and in law, committed the murder.

The fact that the Commission instructed its 26 aides[16] to write an 888-page book stating Oswald was the sole assassin of President Kennedy and therefore no conspiracy existed carries no weight when the evidence in the "Hearings" and in the National Archives supports the existence and completion of a conspiracy.

Historians investigating the Commission must not overlook the various statements made by the Commission's own witnesses or aides after the "Report" had been published. Where two prime aides to the investigation admit facts that would lead to a conclusion opposed to the original "Report," then the Warren Commission's conclusions must be considered a falsification of history.

The primary reason why the Warren Commission must be exposed is due to the political axioms they enunciated. A future president of the United States may be assassinated where friends of the vice president believe the president does not favor their philosophy and the assassinators believe the vice president may be amenable to their philosophy.

---

[15] Marks is distinguishing here between a wound in the back (as reported by the FBI) and the false claim of a wound in the back of the neck.

[16] Not counting James Lee Rankin, the general counsel, the Commission appointed fourteen assistant counsel members and an additional support staff of twelve, which would add up to twenty-six.

The appointees to the Warren Commission was a sign that the seven commissioners would bring in a whitewash. President Johnson appointed six of the seven who were political opponents of the martyred president. The chief justice was nonpolitical. But a Senator Russell? He thought so little of the investigation that he found only 5% of his time to condescend to listen to testimony! There was no commissioner who gave of himself 100%, not one. As the record revealed, only one, the chief justice, attended all the meetings, but he popped in and out; never did he stay a full meeting.

Their conduct was to be a new interpretation of "the basic principles of American justice."

Within one year after the publication of their official "Report," rumors, and then facts, swept the nation. In Europe, the "Report" was greeted with amazement by those who took the time to read the entire "Report." By 1966, no intelligent historian accepted the "Report" as being a true and honest investigation. For example, Dr. Boswell, second in command of the military team of three physicians conducting the autopsy upon the body of the murdered president at the Bethesda, Md. Naval Hospital on November 22, 1963, informed the newspapers on November 25, 1966 that "I never thought the autopsy would be a public record." Or that of the physician in command, Commander Humes, was to state on the CBS program: "The autopsy was never meant to be accurate"!

When one considers that, at the conclusion of the autopsy, Lee Harvey Oswald was alive and being held for trial for the murder of the president, then their explanations can only lead to the conclusion that the autopsy was a fraud. Those two physicians knew that Oswald was alive and under arrest for the murder of the president. They also knew, as physicians, that a legal autopsy was absolutely essential for the proper conduct of a prosecutor in a trial for murder. Yet, why did those physicians deliberately maneuver in such a manner that they knew their conduct would be inadmissible in a court of law? Unless, perhaps, they knew Oswald would never live to stand trial for the murder? In January 1969 at the Clay Shaw trial an autopsy physician was to admit the autopsy report was a fraud!

The work of the Warren Commission was directed at one

objective: to obscure all evidence that revealed the conspiracy and its members, for that evidence would lead directly to various federal agencies, including members of the executive department of the government.

The upholders of the Warren Commission's conclusion that "Oswald was the sole assassin of President Kennedy" rely one hundred percent upon the "prestige" of the commissioners. So did many Frenchmen in the Dreyfus Affaire! Many of those who oppose that conclusion do so on the grounds that the responsibility for the work of the Commission rested solely upon the 26 aides employed by the Commission.

Both defenses are inexcusable and unacceptable!

The evidence is overwhelming that the Warren Commission, within one month of its inception, had in its possession absolute proof from the FBI and the U.S. Secret Service that Lee Harvey Oswald was not the sole assassin of President Kennedy. In fact, that evidence proved he was not the killer in the remotest sense of the word.

The evidence in their possession revealed that a conspiracy murdered President Kennedy; but whether Oswald was a part of the conspiracy cannot be ascertained. Under the "basic principles of American justice," if a person enters into a conspiracy to commit murder, and the murder is committed, then the degree of the participation is of no consequence—that person is guilty of the full penalty. If, however, a person takes some action of which he has no knowledge that his action is part of a conspiracy, he cannot be guilty of any crime. There is evidence that Oswald was used as a "patsy"; that he executed a part of the conspiracy but he had no knowledge of what was to occur. Since the Commission unequivocally stated that no conspiracy existed, and since the evidence proved beyond a reasonable doubt that Oswald was not involved in the murder, he was not guilty of any murder.

The question then revolves around the contention of [who bears the] responsibility for that miscarriage of justice? The seven commissioners or their 26 aides?

The final responsibility rests solely upon the seven commissioners. As had been previously stated, the Commission had in its hand, within three months of its initial meeting, overwhelming evidence that proved Oswald innocent beyond a reasonable doubt. What was that evidence?

In its very first meeting the Commission was in possession of a U.S. Secret Service memo that stated Oswald was an FBI informant, with a code number of "S179," and being paid $200.00 per month.[17] This information had been given to the Secret Service by Mr. Alonzo Hudkins, a reporter for the Houston "Post" who stated he had been given that information by Chief Sweatt of the Dallas Intelligence Service Bureau. The report is published in the illustrated section of this book. It is not published in the "Report." The only legal question, under the "basic principles of American justice," was whether or not Chief Sweatt had given that statement to Mr. Hudkins and, if he did, was the statement true?

Under these "principles," the Commission should have had Mr. Hudkins and Chief Sweatt testify under oath to answer these questions. But the Commission did not desire to place Oswald in the form of an FBI agent. So, the Commission proceeded to rape the principle! They refused to have either Mr. Hudkins or Chief Sweatt testify. They requested the FBI to give their "word" that Oswald was never an FBI informer nor ever on their payroll. However, the FBI never answered under oath.

---

[17] Although it's highly likely that Oswald was an FBI informant, it later emerged that "S172" was a fictitious badge number and part of a hoax played upon the Bureau. Dallas County Assistant DA William Alexander suspected that the FBI was tapping his phones, so he decided to play a trick. He arranged a conference call with his friends Lonnie Hudkins and Hugh Aynesworth, reporters who also suspected that their lines were bugged. (They were said to be investigating the possible connection between Oswald and the FBI.) The trio had prearranged to discuss Oswald's "payroll number": was it S172 or S179? "Within half an hour" of the call, "FBI agents, flashing their badges, showed up at the offices of all three of these marplots asking what they knew about Oswald's government payroll number." Gerald D. McKnight, *Breach of Trust* (Lawrence, KS: University Press of Kansas, 2005), p. 139. Aynesworth was a journalist for the right-wing *Dallas Morning News* who also played a key role in the government's secret media campaign to slander D.A. Garrison.

They gave their "word." As the record and this book will reveal, the "word" of too many agents was not worth a tinker's damn. The strange fact is that the world would never have known of Oswald's capacity as an FBI informer if Congressman Ford had not blabbed in his book relating to his activity as a commissioner. There is nothing in the "Hearings" or the "Report" that would have led to the discovery of the Secret Service memo. (In the conspiracy trial of the "Seven" in Chicago, October 1969, an FBI informer was paid in the identical manner. He was paid $150.00 a month, in cash, by an FBI agent at various locations. This informer was not listed in the FBI records—nor was Oswald.)

Nor is there any statement in the "Report" that revealed that the Federal Bureau of Investigation, in a response to an inquiry by the Dallas Police Department concerning the reliability of Oswald, had informed the Dallas Police Department that "Oswald was all right"! This interesting bit of information can only be found in the National Archives and in the illustrated section of this book. Why not in the "Report"? Why did the Commission conceal it? (Com. Exh. Doc. 950)[18]

---

[18] See Commission Document 950, pp. 138-139: "Mrs. Meller stated that she and George Bouhe went to a small party at the residence of Peter Gregory in Fort Worth during the summer of 1962, where they met Lee Harvey and Marina Oswald. She and Bouhe visited the Oswalds at 2703 Mercedes in Fort Worth two or three times after that to take them food and clothing. Oswald became very belligerent on these occasions, saying that he didn't need or want help from anyone. Mrs. Miller also said that she saw the book, "Capital," which was written by Karl Marx, during one of these visits at Oswald house and became very worried about it. Subject said he checked with the FBI and they told him that Oswald was all right." Signed by F. A. Hellinghausen and P. M. Parks, detectives from the Criminal Intelligence Section. Addressed to Captain W. P. Gannaway, Special Service Bureau, Dallas Police Department, and cc'd to Lieutenant Jack Revill, Criminal Intelligence Section, Special Service Bureau, Dallas Police Department. A photo of this two-page typed letter is available at texashistory.unt.edu and titled "Report to W. P. Gannaway by F. A. Hellinghausen and P. M. Parks, February 17, 1964." Marks probably first came across this information during his

By March 1, 1964 the Warren Commission had in its possession the following FBI documents that proved beyond a reasonable doubt that Lee Harvey Oswald was absolutely innocent of being the "sole assassin" of President Kennedy:

(1) The Italian rifle given to the FBI by the Dallas police had been "planted" as evidence by the police. (2) That rifle was a nonlethal weapon. (3) One of the cartridges allegedly discharged from that rifle was so deformed that it could not fit in the rifle chamber; thus, no bullet was enclosed in that cartridge case. (4) That rifle could only be used by a left-handed rifleman. Oswald was, and always had been, right-handed. (5) The telescopic sight was structurally defective on that rifle and could not be used prior to its repair by the FBI. (6) No ammunition clip was found, and the clip was essential to complete the firing within the time limit specified by the Commission. (7) There were no fingerprints or palm prints on the rifle, on the stock of that rifle, on the cartridges found by the police, or on the ammunition clip. (8) The rifle was delivered to the FBI in a "well-oiled condition," yet no prints of any kind were found by the FBI. (9) The official FBI report that the president had been struck in the back as distinguished from any bullet in the back of the neck. (10) The official FBI report that the "angle of fire" into the president's body and Governor Connally's prevented any rifleman to strike the president from a rifle discharging bullets from the southeast 6th floor corner window of the Depository. (11) That Brennan, the key witness for the Commission regarding the rifleman at that window, had given an affidavit to the FBI saying he could not recognize the rifleman. (12) The FBI analyzed the Hughes photographs taken of the 6th-floor window at the moment the president's automobile was under that window, and there was no person at that window. (13) The FBI had analyzed the Altgens photograph of the person in the doorway when the president

---

reading of Harold Weisberg's *Whitewash II* (Hyattstown, MD: Harold Weisberg). Chapter six of that book is titled "Oswald is 'All Right'" and it contains an in-depth analysis of the letter. Marks acknowledges his debt to Weisberg and the other early researchers both in the present volume and in his previous two JFK books.

was shot, and that person was not Lovelady. As the Commission stated [that] it had to be either Lovelady or Oswald, the FBI, by stating that it was not Lovelady, was affirming the man in the doorway was Oswald.[19] (14) The Commission also had in its possession the official U.S. Secret Service Report that the president was struck once in the back, once in the head, and [that] Governor Connally was struck by a third bullet. (15) The Commission had the official survey of the U.S. Secret Service showing that no bullet fired from a rifle held by a rifleman on the 6th floor S.E. window could strike the president or Governor Connally.

The above is the list of major elements of evidence that proved the innocence of Oswald. Since the Commission had the Reports from both the FBI and U.S. Secret Service, then it is obvious that from April 1, 1964 the Commission and its aides were engaged in mere shadowboxing. From that day until the "Report" was completed and then forwarded to the printer, the of the Commission and its aides was to fabricate a "Report" by selecting words from affidavits or documents which would enable the Commission to say that "Oswald was the sole and only assassin of President Kennedy." However, the most important and vital pieces of evidence were in the possession of the Warren Commission prior to February 1, 1964, which absolutely proved Lee Harvey Oswald innocent: (1) Lt. Day's official report that at no time did he discover fingerprints or palm prints on the Italian rifle. (2) The official letter from the FBI that they had not found any fingerprints or palm prints on the cartridges, the clip, or on Oswald's revolver! These two letters were suppressed by the Commission but are published for the first time in the affidavit section of this book, nos. 11 and 20.

"The Commission wanted it that way!" "I work for the Commission," an aide is stated to have said to Mr. Epstein of "Inquest."[20] True, the aide later denied making these

---

[19] The question of whether it was Lovelady or Oswald continues to provoke a contentious debate within the assassination research community.

[20] See Edward Jay Epstein,. *Inquest: The Warren Commission and*

statements, but the conduct of those aides bears out those statements, regardless of who did the uttering. The work of those aides, as outlined by Mark Lane, Penn Jones, Harold Weisberg, and Sylvia Meagher, gave proof that the aides labored mightily nigh unto six months to select "evidence" that would support the Commission's statement that "Oswald was the sole assassin of President Kennedy." The aides wrote a "Report" that was unsupported by the evidence but they knew, in their hearts, that it was in the "interests of national security" to prove no conspiracy existed.

Within three years after the publication of the "Report," many of the aides were so busy defending themselves that their defense consisted of statements admitting the "Report" was false. One aide, Specter, was to [state] that Bullet 399 was not "indispensable" to the Commission's conclusion! He calmly overlooked [the fact] that Bullet 399 was the main structure that convicted Oswald. Another aide was to say that he knew Brennan saw no man at the 6th-floor window. By stating this, the aide was admitting a conspiracy existed. But President Kennedy had been dead for more than three years, and who was interested in capturing and convicting his murderers?

Is this author correct in stating that the "Report" was written to conform to the Warren Commission's obligation to conduct a whitewash?

In the illustrated section of this book is a memo (Com. File 962) from an aide to the Commission's General Counsel, Mr. Rankin. The implication in the memo is staggering. That memo clearly implies that, months prior to examining prime witnesses relating to both the murders of President Kennedy and officer Tippit, the Commission had instructed its aides to write the "Report"! Notice the date when the memo was circulated and the implied fact that, even prior to the memo, writing of the "Report" had commenced. The "Report" was being written during the week so as not to interfere with the aides' weekend. In other words, the commissioners and their aides were merely

---

the Establishment of Truth (New York: The Viking Press, 1966), p. 145.

going through the motions. No wonder Senator Russell attended a mere eight sessions. He knew the verdict before the evidence was heard!

The moral crime committed by the Commission was that, by their concealment of the conspiracy, the conspirators were permitted to erode the public's faith in their government, for it is now permissible to assassinate elected leaders to obtain a change in the policies of the murdered leader.

J'Accuse!

* * *

AUTHOR'S GRATITUDE to the various members of the Federal Bureau of Investigation, the United States Secret Service, unspoken members of the Central Intelligence Agency, policemen and deputy sheriffs of Dallas, Texas, and Texas Rangers, who furnished, guided, and interpreted vital information that was found in the National Archives.

The author hastens to point out that the information received, or the guidance furnished, was in no manner any violation of any federal statute, for all the information so given can be found in the public records at the Dallas Police Department, the Dallas Sheriff's Office, or in the National Archives at Washington, D.C.

Those men and women believed that no President of the United States deserves to be shot down like a blind animal in any city of this nation. Nor do they believe that the assassins should be free to walk this earth without first receiving the just punishment they so deserve.

Without the assistance of those unnamed persons this book would not have been written.

"Justice is achieved only when those who are not injured are as indignant as those who are."—Anon.

PART ONE

CHAPTER I

The Ananias Club

Ananias was, by mythology, the "father of liars." Thus, the question arises whether seven men can give authorship of a single lie. That lie, in history, is known as the "Warren Report." However, although Ananias was one, the Commission comprised seven men that concocted a single lie that "Oswald was the sole assassin of President Kennedy." It is probably correct to state that the Warren commissioners can be considered as a single entity. The same club also decreed that no conspiracy, internal or external, was involved in a conspiracy that executed the president.

The leaders and citizens of the United States have always proudly proclaimed that the nation is governed by law, not by the whim of men elected to the reins of government. The conclusions, therefore, of the Commission must be upheld by legal procedures and principles that govern the nation. Thus, the only question involved in determining the truth or falsity of their oracle proclaiming [that] no conspiracy existed and [that] Oswald was the sole assassin is whether or not that oracle is supported by the evidence and documents in the 26 volumes titled "Hearings" or in the exhibits and documents now reposing in the National Archives.

The failure of the American people to understand the principles of law governing the nation permitted the Warren Commission to practice deceit, deception, and duplicity in their investigation of the conspiracy that murdered President John F. Kennedy.

Although Lee Harvey Oswald was dead at the time the Commission commenced its investigation, his death did not relieve the Commission of its sworn obligation to ascertain the facts, evaluate them, and announce the truth. The Chairman of the United States Supreme court, proudly informed [the] world that the investigation would adhere to the "basic principles of American justice." The following pages will reveal the interpretation of that ringing phrase by the seven commissioners.

Under the "basic principles of American justice" the Warren Commission, by labeling Oswald the sole assassin of the president, was informing the world that they had, by applying these "principles," located evidence that proved beyond a reasonable doubt Oswald was the sole assassin and no conspiracy existed.

[Under] the "basic principles of American justice," in a trial where a person is being prosecuted for murder the State must prove (1) that the person so accused was at the scene of the crime; (2) that the accused was the person who used the instrument that was the direct cause of death; (3) that the weapon that was the alleged weapon of death was a lethal weapon which caused the death of the victim. The Commission's case against Oswald had to prove beyond a reasonable doubt that Oswald was at the 6th floor S.E. corner window of the Texas Book Depository building at the time the shots were fired at the president. They must also prove that he used the weapon and [that] bullets from that weapon struck the president, which was the direct cause of his death. Finally, the Commission must also prove that the weapon used could discharge bullets through its barrel. In other words, [that] the rifle used was a lethal weapon.

Under the "basic principles of American justice," if the Warren Commission failed in any of these three basic requirements Oswald was not guilty of any crime on November 22, 1963.

The fact that Oswald was at the scene of the crime in the literal sense has no value in his conviction by the Commission. There were several thousand persons at the murder site. In the specific sense Oswald must be proved to have been at the 6th-floor window at the exact time the shots were discharged at the president. It would not be Oswald's function, if alive to be tried in court, to prove he was somewhere else; that would be the sole responsibility of the Commission—acting as the prosecutor for the purposes of this book.

But assuming [that] Oswald was at the 6th-floor window at the time the shots were discharged, the Commission must also prove that the shots came from that specific 6th-floor window. Hence, assuming the Commission proved Oswald was there; but if he was not there at the time the shots were fired, Oswald would be innocent.

Finally, assume that Oswald was at the window at the time the shots were fired. The Commission must prove, under the "basic principles of American justice," that the rifle allegedly used to murder President Kennedy discharged the bullets which caused his death.

The Warren Commission, under its sworn obligation, must prove beyond a reasonable doubt that Oswald was the person who matched those three legal requirements. If the Commission failed to prove a single requirement of any of the three, [then] he was an innocent man and unjustly labeled an "assassin."

Citizens of this nation must remember that the rights of a person accused of a crime must have been obtained only through the long bloody struggles against tyranny. Today there is a retrogression of those rights under the "propaganda" of "law and order." The constant drumbeat by the Nixon Administration that "dissent" is "treason," that "law and order" is of greater value than "justice," is, in English, what dictators have said throughout the ages.

"The streets of our country are in turmoil. The universities are full of students rebelling and rioting. Communists are seeking to destroy our country. Russia is threatening us with her might and the republic is in danger.

"Yes, danger from within and from without. We need law and order. Without law and order, our nation cannot survive.

"Elect us and we shall restore law and order. We will be respected by the nations of the world for law and order. Without law and order our Republic will fail."—Adolf Hitler, 1932.

Every dictatorship has "law and order," but only a democracy has "law, order, and justice." When any nation bases its entire existence upon "law and order," one can be sure that justice does not prevail. The Pledge of Allegiance to the United States says nothing about "law and order." It does say "liberty and justice for all." Without justice, where is "liberty?"

In the case of the Commission vs. Lee Harvey Oswald neither law nor justice was applied.

This book will bring together all these facts as published in the "Report," the 26 volumes of the "Hearings," or the documents in the files of the National Archives. It will be those facts that will evaluate the evidence to prove the truth.

The Commission's indictment, or "Conclusions," was published in such a manner that it is difficult for any investigator to analyze the "Report" in a logical method. For example, as seen below in paragraph (A), last sentence: The Commission alleges the shots rang out between a period of not less than "4.8 seconds and 7 seconds." In an effort to check the accuracy of that time period the investigator was compelled to research in many of the individual 26 volumes, which contained the testimony of the witnesses, and documents in the National Archives, which were suppressed by the Warren Commission. Thus, an investigator had to locate testimony relating to the condition of the rifle, the type of bullets that could fit within that rifle, and the type of cartridges found on the 6th floor near the rifle. Further, whether or not these cartridges could hold bullets. Finally, the investigator had to be positive that the rifle was a lethal operating weapon.

Generally, the standard procedure in any investigation would have been to arrange the testimony, exhibits, and documents in a single section relating to a specific subject matter. But the Commission had no desire to assist any investigator interested in locating the evidence which would have proved or disproved Oswald's innocence. This is why the reader will notice in the reference section of this book that many volumes have been used to locate the testimony.

To understand the "Conclusions" of the Warren "Report" one must first read them carefully. These "Conclusions" were, in reality, the indictment of Oswald by the Warren Commission. This indictment contained eight specific accusations which, in turn, were supported by nineteen additional allegations.

The unanimous opinion of the Commission convicted Oswald as follows:

"Based on the evidence analyzed:"

(A) "The Commission has concluded that the shots which killed President Kennedy and wounded Governor Connally were fired from the 6th-floor window at the S.E. corner of the Texas Book Depository building. Two bullets probably caused all the wounds suffered by President Kennedy and Governor Connally. Since the preponderance of the evidence indicated 3 shots were fired, the Commission concluded that one shot probably missed the presidential limousine and its occupants, and that the 3 shots were fired in a time period ranging from approximately 4.8 seconds in excess of 7 seconds."

(B) "Having reviewed the evidence that (1) Lee Harvey Oswald purchased the rifle used in the assassination, (2) Oswald's palm print was on the rifle in a position which shows that he handled it while it was disassembled, (3) fibers found on the rifle most probably came from the shirt Oswald was wearing on the day of the assassination, (4) a photograph taken in the yard of Oswald's apartment showed him holding this rifle, and (5) this rifle was kept among Oswald's possessions from the time of its purchase until the day of the assassination, the Commission concluded that the rifle used to assassinate President Kennedy and wound Governor Connally was owned and possessed by Lee Harvey Oswald."

(C) "The preponderance of the evidence supports the conclusion that Lee Harvey Oswald (1) told the curtain rod story to Frazier to explain both the return to Irving on a Thursday and the obvious bulk of the package which he intended to bring to work the next day; (2) he took paper and tape from the wrapping bench of the Depository and fashioned a bag large enough to carry the disassembled rifle; (3) he removed the rifle from the blanket in the Paine's garage on Thursday evening; (4) carried the rifle into the Depository building, concealed in the bag; and (5) left the bag alongside the window from which the shots were fired."

(D) "Fingerprints and palm print evidence establishes that Oswald handled two of the four cartons next to the window and also handled a paper bag which was found near the cartons. Oswald was seen in the vicinity of the S.E. corner on the 6th floor approximately 35 minutes before the assassination and no one could be found who saw Oswald anywhere else in the building until after the shooting. An eyewitness to the shooting immediately provided a description of the man in the window which was similar to Oswald's actual appearance. This witness identified Oswald in a lineup as the man most nearly resembling the man he saw and later identified Oswald as the man he observed. Oswald's known action in the building immediately after the assassination is consistent with his having been at the S.E. corner window of the sixth floor at 12:30 p.m. On the basis of these findings the Commission has concluded that Oswald, at the time of the assassination, was present at the window from which the shots were fired."

(E) "The (foregoing) evidence established that (1) two eyewitnesses who heard the shots and saw the shooting of Dallas police patrolman J. D. Tippit, and seven eyewitnesses who saw the flight of the gunman with the revolver in hand, positively identified Lee Harvey Oswald as the man they saw fire the shots or flee the scene; (2) the cartridge cases found near the scene of the shooting were fired from his revolver in the possession of Oswald at the time of his arrest, to the exclusion of all other weapons; (3) the revolver in Oswald's possession at the time of his arrest was purchased by and belonged to Oswald; and (4) Oswald's jacket was found along the path of flight taken by the gunman as he fled from the scene of the killing. On the basis of this evidence the Commission concluded that Lee Harvey Oswald killed Dallas police patrolman J. D. Tippit."

(F) "On the basis of the evidence.... the Commission has found that Lee Harvey Oswald (1) owned and possessed the rifle used to kill President Kennedy and wound Governor Connally; (2) brought this rifle into the Book Depository building on the morning of the assassination; (3) was present at the time of the assassination, at the window from which the shots were fired; (4) killed Dallas police officer J. D. Tippit in an apparent attempt to escape; (5) resisted arrest by drawing a fully loaded pistol and attempting to shoot another police officer; (6) lied to the police after his arrest concerning important substantive matters; (7) attempted, in April 1963, to kill ex-Maj. General Edwin A. Walker; and (8) possessed the capability with a rifle which would enable him to commit the assassination. On the basis of these findings, the Commission has concluded that Lee Harvey Oswald was the assassin of President Kennedy."

In law, the actual indictment of Oswald would be the final paragraph (F). However, this paragraph is the most fascinating [one] written by the Commission. Nowhere in that paragraph does the Commission categorically state that Lee Harvey Oswald was the assassin! In (1) Oswald only "owned and possessed" the rifle but the Commission refused to say that Oswald used that rifle.[21] In (2) and (3) the Commission alleged Oswald brought the rifle into the building and was present at the window from where they alleged the bullets were discharged. Again, the Commission refused to state that Oswald used the rifle, or that he was the rifleman when the shots rang out.

For example, when Senator Robert F. Kennedy was murdered in the kitchen hallway of the Ambassador Hotel, there were more than eighteen persons accompanying him, including several armed bodyguards. Did that mean that those persons were involved in his murder? Of course not. Hence, in law, possession of a lethal weapon and presence at the crime site does not presuppose the commission of the crime.

The Commission then proceeded to involve Oswald in three other criminal acts, none of which had a bearing upon the

---

[21] Cf. "Even if it had been established beyond a reasonable doubt that Oswald's rifle *was* the murder weapon, this would not prove that Oswald was the assassin. Hundreds of crimes have been committed with weapons belonging to others, often for that very reason: in order to incriminate them. The law, taking this into consideration, demands that the prosecution prove that the owner of the weapon had it in his possession at the time of the crime and that it was actually he who used it. The pronouncement in Finding Number 1 that Oswald both "owned and possessed" the rifle seems intended to suggest that ownership constitutes possession, but that is not the case." Léo Sauvage, *The Oswald Affair* (Cleveland: World Publishing, 1966), p. 359. Marks cites Sauvage's work in his previous book, *Two Days of Infamy*.

murder of President Kennedy. Oswald was accused of killing officer Tippit, who allegedly attempted to arrest him for the murder of President Kennedy. The fact that the Commission had in their possession testimony that no description was ever given to Tippit and the further fact that no witness ever identified Oswald either to the police or to the Warren Commission never bothered the Commission.

The second major crime not associated with the murder of the president was the attempted murder of officer McDonald by using a nonexisting weapon. The fact that the police ordered seventeen policemen to arrest a man "sneaking" into a theater or the fact that the "arresting officer" chose Oswald, who did not match the description McDonald had of the murderer of Tippit, did not bother the Commission either. Nor the fact that the Dallas police "arrest charge" sheet on Oswald revealed he had no revolver in his possession! Nor the fact that that same sheet showed Oswald did not resist arrest! Nor the fact that no policeman legally signed that "arrest"!

The third major crime applied to Oswald was his "attempt" to murder ex-Maj. General Walker seven months prior to the murder of President Kennedy. At the time of Oswald's murder he was, in theory, according to the Commission, a psychotic who relished murder. The only reason for attaching that upon Oswald was the Commission's desire to prove his instability. But the Commission would not go so far as to state he was insane. The Commission reasoned that the greater the number of crimes, the greater the opportunity to impress the public.

In analyzing the conduct of the Warren Commission, the investigator must place himself in the position of Oswald's attorney. But, in view of the "prestige" of the Warren Commission, the investigator or attorney had to assume the fact that since the public believed the correctness of the Commission's verdict that Oswald was guilty, the investigator would have to prove Oswald's innocence beyond a reasonable doubt. In legal theory, the "burden of proof" that the prosecution carries upon its shoulders to prove an accused person guilty was shifted to the shoulders of the investigator of the Warren Commission. Furthermore, the investigator had to prove his accusation that the Commission wrongfully convicted

Oswald by more than a mere consensus but "beyond a reasonable doubt."

At the same time, the investigator would be proving a conspiracy which the Commission heatedly denied. For, if Oswald was innocent, the establishment of that condition automatically proved a conspiracy. That is why the Warren Commission was compelled to convict Oswald. The establishment of a conspiracy would prove the involvement of many "Americans"—in and out of the government.

The investigator or Oswald's attorney would have a difficult task to perform. However, if Oswald's attorney could prove by the evidence in the "Hearings" or with the documents in the National Archives that such evidence directly conflicted [with] or then contradicted the Commission's statements in the "Report," then Commission's conclusions would be invalid.

As stated previously, the Commission charged Oswald with the murder of a policeman, the attempted murder of two other persons, and the wounding of Governor Connally. The Commission stated that because of those acts he was guilty of the murder of President Kennedy. The tortuous reasoning of the Commission can readily be seen by reading paragraph (F) of the indictment. The first three accusations relate only to the killing of President Kennedy and the wounding of Governor Connally. Therefore, what have the remaining four accusations to do with 1 to 3? In law, nothing; for one crime does not presuppose the commission of another. Nor can the use of words be used as a substitute for the actual criminal act.

Stated in another manner: assuming Oswald had killed officer Tippit, does that assumption mean he also murdered President Kennedy and wounded Governor Connally? The Commission promulgated its theory by stating that the assumption was proper because Oswald was attempting to escape from being arrested for the president's murder. The Commission had no proof, and this they admit; but by using words as evidence they not only created a killer image of Oswald but, at the same time, absolved the Dallas police of being implicated in the Tippit murder—which they were.

The Warren principle that a person by committing one crime automatically becomes guilty of another crime is not so "under the basic principles of American justice." Thus, the alleged attempt to murder ex-Maj. Gen. Walker was nothing but a smoke screen. Yet, assuming Oswald did make that attempt, that does not prove him guilty of murdering the president.

The reader must remember that the converse is also true. Oswald did not murder Tippit, and he did not attempt to murder Walker, but he could have murdered the president. Thus, the investigator of the Warren Report must not spend much time on the other crimes supposedly committed by Oswald; for, even if the investigator proved Oswald innocent of those crimes, the fact remains the investigator must prove him "not guilty" of the crime of murdering President Kennedy.

Today, the investigator knows that several courts have ruled upon the worthiness of the Warren "Report." In the Shaw trial in New Orleans, January 1969, the courts of that state ruled that the Warren Report was nothing more than "hearsay piled upon hearsay." That ruling was appealed all the way to the U.S. Supreme Court, and they refused to interfere in Shaw's trial. Shaw, it will be recalled, attempted to have the criminal court trying his case rule that his indictment should be declared invalid, since the Warren Commission said (1) that no conspiracy murdered President Kennedy, and (2) the sole murderer was Lee Harvey Oswald. If the court had upheld the Warren Commission, then Shaw would have been freed immediately. But not only did a 3-panel court of judges rule against Shaw, every higher court he appealed to refused to overturn that decision. In other words, hearsay was piled upon hearsay, and the "Report" was nothing more than a story fabricated by 26 aides supported by 7 commissioners.

Legally, the Warren Report is not a legal document and its verdict of entombing Oswald with the label of the president's assassin is a fabrication.

The mass communication media, the TV stations, columnists and authors upholding the Commission have conveniently and deliberately overlooked this important legal decision.

Many persons cannot understand the reason why the powerful newspapers and the ABC, CBS, and NBC television and radio chains have kept a constant drumbeat against the critics of the Warren Commission. The reason is quite simple—when the president was murdered the power structure shifted both economically and politically. It would take a little time, but, since the Kennedy—Johnson philosophies were in basic conflict, the murder of the president gave power to the Johnson philosophy. A reading of history throughout the ages reveals the shifting sands of power. President Johnson and the martyred president were as far apart as today's "generation gap." Although history has shown that the old was disposed of by the young, the assassination proved the exception. Thus, the magnates of the mass communication system simply got on the bandwagon.

Sometimes it is difficult to get off the "tiger's back"! The communication system is now aware of that, for Vice President Agnew's attack on November 13, 1969 against the entire spectrum of television and radio commentators is the opening gun (aimed, however, by President Nixon) to create a subservient press! His speech was reminiscent of Hitler's attacks against the German press in 1932-33.

The following pages will reveal and expose the methods used by the Commission to conceal the conspiracy that murdered President Kennedy. To attain some semblance of order the author will adhere strictly to the form of [the] paragraph[s] of the indictment. Paragraphs A to F will be analyzed in the following chapters, and from the testimony, affidavits, documents, maps, and photographs either in the "Hearings" or in the files of the National Archives will come forth the proof that Oswald was innocent. The conspiracy and some of the conspirators, as revealed from the testimony and suppressed records in the National Archives, will also be discussed.

When the French people were under the heel of the Nazis—who were also great believers in "law and order"—a famous French poet of the Resistance, Jean Tardieu, wrote for an underground newspaper:

> "Puisque les morts ne peuvent plus se taire,
> est-ce aux vivants à garder leur silence?"

"Since the dead can no longer be silenced, Are the living

entitled to keep their mouths shut?"[22]

IF THE DEAD CANNOT SPEAK, SHOULD NOT THE LIVING?

---

[22] In the words of Martin Luther King, "There comes a time when silence is betrayal." For more on Tardieu and the translation of this verse, please consult my Introduction.

CHAPTER II

THE FRAUDULENT AUTOPSY
or How to Lie in a Military Manner

The discussion of law and its application is, unfortunately, considered to be a highly technical subject and difficult for the layman to understand. Yet, the most fascinating literature of all time has generally dealt with some aspect of the law—whether it be fiction or nonfiction. Some lawyers can write beautiful literature; some cannot. Some can write legal tomes that will impress the legal profession but bore the layman.

The investigation of the Warren Commission must, by its very nature, deal with the criminal practice and procedures of the United States. Murder is a criminal act and, to prove that act, legal principles must be used. It is somewhat difficult to reduce criminal law and procedure for the layman, who can easily become bored with the subject. It is hoped that the layman reading this book will bear with the author, for it is the only method that can be used to prove the falsity of the Warren Commission's "Report."

Under American criminal law an accused murderer can be found "guilty" only when the evidence proves beyond a reasonable doubt that (1) the victim died as the result of an illegal act committed by the defendant. Thus, if the accused is indicted for the murder of a person by using a weapon that discharged a bullet from its barrel, then if the evidence revealed that the victim died as the result of natural causes the accused must be given a verdict of "not guilty." In other words, the manner of death must be illegal. (2) The weapon itself must be the cause of death. If the weapon be proven to be nonlethal, then that by itself would create a "not guilty" verdict. A revolver or rifle alleged to have been used must be capable of not only receiving bullets in its chamber but the condition of the gun must be such that it will cause a bullet to go into the chamber, the trigger must be able to strike the bullet, and the bullet must be able to travel through the barrel. If bullets do not fit within the rifle or if there be no trigger, then it is obvious that the rifle is a nonlethal weapon. Or, for example, if a person is arrested for drunken driving of an automobile, then if the evidence revealed that the drunken person was sitting at the steering wheel of an automobile that had no wheels he would be found "not guilty." (3) The accused must be at the scene of the crime unless he is part and parcel of a conspiracy that committed the crime. (4) The accused must be the only person, or one of the persons, who used the murder weapon to slay the victim.

The Warren Commission, in paragraph (A) of its indictment charging Oswald as being the sole killer of President Kennedy, stated that only three bullets were fired from the S.E. corner window of the 6th floor of the Texas Book Depository building. One of those three bullets not only missed the president's automobile but any person standing on Dealey Plaza, the trees, the street signs, Elm Street, the curb, and the earth. It would like saying he shot a bullet in the ground and missed!

Whether that missed bullet ever came to ground, or whether that was the first, second, or third shot the Commission did not discover. But they did state that two bullets created all the wounds: one bullet going through the back of the president's neck and continuing on into the governor's body and the other bullet striking the president in the head, causing his death. The Commission also informed the public that those three shots were fired in a time period of between "4.8 seconds in excess of 7 seconds." What the last quoted phrase means is left to the imagination of the reader of the "Report." It could be interpreted to mean that the killer took in excess of one minute, three minutes, one half hour, or a day.

An investigator immediately knows that the Warren Commission was playing with words, not evidence, for the indictment placed Oswald at the 6th-floor window at a specific time: 12:30 p.m., not 12:45 p.m. or 1 o'clock, or 9:00 p.m.

The Commission asserted that only three shots were fired, two of which caused all the damage. Oswald's defense attorney would have to cross-examine the physicians at both the

Parkland Hospital and the Bethesda, Md. Naval Hospital, for it would be those physicians who knew the condition of the president immediately after being struck by bullets. However, the attorney would also have available for examination the official reports of the FBI and the U.S. Secret Service bureau; photographs; X-rays; motion picture films; TV tape films; and surveys. That is, under the "basic principles of American justice," those persons and documents would be available to an attorney defending Oswald of murdering President Kennedy.

One of the questions that would be raised by Oswald's attorney would be "Is the autopsy report published by the Commission a fraudulent or legal document?" If fraudulent, then the autopsy report is worthless, and Chief Justice Warren and his 26 aides knew the legal principle that a fraudulent document cannot be used to convict an accused person. But the chief justice was compelled to use that fraudulent autopsy report, for without it Oswald was innocent. Thus, the defense attorney had to prove fraud, and this he could do from the testimony and documents in the "Hearings" or in the National Archives.

A person reading pages 516-37 of the "Report" can see for himself that the autopsy report is a deliberate fraud! It is nothing more than a piece of evidence manufactured by the Commission to deceive the people as to the cause of the president's death. The first page is torn or cut in half. What happened to the bottom half of that page? Why was it destroyed? The third page has a typewritten figure of "2" on it, which can only mean that it was not the original third page but in reality page 2. Then, to complete the fraud, page 1 has a type different from pages 2 and 3. To further prove a fraud, that report is unsigned! Comdr. Humes, Lt. Col. Finck, and Dr. Boswell, although experienced physicians who knew [that] the law required their signature to render it a legal document, refused to add their signature to that alleged document published in the "Report."

This so-called Humes Autopsy Report was, as the testimony revealed, not drawn up immediately at the conclusion of the Bethesda autopsy but only after a 48-hour time lag. Then, Comdr. Humes calmly destroyed his "original notes"!

Yet, in volume 3, page 373, Comdr. Humes stated that he

burned "a draft of this report which I later revised." This statement clearly implies that originally he had (1) preliminary notes, then he completed a draft, and (3) from that draft he made a revision (2). But his testimony definitely stated he only burned his "draft notes," not (2) or (3). Hence, where is and who has (2)? Furthermore, why did Comdr. Humes have to revise (2) unless the reason be that he realized that (2) failed to conform to his instructions given to him in the autopsy room by "higher authority"?

This unmedical procedure by the Commander was compounded by his admission that his autopsy report was based upon a newspaper story written in the November 23, 1963 issue of the Washington "Post." This is the first time in medical history that an autopsy of a murder is based on what a newspaper man saw and heard.

In addition to this monstrosity, the Humes' autopsy report revealed many alterations, additions, and subtractions, which, "under the basic principles of American justice," made that report a worthless piece of paper. No American court of justice would permit that "medical" report to be read to a jury or placed in the court record. This "Humes" autopsy report has been attacked by every major medical society in the United States including the "Journal of the American Medical Association". But, the chief justice stated, he was not interested in applying legal principles if, by avoiding them, the "truth" could be obtained.

More than four years would elapse before the truth came forth—not from any of the aides but from sworn testimony given at the Clay Shaw trial held in New Orleans in January 1969. At that trial, Lt. Col. Finck was to admit under oath that the autopsy physicians never had an autopsy upon the president's body! He swore that only an "incomplete autopsy was made." An incomplete autopsy is not an autopsy, either in the medical or legal profession. An incomplete autopsy cannot be used to convict a man indicted for murder. That rule is one of the "basic principles of American justice." (See Lt. Col. Finck's testimony in Appendix.)

Therefore, the first conclusion published by the Warren Commission is based upon fraud and deceit—and the

Commission and its 26 aides knew that fact prior to the publication and release of the Warren "Report."

Leaving the illegal autopsy report, Oswald's attorney would give his attention to the two official documents signed by the U.S. Secret Service which were in the Commission's possession ONE month after they commenced the "investigation." One is the official survey, conducted by R. West,[23] dated November 25, 1963, which revealed the fact that no bullet discharged from a rifle held by a person at the S.E. window of the 6th floor of the Book Depository could strike the president or the governor. This is the reason why the Commission never announced or published this official survey of the Secret Service bureau. It was a scientific and physical impossibility for any bullet from the 6th floor S.E. window to strike the president. (File No. 87, National Archives, suppressed. See illustrated section.)

The second official U.S. Secret Service document given to the Commission was completed on November 28, 1963. [It] stated that President Kennedy was struck by two bullets and Governor Connally by another independent bullet. This evidence was also suppressed by the Warren Commission, but it can also be found in File No. 87, National Archives, under the title: "Preliminary Special Dallas Report #1. Assassination of the President; Assassination Scene." None of the Commission supporters have brought this to the attention of the public. (See illustrated section.)

One of the reasons why the Commission was compelled to adopt the "missed bullet" theory was to negate the sworn testimony of Secret Service Agent Kellerman, who testified he heard President Kennedy exclaim, "I'm hit!" Two agents testified they saw a bullet strike the president in the back—in the right shoulder.

The Commission was then compelled to say one bullet

---

[23] Marks is referring here to Dallas City Surveyor Robert West, who worked under the supervision of Secret Service Agent Elmer Moore. West provided the survey plat of Dealey Plaza for the December 5, 1963 reenactment of the assassination.

missed, for the bullet that entered the front of the president's throat destroyed his power of speech. Thus, how could the president exclaim, "I'm hit!"? However, it can be assumed that the president, hearing a sound like a shot, and then feeling the pain of a bullet hitting him in the shoulder, instinctively cried out, "I'm hit!" A fraction of a second later, another bullet hit him in the front of his throat.

The Commission had to negate the testimony, and they could only do that by evolving their absurd theory of two bullets, with another one missing its human target.

No critic seems to remember that the bullet in the president's right shoulder was not a fatal wound. The statement by the Commission that only two bullets struck the president was a statement unsupported by legal evidence. It is more logical to assume that the bullet in the shoulder was the first bullet to hit the president, in view of the Commission's outrageous perversion of the evidence. The bullet in his back was fired from a rifle on the 3rd floor of the "Dal-Tex" Building from where the rifleman fled and was then arrested on the street, taken to jail, and then released by the police, as shown in volume 19 of the Hearings and reported in the Dallas "Times-Herald" on November 22, 1963, late edition, and in the FBI's official report, which supported an "angle of fire" from the "Dal-Tex" Building.

The question before the general public today as of yesterday: "How many bullets were fired at President Kennedy, and how many struck him?" The evidence proved beyond a reasonable doubt that two bullets struck him in the head, one in the front of the throat, and one in the back of his right shoulder. That totals four. Governor Connally was definitely struck by two bullets, as proven by the testimony. That totals six bullets. One bullet fired at the president missed and struck the curb, portions of which struck a Mr. Tague in the face. Regardless of the fact that the Commission attempted to repeal the laws of science, physics, ballistics, and mathematics, and unless a new "Stalin" rises in this nation, 4 plus 2 plus 1 equals 7. The Warren Commission in its "Report" admitted that seven bullets, let alone 4, could not have been discharged in the 4.5 to 7-second time limit theorized by them from that nonlethal, rusty Italian rifle foisted upon the FBI as the weapon owned, but never used, by the sixth-floor rifleman.

The proof as to the number of bullets can be seen in the official Autopsy Chart No. 397,[24] where that legal chart shows the president received two head wounds, plus a wound in the back near the right shoulder, plus a wound in the front of his throat. At no time did any one of the physicians conducting the autopsy ever testify under oath that Chart 397 was incorrect or misleading. Chief Justice Earl A. Warren of the U.S. Supreme Court, as an attorney, prosecutor, judge, and justice, knew that under the "basic principles of American law" a court of any one of the fifty states of the United States would rule that, since that chart is a legal document, then Lee Harvey Oswald was an innocent man. The Commission never denied the legality of Chart 397.

Dr. Shaw, one of the outstanding thoracic physicians in the United States and an attending physician at Parkland Hospital when the president was brought in, announced that "the first bullet entered the president's trachea, in front of his neck, coursing downward into his right lung." Dr. Perry, an attending physician who operated upon the president, stated: "The bullet ranged downward in the throat and did not exit."[25] Dr. Clark,

---

[24] Commission Exhibit 397.

[25] Fifty years after the assassination, Martin J. Steadman, a former reporter for the *New York Herald-Tribune*, described a quiet evening he spent as a guest at the home of Dr. Perry on the evening of December 2, 1963. "Dr. Perry had become a controversial figure in the assassination story—to his dismay. With the president lying on his back on a gurney, fighting for breath in his dying moments, Dr. Perry tried to create an air passage with an incision across what he believed to be an entrance wound at the front of Kennedy's neck. The president was pronounced dead soon after, but the doctor's incision at the throat had forever foreclosed a conclusion that the wound was an entrance wound or an exit wound.

Late that Friday afternoon, the Parkland Hospital officials held a news conference for the hundreds of reporters who had descended on Dallas. Dr. Perry spoke of his efforts to save the president and his belief that his incision was across an entrance wound. The controversy didn't erupt until government officials in Washington

also a member of that operating team, confirmed the diagnosis of those two doctors by stating that the president "was hit by a bullet in the throat just below the Adam's apple." The two

---

later said all three shots at the president had been fired from a sixth-floor window of a building behind the president's limousine.

So, little more than a week later, three reporters were speaking quietly to the surgeon at the center of the dispute. As far as I know, it was the first and only such private interview with Dr. Perry. None of us in his living room that night took out a notebook or a pencil. It was a conversation with a clearly reluctant surgeon who had done his best in a crisis and who had agonized about it since.

Dr. Perry said he believed it was an entrance wound because the small circular hole was clean, with no edges. In the course of the conversation, he was asked and answered that he had treated hundreds of gunshot victims in the emergency rooms at Parkland Memorial Hospital. At another point he said he was a hunter by hobby, and he was very familiar with guns and ammunition. He said he could tell at a glance the difference between an entrance wound and an exit wound with its ragged edges.

But he told us that throughout that night, he received a series of phone calls to his home from irate doctors at the Bethesda Naval Hospital, where an autopsy was being conducted, and the doctors there were becoming increasingly frustrated with his belief that it was an entrance wound. He said they asked him if the doctors in Dallas had turned the president over and examined the wounds to his back; he said they had not. They told him he could not be certain of his conclusion if he had not examined the wounds in the president's back. They said Bethesda had the president's body and Dallas did not. They told Dr. Perry he must not continue to say he cut across what he believed to be an entrance wound when there was no evidence of shots fired from the front. When he said again he could only say what he believed to be true, one or more of the autopsy doctors told him they would take him before a medical board if he continued to insist on what they were certain was otherwise. They threatened his license to practice medicine, Dr. Perry said.

When he was finished, there was only one question left. I asked him if he still believed it was an entrance wound. The question hung there for a long moment.

'Yes,' he said."

—Martin J. Steadman, "Fifty Years from That Fateful Day in Dallas," *Eve's Magazine* (online), evesmag.com

remaining physicians also testified that the bullet wound in the throat was an "entrance wound." (N.Y. "Times," November 23, 1963.)

Time has solved the mystery of what happened to the bullet that entered the president's throat, in front of his neck, and coursed downward into his right lung. As seven doctors testified to that bullet, the Commission was compelled to seek some method to suppress the news of that bullet. There is no testimony regarding the answer, and over a period of years the question has been forgotten. This author, in his two previous books relating to the conspiracy that murdered President Kennedy, incorrectly assumed that the bullet had remained in the president's body and was buried in his casket.

By returning to the newspapers the answer was located in the November 28, 1963 issue of the now defunct "New York Herald-Tribune." A reader of my former books forwarded an issue of that paper, and in an exclusive story by Martin J. Steadman the answer was obtained. Mr. Steadman was informed by Dr. Shaw that the bullet which had "entered the president's trachea, in front of his neck, and coursed downward into his right lung," had been removed in the Bethesda, Md. Naval Hospital where the autopsy was performed.[26]

Yet, that bullet is not mentioned in the Humes' illegal autopsy report. It can also be stated that this bullet was THE reason why the Commander destroyed his original notes by "command of higher authority." It also answers the reason why Lt. Col. Finck admitted to performing "an incomplete autopsy." His reason conceals the fact that a bullet, a complete bullet, not fragments, was removed from the president's right lung. By deliberately withholding the knowledge of that bullet, the Commission was

---

[26] Steadman's story was picked up by various mainstream papers. For example, on November 28, 1963 it was featured on page 74 of the *Boston Globe* under the headline, "Kennedy's Wounds Described," and includes the following quote: "Dr. Shaw said 'The first bullet entered President Kennedy's trachea, in the front of his neck, coursing downward into his right lung. The bullet was removed in the Bethesda Naval Hospital, in Maryland, where an autopsy was performed.'"

able to confuse and deceive the public as [to] the existence of not less than four bullets striking the president, which made it impossible for Oswald to strike the president in "front of his throat" by discharging a rifle firing bullets into him in his back near his shoulder.

That lung bullet was removed at Bethesda Hospital, and "under command of higher authority" was disposed of so that no ballistic tests could be made. It also permitted the Commission to cynically announce that no conspiracy existed.

The legal Autopsy Chart 397 proved that two bullets struck President Kennedy in the head. The official cause of death was announced by Dr. R. N. McClelland of Parkland Hospital, who testified that the cause of death was "a massive head and brain injury from a gunshot wound of the left temple." To support the statement that the two head bullets struck the president, the Director of the FBI, Mr. Hoover, admitted that one bullet struck the president's head and pushed it forward while a second bullet made the president's head go backwards. (Zapruder film, frames 311-315.) The FBI director was admitting, indirectly, that a conspiracy murdered the president when one joins this admission with the statements made by the FBI in their official report in December 1963 and January 1964. Every Parkland physician testified that there was a wound over the left side of the president's head; and Catholic Father Huber, who offered the last rites, stated "he noticed a terrible wound over the left eye."

Conclusive proof that the Commission knew, beyond a reasonable doubt, that a conspiracy murdered President Kennedy can be found in volume 2, page 30, of the "Hearings," where an aide asked a physician to describe the wounds. The physician, due to the vagueness of the question, asked, "Which wound?" The aide replied, "Start with the HEAD wound, or the BACK wound, either one." As the investigation was conducted in the English language, and as all the "legal beagle" aides were lawyers who passed the Bar Examination in English, it must be assumed that they understood English. Common sense, therefore, dictates the assumption that by describing two different types of wounds, and then by using the phrase "either one," the aide was admitting there was a "back wound" as distinguished from a wound at the back of the neck. A wound at the rear of the base of the skull cannot, under any stretch of the imagination or use of English, be considered identical to a "back wound."

Far too many supporters and critics of the Commission have carelessly or conveniently overlooked the Commission's adoption of a "back wound" on pages 95, 105, and 111 of the "Report." As any law student should know, "secondary evidence" is permitted in a court practicing the "basic principles of American justice," and, therefore, under these principles, testimony and legal charts can be used where the primary evidence, in this case, the X-rays, is suppressed or not subpoenaed by the prosecution, i.e., the Warren Commission.

The autopsy chart, Com. Exh. 397, is an authentic, legal document. It proved that the president did have a wound in his back "approximately 6 inches below the top of the collar, and 2 inches to the right of the seam." The location of the wound on the autopsy chart by Dr. Boswell conformed to that description. The bullet hole in the back of the president's jacket conformed to that description. So did the bullet hole in his shirt. The official FBI photographs, suppressed by the Commission, can be found and seen in FBI File No. 60, National Archives. (See illustrated section.)

The Warren Commission, ever on the alert to suppress evidence that proved Oswald innocent, suppressed the official FBI report of December 1963 and January 1964, for that report stated that a bullet entered "below his (the president's) shoulder to the right of the spinal column at an angle of 40 to 60-degrees downward; there was no point of exit and the bullet was in the body." Again, this location is supported by the legal Autopsy Chart No. 397. Even the Commission's own physician expert, Comdr. Humes, supported the FBI's official report and, in turn, the official report of the U.S. Secret Service, signed by Agents Hill and Kellerman.

Yet, the 7 commissioners and their 26 aides, none of whom were in Dallas, Texas, on November 22, 1963; none of whom were at Parkland Hospital; none of whom were at the Bethesda, Md. Naval Hospital; unanimously signed a report that categorically and unequivocally branded every physician, every

FBI and U.S. Secret Service agent who signed their reports to their respective bureaus, as either incompetent or a perjurer!

The only choice before the American people is who to believe? Men who had no ax to grind at the time of their medical examination, plus the federal agents, or 33 men who had to protect a preconceived theory that fabricated an 888-page story that no conspiracy existed because it was not in the national interests to proclaim the existence of an American conspiracy? The American people cannot have it both ways! Either the 33 were writing the truth or the agents and physicians were; but one or the other had to be deliberate perjurers or liars.

Regardless of the testimony proving President Kennedy was struck by four bullets, the Commission then had to proceed with the testimony relating to the wounds suffered by Governor Connally. Again, the same procedure was adopted by the Commission: every FBI or Secret Service agent and physician was branded a liar or perjurer by the Commission.

The aide conducting the investigation of the wounding of Governor Connally was Mr. Specter. He was quite an aide, and his idea of how to obtain the facts so that the truth could be ascertained was novel in the manner he interpreted his duty.

Specter's idea of "ascertaining the truth and evaluating the facts" was to pervert the witness statements or manufacture a set of "facts" from the words he uttered! Using his own words, he then proceeded to manufacture evidence based on those words. What an attorney; and he was twice to be elected as the Philadelphia district attorney. God help the accused! Specter's main prop on his pedestal of history is his infamous Bullet 399. As reported in the "Hearings," Specter originally informed Allen Dulles, a commissioner, that although he did not have any information or facts regarding Bullet 399 when questioned, he would go down to Dallas and find it. He did! First he gave birth, then he became pregnant!

Bullet 399 is, without question, the most remarkable bullet in the history of bullets and ballistics. This was the bullet that not only went into the president's back a "finger length" (FBI Agent O'Neill—Siebert Report, November 26, 1963), but then reversed itself, straightened up, flew up the president's back, entered the base of the neck at the rear, proceeded through his neck at an approximate angle of 90 degrees, went through his neck, and at a 27-degree angle entered the governor's body with such havoc that it "tumbled" through his wrist and then his thigh!

And this fairy tale, this concoction, this utter fabrication of evidence, was calmly swallowed by prestigious lawyers and heavy thinking newspaper and TV columnists!

The conduct of this Bullet 399 was admitted by Specter to be an utter fabrication; but it took him nearly three years to confess—in an interview to "U.S. World News." Chief Justice Warren, a firearms devotee, and Allen Dulles, ex-chief of the CIA, knew perfectly well that there is no bullet, past, present, or future, that can "tumble" within a human body or reverse itself. But, being men of high "honor," they signed the "Report." The reason why they accepted Specter's fairy tale was to create the "proof" that a conspiracy did not exist. The Commission succeeded beyond its wildest hope, for by the time that lie had been exposed the coup d'état had succeeded.

What was Bullet 399? That bullet was a substitute bullet which had been originally planted "under the floor mat" of the hospital elevator by (1) the conspirators, (2) a member of the Dallas Police Department, (3) Jack Ruby, or (4) by an "unknown" CIA agent who was knocked down and out by Secret Service agents guarding the operating room where the physicians were struggling to save the president's life.[27]

---

[27] Secret Service Agent Andrew E. Berger (stationed with Agent Richard E. Johnsen right outside Trauma Room One) reported that he encountered the following four figures at Parkland Memorial Hospital, who each attempted to gain entry to the room: FBI Agent Drain, accompanied by a "doctor friend." An "unidentified CIA agent," who possessed credentials. And an "unidentified FBI agent," who did not possess credentials. See Vincent Palamara, *Survivor's Guilt: The Secret Service and the Failure to Protect President Kennedy* (Walterville, OR: Trine Day, 2013), pp. 271-272. Palamara concludes: "Berger's report was totally ignored by just about everyone." Author Gerald McKnight adds that the unidentified FBI agent who attempted to push his way past the Secret Service "was instantly slammed to the wall and fell to the floor after receiving a haymaker from one of the Secret Service agents. The FBI agent was

Bullet 399 was found on an elevator containing a stretcher, by the building engineer, Mr. Tomlinson. He had entered the elevator between 1:00 and 1:30 p.m. and, as he did so, his step caused a bullet "to roll out from under the floor mat." He immediately took it to Mr. Wright, the hospital personnel director.[28] Mr. Wright, in turn, gave it to Secret Service Agent Johnsen, who gave it to Chief J. J. Rowley of the U.S. Secret Service bureau. From that point on, that bullet was treated like the proverbial "hot potato." The chief took "A" bullet with him to Washington, D.C., and on that night, November 22, 1963, gave "A" bullet to FBI Agent Todd.

Now, Agent Todd, conforming to FBI procedures, placed his initials upon A bullet and gave it to Agent Frazier, who did the same. Thus, A bullet should have the initials of two FBI agents. During that night, Agent Frazier gave A bullet to Agent Gallagher of the spectrographic department.

Ninety-two days pass, and A bullet is given to Commission aide Eisenberg, who then gave A bullet to Mr. J. D. Nicol, an Illinois ballistic expert. He conducted experiments upon A bullet at his ballistic laboratory in Illinois and, in April 1964, testified before the Commission concerning A bullet given to him by aide Eisenberg. However, the "Hearings" does not say when that bullet was ever returned to Washington, D.C. or by whom. What is known is that on June 24, 1964, FBI Agent Odum was in Dallas, Texas, where he asked both Mr. Tomlinson and Mr. Wright if the bullet he was showing them was the bullet they had given to U.S. Secret Service Agent Johnsen on November 23, 1963. Bingo! The answer was a definite "no" by both men. Not being disturbed in the slightest by the positive refusal of these two witnesses, Agent Odum took the bullet he had shown these two witnesses to the Secret Service headquarters in Washington, D.C. and showed A bullet to both Chief Rowley and Secret Service Agent Johnsen. Odum asked them if it was the bullet they had given FBI Agent Todd.

---

later identified as J. Doyle Williams." See McKnight, *Breach of Trust*, pp. 272-273.

[28] O. P. Wright was the Parkland Memorial Hospital personnel director of security.

Bingo! Again, a definite "no"! Four witnesses, all of whom had refused to identify Bullet 399 as the one they had at Parkland Hospital on the afternoon of November 23, 1963.

In law, as Chief Justice Warren very well knew, Bullet 399 was a worthless bit of evidence. It was evidence that was "'planted" to conform to the theory that it was discharged from the planted Italian Carcano rifle even though the FBI testified that the rifle was never "used" by Oswald at any time. (FBI Report, vol. 5.) There is no evidence in the "Hearings" that the two FBI agents' initialed bullet was the bullet given to expert Nicol to use in his ballistic tests. The evidence published in the "Hearings" also revealed that no nurse, physician, or orderly saw any bullet when they removed the clothes from Governor Connally prior to operating upon him, nor did they see a bullet on the stretcher, nor did any person see any bullet on the president's stretcher when he was taken into the operating room. The only person whose testimony could be accepted by a court of law would be that of Mr. Tomlinson, who testified that "a spent cartridge or bullet rolled out that had apparently been lodged under the edge of the mat."

As the Commission was not operating under the "basic principles of American justice," aide Specter, in an attempt to negate testimony which proved Bullet 399 was a plant, simply lied in the statement he made to a physician that Bullet 399 was found on the governor's stretcher. Then Specter used his own lie to substantiate the statement he made to a witness who was never involved in the finding of Bullet 399. The only witness who found that bullet swore under oath where he found it, but then that would prove a conspiracy. And that was what the 26 aides were instructed not to find!

Conclusive proof that Bullet 399 was a deliberate fraud perpetrated upon the American people by the Warren Commission can be found in the willful machinations of the FBI regarding that bullet.

In all ballistic tests, the bullet when going through the barrel of the rifle, or gun, will have marks made upon it. The marks on the bullet must match the marks that exist within the barrel. No two gun barrels will make the identical marks upon a bullet. Therefore, to conduct a legal ballistic test, the expert must have both the rifle and the bullet.

Secreted by the Warren Commission is the testimony of Mr. Nicol that at no time did the FBI give the Italian 6.5mm Mannlicher-Carcano rifle to him for testing purposes! At the time [that] Mr. Nicol was permitted to test A bullet given to him by the Commission, the FBI knew that several rifles had been in the possession of the Dallas police. One was a German Mauser seen by Deputy Sheriff Weitzman, Deputies Boone and Mooney, Lt. Day, and Captain Fritz; and several were Italian Mannlicher-Carcano rifles. The FBI did not know what rifle the Dallas police had given to them. They did know that the Italian Mannlicher-Carcano rifle they had received was a nonlethal weapon.

The FBI knew that the rifle sent to them by Lt. Day did not have any of Oswald's prints upon it; they did know that the ammunition clip "found" by Lt. Day was planted evidence; and they did know that they had received a rifle "in a well-oiled condition" but one which left no stains or indentations upon that bag. The FBI thus knew that the police were setting up the Bureau as another "patsy."

The FBI was placed in a terrible predicament. The Dallas police Italian rifle could not be given to Mr. Nicol, for he would discover that it was a defective, nonlethal weapon. He would see that the rifle could only be used by a left-handed rifleman. He could see that the telescopic sight was defective. He could see that the trigger mechanism was of no value. How did the Bureau solve that problem? That problem had to be solved quickly, for if that Italian rifle was given to Mr. Nicol the conspiracy would be exposed.

The solution was simple. The Bureau gave 100 bullets to Mr. Nicol and informed him that these 100 bullets came from the Mannlicher-Carcano rifle. Then, based upon the assumption that A bullet he had received from the Commission was the bullet found by Mr. Tomlinson from under the elevator floor mat in Parkland Hospital, the ballistic expert simply testified that the bullet he received from aide Tomlinson matched the 100 bullets given to him by the FBI. In law, as will be seen, the testimony proved a conspiracy. It also proved that the FBI accepted a role as being "an accessory after the fact" in the murder of President Kennedy.

Mr. Nicol revealed that prior to receiving the 100 bullets from the FBI, the FBI repaired the Italian rifle, shot 100 bullets through the new barrel, and then only gave him those bullets to compare with the bullet he received from Commission aid Eisenberg. There is no ballistic expert in the world that can match a bullet that has been discharged prior to the internal repairs made upon a rifle barrel with a bullet that has been discharged after the repairs have been completed.

The Commission knew that fact; the aide knew that fact; the FBI knew that fact; and so did Mr. Nicol. In law, every one of them knew that Bullet 399 had never been legally identified. The Commission, its 26 aides, and the FBI knew that Bullet 399 was a fraudulent piece of evidence. As the evidence revealed, only two federal agencies were involved in the substitution of a bullet that was used to plant evidence. The FBI or the U.S. Secret Service. There is no testimony in the "Hearings" that any federal agent gave the "initialed" bullet by Agents Todd and Frazier to Mr. Nicol. All four men who handled the bullet in the hospital refused to identify Bullet 399 as the bullet they had handled. What happened to the bullet found by Mr. Tomlinson? No one knows! In law, a court acting under the "basic principles of American law" would decree that Bullet 399 is manufactured evidence and, as such, is illegal. Being illegal evidence, it could not be used to convict a person accused of murdering the president and wounding the governor.

The Commission not only violated the principles of law but also lied concerning the path the bullet took between the president's body and its entry into the governor's. The angle of fire into the president's back was at a 40 to 60-degree angle. The path of the bullet into the governor's body was at a 27-degree angle. Thus, the Commission, like the pope, attempted to overrule the laws of science. (FBI Report, vol. 1.)

In an attempt to prove their statements regarding Bullet 399, the Commission published a photograph in the "Hearings" which can be seen in the illustrated section of this book. The cut-off portion was made by the FBI ballistic section to conduct tests. But, as can be seen, that bullet remained in a pristine condition. This bullet, according to the Commission, not only smashed the governor's wrist but "tumbled" through it, and then destroyed a rib in his rib cage; and, after creating all that damage, the loss of weight of that bullet was 1/180th of an ounce!

The two physicians who treated Governor Connally, Dr. Shires and Dr. Shaw, were cross-examined by ex-CIA Director Allen Dulles. Both of them, under oath, testified that the governor was struck by TWO bullets. In fact, the physicians stated that it was entirely possible that three bullets struck him. Dr. Shires testified that there remained metal fragments in the governor's body at the time he was testifying. After dismissing both physicians, Dr. Humes, the Commission's own medical expert, supported the testimony of those two doctors. Read and compare R95 to R93 where the "Report" itself stated that the governor had a wound in his leg which was not the result of a fragmented bullet in his ribs, nor the fragments of that bullet, but from another independent missile!

Dr. Shires had also testified that bullet fragments were still in the governor's chest. The believers of the Warren Commission have never answered the question brought forth by the Commissioners, for how could a bullet which left bullet fragments exceeding the weight of 1/180th of an ounce be as nonfragmented as Bullet 399, pictured in the "Report"? The Commission, in its contempt for the intelligence of the American people, went so far as to publish photographs of a bullet smashed beyond ballistic testing when fired into goat skins and gelatin.

Not being satisfied with the testimony of the physicians that proved a conspiracy murdered President Kennedy, the Commission decided to use a few fabricated sketches relating to location of the president's head wounds. A close scrutiny of those exhibits, labelled Com. Exh. 385 and 386, revealed that No. 385 has no head wound at all, while No. 386 shows the president's head in an entirely new position from that of No. 385 and, in addition, there is no hair on the back of the head.

As the Commission swore, on their "honor," that the president was struck by only one bullet, it would be a physical and scientific impossibility for the exhibits to show two different positions for the identical wound. Therefore, these two exhibits were fabricated by the Commission in an effort to conceal two head wounds which, in turn, revealed the existence of a conspiracy. Upon reading the testimony relating to those two exhibits it was revealed that an enlisted Navy man had been instructed by Comdr. Humes, after the commander had destroyed all his original notes and long after the autopsy had been performed, to draw the illustrations to conform to Comdr. Humes' "memory." The commander's "memory" was so clear that he had to read a newspaper to remember what he had done at the autopsy! The enlisted man, acting under orders from the commander who, in turn, was acting under orders from "higher authority," was informed to draw the sketches to conform to what Comdr. Humes thought should be the position of the head if the president was struck by bullets fired from the 6th-floor window. Unfortunately for Comdr. Humes and Dr. Boswell, the other physicians were on hand to testify; and, since those two exhibits contradicted each other, the remaining physicians corrected the exhibits properly.

The testimony of the doctors relating to the governor's wounds also brought forth additional manufactured evidence by the Commission. Two Secret Service agents, who never studied medicine and who were never at Governor Connally's bedside, made three exhibits, Numbers 679, 680, and 689. They were shown to Dr. Shires, Dr. Gregory, and Dr. Shaw; and every one of them said those exhibits were improper and fraudulent. These physicians were permitted by the Commission aides to draw the proper angle of fire into the governor's body, and all of them agreed that no bullet fired from the 6th-floor window could enter the governor's body. Although the U.S. Secret Service wrote to the Commission that the sketches of their agents were incorrect, the Commission published the incorrect sketches as proof of their theory! (See also Secret Service Report CD 381.)

In summarizing the testimony, exhibits, and evidence published in the "Hearings" and in the National Archives, a definitive statement can be made that the Commission's accusations in paragraph (A) of the Commission's indictment were totally false. Being false, Oswald was innocent.

The FBI and the U.S. Secret Service proved that no bullets were fired, and no bullets had been fired, from the S.E. corner window on the 6th floor of the Book Depository.

The medical testimony supported the testimony of the FBI and the Secret Service. That testimony proved that President Kennedy was struck by two bullets in the head, another bullet hit him in the back, and one more entered the front of his throat and coursed downward into his right lung. Four bullets proved the conspiracy. Uncontradicted medical testimony proved that Governor Connally was struck by a minimum of two bullets, and fragments of another bullet struck him in the leg. Thus, a minimum of 7 bullets were legally and medically proven to have been fired at President Kennedy. 7 bullets confirmed the conspiracy.

History has revealed the acknowledgement by several Commission aides that they knew a conspiracy murdered President Kennedy. Unfortunately, as [with] the French in the Dreyfus Affaire, these aides admitted their errors several years after the publication of the "Report."

But when their admissions were openly confessed, investigators had already proved beyond a reasonable doubt that a conspiracy existed. With the testimony of the medical profession and the FBI and Secret Service bureaus, Lee Harvey Oswald's attorney would have had no difficulty in proving to a court believing and practicing the "basic principles of American justice" that Oswald was an innocent man.

CHAPTER III

NONEXISTING EVIDENCE
The Rifles, Palm Prints, & Photographs

Paragraph (B) of the Commission's indictment alleging involvement of Oswald as the murderer of President Kennedy uses language that, in law, involves him in not doing anything! True, the Commission alleges he (1) purchased the rifle used in the assassination; (2) his palm print was "found" on the rifle. Thus far, Oswald had committed no criminal act, for the purchasing of the rifle and the disassembling of it violated no law. The fact that the Commission stated he "owned" a rifle "used" to commit the crime means nothing unless he "used" it for that specific purpose. The palm print also denotes no crime, for any man may disassemble a rifle without using it for a crime. The Commission, in an effort to connect ownership to actual use of the rifle by Oswald, wrote that the fibers on the rifle butt "most probably" belonged to Oswald's shirt. That statement in a law court also meant nothing. The Commission also stated that Oswald had possession of that Italian rifle from the day it was purchased to the day it was "found" on the 6th floor. Again, in law, that statement cannot support a conviction unless there be evidence to prove their statement. In conclusion, the Commission said this specific rifle was used as the assassination weapon because it was "owned" and "possessed" by him. Notice the switch of terms from "used" to "owned" and "possessed."

One is again struck by the language the Commission used to convict Oswald. The Commission, neither in paragraph (A) or (B), ever made the specific allegation required by law that Oswald "used" that rifle on that day to murder another human biting. As will be seen, the Commission waited until paragraph (E) of the indictment to specifically name Oswald as the murderer: not of President Kennedy, but of officer Tippit. Why the distinction?

Under the "basic principles of American justice" was there any proof that Lee Harvey Oswald did purchase a 6.5mm Italian Mannlicher-Carcano rifle which was used as the weapon to murder President Kennedy?

The answer to that question must be an unequivocal "no."

There is absolutely no evidence available to a law court in the testimony or in the National Archives that proved, beyond a reasonable doubt, that Oswald purchased, possessed, or used the rifle allegedly used to murder President Kennedy. In its official report the FBI never accused Oswald of "using" that rifle or any rifle on the day of the murder. The Bureau only stated that he "owned" the rifle. (FBI Report, vol. 1.)

Proceeding from that FBI official report directly to the testimony given under oath by the finder of that rifle, Deputy Sheriff Weitzman swore that the rifle he found was a 7.65 German Mauser, with a 4/18 telescopic sight, and "a brownish-black sling on it." Under tremendous pressure the Deputy recanted his affidavit; but at that time, although the Italian rifle was in the Commission's room, he was not shown that Italian rifle, Com. Exh. 139. Under the "basic principles of American justice" the deliberate refusal of the Commission to show Com. Exh. 139 to Weitzman for purposes of identification proved Com. Exh. 139 was not the weapon seen by the deputy.

However, Deputy Sheriff Weitzman's partners, Deputies Mooney and Boone, swore under oath that Capt. Fritz, in their presence, examined the rifle found on the sixth floor and pronounced it a 7.65 German Mauser. District Attorney Wade was to announce to the press, on November 24, 1963, that the rifle was a German Mauser. The Deputy who was with Weitzman when he found the rifle was shown the 6.5 Italian Mannlicher-Carcano during his examination, and that Deputy flatly rejected the German Mauser as the one he had seen when Capt. Fritz was examining it.

In violation of every principle of American Criminal law, the Commission, instead of accepting the sworn testimony of every police officer who testified the rifle was a German Mauser, used the "testimony" of Lt. Day as "proof" that the rifle was an Italian Carcano. In volume 4, page 260 of the "Hearings" is his testimony that he dictated a memo to his secretary at police headquarters where he had taken the rifle for examination. At 9 p.m. of the same day, another police officer wrote a description of that rifle. Both of these reports are missing from the files of the Dallas Police Department and from the National Archives! It can be stated that since Lt. Day was a perjurer on other matters that he was a perjurer on this matter. As they say in Latin, translated into English: "Once a liar, always a liar." That two vital documents, the only two outside of the Weitzman affidavit, should be missing is far too much to ask when the investigation deals with the murder of a president of the United States. In an attempt to take himself "off the hook" for perjury, Lt. Day said that when he was taking the rifle back to police headquarters he rode with FBI Agent Odum, and the agent radioed FBI Dallas headquarters and Agent Odum notified them that the rifle was a 6.5 Italian Carcano. Was this true? Of course not! When Agent Odum testified before the Commission, he was never questioned by the Commission concerning this vital evidence. Nor did the Commission ask the FBI to search their radio tapes for that conversation, nor did the Commission ask any FBI agent working out of the Dallas office if they discussed the type of rifle Lt. Day had in his possession in the agent's car.

Under the "basic principles of American justice," the rifle found by Deputy Weitzman was a 7.65 German Mauser, "equipped with a 4/18 telescopic sight, with a brownish-black sling," and his affidavit, in turn, was substantiated by every police agent on that floor and further substantiated by the manner in which the Warren Commission attempted to conceal that knowledge from the public.

Mark Lane, of "Rush to Judgment," was to expose the switching of the rifles by the Dallas Police Department. For he pointed out to the Commission that on the stock of the rifle were the words: 6.5 Cal. Made Italy." Yet, Capt. Fritz who examined that rifle and Lt. Day, who had that rifle in his possession for more than 10 hours, never saw those words. They never saw them, for they were not on that rifle taken from the Depository. At no time did Lt. Day or Capt. Fritz ever notify the press that it was an Italian rifle found on the 6th floor. Would one believe that they also never notified District Attorney Wade at any time, for he reiterated the statement that it was a German Mauser. Only when the FBI announced on the 23rd of November that they had received a 6.5 Italian Mannlicher-Carcano rifle did the police change their minds. But then, as the evidence will reveal, the police had that rifle in their possession prior to the murder, just as they had Oswald's revolver prior to the murder of officer Tippit.

In an effort to support their accusation that Oswald had purchased the Italian rifle given to the FBI by the Dallas police, the Commission relied upon evidence which proved the contrary. The Commission published a statement that Oswald's wife swore she saw that specific rifle and that the wife's statement was substantiated by her landlady, Mrs. Paine.

However, when one examined her statement published in the "Report" to the one she also signed under oath to the U.S. Secret Service bureau, the investigator can immediately see the perjury she committed—either deliberate or made under the pressure that she would be deported to her former country, the USSR, without her two children. This document was not published in the "Report" but was suppressed under the Code No. 344 in the National Archives.

Mrs. Marina Oswald, the wife of the accused, signed her affidavit containing the statement that from February 1963, which was more than a month prior to Oswald allegedly purchasing the rifle from Klein's of Chicago, she saw a rifle "either standing in the corner or on the shelf" in her New Orleans apartment. The Commission showed no concern that the alleged rifle was in the Oswald home a month prior to its alleged purchase. Mrs. Oswald's testimony was corroborated by none other than Mrs. Paine, the FBI informant concerning matters relating to the Oswalds.

This rifle "either standing in the corner or sitting on the shelf in the closet" was seen by both Mrs. Paine and Mrs. Oswald to have on it no telescopic sight! Yet, Klein's forwarded a rifle with a telescopic sight attached, for the money order specified a sight attached to the rifle. Thus, in a court of law, the presumption is that Oswald never owned a rifle with a telescopic sight. However, there is more evidence that Oswald never received any type of rifle, at any time, from Klein's of Chicago.

An examination of the files of the National Archives and of the testimony in the "Hearings" revealed the undisputed fact that the FBI had conducted a surveillance of Oswald's post office box from the very day he leased that box in October 1962, until he surrendered the lease in May 1963. That P.O. Box 2915 was watched not only by an Inspector of the Post Office, Mr. Holmes, but when he was not there, by the employees who notified the FBI of every bit and kind of mail Oswald received. At his examination before the Commission, the inspector admitted that under Postal Regulations no person, other than the lessee, could obtain any kind of mail from a box registered to the box lessee. (P.O. Regs. 355.) The Commission and the inspector admitted that no other person than Oswald was legally permitted to obtain any mail or package. There is no evidence or proof that Oswald ever received any type of package the size of which could have enclosed an assembled or even a disassembled rifle. As the chief justice proclaimed his intentions to follow the law as practiced "under the basic principles of American justice," there is not the slightest aroma of proof that Oswald received a rifle from Chicago.

In their last desperate attempt to prove that Oswald purchased a rifle in March 1963 from Klein's, the Commission suppressed one of the key documents submitted to them by the FBI. Hidden from the reader of the "Report" was a letter to the Commission signed by Mr. J. Edgar Hoover of the FBI. That letter informed the 7 "honorable" commissioners that every rifle manufactured in Italy from 1930 to and including the World War II years had stamped on all Italian Mannlicher-Carcano military rifles the number "C 2766"! The "Report" had given the impression that "C 2766" was used only once and that every Italian rifle of that make received a different code number. Thus, the Commission lied, deliberately lied, for they had Mr. Hoover's letter months before the "Report" was in the hands of the publisher.

One of the most intriguing and unanswered questions is: "How did the FBI associate the name "Hidell" to Lee Harvey Oswald?" The Commission simply printed a statement that the FBI, between 1 a.m. on the morning of November 23rd and late afternoon of the same day, connected "Hidell" to Oswald.

The evidence in the "Hearings" had revealed that the Dallas Police Department had in their possession the "Hidell" name card prior to the arrest of Oswald! The testimony is overwhelming that the "Hidell" card was not taken from Oswald's person or found in his Berkley rooming house. Neither the FBI nor the U.S. Secret Service knew of Oswald's "association" until the day following the arrest; and the Secret Service testified that none of their agents knew of the alleged connection until November 24th.

Due to the fact that the agents of the FBI confiscated ALL records relating to this mysterious "Hidell" money order—including Klein's record books, which would show the return of any "Hidell" package mailed to Oswald's post office box—until the year 2038 when the assassination will be a footnote to history, no person will be able to contest the FBI's statement that the "Hidell" signature was made by Lee Harvey Oswald.

No court of law operating under the "basic principles of American justice" would permit the Warren Commission to connect Oswald with the "Hidell" signature; nor would the same court, under any stretch of the imagination or under any ruling by the U.S. Supreme Court, permit any prosecutor to state that the rifle was delivered and accepted by Oswald in view of the uncontradicted testimony of the post office employees that no such package was ever placed in Oswald's post office box.

The Commission never explained how the alleged Oswald order for the Italian rifle led to Klein's shipping to him a rifle that was not ordered by Oswald. The rifle "sent" to Oswald was not the one in the advertisement in the February 1963 "American Rifleman" but one that was 4.2 inches longer and 2.5 pounds heavier. Klein's runs a multimillion-dollar legal weapon business, and it is slightly more than incredible that the only time Klein's mailed the improper type of weapon was one that was ordered by Oswald "using" the name "Hidell."

The evidence that the Commission produced to associate Oswald with "Hidell" was manufactured by the Dallas police. The Dallas policemen who arrested Oswald and searched his billfold at the police station testified that they never saw any

"Hidell" card. The Justice of Peace Johnston Exhibit No. 1 does not list "Hidell" as an Oswald alias. Nor do the interrogation reports signed by the FBI mention "Hidell" as one of Oswald's names! Nor did the Dallas police sent to arrest him at his rooming house on Berkley Street ask Mrs. Roberts if "Hidell" lived there. They asked only for "O. H. Lee." The FBI testified that for anyone to forge a Selective Service card he must be a highly experienced person in the use of a camera used in graphic arts. Oswald had no such experience. Thus, how did the FBI know to associate Oswald with "Hidell" so that they could "search" the Klein's business records? The only logical answer is that (1) the FBI had prior knowledge within their Bureau which, if true, would make the Bureau an "accessory before the murder;" or (2) the Bureau was informed by the Dallas police, and this must be interpreted that the "Hidell" card was a "frame-up."

One thing is certain: Captain Fritz committed. perjury regarding the "Hidell" card. However, the Warren Commission was not concerned with forgery, planted evidence, or manufactured evidence as long as that type of evidence would confuse the public. After all, the Commission said "national security was involved," and to make safe that "security" a little more, or less, fake evidence was immaterial.

An investigation and an analysis of the methods and conduct used by the Warren Commission and its 26 aides can only lead to the conclusion that the Commission had no concept of "honor." They did reveal their enormous contempt for the intelligence of the average American and this contempt was revealed in the manner the Commission used to bypass evidence that more than three types of rifles were used by the Commission to "convict" Oswald.

There is no question that the Dallas police were deeply involved in the conspiracy that murdered President Kennedy. That department was an active participant prior, during, and after the assassination. This participation was no secret to the Commission or their aides. In fact, as the testimony revealed, the Commission, time and time again, accepted deliberate perjury committed by members of that department. The Commission, time and time again, knowingly accepted evidence manufactured by the police. Why? The only answer to that question can be traced to the transfer of power in Washington and the fact that the rulers of Texas were extremely bitter toward President Kennedy's program; and those rulers ruled the Dallas Police Department. As will be seen in a later chapter of this book, the police were to murder several witnesses and also commit great physical injury upon the family of one witness.

In view of the involvement of the police, it should not be strange that the Commission conveniently overlooked the overwhelming evidence that the Dallas police "switched" rifles from the 7.65 German Mauser found on the 6th floor to a 6.5 nonlethal, nonoperating Italian Mannlicher-Carcano rifle.

In the National Archives are three vital pieces of evidence that proved beyond a reasonable doubt that Lee Harvey Oswald never received any type of rifle from Klein's, never possessed that type of rifle, and never used that rifle on November 23, 1963!

The evidence was suppressed for only one purpose: to convince the American people that no conspiracy existed, for the Commission knew not only the names of several of the conspirators and the murderers of President Kennedy but they also knew that the conspiracy involved, on a direct basis, men of "prestigious" caliber.

The Commission in its "Report" characterized Mrs. Oswald and Mrs. Paine as truthful witnesses whose testimony was unqualifiedly accepted by them. These two witnesses not only testified that they saw no rifle with a telescopic sight in Oswald's possession, but when they were shown the Italian rifle both women testified, under oath, that they never saw the type of sling attached to that rifle! In support of their testimony, [an] FBI firearms photographic expert testified that, when he examined the "Life" photograph purporting to show Oswald holding that rifle, that rifle had a different type of sling than Com. Exh. 139.

This photograph published by "Life," although retouched by "Life," was accepted by the Commission as a "true and authentic" photograph. It becomes more and more sickening as the interpretation of the Commission's "basic principles of

American justice" is exposed to the light of day. The "Life" photograph, after retouching, showed Oswald holding a rifle in his right hand with the butt of a small pistol sticking outside his belt. However, during the late afternoon of November 22, 1963, the United Press International (UPI) had taken several photographs of a police officer, at police Headquarters, holding the alleged murder weapon by the rifle butt and barrel. A photograph allegedly found in Oswald's Paine garage was also shown to Oswald by Capt. Fritz during his "interrogation." Oswald immediately denied that the picture was of him; Oswald (and the captain admitted this fact) shouted that his face on the photograph had been superimposed on another person's body.[29]

Those photographs served the purpose of proving that the Dallas police had switched rifles, from the German Mauser to the nonlethal Italian Carcano at the police station.

An examination of the photographs of "Life" and "Associated Press" rifles reveals outstanding differences. Both of those photographs have been labeled "authentic" by the Warren Commission, for both are published in the "Report" as being the actual authentic photographs of the murder weapon.

The major differences between the "Life," Com. Exh. 139, and "AP" rifle photographs are: (1) The front end of the telescopic sight on Com. Exh. 139 is 1/4th of an inch behind the barrel. (1b) The same front end in the "AP" picture is directly in line. (2) The front sight of that rifle, Com. Exh. 139, has a tapered sight. (2b) The "AP" rifle has a round sight. (3) The Commission's exhibit rifle shows the rifle bolt to be even to the telescopic sight mount. (3b) The "AP" rifle bolt is directly behind the mount. (4) In Com. Exh. 139 the telescopic mount is slanted. (4b) On the "AP" rifle the mount is vertical!

To assist the reader in analyzing the various rifles used by the Commission to "convict" Oswald, all the rifles are in the illustrated section. In addition, there is a UPI photograph of Capt. Fritz holding the alleged murder weapon in both of his hands. When the FBI analyzed the rifle sent to them by the Dallas police as the weapon they found on the 6th floor, the FBI

---

[29] A likely supposition, since the size of the head in comparison to the body is far too large.

was flabbergasted that they found none of this officer's fingerprints upon the rifle! The FBI informed the Commission of that fact, which could only be interpreted, under the "basic principles of American justice," that the police had forwarded a weapon that was not used by anyone on that day.

An examination of those photographs also revealed under magnification that on the first three photographs of the alleged murder rifle a white sling can be seen; on the fourth photograph there is a two-piece sling. The magnifier also brought forth the evidence that the trigger guards are different, the sights are different, and the stock on rifle number 3 is different from the others! Yet, another mystery remained unsolved, for the FBI in its suppressed five-volume report stated that if Oswald used that Italian Carcano rifle to shoot at ex-Maj. Gen. Walker, he must have changed the barrel! When and where do old rifle dealers in 1963 obtain the barrel of a 1930 Italian military rifle? It was absolutely amazing, the fairy tale the Commission concocted. For now Oswald not only purchased this barrel of an ineffective nonlethal weapon, but he also used a rope as a sling.

The Warren Commission deliberately and willfully lied, for they knew that the evidence proved the Dallas police had substituted several rifles for the 7.65mm German Mauser rifle found on the 6th floor. To protect whom?

With the false photographs being acknowledged by "Life" that It had deliberately retouched—the so-called "Oswald" photograph—that photograph was, under the "basic principles of American Justice," a forgery. Although Mrs. Oswald testified she took only one photograph of that pose, the Commission published two photographs with Oswald in a different pose. Mrs. Oswald also testified that she never saw the camera that the Commission said took the photograph, but the Commission overruled her statement. The Commission never asked Oswald's brother, when he was on the witness stand, if he had ever seen that camera.

This camera was supposed to have been found in the Paine garage, but not a single Dallas police officer who originally searched that garage saw that camera. The garage had been searched on November 22 and 23, and there is no testimony as to how that camera came into the possession of the Dallas police. That camera, furthermore, is not on the police property list relating to the property taken from the Paine garage on those two days!

Those negatives of Oswald were also "mysteriously" found by officers, some of whom committed perjury. The negatives were not discovered by the police on the first day of the search of Oswald's premises in the Paine home. The next day Mrs. Paine conveniently left her home and, lo and behold, the police say they found them. There were no witnesses to see this discovery. But who was the lucky finder? A Detective Rose found two negatives; and Detective McCabe who, not under oath, said he found the camera. Yet, it was McCabe who never thought that the camera he "found" then was not there on November 22. That camera just walked from nowhere right into his hands. Another mystery is the fact that the Commission called the police liars; for on Page 127 of the "Report" the Commission said only one negative was found, and here was Det. Rose saying he found two negatives!

Concluding this sad state of affairs for the Commission was their pet witness, Mrs. Paine, who testified that although she was to be the "scout mistress" for the Oswald family, at no time did she ever see any pictures of Oswald that were taken while he resided in New Orleans, Dallas, or Irving, Texas. Neither Oswald nor his wife, his mother or brother, ever took pictures of Oswald or any member of his family at any time. Would a jury of common sense believe that Commission supposition? But the police found that he took one, two, or three incriminating pictures of himself and retained them so that they could be used to stretch his neck.

The second piece of vital evidence suppressed by the Warren Commission was the planting of an ammunition clip by Lt. Day as evidence against Oswald. The Commission had been informed by the FBI that the rifleman using the Italian Carcano rifle would have to pull the trigger within a time limit of 7 seconds, or the president's body would be out of the telescopic sight.

To meet that time period the Commission requested the FBI to conduct firing tests. As usual, the Commission deliberately lied in its "Report" that three rifle marksmen from the American

Rifle Association had successfully pulled the trigger within that period. As usual, an examination of the testimony in the "Hearings" revealed the tests were as phony as plastic baloney! The tests were fraudulent per se in that not a single one of the marksmen was able to hit an enlarged nonmoving target simulating the president's head at height fifty percent less than [that of] the 6th-floor window to the street below.

Thus, to meet that specified time limit the Commission knew that the only way to do this was to state that Oswald used an ammunition clip. Unfortunately, the Commission forgot that many historians and investigators would look to the testimony and exhibits to see if an ammunition clip had been sent to "Hidell" with the rifle he allegedly purchased from Klein's. Repetition may be boring, but as usual the testimony proved that Lt. Day had planted or manufactured the ammunition clip. The Commission admitted that no ammunition clip or ammunition had been sent to "Hidell" with the Italian rifle. But in the Commission "bullpen" was none other than their pinch perjurer, Lt. Day. The Commission could always rely upon Lt. Day when the Commission needed evidence, any evidence, to tighten their rope around Oswald's neck. He was consistent; he was a consistent perjurer!

Without an ammunition clip in the rifle the Commission knew that no rifleman could have murdered the president in the time limit specified by the FBI tests. Therefore, that clip was absolutely essential to "convict" Oswald. However, the testimony and exhibits in the National Archives revealed that every officer of the Dallas Police Department, the sheriff's office, the state police, the agents of the FBI and U.S. Secret Service, and members of the press searching the area near and around the 6th-floor window found no ammunition clip. Thus, more than 21 men, with 42 eyes, searched and searched, and found no ammunition clip. The cartons that formed the shield and those that did not were moved, but no ammunition clip was discovered.

That is, until Lt. "I see it" Day arrived at the scene. Bingo! He saw it, he said, and picked it up—secretly! No police agent saw him pick it up, or from what spot he picked it up. Lt. Day kept that secret from his superiors in the police department, from the sheriff, from the FBI, the Secret Service, and the press. He was so secretive that he placed no identification tag on it showing the time, the day, and the place where he found it. But, according to his testimony, Lt. Day wrote to himself a memo, and the memo identified the numbers on that clip as being "SMI, 9x2." When the FBI examined the clip that had been forwarded to the Bureau by the Dallas police, the Bureau found that the clip's identification was "SMI 952"! The reliability of Lt. Day as an expert in reading is again subject to doubt. He could not only not read correctly, but he also failed to see the words "Made Italy, 6.5 Cal." that were on the stock of the rifle! How could the Commission accept the testimony of a "witness" who could not see and could not read? At times, his testimony revealed he could not hear!

Lt. Day testified that he had written a memo relating to that clip, but when asked to produce it for the record he had none, for an examination of the records kept in the National Archives revealed the fact that it is "missing"! If one reads the "Report" or the "Hearings," one can see how the "clip" was cleverly slipped into the testimony without any verification. "Three spent shells were found under the window. They were picked up by Det. Sims and witnessed by Lt. Day and Studebaker. The clip is stamped 'SMI, 9x2'" What was picked up? Three shells, not an ammunition clip! There is nothing in the testimony of Sims or Studebaker that [indicates] they saw an ammunition clip.

Further proof of the Commission's deceit and Lt. Day's perjury can be found by analyzing the official Dallas police list of the material evidence taken from the 6th floor by various police agents. That official list, signed by officer Hicks, contains not a single word concerning the finding of an ammunition clip by any officer, let alone Lt. Day.

Conclusive proof that Lt. Day was a perjurer was furnished by the FBI to the Commission when the official FBI report stated "there was no ammunition clip, for the third shell had been loaded into and extracted from the rifle chamber." Lt. Day was a perjurer. "Once a perjurer, always a perjurer!"

The final collapse of the Commission's case against Oswald using an Italian rifle (Com. Exh. 139) was again dealt by the

FBI. In an FBI letter found in the National Archives, the Bureau informed the Commission: (1) the live bullet in the rifle chamber has "marks on it which were not identified with the rifle. (2) Three sets of marks were on the cartridge base which cannot be found on the other two. (3) The third shell had been loaded into and extracted from the weapon at least twice."

The Commission knew that it was a physical and scientific impossibility for any rifleman, using a military rifle, to attempt to load and reload bullets in an ammunition clip while firing. The commissioners, in [the] face of all the FBI evidence informing them that there was no ammunition clip attached to the rifle, had to accept the testimony of a perjurer. These Commissioners knew that when the last bullet from an ammunition clip goes into the rifle chamber the clip is ejected automatically. These men knew that no rifleman would calmly remove a bullet in the ammunition clip, replace it, and then use the clip; for when the final bullet moved into the chamber the clip would fall from the rifle. Thus, the greater question would be: "Who was the greater perjurer, Lt. Day or the commissioners?"

The Warren Commission had additional testimony from the FBI, for the FBI ballistic expert testified (1) one of the shells was so deformed it could not fit within the chamber! (2) There were no fingerprints of any person found on the shells, rifle belt, or stock of that rifle. (3) No fingerprints of any person were found on any of the three cartridges or on the live bullet.

The FBI was informing the Commission that the Bureau had received planted evidence from the Dallas police; for by informing them that (1) no fingerprints were found on any of the cartridges [one must conclude that] the police had switched the cartridges, as Lt. Day admitted [that] two of his fellow officers had picked them up with their fingers. (2) Furthermore, by informing the Commission of the "deformed shell," the FBI was also telling the commissioners that, since that shell did not fit within the rifle chamber, that shell held no bullet. Now, can you kill a man with a bullet that was not fired from a shell? And how can a shell not holding a bullet fire that bullet through a rifle chamber?

Why did the Dallas police conceal and destroy the cartridges seen by the police on the 6th floor which were given to Lt. Day? Were these bullets substituted for others? In a seldom-read exhibit, Coded Exh. No. 705, page 492, suppressed by the Warren Commission, is the statement that at 12:45 p.m. on November 22nd, 15 minutes after the shooting of the president, a police officer notified his superior officer that he found 3 spent cartridges on the third floor of the Depository. Not the 6th floor but the 3rd floor! He was instructed to take them to the station, which he did. The question remains: "What happened to those 3 spent cartridges? Were they substituted for those found on the 6th floor? Why did the Warren Commission keep a deathly silence about those 3rd-floor cartridges? Was there an assassin also on the third floor? Whose prints were on those cartridges?"

In all the FBI testimony and documents submitted to the Commission, the Bureau at no time stated that Oswald "used" the Italian rifle given to them by the Dallas police; nor did the Bureau at any time corroborate the Dallas police regarding the photographs taken by the police of the 6th-floor window area; nor substantiate the finding of fingerprints or palm prints on the rifle or revolver; nor did they corroborate the Dallas police regarding the finding of the three 6th-floor cartridges given to the FBI by the Dallas police; or the "brown paper bag." In view of the outright perjury committed by the various police officers, there is no evidence that could be given to a jury in a courtroom where the "basic principles of American justice" were practiced.

The Federal Bureau of Investigation, contrary to every published story relating to the President Kennedy murder, provided the Commission with twelve (12) major pieces of evidence that proved, beyond a reasonable doubt, that the Italian rifle was not "used" by any person on November 22, 1963. The Bureau, both by letter and testimony, proved the following:

(1) There was no ammunition clip. (2) The telescopic sight was structurally defective [and] had to be repaired by the FBI prior to testing by FBI agents. (3) The same telescopic sight was mounted on the Italian rifle for a left-handed rifleman. Oswald was right-handed. (4) The trigger had to be repaired by the FBI

before the rifle could be used. (5) The firing pin on that rifle was worn down by rust on both the pin and spring. (6) To support the telescopic sight, the FBI had to use three shims before the sight could be used. (7) There were no scratches or abrasions on that rifle, which proved no shims had ever been used. (8) The rifle barrel was so worn and corroded that it had to be repaired internally. (9) No ammunition was ever located by the FBI in any area where Oswald had resided in 1963. (10) No FBI rifle expert was able to aim and pull the trigger within the time limit specified by the Commission. (11) The marks on the three cartridges did not conform to the internal and external markings of the rifle. (12) The rifle barrel may have changed.

All of the above evidence was not published in the "Report" for obvious reasons. The publication would have proved Oswald was innocent, since no person can commit a murder by using a defective, nonlethal weapon. It can honestly be said that the 26 aides became associate members of "The Ananias Club."

The evidence proved beyond a reasonable doubt that Lee Harvey Oswald was framed by the Dallas Police Department. The responsibility of the Warren Commission was as great, if not greater, than the police; for the Commission knew that the testimony and documents of the FBI proved him innocent. The evidence outlined in this chapter supports that charge.

J'Accuse!

Knowing that the photographs showing Oswald with a rifle were worthless as evidence to prove he owned the Italian Carcano, the Commission again summoned its pinch-hit perjury witness from their bullpen. He testified that on the night of November 22, 1963, he disassembled the Italian rifle and found a palm print on the underside of the rifle stock.

As he was calmly perjuring himself, the Commission had in its file a letter from the Federal Bureau of Investigation, which was subsequently verified under oath by the number-one FBI fingerprint expert, Mr. Latona. He testified that "no fingerprints were found on the shells, rifle bolt, or stock of that rifle" (the 6.5mm Italian Mannlicher-Carcano rifle given to the FBI by Lt. Day and the Dallas Police Department)."

With that palm print playing a key role in condemning Oswald as the president's killer, the Commission was placed in an embarrassing position. Both men had testified under oath; both could not be correct. That palm print was or was not on that rifle, and that palm print was essential to convict Oswald.

To locate the perjurer, let the testimony speak.

At no time, according to Lt. Day, did he photograph the palm print. He made that statement to the FBI. He did take a photograph of "partial" unidentifiable fingerprints but not of the palm print. At approximately 8 p.m., within the sanctuary of his office, with no other witnesses to see this historical event, he raised a palm print from the understock of the Italian rifle.

But did he take a photograph of this palm print? Not Lt. Day. He took photographs of the fragmentary fingerprints which were unidentifiable. Apparently having some qualms because he did not take a photograph of the palm print, he again took photographs, at 9:30 p.m., but his camera ability was poor and he was only able to take the same prints he took at 8 p.m. Lt. Day, although he had taken the FBI "advanced fingerprinting course" given by FBI expert Latona, did not believe the FBI knew what they were talking about when the Bureau instructed its students that a photograph of a print must always be taken prior to lifting.

Lt. Day testified that at 11:45 p.m. he forwarded the Italian rifle to the FBI, and at that time he "could still see the palm print on the rifle." The Commission called this witness a perjurer; for, on page 123, the Commission's "Report" stated that when Lt. Day made the "lifting" of the palm print, such lifting was done at the 8 p.m. session, and at that time the "lifting" had completely disappeared. How could Lt. Day see something that had completely disappeared from his eyesight? Lt. Day testified that "I photographed them (the partial prints, not the palm print) only. I did not try to lift them." Then how could he send a photograph of Lee's palm print four days later?

Lt. Day was a perjurer and the Commission knew he was one. J' Accuse!

The rifle was forwarded to the FBI Washington fingerprint bureau at 11:45 p.m. and was examined by Lt. Day's former teacher, Mr. Latona. He testified that not only was there no palm print of Lee Harvey Oswald on any part of that Italian rifle but no fingerprints of any person, including Capt. Fritz, who held the rifle with his fingers for press photographers on the afternoon of November 22nd. Mr. Latona went further, for he swore that he saw evidence of any attempt by Lt. Day to "lift" the alleged palm print seen by Lt. Day.

When the FBI requested police photographs, Lt. Day was compelled to take three additional days so he could forward one to the FBI. The police had "leaked" the news of the palm print via District Attorney Wade, and the FBI was not only puzzled but embarrassed; for its number one expert, Mr. Latona, had informed his chief that there were no fingerprints or palm prints on that rifle sent to them by the Dallas police. The student had evidently outshone his teacher in a ten-day lecture course.

After analyzing this photograph received from Lt. Day, smiles broke out in the FBI fingerprint bureau. The puzzle was solved. A beginning student of fingerprinting could have seen the solution immediately. Therefore, the Bureau wrote its now famous letter to the Commission, which was so devastating that the Commission buried it. The letter stated that "there were no fingerprints of any person found on the shells, rifle bolt, or stock of that rifle."

However, in the belief that no sane person would doubt their "honorable words," the Commission published this photograph in their Exhibits 638-40. Any fingerprint student knows that a palm print that was wrapped around a round surface – as a rifle barrel – has to be, by the laws of science, round! The Commission's exhibits quoted above revealed a flat palm print! This roundness of either a fingerprint or palm print squeezes together the image or whorls that are on the hands; and, by squeezing together, the whorls are lost for purposes of identification.

Involved in the solution of perjury is the question: Where did the Dallas police obtain the "flat" palm print of Oswald? The answer is obvious when the testimony is read. Oswald's palm print was taken in Capt. Fritz's office at 6:00 p.m. on November 23, 1963. When Lt. Day reported to Capt. Fritz that there were no prints on the Italian rifle, Oswald's palm print was retaken in the fingerprint office.

There is no testimony from any FBI agent or any other police agent that stated that the prints shown to them by the

Commission were those taken from the curved underside of the Italian rifle. The only question asked of them by the Commission was whether or not the palm print shown to them was that of Lee Harvey Oswald. Of course it was Oswald's palm print, but that palm print was flat and was the one taken by the police at either the 6 p.m. or 8:55 p.m. fingerprint session.

Further evidence that Lt. Day committed perjury can be found in volume 26, page 829, where the FBI requested Lt. Day to sign a statement under oath that he found Oswald's palm print on that rifle on November 22nd. Lt. Day refused! Of course he refused, for the FBI had a copy of his letter of January 8, 1964 admitting there were no Oswald prints on that Italian rifle!

The Commission's final attempt to link the Italian rifle to Oswald was their statement that shirt fibers found attached to that rifle came from Oswald's shirt. The FBI testimony refused to uphold the Commission, for the FBI testified that too many of that type of shirt existed to make a positive statement that these fibers came from his shirt. (See illustrated section.)

With the testimony of the rifle, the ammunition clip, the internal and external condition of that rifle; with no fingerprints or palm prints on that rifle, [and] with the admitted statement from "Life" that the photographs had been "retouched," the only conclusion regarding paragraph (B) of the Commission's accusation against Lee Harvey Oswald was that the Commission knowingly used manufactured evidence to pronounce him "guilty."

Under the "basic principles of American justice" Oswald was innocent.

J'Accuse!

CHAPTER IV

*THE NONEXISTING PAPER BAG
or How to Manufacture Evidence*

Paragraph (C) of the Commission's indictment vs. Lee Harvey Oswald related to a paper bag which he allegedly manufactured from tape and paper stolen from the Book Depository's workroom and which was used by Oswald to wrap the rifle which he then carried into the Depository.

In this portion of the indictment, the Commission established a new rule of law, as the commissioners could not operate under the "basic principles of American justice." The Commission overruled the eyewitness testimony of the only persons who had seen Oswald carry a package in his hands on the morning of November 22, 1963—from his residence in Irving, Texas, to the entrance of the Book Depository. In other words, the Commissioners and their 26 aides, none of whom were in Dallas on that day, knew in their hearts that Oswald carried a disassembled rifle into the Depository.

There was not a single witness who visited or worked in that building during the morning of November 22 who saw Oswald carrying a package with him; nor did any witness see him assemble a 6.5mm Italian Carcano rifle between 8 a.m. and 12:30 p.m.

Although there were some 98 workers on the floors that Oswald covered as a stock clerk, the Commission would have a person of common sense believe that from 8 a.m. until 11:55 a.m. only one person saw Oswald. Ninety-seven never saw him; they never saw him carrying a package or a disassembled or assembled rifle.

The only persons who saw Oswald carry a package on the morning of November 22 were Mr. Wesley Frazier, the man who drove Oswald to work, since Frazier worked in the same building, and Frazier's sister, Mrs. Randle. Mrs. Randle saw

Oswald carrying a package when he first appeared from his home, which was near the Randle home. According to her sworn testimony, the package she saw in Oswald's hands was approximately 27" long. When Oswald got into Frazier's automobile for the drive to the Depository, Frazier asked him what the package contained, and Oswald said "curtain rods."[30] Mr. Frazier testified that the size of the package was between 24 and 26 inches.

The length of the disassembled Italian Carcano rifle was 34.5 inches.

Thus, the only witnesses who saw the package Oswald was carrying were to be labelled "liars," since it was obvious that a rifle 34.5 inches in length could not be contained in a package that was not longer than 27 inches.

The testimony also revealed that the last person to see Oswald enter the Depository was a Mr. Dougherty, who testified that he saw the package in Oswald's hands as he entered the building. Mr. Frazier testified that Oswald had tucked the package of curtain rods under his armpit, and the bottom of the package was hidden in his palm. Neither of them saw any package the size of 34.5 inches in length which would have extended from his palm to several inches above his shoulder. However, the Commission, in its inherent wisdom, simply knew that Oswald carried a disassembled rifle in his right hand.

The Commission stated that Oswald, during the night of November 21, entered his garage, unknown to his wife or his landlady, and manufactured a paper bag from paper and tape he had stolen from his shipping room. The Commission admitted they had no witnesses, but that circumstantial evidence supported their statement.

Neither circumstantial evidence nor evidence supported the Commission's statement. The superintendent of the shipping room, Mr. West, testified that as long as Oswald was working he never saw Oswald steal any material at any time. Mr. West further stated that even during lunch hours he watched his

---

[30] Without curtains, which normally require rods, Oswald would have been afforded no privacy in a room that looked directly out onto the street.

supplies, since he ate his lunch in that room. To demolish the Commission's circumstantial evidence, Mr. West gave the commissioners a lesson in the use of tape. He stated that, to steal the tape, Oswald would have had to pull the tape through the water in the taping machine. The Commission never did explain how Oswald was able to walk around with three to four feet of wet tape in his pockets for a period of three days prior to the day of the murder.

Thus far, every witness who had been examined by the Commission relating to events surrounding the "brown paper bag" had failed to support the Commission's theory. The only three witnesses who saw Oswald going to work and entering the building testified contrary to the Commission's statement.

An investigator of the Warren Commission's "Report" must attempt to solve this mystery; for how can three witnesses see the accused and yet fail to see a package 34.5 inches in length, which supposedly contained the murder weapon—an Italian Mannlicher-Carcano rifle with a telescopic sight?

Returning therefore to the statement of the original witness, Mr. Frazier. He testified that the bag he saw lying on the back seat of his automobile was a bag "as you get out of the grocery store ... but it was a package roughly two feet long." Mrs. Randle saw a bag that was about 27" long. The FBI, when they checked the rear seat of Frazier's automobile, discovered that it was 28" overall. Thus, the official agency investigating the facts surrounding the murder of President Kennedy verified that the package Oswald was carrying on the morning of November 22 was not more than 28 inches. That bag did not contain a disassembled rifle that was 34.5 inches in length. The Commission lied to the American people that Oswald carried a disassembled rifle into the Book Depository.

The next step in the investigation of this mystery would depend upon the facts of whether or not a 34.5-inch paper bag was actually found by policemen searching the 6th floor of the Book Depository. The testimony revealed that when the first party of police agents searched that area between 12:50 and 1:22 p.m. (when the rifle was discovered hidden between cartons comprising the "shield of cartons"), they neither saw nor picked up any "brown paper bag" 34.5 inches in length.

These agents discovered a German rifle, three cartridges, remains of a chicken lunch, a pop bottle, and a small crumpled lunch bag that had contained the chicken eaten by an employee during his lunch hour while sitting near the 6th-floor windows between 12:00 noon and 12:22 p.m.

With the negative testimony of those policemen and deputy sheriffs, the Warren Commission decided to summon from their witness bullpen the ace perjurer, Lt. Day—he of the enormous eyesight of 40/40 or 100/100. With perjury as his weapon, this police officer swore that he saw a brown paper bag the exact size to conceal a disassembled rifle 34.5 inches long. Lt. Day testified that this large paper bag was lying on the floor near the 6th-floor window in full sight. When he was given the bag, Lt. Day wrote: "A handmade bag of wrapping paper and tape found in the southeast corner of the building within a few feet of the cartridge case. Found next to the sixth-floor window fired from. May have been used to carry the gun." Signed: "Lt. J. C. Day." The Commission deliberately overruled the "basic principles of American justice" in accepting this writing as evidence, for no court of law practicing these "principles" would accept a label that had no date, no time, and no name of the person who found that evidence.

As the Commission relied heavily upon Lt. Day's mysteriously written note that just by chance supported their position regarding the brown paper bag, the testimony that proved perjury was suppressed by the Commission from its "Report." It can be located either in the "Hearings" or in the National Archives.

The first point that made Lt. Day's testimony relating to his "note" perjurious was the fact that there is no 34.5-inch paper bag listed on the official Dallas police list pertaining to the objects found on the 6th floor. J. Hicks, the officer-in-charge of listing these 6th-floor objects, saw no such paper bag and thus made no entry on his official list. The second point would be that none, not one, of the original five policemen and deputy sheriffs saw a bag that size; nor did any of them, including officer Hicks, see a bag that size in the possession or hands of Lt. Day. According to Lt. Day's testimony, the bag was lying in full sight of anyone in the S.E. corner near the window and near which were found three cartridges approximately 3 inches long.

The third point is that Lt. Day arrived on the scene with a retinue of followers which included Det. Studebaker, who acted as the official police photographer, Det. Sims, and policemen Montgomery and Brewer. With inward laughter but innocent of face and eyes, Det. Studebaker swore that although he took approximately 50 photographs of everything in the window area, he failed to take a photograph of that "brown paper bag"! Of course, the fact that no large 34.5-inch paper bag existed anywhere on that floor at any time during that day of the murder prevented his camera from taking a photograph. It is a well-known fact of science that a camera cannot take that which does not exist.

In an effort to support Lt. Day's perjury the Commission, out of necessity, had to support the perjury given to them by several Dallas policemen. Policemen Montgomery, Brewer, and Johnson each gave conflicting evidence. They had the gall to swear under oath that as soon as they saw that "bag" they "assumed that the bag contained a rifle." At the time they saw this bag, the rifle had yet to be found! What an imagination! What perjury!

The Commission knew that perjury had been committed; for they had in their possession an official statement from the FBI that (1) the rifle received from the Dallas police was in a "well-oiled condition." (2) When the "bag" was received by the FBI in their scientific laboratory, they were amazed to discover that that bag had no oil stains in or on it, and that there were no rifle indentations on that "bag." The bag was evidence manufactured by the Dallas police.

The policemen even contradicted each other, under oath, as to the one who discovered this marvelous creation of Lt. Day's. Montgomery said he did not pick up that "bag," it was Det. Studebaker; however, Johnson said it was Montgomery. Studebaker testified he picked it up. Regardless of who was lying, the fact remains that although one of those three policemen picked up that paper bag he left no fingerprints. Lt. Day testified to the fact that on November 22 no Dallas policeman or member of any police agency left fingerprints on any object that was picked up with the finder's bare fingers!

When Det. Studebaker took the witness stand he swore that he would tell the truth, but his fingers were crossed. He said that "he picked up a piece of paper ... doubled over." As he gave this information, the witness said the paper was "about this long," which he established by using his fingers to show the length. The aide then asked Studebaker: "How long was it, approximately?" The absolutely amazing answer was: "I don't know," and the aide deliberately refused to let Studebaker quote a figure. Why? For Studebaker revealed the size to be far less than 34.5 inches. Was the aide too lazy or too scared to measure the distance between Studebaker's fingers?

After dusting this paper for fingerprints, Studebaker testified he gave this "doubled over piece of paper" to "they." Who were "they"? Leprechauns? "They" were unknown. But it was not given to Lt. Day, for Studebaker personally knew his superior officer. Nor was it officers Hicks, Hill, Mooney, Boone, Weitzman, Montgomery, Johnson, or Brewer; for he knew all of them. Of course, the reason he could not identify the "they" is the fact that no paper bag [of] the size sufficient to contain a rifle was ever found on the 6th floor, for it was to be manufactured in the police station between 1 p.m. and 9 p.m. Why would Studebaker give a 3-ounce "piece of paper doubled over" to "they," which is plural, to carry it is slightly incredible.

It should be noticed that at no time did Studebaker ever speak of a paper bag as what he picked up from the floor. It was always a "piece of paper, doubled over." A piece of paper, even in a court of law, cannot be synonymous with a 'brown paper bag, 34.5 inches long."

In an attempt to make the perjury of their witnesses more pervasive, the Commission willfully overlooked the testimony of their fingerprint experts, Lt. Day and Det. Sims, and accepted that of the FBI, although the Dallas police or the FBI had to be lying. An analysis of the "Hearings" always revealed that where the testimony of the police, the FBI, or the Secret Service conflicted, the Commission always published that testimony which supported [its] theory.

Studebaker testified that when he was handling the "bag" with his fingers, he was also examining the bag for fingerprints.

However, he found no prints "but just smudges" on it. He also discovered there "was one little ole piece of print.... I put a piece of tape on it to preserve it.... just a partial print." He swore that the print was so small that he could not tell whether it was a finger- or palm print. Lt. Day supported Studebaker's testimony.

This "bag" was forwarded to the FBI by the Dallas police after the unknown "they" had received it from Studebaker. The evidence, beyond a reasonable doubt, is that the "they" switched the "piece of paper, doubled over" into a bag that was received by the FBI.

The FBI had testified that when they examined this bag forwarded to them by the Dallas police, not only had the tape, which had been placed over the partial print, disappeared, but the Bureau discovered a completely legible fingerprint of Lee H. Oswald! The FBI was also mystified when they failed to discover any oil stains on or in the bag, which supposedly contained a rifle "in a well-oiled condition." It must not be forgotten that no FBI agent, as the Commission implied, testified that the bag they received from the Dallas police was the identical "piece of paper, doubled over" that was handled by Det. Studebaker.

In spite of the double and triple falsification of evidence, an investigator, if he seeks, shall find! Buried in the National Archives is the FBI File Com. Doc. 205, and in that file is the evidence that the Commission knew that the Dallas police had not only committed perjury but had also manufactured evidence of the "brown paper bag."[31] That same document also revealed the existence of the conspiracy that murdered President Kennedy. To conceal the conspiracy the Commission concealed this FBI file.

FBI agents were notified by post office employees in the Irving, Texas Post Office that a package addressed to "Lee Harvey Oswald" was being held for "postage due." When the FBI had rescued that package they unwrapped it, and in it was

---

[31] Marks is referring to pp. 145-150 of this document: a section titled "Wrapping Paper in Shape of a Large Bag and Shirt of LEE HARVEY OSWALD."

a "brown paper bag," a grocery bag, 26 inches long, with indentations representing "curtain rods." The question then arises: What type of bag was shown to the various witnesses before the Commission? A reading of the testimony revealed that Mrs. Randle and Mr. Frazier were shown a "paper bag" that had been manufactured by the FBI agents working in the Dallas, Texas office! What happened to the paper bag which revealed Oswald's prints? Why, for the first and only time, the FBI Laboratory had so crudely handled and examined that "bag" it was destroyed in the laboratory. The Commission said the "bag" shown to Mr. Frazier and Mrs. Randle were "replicas" but that the agents had used the tape and paper taken from the Book Depository shipping room. The fact that Mr. Frazier testified, uncontradicted, that the bag he saw was one "as you get out of the grocery store" did not agitate the Commission. They wanted Oswald "guilty," and they were going to "prove it" even if they had to use manufactured evidence, which they did.

The remaining problem that an investigator must solve is whether or not Oswald was telling the truth to Frazier when he said that the package contained "curtain rods."

In the 9th volume, page 425 of the "Hearings," is the evidence that Oswald was being truthful concerning the "curtain rods." Involved in this suppression of evidence was the Commission's subversion of testimony not only of a U.S. Secret Service agent but also a Commission aide. Withheld from the "Report" was the evidence that those two men found a pair of curtain rods in the Paine garage! The rods did not exceed 28 inches in length. Yet, according to the Dallas police list showing the objects in the Paine garage on November 22, 23, and 24, no curtain rods were found by the police search team or by the other federal agents. Although Mr. and Mrs. Paine both disagreed as to whether she had purchased those rods, the proof remained that no rods were found in that garage on three vital days. Those rods were placed in the Paine garage by a conspirator who had removed them from the Book Depository after Oswald had taken them into the building and placed them in his locker.

The mystery has been solved from the testimony available in the "Hearings" or in the National Archives. The Commission never did examine the FBI agents regarding the size and width of the paper bag that had on it the complete print of Oswald. Nor did the Commission ever ask Studebaker the size of the "doubled over" piece of paper. The Commission never asked the FBI whether the bag they found in the Irving, Texas, Post Office was mailed in [a package addressed in] handwriting or [if it was] typed, and from what area it was mailed.

There can be only one implication in the conduct of the Warren Commission concerning this "brown paper bag." From the testimony given to them, from the perjury they knowingly accepted from various Dallas policemen, [the Commission knew there was conspiracy.] The reason they conducted themselves in such a manner was due to their knowledge that a conspiracy murdered President Kennedy. This fact had to be concealed.

In regard to the evidence relating to the brown paper bag, there was no evidence that supported the Commission's conclusion.

Manufactured evidence and perjury cannot be used "under the basic principles of American justice" to convict a man accused of murder.

J' Accuse!

CHAPTER V

"LSD"—HALLUCINATIONS AND CHARADES

With the complete demolition of their alleged material evidence regarding the Italian rifle and the "brown paper bag," the Commission attempted to prove Oswald was on the 6th floor at the exact time the shots were fired. Although this location of Oswald on the 6th floor at that time would, in view of the previous evidence, prove nothing in a court of law, the Commission used its imagination to secure Oswald's placement. From a review of the evidence in the "Hearings," the Commission's imagination, based on Oswald's fingerprints being found on two cartons, must have been induced by the Commission's use of "LSD"—figuratively speaking. Paragraph (D) of the Commission's indictment states that the fingerprints "proved" Oswald was at the 6th-floor window from where the shots were fired. However, the use of words, under the "basic principles of American justice," cannot substitute for that of evidence secured under oath in a law court.

If there be definitive proof that Oswald was not on the 6th floor at the time the shots were fired, then he must be found "not guilty" regardless of the fact that the Commission discovered hundreds of Oswald's prints all over the 6th floor. This holds true even if the FBI had proved that the Italian rifle was the lethal weapon. The law remains the same; that is, Oswald must be proved beyond a reasonable doubt to have been the rifleman who fired those bullets. The law operates in a slow and majestic manner, and the attainment of justice should not be crushed temporarily by the hue and cry of "law and order." Nor is a person "guilty" simply because he is arrested by the police. However, this concept is now being denied to the poor. Under a law proposed in December 1969 by Senator George Murphy, the other half of the California "song and dance" team,[32] federal money will be denied to the poor under the various welfare laws. If that "team" had their way, the poor should be eliminated from the American scene à la Hitler vis-à-vis with the Jews! The manner in which the Commission conducted its investigation acted as a knife thrust into the body of "justice."

Oswald's attorney, by simply relying upon the FBI evidence given to the Warren Commission sixty days after its initial meeting, knew that Oswald was nowhere on the 6th floor when the president was struck by four bullets and the governor by not less than two.

In paragraph (D) the Commission attempted to prove that because Oswald's fingerprints and palm prints were found on four book cartons, that fact, ipso facto, proved he was at the 6th-floor window at 12:30 p.m. on November 22, 1963.

The Commission cleverly refrained from stating in its "Report" that Oswald's prints had to be found on various cartons, since his work as a shipping room employee compelled him to handle these cartons. There was nothing sinister concerning his fingerprints or palm prints [being found] on any carton.

For the benefit of the reader, it is recommended that he (or she) glance at the illustrated section of this book for the location of cartons "A," "B," "C," and "D," which is illustration no. 14. Carton "D" had on it Oswald's palm print, but the manner by which it was selected and the number of fingerprints on the other two cartons proved that Oswald was framed by the Dallas police.

---

[32] Beginning in the 1930s, George Lloyd Murphy was a leading song-and-dance man in Hollywood musicals until his entrance into politics in 1952. He defeated JFK's former Press Secretary Pierre Salinger in the 1964 race for the California Senate, paving the way for that other Hollywood "song-and-dance" man—Ronald Reagan—to be elected governor of California two years later. In Marks' play about the JFK assassination, *A Murder Most Foul; or, A Time to Die, A Time to Cry* (February 1968), one of the lead characters correctly predicts the eventual presidential election of Ronald Reagan: "Don't underestimate him [Governor Reagan]. He may one day become our chief of state."

The police officers who gave the game away were none other than the Commission's Lt. Day and Det. Studebaker, and from nowhere, an FBI agent named Lucy. Carton "D" was to be Lt. Day's nemesis, and it was the statement in the Warren Report which said: "During the afternoon of November 22, Lt. Day of the Dallas police dusted this carton ("D") with powder and developed a palm print on the top edge on the side nearest the window. This print which had been cut out of the box was also forwarded to the FBI, and FBI fingerprint expert Latona identified it as Oswald's right palm print." This palm print was also a fake, for if the reader will look at picture nos. 14, 17 in the illustrated section, he will see the palm print is on two sides of the carton, and thus the palm print would be bent, making the whorls again distorted. Notice the Commission stated it was a palm print, not fingerprints. Why the police did not identify the fingerprints but a distorted palm print is due to the fact that the police had a full-size Oswald palm print, but the fingerprints on that carton were unidentifiable!

In Appendix 10 of the "Report," the Commission stated that thirteen identifiable prints were on carton "A," nine on carton "B," three on carton "C," and three on carton "D." The impression would be that those were all prints belonging to Oswald. But no! Twenty-four of those prints belonged to either FBI Agent Lucy or Det. Studebaker;[33] only three belonged to Oswald—two on carton "D," plus one palm print. These were

---

[33] As noted in the Warren Report, p. 566. Forest L. Lucy was an FBI clerk. The Bureau reported finding five of Lucy's "latent" fingerprints and one of his "latent palm prints" on the cartons. In the same FBI report, Studebaker scored fourteen "latent fingerprints" and four "latent palm prints." One palm print remained "unidentified." (See "FBI 105-82555 Oswald HQ File, Section 211," pp. 17-18). As James DiEugenio points out in his article "Dead Men Talking: An Update" (November 29, 2012, Kennedys and King website), a careful reading of the FBI reports leads one to the conclusion that "the Bureau is equivocating. They are leaving out what seems to be one identified fingerprint. I should add that there are three other prints, which they disguise by labeling 'not identifiable' or having 'indistinct characteristics.'" They were also known to misrepresent the actual number of prints in their possession.

found on the "Rolling Readers." There were no prints on the carton on the windowsill or on the heavy carton below it. How did Oswald avoid placing any kind of print on those two cartons when the Commission said he used all those cartons to form a gun rest? The Commission admitted Oswald wore no gloves at any time!

Now, referring back to Lt. Day's work quoted in the first paragraph above, there is a clash of language. The "Report" states that the palm print on carton "D" had been "cut out of the box.... forwarded to Latona." Lt. Day is not credited with identifying that palm print as Oswald's; only that a palm print was developed. When did he forward that print to Mr. Latona? Lt. Day did not identify that palm print as Oswald's, for the language specifically states that Mr. Latona did that work. Therefore, how did Lt. Day know that that palm print was Oswald's or the alleged assassin's? How was Lt. Day able to distinguish that one palm print from those of Agent Lucy and Det. Studebaker? Why did Lt. Day fail to send the other fully developed unidentified palm print? Was he gifted with Merlin's power? Or did he have preknowledge that the palm print cut from carton "D" was Oswald's?

Thus, three questions arise: (1) Why and how did Det. Studebaker and FBI Agent Lucy know that, out of all the prints on those two cartons that they selected, they cut the only print that identified Oswald? Why did those two police agents cut only that palm print and not the other palm print? (2) Why did an FBI agent, long experienced in police investigative procedure, permit himself to place his own prints all over those cartons, which smeared any prints that could be used? Only three Oswald prints were found, but 24 prints of Lucy's and Studebaker's were found! (3) Why did the police and the FBI fail to identify that palm print that was readable but not identified? By a strange coincidence, Lt. Day sent the Oswald print which had to be raised by silver nitrate in the FBI laboratory but not the one that remained unidentifiable.

Again, referring to the illustrated section, which shows the location of the Oswald prints, one can logically ask, "How could any person lift those cartons: one carton with his palm, the other with his palm and one finger?" Those cartons weighed approximately 30 pounds, and not even an "Atlas" could lift those cartons with his palm or finger.

After the sentence following that ridiculous assumption by the Commission, they then asserted that Oswald was seen at 11:55 p.m. in the "vicinity" of the S.E. 6th-floor window, and from that time on he was seen by no other person until 12:30 1/2 p.m., in front of the "Coke" machine at the entrance to the lunchroom.

The use of the word "vicinity" is as valid and relative in this case as one would say of a person living on Staten Island [that Staten Island] is in the vicinity of New York City. Oswald was never seen in the "vicinity" of that window, for the Commission's chief witness testified he saw Oswald at 11:55 p.m. standing in front of the 6th-floor elevator. The elevator is not in the "vicinity" of the window, for it is more than 50 feet away from the window. Compared to Los Angeles, Fort Worth is in the vicinity of Dallas. Strangely, Givens, the man who placed Oswald at the elevator, was a member of a six-man maintenance crew working on the 6th floor, and only he, none of the other 5, saw Oswald. None of the 5 were called to testify by the Commission to substantiate Givens' testimony. The evidence revealed that Givens was an ex-convict on parole, subject to revocation by the Dallas police!

Thus, at 11:55 p.m., Oswald was on the 6th floor going down toward the employee's lunchroom. The "Report" definitely stated he then disappeared from sight until 12:31 1/2 p.m. But in the files of the National Archives are several suppressed affidavits which proved his whereabouts from 11:55 a.m. until 12:31 1/2 p.m. These suppressed affidavits conclusively proved that Oswald was nowhere on the 6th floor when the shots rang out.

One of those affidavits was given to the Warren Commission by the FBI, who interviewed Mrs. Arnold, an employee of the Book Depository. She signed an affidavit that between 12:15 and 12:25 p.m. she saw Oswald on the first floor near the building entrance. After the Commission read her affidavit of November 26, 1963, the FBI was ordered to obtain another sworn statement from her. The FBI, fully understanding the reason for this request, asked her whether or not she "had seen

Oswald at the time the president was shot." She answered that she did not see Oswald when the president was shot. Of course, several billion people did not see Oswald either!

The eager-to-please FBI had overreached itself. Mrs. Arnold's first affidavit had merely said she had seen Oswald between 12:15 and 12:25 p.m. Where? At the front entrance to the Book Depository. She never said she saw him shoot the president. The question was not if she saw Oswald shoot the president (for she was at the Depository entrance) but when and where did she see him. The Commission was thus lying when it said no person saw Oswald between 11:55 a.m. and 12:31 1/2 p.m. She was one witness.

Mrs. Arnold's testimony placing Oswald near the Depository entrance was to be supported by another document in the National Archives, No. 354. Oswald, during his interrogation periods, informed Capt. Fritz that he had spoken to a man claiming to be a Secret Service agent who had asked Oswald where a telephone was located near the entrance so that he could telephone his story to the station.[34] In Com. Doc. 354 the man was named Mr. Allman, and he did admit that he had asked some young man about a telephone right after the shooting. Mr. Allman was not summoned by the Commission for the reason that Oswald could not have concocted such an incident unless he had been the man involved. Thus, Oswald was seen and spoken to immediately after the shooting. From the Depository entrance, Oswald went up the stairs to the Coke machine, where he was drinking pop when officer Baker stuck a gun in his belly. This document 354 was one given to the Commission by the

---

[34] The Secret Service "report noted that Allman had a 'crew cut'" (just as Oswald had described) and "'carried his press pass in a leather case similar to cases carried by Federal agents and police officers.' By the time the report was filed on February 3, 1964, the Secret Service was satisfied that [Pierce M.] Allman and [Terrance] Ford were the men 'referred to by Oswald in his interview.' The report concluded, however, that since there was no indication that either Allman or Ford had 'identified themselves as Secret Service agents,' the investigation was closed!" Gerald D. McKnight, *Breach of Trust*, pp. 115-16. Allman was program manager at Dallas WFAA-TV and Radio.

Secret Service, and that agency supported Oswald's statement. (See illustrated section.) Now the Commission had two sworn statements that Oswald was seen at places which proved [that] he was not at the 6th-floor window when the shots rang out.

In addition to Mrs. Arnold and Mr. Allman, the Commission had yet another affidavit signed by a Mr. Piper. This witness saw Oswald at approximately 12:10 p.m. on the first floor of the Book Depository. Finally, Oswald informed Capt. Fritz that he also saw and spoke to a black employee who he knew only as "Junior." This employee, Junior Jarman, admitted being near the lunchroom between noon and 12:15 p.m., as Oswald stated.

From the testimony, none of which was contradicted by any other witness, the Commission had conclusive proof that Oswald was seen by not less than four unimpeached witnesses: Mrs. Arnold, Mr. Piper, Mr. Allman, and Jr. Jarman. It is not necessary, under the "basic principles of American justice," [to provide] hundreds of witnesses to prove that an accused person is somewhere else at the commission of a crime.

However, if Oswald's defense attorney did not believe that those four witnesses were sufficient to prove beyond a reasonable doubt that Oswald was not at the 6th-floor window at 12:30 p.m. when the shots were fired, then the defense attorney had available two federal agencies, the FBI and the U.S, Secret Service, to prove that Oswald was innocent. In addition to those agencies, there were to be two photographs which substantiated Oswald's location at the time the shots were fired.

As the question of Oswald's location at the time of the shooting is necessary for either a "guilty" or "not guilty" verdict, his presence or nonpresence being one of the three elements involved in solving the crime, that evidence was suppressed deliberately by the Commission in its "Report." The commissioner who ironically gave the game away was none other than the former chief of the CIA, Allan Dulles.

The tip-off that the Commission was concealing evidence was originally given when Mr. Dulles cross-examined Bonnie Ray Williams, a black employee who testified that between 12:00 noon and 12:22 p.m. he was eating his lunch on the 6th floor near the third and fourth windows. His view of the S.E. corner window was not blocked by any object. After his examination by an aide, Mr. Dulles asked Mr. Williams four vital questions that destroyed the Commission's theory. The former Chief asked the black employee whether during his 22-minute lunch he had (1) seen anyone, (2) seen anything, (3) heard anyone, (4) heard anything? Mr. Williams answered "no" to all four questions! No hesitancy, no doubt, he was emphatic in his "no."

Thus, under the "basic principles of American justice," Lee Harvey Oswald, between 12:00 noon and 12:22 p.m., was not on the 6th floor. From the files of the National Archives, it is known that at that time he was seen by four witnesses at the lunchroom or near the Depository entrance. However, Oswald's attorney would have to do more than rely upon negative evidence given by Mr. Williams, for the attorney would have to prove to the jury that between the time established by Mrs. Arnold and the time the shots rang out Oswald was definitely not at that 6th-floor window. There are approximately 8 minutes to be accounted for.

Although the Warren Commission said Oswald was there at the window, the Commission also admitted that Oswald, according to the evidence uncovered in the National Archives, had to complete the following physical acts between 12:22 and 12:30 p.m.:

(1) He had to construct a shield of cartons, consisting of approximately 32 book cartons, averaging 50 lbs. (2) After constructing that shield, which was approximately 5-1/2 feet high, Oswald then went somewhere not on the 6th floor to obtain his package containing a disassembled Italian rifle. (3) He returned from the rifle's hiding place, or he first unwrapped the rifle from the "paper bag," leaving no fingerprints, threw the bag on the floor near the window, but put the tape in his pocket, and in the hiding place assembled that rifle by using a 10-cent coin, which took him not less than 6 minutes. The coin and the 6 minutes was stipulated by the Commission, not by this author. (4) With the assembled rifle in his hands, this miracle man then, from a standing position, jumped between 5 1/2 feet and 5 2/3 feet high, soared across the shield of cartons, and landed on his feet in a two-to-three-foot space! (5) After making this soft landing, which made no noise to disturb anyone or anything,

Oswald calmly waited until he could use his nonlethal weapon that could be used only by a left-handed rifleman. Strange, is it not, that the three Commission's witnesses who heard three rifle cartridges falling on the floor above them after being ejected from a rifle did not hear the sound of a 145-lb. man landing on the same floor after jumping a 5 1/2 foot barrier? Nor did this 145-lb. "jumping" rifleman disturb any dust from the ceiling above those men, although three 2-oz. cartridge shells did! (6) As the rifleman had no ammunition clip, he hand-loaded three bullets each time he pulled the trigger. (7) After placing an unneeded 4th bullet in the rifle chamber, the rifleman stood up and threw (!) that rifle in such a manner that it squeezed itself into an upright position between two convenient cartons. (See illustrated section.) (8) However, prior to throwing away the Italian rifle, the assassin calmly wiped off the entire rifle, without using a cloth or paper, so that he would leave no fingerprints. (9) Then, with a sudden, huge intake of breath, with a tremendous spring, he soared from the ambush site across the top of the shield of cartons, and ran down to the Coke machine in front of the lunchroom.

The above activity was not manufactured by the author, for the Commission had testimony from Mr. Williams that between 12:00 noon and 12:22 p.m. he left the 6th floor "because it was too quiet there," and he saw and heard nothing. Therefore, those 9 requisites had to be completed by the assassin. Mr. Truly—the Depository manager and the man who hired Oswald—testified that when he inspected the work of the maintenance crew at midmorning he saw no "shield" of cartons, and that those cartons were on that floor lying about in a "random fashion." No one else saw that "shield" prior to 12:00 noon.

Therefore, the Commission had to imply that their "assassin," Oswald, constructed that shield. Then, the question remains for the jury to answer: "How many minutes would it take an average man of 145 lbs. to construct a 5-1/2-foot shield of cartons which had an approximate total weight of 1, 500 pounds?" The Commission said: "Two minutes!" The Commission admitted that it took Oswald not less than 6 minutes to assemble the rifle. He was last seen on the first floor between 12:15 and 12:25 p.m. by Mrs. Arnold. Using the best possible figure that would not conflict with Mr. Williams' testimony that he was leaving the 6th floor at 12:22 p.m., Oswald had to be running up 5 flights of stairs, because Mr. Williams was using the elevator to go down from the 6th floor to the 5th floor. The elevator is an open cage type, so he would have seen Oswald running up to the 6th floor, but he did not. Thus, Oswald could not have reached the 6th floor until after Williams had stepped out of the elevator and walked out of sight.

Giving the Warren Commission the benefit of the doubt, and not the accused, Oswald arrived at the 6th floor at 12:22 p.m. But, hold on! He had to have time to assemble the rifle, and that time was 6 minutes. Therefore, the time is now 12:28 p.m. Would any jury with the slightest amount of common sense believe that Oswald, in two minutes, completed 4 acts of extreme physical activity? Including the lifting of 32 book cartons totaling 1,500 pounds?

To render complete the stupidity of the Commission's statement or fairy tale is the fact that at no time did Lee Harvey Oswald, or any employee of the Book Depository, know the exact time President Kennedy's automobile would be below the 6th-floor window! As a matter of fact, his cavalcade was running behind schedule; and only if Oswald was part of a conspiracy would he know that fact, for there were no civilian or police radios in the building to notify Oswald of the location of the cavalcade as it approached the Book Depository. Therefore, if Oswald was a member of a conspiracy, he would have had to be in that ambush site from 12:00 noon until the president's automobile appeared.

From theory, let us proceed to actual evidence suppressed by the Warren Commission that reveals the actual whereabouts of Lee Harvey Oswald at the exact moment when the shots were discharged.

A Secret Service agent, holding the rank of inspector, and head of the Dallas Secret Service bureau, swore under oath that, at the time of the shooting, he "never saw any object or anything like that in the window, such as a rifle or anything pointing out of the 6th-floor windows. There was no activity, no one moving around that I saw at all." Inspector Sorrels was the Secret

Service agent in the lead automobile, being driven by Chief Curry, and he was not looking into the sun. This testimony is positive testimony by the chief of the Dallas bureau—a man whose job [it] was to protect the president and who was watching and searching the buildings as the cavalcade drove down the streets. He was watching that window from the time the shooting commenced until it ceased within 10 seconds.

The Oswald defense attorney now has another witness that proved his client innocent, but since that is not what the Commission desired it suppressed all of that testimony from its "Report."

The final federal agency that would prove Oswald innocent would be none other than the Federal Bureau of Investigation. But their letters would also be buried in the National Archives, far from the written pages of the "Report."

The FBI gave to the Commission a formal letter analyzing two photographs: one of which substantiated Inspector Sorrels' testimony, the other to prove the exact location of Lee Harvey Oswald at 12:30 p.m. The letters and the photographs are published in the illustrated section.

The N.Y. "World-Telegram," on February 24, 1964, published a photograph which showed the upper portion of a man's body standing in the entrance to the Book Depository at the exact time the shots were fired. The man's face resembled Oswald's; and, if it were his, then he was innocent.

The Commission, contrary to evidence as now revealed by the FBI testimony in the National Archives, published a statement that the "man in the doorway" was a Billy Lovelady. That Lovelady was proved to have perjured himself did not bother the 7 commissioners who gave their [word of] "honor" that Oswald would be tried "under the basic principles of American justice." If perjury was necessary, then perjury would be used.

The Commission had admitted that the person in question had to be either Lee H. Oswald or Billy Lovelady. They therefore instructed the FBI to conduct a thorough investigation. That Bureau presented to the Commission two vital affidavits. (1) A sworn statement of Billy Lovelady that [at] the time the photograph under investigation was taken he admitted that he was wearing a "red-and-white vertical striped short-sleeved shirt, buttoned up to the top." (2) The other affidavit was signed by Billy Lovelady's foreman, William Shelley, that at the time of the shooting Billy Lovelady was "seated on the steps of the entrance."

The photograph published in the "Herald-Tribune" is published in [this] book, and this photograph is the famous Altgens photograph. The "man in the doorway" is wearing a long-sleeved shirt, [which] is unbuttoned down beyond his chest and is a solid color. Furthermore, a "man seated on the steps" was not in the photograph, since he was hidden by the people standing up.

The "man in the doorway" was Lee Harvey Oswald. The Commission had deliberately and willfully lied to convict an innocent man.

The FBI also had one more arrow that pierced the heart of the Commission's fabricated story of Oswald being at the 6th-floor window at the exact time the shots were fired.

The FBI letter was also buried in the National Archives, for that letter interprets the famous 9th frame of the Hughes photograph. That photograph unqualifiedly substantiates the testimony of Inspector Sorrels of the U.S. Secret Service that, at the exact time of the shooting, he saw no rifle and nobody at the S.E. corner 6th-floor window! Photographs taken by Mr. Hughes showed not only that the photograph captured a portion of the president's automobile but, also, because of the tilt of the camera and the location of Mr. Hughes and the automobile, the S.E. corner window of the 6th floor. The FBI was given the various photographs taken from the Hughes film; and on Frame No. 9, the exact moment the president's automobile was passing the entrance, Hughes was filming it. In an official letter signed by Director J. Edgar Hoover, on January 20, 1964 he said that the president's automobile is shown to be "directly in front of the Texas Book Depository building." The letter and the Hughes photograph is published in the illustrated section. There is no rifle; there is no person at that window. QED Oswald was unjustly accused and convicted by a Commission established to "evaluate the facts so that the truth can be ascertained."

In the face of the evidence never questioned or contradicted by either the Commission or a witness, the Commission placed on the witness stand a witness who either deliberately committed perjury or who was subjected to such pressure that he perjured himself under threats given to him by the Dallas police. His name: Mr. Howard Brennan—the Commission's key witness.

The reader must remember that, at the time Brennan testified, the Commission had in its possession the uncontradicted testimony [of] (1) the U.S. Secret Service Inspector, Mr. Sorrels. (2) The official report of the Federal Bureau of Investigation; [the Bureau] had proved Oswald was the "man in the doorway" and [it had] photographs proving that no rifle or person was in the S.E. corner 6th-floor window, thus corroborating the inspector's testimony. (3) The testimony of Mrs. Arnold, who saw Oswald between 12:15 and 12:25 p.m. at the entrance to the Book Depository. (4) Mr. Allman, who was spoken to by Oswald at that entrance. (5) Jr. Jarman, who spoke to Oswald or was seen by Oswald between 12:10 and 12:15 p.m. (6) Mr. Piper, who saw Oswald at approximately the same time near the lunchroom.

In spite of all the above evidence, the Warren Commission deliberately and impliedly stated that every one of those witnesses, including the agents who analyzed the Hughes photograph, and including J. Edgar Hoover, who signed a letter relating to Billy Lovelady, were either liars or perjurers!

And upon whom did they base their accusations against these persons?

By accepting the testimony of a person who was an admitted liar and possibly a perjurer! That is how the 7 commissioners interpreted the "basic principles of American justice."

The value of this "eyewitness" can be seen by the fact that although he testified he could identify "Oswald's facial features, which were six floors above the street level, Brennan failed to identify the man who received that description when he was a mere three feet away from his eyes at the street level! Moreover, at the 4 p.m. police identification "lineup," he refused to identify Oswald as the man he saw at the window.

The FBI also examined Mr. Brennan, and he gave a statement to that Bureau on two occasions. The first statement acknowledged that he could not identify Oswald, thus confirming his statement at the police lineup. The second affidavit said he could identify Oswald as the rifleman. Prior to those two statements, Brennan signed an affidavit in the Dallas Sheriff's Office. This affidavit is of such interest that it is published in the illustrated section. In one portion of the affidavit Brennan stated that he "saw" the rifleman "step down out of sight" at the conclusion of the firing of the three bullets.

In the official photograph published by the Commission (the situation of the various cartons proved that the photograph may have been "official," but, as explained later in this book and in the illustrated section, that photograph is not "authentic"), the only manner by which the rifleman could have "stepped down" would have had the rifleman shooting in a standing position on the windowsill! To add insult to the intelligence of the reader of the "Report," by standing up to fire that rifle, the rifleman would have had to shoot through two panes of glass, since the lower window is open.

Comparing Brennan's affidavits to his testimony given to the Commission, he committed four acts of perjury: (1) The Commission stated that the rifleman shot at the president while in crouched position, using two cartons as a "gun rest." (2) Brennan saw no "white smoke" as the shots were fired, although the FBI, in testing that weapon after they had repaired it, stated that white smoke was emitted every time a shot was fired. (3) Brennan testified that he saw 70 to 80 percent of the rifle, yet he saw no telescopic sight. (4) Since Brennan's "rifleman" had to shoot through two panes of window glass, that glass should have been shattered. No glass window was shattered, as the photographs revealed. As the Commission accepted Brennan's testimony upon which to base their "identification" of Oswald, that identical testimony freed Oswald! The Commission stated that the rifle used had to have on it a telescopic sight. Brennan saw no telescopic sight. QED the Italian rifle [designated] by the Commission as the weapon used by its named killer was not the murder weapon. And since that was the killer's weapon, then Oswald could not have used that Commission's designated weapon.

The FBI thought so little of Brennan's identification of Oswald as the assassin that his name is not published in any one of the five volumes submitted to the Commission by that Bureau as a witness to any feature or fact relating to the assassination. That is what the Commission's own investigating agency thought of Mr. Brennan. As previously stated, Brennan's testimony may have been the result of pressure exerted upon him by outside forces. At the time he did testify before the Commission, several witnesses whose testimony was favorable to Oswald had mysteriously died, another one was shot in the face, another one's brother was murdered, another one's son was thrown out of a bathroom window by the Dallas police, another "hung" herself within 30 minutes after being placed in a police cell, another fled to California, and so forth.

If this small book were to conclude at this point, and if the Commission had operated under "the basic principles of American justice" in an American court of law, Oswald's defense attorney would have made a motion to have the court direct the jury to issue a verdict of "not guilty."

The thousands of words uttered by the Warren Commission had been swept away by the testimony of its own witnesses. The letters and photographs given to the Commission by the FBI and the U.S. Secret Service proved beyond a reasonable doubt that Lee Harvey Oswald was not "the sole assassin" of President Kennedy. The Hughes photograph plus the testimony of U.S. Secret Service Inspector [Sorrels] that no person was at that S.E. 6th floor corner window would have freed Oswald. The Altgens photograph proving Oswald on the step of the entrance to the Book Depository, and the testimony of Mrs. Arnold, Bonnie Ray Williams, and TV reporter Mr. Allman, plus the FBI examination of Billy Lovelady, proved Oswald was not at the 6th-floor window at the time—12:30 p.m.—of the shooting. The letters and testimony of the FBI regarding the nonlethal capacity of that Italian rifle would have freed Oswald. The testimony of the four witnesses who saw Oswald between 12:00 noon and 12:30 p.m. would have freed him. The manufacturing of the palm print evidence by Lt. Day, his manufacturing of the "brown paper bag," and his same activity regarding the ammunition clip, would have destroyed the Commission's case against Oswald.

By concocting a myth that the security of this nation was

involved, or [by] using the phrase "in the national interests," the Commission deluded and deceived the people from whom they had accepted an "obligation of honor."

J'Accuse!

CHAPTER VI

WHOSE BODY? TIPPIT'S?

Paragraph (E) of the Commission's indictment against Lee Harvey Oswald deals with the mysterious murder of officer Tippit. This paragraph was subdivided into four specific areas: (1) Seven "eyewitnesses" saw "Oswald" flee the murder site, and two of those seven clearly saw Oswald murder Tippit. (2) The shells found near and around the murder site were identified and matched to Oswald's weapon used to murder the policeman. (3) The revolver "taken" from Oswald at the Texas Theatre was purchased by him and in his sole possession at all times. (4) "Oswald's" jacket was found near the murder site.

This murder in no way related to the murder of President Kennedy and Governor Connally. Nor does that murder apply to the attempt to murder ex-Gen. Walker way back in April 1963. The Commission was creating an image of Oswald as being a man who just liked to kill people.

Everyone knows that where a person is accused of murdering one person, then the body of that person is sufficient. However, in the Tippit murder, the Warren Commission calmly used five different bodies to prove that there existed one Tippit body. Under the "basic principles of American justice," no court would permit the prosecution to simply go to the police morgue and select any body waiting for identification and burial. As the testimony showed, that is exactly what the Dallas police and the Warren Commission did.[35]

---

[35] Here Marks states this as a literal fact, but at other times when discussing the Tippit case his tone appears to be more rhetorical, i.e., that it is *as if* the Commission is presenting evidence culled from four separate corpses, since so many police witnesses cited different numbers and types of bullet wounds. All this leads Marks to conclude (below): "True, officer Tippit is dead—but how he died, legally, no one knows."

In the Tippit murder, the Commission had full knowledge of the deceit practiced by the police in pinning the Tippit murder on Lee Harvey Oswald. The Commission listened to testimony from the FBI, the U.S. Secret Service, and the Dallas police that a minimum of five (5) bodies were used and labelled to be "Tippit"! There is even a possibility that six (6) were used.

Which of the five belonged to Tippit? To this day, no one legally knows. In law, the Commission has yet to prove that one of them was Tippit's. Thus, "under the basic principles of American justice," the complete failure, or evasion, by the Commission to prove that one of those bodies was Tippit's would compel a court of law operating under those principles to grant a verdict of "not guilty" to Lee Harvey Oswald.

The reader should not be surprised to learn that there is no death certificate or autopsy report relating to officer Tippit in the Warren "Report." There exists no record, either, in the National Archives. True, officer Tippit is dead—but how he died, legally, no one knows.

There is a suppressed document in the National Archives that was in file No. 87 of the U.S. Secret Service. The code number is M-63-352, and that paper contains the statement by Dr. Rose, the coroner of Dallas County, Texas. The document is signed by Secret Service Agent Moore.

His report to his agency said that three bullets penetrated the body and a 4th bullet merely "hit a button on the officer's (Tippit's) coat." This "is Body No. 1. But, is it Tippit's?

Agent Moore's statement does not end there, for he goes on and says: "Three bullets hit Tippit in the chest, and one in the head." Now, there are four penetrating bullets, one of which is a head wound. That is Body No. 2. But, is it Tippit's?

Agent Moore continued his investigation, and he wrote in the same report: "Police officer R. Davenport informed him (Moore) that a .38 caliber bullet was taken from the stomach of officer Tippit." Now this body has a different bullet hole, a stomach wound. That is the third body! But, is it Tippit's?

The Secret Service evidently became as confused as the Commission; for Inspector Kelly of that Service testified that "Tippit was shot once in the head and twice in the chest." This body now has one less bullet hole in the chest. That is the fourth body. But, is it Tippit's?

Showing no qualms, the Commission summoned a representative of the Dallas Police Department, and although the U.S. Secret Service testified there were four bullet holes, the Dallas representative testified that the body he saw was "shot three times, [once] each in the hand, chest, and head." Body Number 5 now has a hand wound! But, is it Tippit's?

Still undaunted, the Commission plunged ahead: they would "pin" Tippit's murder upon Lee Harvey Oswald if they had to use every body in the Dallas police morgue. The FBI was summoned to give testimony that the body they were shown by the Dallas police had a portion of Tippit's coat button driven into the bullet hole. In Body Number 1, Dr. Rose never stated that one of the bullets carried portions of the button into the body. Thus, Body Number 6. But, is it Tippit's?

A first year law student studying criminal law and evidence would know that there is no evidence as to the cause of Tippit's death. He may have died of a galloping cold like Jack Ruby did;[36] he may have died of the measles, or the smallpox, or a

---

[36] Regarding his "timely" death, Ruby himself believed that he was injected with cancer cells. In Jim Garrison's 1967 *Playboy* magazine interview, Garrison addressed the deeper significance of this claim: "We have discovered that David Ferrie had a rather curious hobby in addition to his study of cartridge trajectories: cancer research. He wrote a medical treatise on the subject and worked with a number of New Orleans doctors on the means of inducing cancer in mice. After the assassination, one of these physicians, Dr. Mary Sherman, was found hacked to death with a kitchen knife in her New Orleans apartment. Her murder is listed as unsolved. Ferrie's experiments may have been purely theoretical and Dr. Sherman's death completely unrelated to her association with Ferrie; but I do find it interesting that Jack Ruby died of cancer a few weeks after his conviction for murder had been overruled in appeals court and he was ordered to stand trial outside of Dallas." Ruby was surrounded by a strange crew of medical practitioners. His defense psychiatrist was the notorious Dr. Louis Jolyon West, a key figure in the CIA's mind control operation, MK-ULTRA. "Jolly" West, an LSD proselytizer, specialized in the use of hypnosis combined with LSD, which had the effect of "locking in" a posthypnotic trance and preventing the subject

stroke which affected his brain or heart. The only thing that is known in a legal manner is that the death certificate said the body applicable to it was dead! Did Tippit die as the result of an illegal act committed by another person? There is not one shred of legal proof that he died as the result of a criminal act committed against his person. This statement is not made in jest, for the Commission was to charge for eternity the crime of murder upon Lee H. Oswald.

Only by a court of law perverting the "basic principles of American justice" would a criminal court judge permit the Commission to continue its case against its alleged murderer—Lee Oswald. No court would permit any prosecutor to use five or six bodies as proof that the victim was one of those bodies. Nor would a court of law permit the prosecutor the liberty of stating to the jury, with no proof, that the victim was shot 3, 4, or 5 times and that the jury should conduct a vote to determine the cause of death.

It is well known in forensic medicine that a bullet hole, or bullet holes, per se, does not cause death. Nor do chest wounds necessarily cause death, nor stomach wounds, nor hand wounds. Lack of blood due to bullet holes can be the cause of death, but did Tippit die from lack of blood? It should be noticed that Dr. Rose only said the body he examined had three "penetrating wounds," but that phrase does not explain the cause of death. As a coroner, why did he fail to say that one of those wounds was the cause of death? His report to the Secret Service agent is not only unmedical but purposely vague. Why? Where were those "penetrating wounds" located in the body? Dr. Rose remained silent; nor did the Commission examine him on that vital point of medicine and law. Why? A "penetrating" wound can be in the leg, legs, thigh, rib cage, stomach, head, shoulder, back, chest, arm, arms, or hand. But Dr. Rose

---

from being mentally "cleared" from the trance by any other hypnotist. Ruby's erratic behavior while in jail has led a number of researchers to the hypothesis that Jolly injected Ruby with massive doses of LSD. (For more on Dr. West and Ruby, see Lisa Pease, *A Lie Too Big To Fail: The Real History of the Assassination of Robert F. Kennedy* (Port Townsend, WA: Feral House, 2018), pp. 403-07.

remained silent! Why?

Nor is there any testimony from any police agent as to the person who identified the "Tippit" body at the morgue. Why? Under those circumstances, an investigator of the "Report" has a right to raise those unanswered questions when that investigating body had the authority to demand the answers. When that Commission failed in its responsibility, then it is entirely proper for any person to doubt the veracity of the commissioners. Nor should the "prestige" of those seven commissioners prevent any person from raising those questions.

Assuming that one of those five or six bodies was Tippit's, and assuming that he died as the result of an illegal act, Oswald's defense attorney would be able to prove his client innocent "beyond reasonable doubt" simply by using the testimony of the Commission's own witnesses and the FBI testimony.

The Commission stated that the Tippit murder case commenced at 12:45 p.m., when the Dallas police flashed a Code 3 that contained the description of the man wanted for the murder of President Kennedy. The Commission admitted that the following words were the only ones used to describe the "wanted man": "a slender white man, about 30, 5' 10", weighing 165 pounds, carrying a .30-30 Winchester."

From that description, the Warren Commission, 7 "honorable men," informed the American people that officer Tippit immediately recognized Lee Harvey Oswald. In spite of the fact there were no facial features, no clothing description, no extraordinary manner in walk or talk, no blemishes, officer Tippit immediately stopped "Oswald" who was not 5' 10" tall, who did not weigh 165 pounds; and the person who was halted by Tippit was not carrying a .30-30 Winchester—or any other type of rifle. Oh, yes, Tippit did stop a "white man"! Of course, the Commission implied that the white man brought to a halt by officer Tippit was the only white man in the city of Dallas, on November 22, 1963, who was the height and weight of the suspect.

What was concealed by the Commission was the fact that the

Dallas police arrested not less than eight white men who were carrying rifles, and who were 5' 10", and who weighed between 160 and 165 pounds. What happened to them? Two of them were the conspirators, as will be shown in the conspiracy chapter, and those two were mysteriously freed by the Dallas police. But the Commission was not interested in those two killers, for they had a ready-made "patsy," and he had the name of Lee Harvey Oswald. True, he was also murdered with the connivance of the Dallas police, but he was conveniently dead with no opportunity to defend himself.

The Warren Commission accepted as authentic the testimony of Mrs. Markham, who was the chief "eyewitness" in identifying Oswald as the killer only when that testimony conformed to their fairy tale. But this same witness, who placed a noose around Oswald's neck, swore that she heard Tippit speaking as he lay on the ground waiting for the ambulance to arrive. The Commission said she heard nothing, as he was already dead.

Why did the Commission utter such a statement, saying Tippit was dead? Was it because Mrs. Markham heard something she should have forgotten? The manner in which the Commission deliberately refused to summon the hospital ambulance drivers who took Tippit from the street to the hospital is more than a suspicion that Tippit was alive and did speak to those two ambulance men.

The only witnesses who knew whether Tippit was dead or alive when the ambulance arrived at 1:22 p.m. would be those ambulance hospital orderlies. Yet, at no time did the Commission summon them to testify. Why? Their statements to the FBI cannot be found in the National Archives, nor their statements to the Dallas police, who were at the hospital during Tippit's short stay. The Commission has securely prevented the public [from] receiving any information regarding the Tippit affair in this important matter. It is utterly inconceivable that the 7 commissioners and their 26 aides paid no attention to the matter involving six totally different bodies; whether Tippit was alive or dead when the ambulance arrived; and whether or not he spoke in the privacy of the ambulance. Nor is there any evidence as to whether or not a physician at the hospital examined Tippit as to his condition when he was brought into the hospital.

In view of the various bodies to "prove" one Tippit was dead, various investigators both in Western Europe and in this country have asked: "Is Tippit dead?" According to the press stories relating to Tippit's death and funeral, the family never saw the open casket in which "he" was buried. From the testimony quoted above by the Dallas police, the FBI, and the U.S. Secret Service, none of them stated that they personally knew officer Tippit. They were given a report that "said" the body was that of Tippit; and certainly the testimony revealed above does not, in any manner, prove one of those six bodies was legally that of officer Tippit. Who identified the body placed in the Tippit casket as that of Tippit?

This book does not involve itself in conjecture or speculation. How any person interprets the above testimony from the three police agencies is their concern. This book deals only with hard, cold testimony. Based on that testimony, the questions asked in the previous two paragraphs are legitimate questions that would be asked by any ethical attorney representing Lee H. Oswald on trial for his life for murder.

The major witness used by the Commission to label Oswald as the murderer of officer Tippit was a Mrs. Markham. The Commission stated that she was a "reliable" witness and that her testimony convicted Oswald. However, in spite of what the Commission published in its "Report," her testimony did not say she identified Oswald. Even when her son, an ex-convict, was pushed out the bathroom window of her home by two Dallas policemen, Mrs. Markham refused to make a positive identification. The Dallas police were using the Gestapo "attempting to escape" ploy to convince Mrs. Markham to [definitively] identify Oswald as Tippit's killer. The Commission, as it had and would continue to do, showed no concern that witnesses whose testimony was favoring Oswald had constantly received uninvited punishment toward themselves or members of their families.

With Mrs. Markham's testimony on the negative side of the ledger, the Commission summoned a male witness, Mr. Benavides, who originally informed the police that he could not identify the man who shot Tippit. The police believed him and did not take him to witness the police line-up, which included Oswald dressed in a fashion to "pinpoint" him as the suspect.

Mrs. Markham's original description of the Tippit killer was supported by Mr. Benavides, who informed the police that the murderer had "curly" hair and was "dark complected." In fact, the police were to use one of their descriptions as a police bulletin to alert all police to be on the lookout for a dark complected man with curly hair. Although Benavides was less than 15 feet away from the killer, he could not give the police a facial description. This witness's brother was to be murdered when the killers mistook him [for] the witness.

When Oswald left his boarding room at 1:00 p.m., he was wearing a tan shirt and a dark jacket. Mrs. Markham and Mr. Benavides said the killer wore a light-colored jacket. Oswald, the Commission admitted, was not dark complected and did not have "bushy" or "curly" hair. Thus, the two main witnesses used by the Commission denied the Commission's accusation that Oswald was the killer. The Commission, therefore, produced another "eyewitness" and seven other witnesses who said they saw the killer flee but that they could identify him.

The number one "eyewitness" to the killer fleeing the murder site was a cabdriver who never saw the killer's face. When the FBI showed him several 8 x 11-inch pictures of Oswald, he refused to say to the agents that Oswald was the man he saw fleeing from the murder site. He also told the Commission a strange story. Immediately after the killer fled, the cabdriver went to Tippit's squad car. While waiting for the police to arrive, he looked around, but he never saw Mrs. Markham. Nor could he identify her to the Commission. Yet, she was there, for the police had taken her name, address, and telephone number. The cabdriver was standing within two feet of her, yet he never recognized her. As an "eyewitness," his eyes saw nothing.

With no face or body identification of the man fleeing the Tippit murder site, the Commission was reduced to witnesses who, the Commission said, identified the jacket discarded by the killer as he fled. But the Commission's own statement in the "Report" is refuted by the testimony those witnesses gave in the "Hearings." Mrs. Markham refused to identify the

Commission's jacket, Com. Exh. 162, alleged to be Oswald's. Mr. Benavides swore the jacket he saw was "blue," the cabdriver said "no" as did the two Davis sisters;[37] so did Ted Callaway. Oswald's landlady, the only person to see Oswald in her home, and also when he stood at the streetcar bus stop near her home at 1:03 p.m., testified it was not his jacket. She should have known, for she straightened out his room and knew his clothes. Finally, a person who knew Oswald quite well since he was his next-door neighbor and drove Oswald to work, Mr. Frazier, testified that he never saw Oswald wear that jacket at any time.

What was Com. Exh. 162? Upon an analysis of all the testimony and affidavits residing in the files of the National Archives, a positive statement can be made that the jacket was planted by the Dallas police as evidence that Oswald was at the Tippit murder site. The police committed perjury, and the Commission, from the testimony and exhibits, knew they lied,

The Commission's contortions in their attempt to associate an unknown jacket to Oswald were clearly seen in its fraudulent attempt to conceal the fact that the Commission never discovered who found it and how it was discovered. Captain Westbrook testified that he did not find the jacket; that it was given to him by an "unknown" policeman who, according to the police radio log, wore Badge No. "279." There is also a statement by an officer Hutson that it was not Capt. Westbrook who picked up the jacket but another officer; and, unfortunately, Hutson did not know the name of that officer. In Dallas, the presumption must be that any person who wants to be a Dallas policeman simply goes into an Army-Navy retail store and purchases a Dallas police uniform. This is not as funny as it reads, for the activities of the Dallas police made the Mack Sennett "Keystone Cops" look serious. The testimony revealed that Badge No. "279" was worn by an officer J. Griffin who, in turn, was a police officer in a 12-man motorcycle squad of which both Hutson and Griffin were members! Yet, Hutson testified he never knew [that] Badge No. 279 belonged to his

---

[37] Mrs. Virginia Davis and her sister-in-law Barbara Jeanette Davis.

friend in his own motorcycle squad. Who was committing perjury? Was that jacket, Com. Exh. No. 162, found, or was it a plant by the police in the Dallas police headquarters?

The evidence proved, beyond a reasonable doubt, that no jacket was ever found in the Tippit murder area. It was a plant made by the Dallas police.

What the Commission had concealed is that both Griffin and Hutson testified that the jacket they "found" was "white," not gray. No police officer ever admitted [that] he located or picked up the Commission's grey jacket, nor did any officer admit he picked up a jacket and gave it to another policeman. Thus, the question never answered by the Warren Commission was: "If no police officer admitted finding or handling that jacket, how did it get into the hands of the police department?"

Now reduced to an absolute zero in their efforts to have that jacket belong to Oswald, the Commission summoned their most expert witness on the life of Lee Harvey Oswald—his wife, Marina. Knowing that she would lose the custody of her two children, and facing deportation, Mrs. Oswald promptly acceded to their "request" that she identify Com. Exh. 162 as belonging to her husband.

This Commission jacket, when given to the FBI by the Dallas police, had attached to it a laundry code number "B-9738." The jacket was a "medium" size, and Oswald always wore a "small" size. The FBI, the Dallas police, and the Secret Service visited every cleaning and laundry shop in the Dallas; Irving, Texas; and New Orleans area, and they never located, out of those 600 shops in those areas, any shop that used that code number. Mrs. Oswald, prior to her statement to the Commission, informed the FBI and Secret Service that she never took her husband's clothes, at any time, to any dry cleaning or laundry shop during their married life!

Thus, Oswald's attorney, based on the testimony given to the Commission, would have had no trouble in securing a "not guilty" verdict from a court following the "basic principles of American justice." However, assuming that the trial judge and jury believe that more evidence would be necessary to give a "not guilty" verdict, the attorney would then develop Oswald's defense by presenting or cross-examining the testimony and exhibits relating to the very start of the Tippit murder case.

By using both positive and negative testimony, Oswald's defense attorney would have destroyed the Commission's case against his client Oswald.

The uncontradicted testimony of Oswald's rooming house manager, Mrs. Roberts, stated that he left the rooming house at 1:00 p.m. and that she [saw] him standing at a streetcar bus stop at 1:04 p.m. Her evidence is positive evidence, since she saw him at that bus stop, and it is interesting to note that the Commission made no indication that Mrs. Roberts was mistaken or lying. Since Mrs. Roberts gave positive evidence, the burden of proof remained upon the Commission to prove that from 1:04 p.m. Oswald could, and did, walk to the Tippit murder site within 4 to 5 minutes.

[From] the Tippit murder site [to] the rooming house was nine-tenths of a mile. The Commission, therefore, had one of its aides make a walking test to determine the length of time it would take a normal walking man, crossing all the streets without attracting attention, to arrive from the Oswald bus stop to the Tippit murder site. The time was 17 minutes, 45 seconds. By positive testimony of its own, the Commission proved Oswald was not at the murder site when Tippit was killed. With this evidence in its possession the Commission resorted to the hat trick and, with the use of words, informed the American people that Tippit was not murdered between 1:06 and 1:08 p.m. but at 1:16 p.m.

With the use of words, not evidence, the Commission informed the public that Tippit was shot at exactly 1:16 p.m. The Commission arrived at this time schedule by willfully and deliberately overlooking the sworn testimony of two witnesses, whom the Commission said gave the truth and nothing but the truth. When the testimony of those two witnesses was read and analyzed, it revealed the fact that one witness was a liar and the other never said what the Commission said he said!

Mrs. H. Markham was the prime witness for the Commission relating to the identity of Oswald as the killer, and she committed perjury several times during her testimony. Again, as in the Brennan testimony, the Commission impaled itself on the horns of a dilemma. Her testimony was the "testimony" used by the Commission in its attempt to place Oswald at the Tippit murder site. Their dilemma occurred when she testified that she saw "Oswald" shoot Tippit at exactly 1:06 p.m. However, Mrs. Roberts' testimony placed Oswald at a bus stop at 1:04 p.m., and the Commission's expert walker took slightly more than 17 minutes to walk from the Oswald room to the Tippit site. Thus, the Commission, by Olympian feat, concluded that Oswald was the world's fastest human being on November 22, 1963! According to the Commission, Oswald could have given Man o'War or Kelso a hot race before Oswald faded in the stretch.[38]

Realizing that it could not afford to have Mrs. Markham's testimony impeached, the Commission decided to solve its dilemma by fabricating an entirely new time schedule but overlooked its tester's walking time. In police circles it is well known that the vast majority of hardcore criminals use the same "modus operandi." The Warren Commission, according to the Dallas police records, was no exception, since it adopted the identical pattern when the Commission determined the time of the president's murder by moving the clock ahead, from 12:25 p.m. to 12:30 p.m. In that murder they used five minutes, in the Tippit murder 10 minutes. The Commission decided, "in the interests of national security," that its chief witness, Mrs. Markham, was mistaken. Her 1:06 p.m. time was really 1:16 p.m. It was flabbergasting that the Commission should have stated that the time of the killing was between 1:17 and 1:18 p.m., for their own tests revealed that "Oswald" could not have reached the Tippit murder site until 1:17:45 p.m. Where did "Oswald" pick up one and three-quarters minute? In the Tippit murder the Commission proved that not only were they liars but poor liars—and that is unforgivable to readers of detective stories. What proverb has said that a liar manufactures the web by which he is caught?

This time element never bothered the Commission, as it never took the time to refute it. What is important to Oswald's defense is whether or not there is any evidence in the "Hearings" or the

---

[38] Kelso and Man o'War were two American Thoroughbred racehorses that were considered to be among the best in history.

National Archives which would substantiate a time closer to Markham's time of 1:06 p.m. than the 1:16 p.m. false time created by the Commission. If there be any evidence corroborating the 1:00 p.m. time, then Oswald must be found "not guilty."

On page 202 of the 24th volume of the "Hearings" is corroborating testimony that Mrs. Markham's time of 1:06 p.m. was correct. A Mr. Bowley testified that, at 1:10 p.m., he was driving his automobile when he approached the Tippit murder site and saw the body of officer Tippit "next to the left front wheel of the squad ear, on the street."

He further testified that he got out of his automobile and called the police on the squad car radio. The Dallas police radio log recorded his message: "A policeman has been shot. He is lying out there in the street. I think he is dead." The police then "logged" this conversation as to the time when they received the Bowley message—not the time of the murder but the time of the message—as 1:16 p.m.

In law, there is no discrepancy between Mrs. Markham's time, Mr. Bowley's, or the police log. The police recorded the time of Mr. Bowley's message. Thus, when the police received the Bowley message, officer Tippit was already dead or dying. Since Mr. Bowley, at 1:10 p.m. never witnessed the shooting or even saw the murderer flee from the scene, time had elapsed. Mr. Bowley's uncontradicted testimony revealed that he had looked at his wristwatch, which showed 1:10 p.m. Therefore, since the act of murder had been completed and the murderer had fled, common sense, not legal mumbo jumbo, proved that Mrs. Markham's time of 1:06 and 1:08 p.m. was correct. In law, in spite of the fact [that] she committed perjury on other substantive matters, her time of 1:06 p.m. is lawful testimony when that same testimony was upheld by an impartial witness.

What must be remembered is that without Mrs. Markham's testimony, the evidence of Mr. Bowley was sufficient to absolve Oswald of being the killer of officer Tippit. Oswald could not be at the bus stop at 1:04 p.m. and also be the killer of a police officer killed nine-tenths of a mile away from that bus stop at 1:06 or 1:08 p.m. Add the Commission's own tests to the time element, and Oswald was proved innocent by the

Commission.

The Commission willfully deceived the American citizen by implying that the police "logging" of 1:16 p.m. was the actual time of the Tippit murder. The Commission's reasoning would be the same as if saying the time of a murder is the identical time when the police received information that a murder had been committed. The stupidity of the Commission's reasoning is easily pierced, for to use that reasoning would mean that a dead body found ten hours, ten days, or ten years after the police were informed of the finding of the body would, ipso facto, also be the time of death. The Commission published its fabricated statement because it knew that the general public had little knowledge of law.

The testimony was slowly but surely destroying the Commission's accusation that Oswald was the killer of officer Tippit. In spite of the testimony, the Commission was determined to "convince" the people that Oswald was the killer even if that investigating body had to use the perjury of the Dallas police. And they did!

After the arrival of the police upon the Tippit murder site, they attempted to obtain witnesses for the description which they could broadcast. Upon analyzing the radio logs it seems clear that the original police broadcast used the information given to them by patrolman Summers: "I got an eyeball witness to the getaway man. He is a white male, age 27, 5' 11", black wavy hair, fair complected, wearing a light Eisenhower-type jacket, dark trousers, and a white shirt.... apparently armed with a .32 dark-finish automatic pistol which he had in his right hand." Oswald, when captured some 20 minutes after that broadcast of 1:33 p.m., was wearing a tan shirt [and] did not have black wavy hair. The Commission admitted that Oswald wore a tan shirt at the Depository and at the Texas Theatre!

In addition to the description that did not match Oswald, two other facts appeared: (1) the police, as per their custom, failed to obtain the name or address of the "eyeball witness," and (2) the killer was armed with a .32 automatic pistol, not a revolver allegedly taken from Oswald when arrested. Furthermore, Sgt. Hill, immediately after Summers' talk to the radio dispatcher, also informed his radio contact that the killer was armed with an automatic .38, as indicated by a discharged shell left at the murder site. Thus, both policemen informed the radio dispatcher that an automatic gun was used, or was one of the weapons used, to murder officer Tippit. Another indication that two killers were Involved was the testimony of cabdriver Scoggins, who saw the killer flee with the gun clutched in his left hand.

In summation relating to the identity of Oswald as the "killer," the Commission had no witness who identified Oswald as the murderer; the Commission had no evidence that not only was the jacket "found" under mysterious circumstances but that no witness identified the jacket to the man they saw flee from the actual scene of the murder; and at no time was the jacket associated with Oswald under any circumstances in spite of the testimony of Mrs. Marina Oswald, who admitted that at no time had she ever sent or seen Oswald's jackets in a dry cleaning or laundry shop.

Of course, the perversion of the time of the murder from 1:06 p.m. to 1:16 p.m. was conclusive proof beyond a reasonable doubt that Oswald was never at the Tippit murder site.

The Commission, having failed in its endeavors to link Oswald as the killer, was now reduced to relying upon (1) an unknown pistol, and (2) bullets allegedly recovered from one of five bodies in the Dallas morgue.

Within twenty minutes after the police broadcast of the Summers description, Oswald was arrested in the Texas Theatre. What occurred during his arrest is not known, as the Dallas police carefully screened approximately 10 to 15 patrons and selected only two—who promptly gave contradictory statements regarding those events. Why those, and only those two witnesses, were selected was never asked by the Commission; although the captain in charge testified that he directed his lieutenant to make a list of all of the patrons. What happened to that list, if taken, is unknown. The Commission never subpoenaed that list. Why? Could the answer be that the uncalled witnesses would reveal the fact that Oswald never drew a revolver from his waist belt? Thus, an investigator of the Tippit affaire is reduced to analyzing the testimony of the Dallas police, many of whom gave perjured testimony.

Now, proceeding to point out the lies. At the time of the shooting of President Kennedy, McDonald was instructed, as were many other police squad cars, to go to the Book Depository to render assistance. (He was not cruising around.) He arrived at the Depository at 12:40 p.m. and remained there until 1:16 p.m., when he said he heard the police radio flash that a policeman had been murdered. Without notifying any of his superior officers, he got into his squad car and drove toward the Tippit murder site. On the way there, he testified, he heard that the man suspected in the Tippit murder was "a white male, 5' 10", 27 years old, wearing a white shirt." Note that the suspect is wearing a "white" shirt. He admitted he never heard the Summers description.

Although McDonald admitted that "at the time of Oswald's arrest he (Oswald) was wearing a dark brown shirt, a T-shirt, and dark trousers, "the Commission never asked McDonald how he reconciled a "white shirt" with a "dark tan" one. Nor did the Commission ask the patrolman how his theater "tipster" knew that he was looking for a man on the first floor instead of a man in the balcony. Now can be seen the reason why the police lieutenant never submitted the list of patrons he was ordered to take by the police captain. The "informer-tipster's" name would be on it!

McDonald, upon hearing that there was a suspect in the Texas Theatre, then hurried to that place. Although there were some 20 to 25 police at the theater, McDonald rushed into the theater accompanied by the shoe salesman and manager. The lights were put on and Mr. Brewer pointed out Oswald. He [McDonald] went down the stairs, conversed with the two patrons (what they said was not told by McDonald to the Commission), then approached Oswald with his cocked pistol in his hand. This "suspect" then got up from his seat, and, despite the fact that McDonald already had a cocked pistol pointing at him, deliberately drew from his waist a revolver but did not fire, only struck out at McDonald. McDonald used one hand to hold the gun, another one to grab Oswald's gun, which did not fire because "the primer was dented," and with his third hand grabbed Oswald around the body. While all this was going on, Special Detective R. Carroll "jerked" a gun from someone's hand.

McDonald's "epic" testimony never answered several pertinent questions: (1) Since when does any police department send 15 to 20 policemen to answer a call to apprehend a man "sneaking" into a theater? (2) Since Oswald's description in no shape, manner, or form matched the suspect in the only description given over the Dallas police broadcast, why did the Dallas police send that many men to arrest a man for a misdemeanor? (3) How did the police rationalize that overwhelming force when no one saw Oswald enter the theater with a gun in his hands or clothes? (4) How did McDonald rationalize the only description he received with that of Oswald?

The only answer with any common sense applied to it would be that Oswald was ordered to the theater by his fellow conspirators and they, in turn, believed that Oswald would, in panic, seek to escape and be shot down by the police stationed in the rear of the theater.

What actually occurred can be placed together after the reading of all the testimony. The commissioner who destroyed the Commission's case regarding the question of whether or not Oswald had a revolver in his possession when arrested was Senator Cooper. In his cross-examination, to establish the legal requirement that the weapon "taken" from Oswald was the identical weapon before the Commission, Senator Cooper asked Det. R. Carroll from whom did he "jerk" the revolver. To the consternation of the other commissioners and aides, the special detective calmly testified he "jerked it" from someone's hand, but he did not know whose hand.

Previous to Carroll's testimony, McDonald testified that he had put his "mark" upon the weapon he had "taken" from Oswald; but, on cross-examination, the patrolman admitted that he had put his "mark" on a weapon given to him by an "unknown" policeman at the police station. Thus, in fact and in law, McDonald was admitting that he had not recognized Oswald's weapon, since the weapon he identified was given to him at the police station. Again, one is impressed by the tremendous number of policemen who do not know their fellow policemen in Dallas, Texas. Unidentified "cops" float all over

Dallas and all over the head of the Commission. Whenever the Commission desired "evidence" needed to draw Oswald into its net, the Commission was always able to locate that essential "unidentified" policeman right at its elbow.

In view of the testimony of McDonald and Carroll, the only implication that can be made, based upon their testimony, is that the Dallas police had Oswald's revolver in their possession prior to his arrest and prior to the murder of officer Tippit. Which, in turn, implies that officer Tippit was primed to be murdered with the knowledge of some Dallas policemen.

Perjury was immediately presented to the Commission, for (1) McDonald testified that when he "took" the revolver from Oswald's hand after he had been subdued, McDonald immediately opened up the revolver chamber and put his "mark" upon one of the six bullets in that space. He lied, for he put his "mark" upon "A" revolver given to him at the police station. (2) But Det. Carroll testified that when he "jerked" the revolver from an unknown hand, he immediately gave the revolver to a Sgt. Hill, who, in turn, while seated in the squad car outside the theater, opened the revolver, saw six bullets in the chamber, and made his mark upon the bullets. (3) A revolver was then taken to the police station, and that is all those two men know about A revolver. This scenario is the exact duplicate of the one enacted over Bullet No. "399." A bullet is found; a revolver is found; and in both cases no legal identification can be made in a court of law. Thus, one of the questions to be answered is: "Was a switch made?" Of course, the question could also be asked: "Since no one, except McDonald, testified that Oswald had a revolver when he was arrested, and he [McDonald] had committed perjury and had also lied, his credibility was under a severe strain. Was the revolver at the police station a plant?"

Further evidence of perjury can be found in the deeply suppressed affidavit signed by Deputy Sheriff Buddy Walthers. This affidavit shook the Commission down to its very core, and it was buried way down in the 19th volume. The deputy stated that (1) he was informed by [the] Chief of the Sheriff's Criminal Division, Mr. Sweatt (he was the same one involved in the statement made by [Lonnie] Hudkins to the U.S. Secret Service that Oswald was an FBI informant), to investigate the murder of officer Tippit, which was given to Deputy Walthers fifteen minutes prior to the shooting of the policeman! (2) First, the deputy was told to go to the public library to search for the killer (that is where several other officers went!). When the deputy got to the library, he was told to go to the Texas Theatre. (3) When he arrived at that theater, he was informed that the killer was in the balcony. (4) He heard shouting, and looking down he saw a struggle on the first floor. Dashing down there to assist in the capture of Oswald, he saw several officers, at least five, not just McDonald, struggling to subdue Oswald. Then, glancing down on the floor, he saw a gun which was being pushed out by several police officers, who were putting their fingerprints all over that weapon.

He did not see Det. Carroll "jerk" that gun from McDonald or Oswald, as it was on the floor! The deputy also admitted that not only did he have his shotgun with him, but at least five other officers also carried shotguns into the theater. Thus, the Commission deliberately lied when it said Oswald had not seen any shotguns; and the two witnesses who testified that several cops struck Oswald with the butt of the shotgun were not lying, as the Commission claimed. The commissioners were the liars, not the witnesses!

The same deputy was the one who found the bullet in the ground in Dealey Plaza at 12:40 p.m., and he is also the same officer who went to the Oswald home in Irving, Texas and gave the startling testimony that Mrs. Paine admitted to him that "she expected him"!

The evidence supporting both a "switch" and a "plant" of the revolver was admitted, by error or mental strain, by Capt. Fritz. After the arrest of Oswald and his booking by the police, the captain held a press conference; and, in addition to his comments concerning why Oswald was the killer of President Kennedy, announced that Oswald was "guilty" in the Tippit murder because Oswald's gun had "two empty shells in it." According to McDonald, Carroll, and Hill, six live shells were in the revolver; but the revolver that the captain had in his office, which was given to him by Sgt. Hill, had only four live shells and two empty ones. QED the revolver taken or "jerked" by Carroll from an unknown hand was not the revolver in the possession of the Dallas police, which they said was the one used by Oswald to kill Tippit.

In a further attempt to connect Oswald with that revolver, the Commission accepted the "word" of the police that they found a gun holster on Oswald's bed when they illegally searched his room after his arrest. Mrs. Roberts, whose testimony was never contradicted, testified that at no time as long as he lived in her home did she ever see Oswald have a revolver or holster. She testified that she cleaned his room and changed the sheets. The police again "found" the evidence which the Commission needed to draw the "net" a little tighter around Oswald.

McDonald, as previously mentioned, testified that Oswald attempted to murder him when Oswald pulled the trigger of his "gun" and the "primer misfired because it was dented." It was this testimony which led the Commission to accuse Oswald of "attempting to kill a police officer while resisting arrest"! (Commission Conclusion No. 5.) The reason why they made this charge is absolutely baffling, for they had the testimony of the FBI Ballistic Bureau that said McDonald was mistaken. McDonald testified that he heard the "click" and the revolver misfired, not that he put his finger or part of his hand between the trigger and the chamber. The FBI testified that, when they examined the revolver given to them by the Dallas police, they found that "none of the cartridges found in that revolver bore the impression of the revolver firing pin." That disposes of the Commission's 5th Conclusion. Oswald never pulled that trigger, and it casts further doubt on the credibility of patrolman McDonald.

What did the FBI seek to achieve by using the language "none of the cartridges found in that revolver bore the impression of the revolver firing pin"? The only logical answer is that the FBI was warning the Commission that that revolver was never used in any murder on November 22, 1963! "Oswald" was supposed to have reloaded 6 bullets in that revolver when he fled. Capt. Fritz testified that that revolver had 4 live bullets and 2 expended shells. Now, the FBI was saying that none of the cartridges had any impression of the revolver's firing pin. Then, what force compelled the bullets to leave the cartridges?

During the entire investigation conducted by the Commission in the Tippit murder they never produced a scintilla of evidence that the theater revolver was ever taken from Oswald, or that he had one in his possession, or that the revolver sent to the FBI by the Dallas police was the identical revolver "taken" from Oswald. Thus, in a court of law, the Commission only proved that Oswald "owned" a revolver known as Com. Exh. No. 143, but they never legally proved by the evidence published in the "Hearings" that that revolver was "used" in the Tippit murder.

With the evidence blowing up in their collective faces regarding the revolver, the commissioners were reduced to the bullets and cartridges given to the FBI by the Dallas police; for, in a court of law, those bullets and cartridges must match the bullets taken from "Tippit's body(s)," and the cartridges must also match the Tippit revolver. From a legal point of view, to this day, no one knows that exact number of bullets used to kill officer Tippit—if, in fact, he was killed by bullets.

That the Commission willingly and knowingly accepted perjured testimony from the Dallas police is seen by their statements that only three (3) bullets were fired into officer Tippit's body. Det. Leavelle and Capt. King swore there were only three bullets. In view of their sworn testimony, the ballistic expert for the FBI, Mr. Cunningham, testified: "For the record, I would like to state these 4 bullets, C251, C252, Q13, and C253 were recovered from the body of Tippit." Here were the Dallas police being charged with perjury by the FBI, yet the Commission said nothing, did nothing. Thus, who was committing perjury? Did the Commission know for a certainty who was committing the perjury—the FBI or the Dallas police? The Commission knew that the police were committing flagrant perjury, since a Commission aide directly informed the Commission in response to Commissioner Boggs: "How many bullets were recovered?" Aide: "Four were recovered from the body of the officer.... that does not mean four bullets were found, because there is a slight problem here."

Slight problem? What a problem!

It was a problem that was taxing to the brain. For in the development of attempting to reconcile the testimony of the Dallas police with that of the U.S. Secret Service suppressed autopsy report, which revealed the existence of five (5) different Tippit bodies, and with that of the police testimony of only three bullets, while at the same instance right on the top of the Commission's table were 4 bullets, was the "slight problem." With those four bullets on the Commission's table, to what did the aide think Agent Cunningham was referring? Cats and dogs? Why did the police commit this obvious perjury, and why did the Commission agree to accept their perjury?

As the investigator digs into the "Hearings," he becomes amazed at the duplicity practiced by the Commission. In the "slight problem" enunciated by the aide, the problem was stated but never solved. The Commission's fourth bullet on its table was none other than a bullet from a .38 automatic, which could not be discharged from the revolver "taken" from Oswald at the theater. Two policemen, as had been stated, found an automatic shell, recently fired, at the Tippit murder site. Thus, either the killer was a "two-gun" man or there were two killers. Yet, the two key witnesses, Mrs. Markham and Mr. Scoggins, only saw one killer. One killer, one gun. Oswald's weapon was not an automatic pistol. Using common sense, the automatic shell proved Oswald was not the killer.

There is now no doubt that the Dallas police never proved Oswald had a revolver in his possession, nor an automatic. In addition, if there was a pistol taken from him it was not the weapon used to murder Tippit. Therefore, the police switched that weapon for another weapon in the police station. When the FBI asked the police for the bullets that killed Tippit, they gave the FBI a bullet and a statement that only one bullet was recovered. That was on November 23, 1963; but, as rumors swept the country that more than one bullet was involved, the Commission demanded that the police surrender the other ones. Lo and behold, after searching their "dead" files, the police "found" three bullets. The FBI did not testify that those 3 bullets came from a specific revolver, just that the Dallas police gave them those 3 bullets.

Upon an examination in the FBI Laboratory the Bureau knew that they were being asked to act as the "fall-guys" for the Dallas police. In the FBI's testimony they said: "It is not possible from an examination and comparison of those bullets to determine whether or not they had been fired—those bullets themselves—had been fired from one weapon or whether they had been fired from Oswald's revolver." The meaning of that testimony was loud and clear, for the Bureau warned the Commission that the police were involved in (1) switching revolvers; (2) planting false evidence; (3) suppressing evidence connecting someone in the Dallas Police Department with the Tippit murder. In the "Hearings" the FBI testified that (a) three of the four bullets given to them by the police were manufactured by the Winchester-Western Corp.; (b) the fourth bullet was a Remington-Peters; (c) only two shells of the three bullets were found; and (d) two shells of one bullet was found."

"How can," asked the FBI, "one bullet be discharged from 2 shells?"

Damaging evidence from the FBI was suppressed by the Commission, but it can be found in FBI File No. 87, Doc. No. "774," in which Mr. Hoover wrote: "that the bullets sent to the FBI Laboratory were too mutilated to be tested.... That three of the four bullets may have come from the revolver (given to the Bureau by the police), from Oswald's pockets, or the U.S. Secret Service." In a court of law, a judge would have given a "not guilty" verdict to Oswald. Since none of the bullets could be matched to that "Oswald" revolver, the prosecution had no case. Having relied upon the FBI as its only witness and agency to test the bullets, the Bureau's answer was complete clearance of Oswald. True, the chief's letter is an amazing one in that he impliedly implicated the U.S. Secret Service, but the fact remained that the FBI said those bullets could not be ballistically tested so that the Bureau could not, beyond a reasonable doubt, say those bullets did in fact and in law come from that alleged Oswald revolver given to the FBI by the Dallas police. Mr. Hoover knew that no revolver could discharge a .38 automatic bullet from that "Oswald" pistol, and he was not going to place his head on the chopping block when the Oswald affaire was to be examined by historians as the years passed.

The evidence is overwhelming that, as with the rifle cartridges, the Dallas police were submitting "faked" cartridges to the Commission. According to FBI Agent Cunningham's testimony, the bullets given to him by the Dallas police as being discharged from the "Oswald" revolver were too small a caliber to fit properly within that revolver. As to the 4 cartridges, two of them were found by the man who could not identify Oswald as the killer, Mr. Benavides, and one each by the Davis sisters. Benavides' two cartridges were taken by patrolman Poe, who marked those two with his initials "JMP." He then gave them to Sgt. Barnes, who also placed his initial "B" upon those two, plus the other two cartridges. What happened at the Hearings? As usual, both policemen refused to identify the cartridges shown to them by the Commission as coming from the "Oswald" revolver! Their initials had disappeared. In a court of criminal law, no [self-]respecting judge would convict a man accused of murder on the cartridges which had been either "planted" or "switched" by the Dallas police. In law, those four cartridges given to the Commission were outright fakes.

One of the most intriguing questions in the Tippit murder is: "How did the Dallas police know Tippit was to be slain approximately 30 to 40 minutes prior to its occurrence?" The reader is advised to read Com. Exh. No. 2003, Nos. 78 to 85 inclusive. No. 79 is a police statement that a Dallas policeman was stationed at the Trade Mart, where the president was to give his luncheon address. At 12:40 p.m., after the announcement the president was shot, the policeman was ordered to go directly to the Book Depository to render assistance. The Depository is less than 4 miles from the Trade Mart. The officer immediately left at 12:45 p.m. to go to the Depository, but then this officer, between the Trade Mart and the Depository, heard the police announcement that a policeman had been shot in the Oak Cliff district. The time? Not later than 1 p.m.! Tippit was shot at 1:06 p.m. but no announcement was made, according to the Dallas police, until 1:18 p.m., when it was flashed over the Dallas police radio band.

This same officer, although the president of the United States was dying from gunshot wounds, and although being ordered by a superior officer to assist in the investigation of the shooting of the president, decided to investigate a shooting of a fellow officer, although no police radio call had summoned any police from the Trade Mart or Book Depository to go to the Oak Cliff murder site. The same officer, violating his instructions, continued on the way to Oak Cliff; but on the way he heard, by police radio, that a suspect was being sought in a Dallas branch public library some 5 miles away from the Tippit murder site. Therefore, to assist his competent (?) fellow police to search the library, this police officer dashed to the library. Arriving there, he was informed by a man representing himself to be a "U.S. Secret Service agent" that it was a false alarm and to go to the Texas Theatre! This patrolman then drove to the Texas Theatre.

Thus, in this Com. Exhibit No. 2003, can be seen (1) a statement that can only be labeled "perjurious," for if that policeman left the Trade Mart at 12:40 p.m., and since the Book Depository is less than 7 minutes by siren-sounding police-radio squad car, how did this patrolman hear the shooting of officer Tippit at not later than 1 p.m.? (2) Who was the "U.S. Secret Service agent" at the Dallas branch public library that notified this patrolman that the library "tip" was false and the alleged killer of Tippit was somewhere else? (3) Why did the Warren Commission fail to cross-examine this officer who heard the Tippit alarm some 40 minutes prior to its occurrence, and why did they fail to ask him about the Secret Service agent?

In the same exhibit, No. 2003, #83, a Lt. Cunningham was also at the Trade Mart. He also heard of the Tippit shooting at the same time the first policeman said he heard the announcement. Lt. Cunningham also said he heard that the suspect was in the Texas Theatre. He hurried to that place and entered it, where some unidentified officer notified him that the suspect was in the balcony. While searching the balcony, Lt. Cunningham heard someone shout that the suspect was on the first floor. Another exhibit, #81, was signed by Special Detective Carroll, the man who "jerked" a revolver from an unknown person during the Oswald "struggle." When Carroll entered the theater, an "unknown white female" informed him that the suspect was in the balcony, so he went to the balcony. While in the balcony, Carroll heard another "unknown" voice shout that the suspect was on the first floor! Who was the unknown "tipster" that knew that Lee Harvey Oswald was wanted for the Tippit murder? Who knew that Oswald was on the first floor and not in the balcony? The only answer must be:

a conspirator.

The outstanding feature of the police affidavits in Com. Exh. 2003 is the salient fact that the police at the Trade Mart were informed by some voice over the police radio band that Tippit had been shot 30 minutes prior to the actual statement made by Mr. Bowley from Tippit's radio squad car. The police radio announced the shooting of President Kennedy at 12:30. Between 12:30 and 12:45 p.m. the police at the Trade Mart were instructed to go to the Book Depository to render assistance. The Trade Mart police said they left immediately, and on the way to the Depository, a mere 5 miles away, they all heard the police radio announce the shooting of officer Tippit. Therefore, the absolute maximum time they heard that announcement was 12:55 p.m.

This time element was substantiated by Police Chief Curry's testimony that he was notified "a short time after 1 p.m." that an "officer had been shot" in the Oak Cliff area. He was informed by "unidentified" policemen at the Parkland Hospital. This notification was also prior to the time of Tippit's death!

Now it can be seen why the Dallas Police Department submitted false transcripts of their radio tapes between 12:00 noon and 2:00 p.m. This falsification was so obvious that the Commission asked the FBI to attempt to obtain the truth, but the police so garbled the original tapes that the FBI had no success. Of course, what could have occurred was the same situation in the Dr. King assassination when the conspirators intervened on the Memphis, Tenn. police radio band and directed the Memphis police away from the killer's automobile. However, in the Dallas murder, the conspirators directed the police toward their "patsy," Lee Harvey Oswald.

Further evidence that Tippit was also slated to be murdered is the undisputed fact that fake Secret Service agents were "assisting" the Dallas police in seeking Oswald, both at the public library, at the Texas Theatre, and at the Book Depository. Yet, the Commission said "no conspiracy."

Summarizing the testimony in the "Hearings" and the National Archives, a court of law ruled by an impartial judge would instruct [a] jury of impartial Americans to bring forth a verdict of "not guilty" if Lee Harvey Oswald had lived to face trial for the murder of officer Tippit. Captain Fritz testified that Oswald never admitted that he killed the police officer. He did admit owning a revolver, but he never admitted, according to the same police captain, that he ever used that weapon to kill anyone. Oswald never admitted that he had any revolver in his possession when he was arrested in the Texas Theatre. In fact and in law, there is no evidence that proved any policeman took a revolver from him in that theater. McDonald was proved to be both a liar and a perjurer, and his testimony that he saw Oswald with a revolver in his possession and that Oswald attempted to shoot him was not verified by any police officer in that theater or by an FBI examination of that gun.

The evidence proved that the jacket "found" near the murder site was not worn by Oswald; nor did the evidence reveal the finder of that jacket; nor did the evidence show that the jacket fitted Oswald. As a matter of fact, although the police had that jacket for the two days while they were interrogating Oswald, the evidence revealed that not once did the police ask or show Oswald that jacket. The evidence revealed that the jacket label was "medium" when all of Oswald's clothes bore a "small" label.

Oswald was never legally identified as the man fleeing from the Tippit murder site, nor was he identified by the two key witnesses used by the Commission as the man who fired bullets into Tippit's body.

The Warren Commission's allegations in paragraph (E) and its "Conclusion No. 5" were never proved with the slightest aroma of legal evidence. QED Oswald was innocent, and a verdict of "not guilty" would be upheld in any court of this land.

Paragraph (F) contained eight (8) conclusions of which (1) to (5) have been analyzed in proportion to the space used by the Commission to convict Oswald of various and sundry crimes.

In an effort to prove Oswald's character was that of an amoral person, the Warren Commission gratuitously placed another crime on his back—that of attempting to murder ex-Maj. Gen. Walker. The picture created by the Commission was that Oswald had murdered President Kennedy, attempted to murder Governor Connally, attempted to murder officer McDonald, did murder officer Tippit, and attempted to murder the ex-Major

General. That is a lot of murder in one's lifetime. As the testimony from the Dallas police proved that two men drove away from the Walker home in two separate automobiles, that eliminated Oswald, for he could not drive. When the same police removed the slug from the Walker home, they found that it was fired from a rifle different in caliber from the Italian 7.65mm Carcano. The FBI added their little bit to the mystery, for when they examined that Italian rifle they said that the barrel of that Italian rifle given to them by the Dallas police may have been changed. Where any rifleman could purchase just the barrel of a 1941 rifle was not discussed by the Commission or the FBI.

If the assassination of a President was not a serious matter, then the Commission's attempt to prove Oswald guilty because he "lied on substantive matters" would have been a laughing matter in a law court. Where was the evidence that supported that statement? There was none.

Although Lt. Fritz had available a secretary who took his various "memos," the top-ranking homicide chief of the Dallas Police was unable to secure the services of a stenographer. Nor did the wealth of the rulers of Dallas permit the police department to have a tape recorder available for the department. Therefore, Captain Fritz did the best he could; he used a pencil and made notes. What did he do with those notes? According to the "Report," he destroyed them—but later in the same book "he kept rough notes."

As to the "notes" written by various FBI and Secret Service agents, many of them relative to substantive matters contradicted each other. To say the accused "lied on substantive matters" is one thing; to prove that statement is another!

The substantive matters that could affect Oswald's credibility would only be those matters that are positively connected with the two murders, the wounding of Governor Connally, and the two attempted murders upon Walker and McDonald. Oswald denied murdering President Kennedy and officer Tippit. Was he lying? The evidence proved he was telling the truth. He denied wounding the governor. He was stating the truth. He denied attempting to murder Walker and McDonald. He was again truthful. He admitted visiting Mexico City contrary to the statement published by the Commission that he denied going to that country. His admission was testified to by Holmes of the Post Office Inspection bureau. He denied purchasing the Italian Carcano rifle. The evidence supported him, not the Commission. He denied that he was in the "Life" photograph. That magazine admitted to the Commission that the photograph had been "retouched." A "retouched" photograph is fraud in a court of law and no judge would permit a prosecutor to state to the jury that the photograph is an authentic piece of evidence. Oswald was stating the truth, as proved by the FBI, that at the time of the shooting of President Kennedy he was standing on the steps of the Book Depository. He denied attempting to murder Walker with the Italian Carcano, or with any rifle, and the Dallas police produced the evidence that two other men were seen at that time, and neither of them was Oswald. Oswald stated the truth when he said he had seen Jr. Jarman and TV reporter, Mr. Allman, which also proved he was not at the 6th-floor window or even on the 6th floor between 12:00 noon and 12:30 p.m.

Thus, on those substantive matters which relate directly to the murders or attempted murders, Oswald committed no falsehoods. As to the "attempt" on McDonald's life, that was dreamed [up] by that policeman. The FBI proved that the revolver foisted on Oswald by the same policeman was incapable of discharging bullets. QED how could that same revolver be used to murder officer Tippit?

The final conclusion (8) published by the Commission was that Oswald possessed the capability with a rifle that enabled him to consummate the assassination. It is a well-established fact that any person with a rifle has the capability to murder another person—unless the former is totally paralyzed! Yet, in the rifle tests conducted by the FBI, any rifleman holding the rank of "marksman" with the American Rifle Association failed completely in matching the alleged marksmanship of Oswald! The Commission was so positive that Oswald was the world's greatest marksman on that tragic day that they suppressed the official statement by the U.S. Marine Corps that Oswald's marksmanship was "poor"! The Commission perverted, or converted the Corps report from "poor" to "superior." The

Commission also suppressed the affidavit of a defector from the USSR intelligence bureau who stated that Oswald's marksmanship was so poor that when Oswald went hunting in the Soviet Union his companions had to shoot the hunted animals and give credit to Oswald!

Thus, the case of the Warren Commission against Lee Harvey Oswald for the murder of President Kennedy, the wounding of Governor Connally, the murder of officer Tippit, and the attempted murder of two other persons, ended on the same note that the Commission sounded when it opened its case: with the perversion of the testimony, with the planting of evidence, and with the manufacturing of evidence. All those acts committed "in the interests of national security" under the "basic principles of American justice"!

The callousness with which the Commission and its aides accepted perjury proves the statement that the Commission was conducting a "whitewash": a "cover-up" of the actual conspiracy and the members of that criminal act. When sixty witnesses under oath openly inform the commissioners and their 26 aides that the FBI agents had deliberately perverted statements given to those agents, then it can be honestly assumed that the Commission was not interested in obtaining the truth when, at no time, did the Commission summon any FBI agent so indicated to confirm or deny the charge of perjury. When those same agents are also called "liars" by U.S. Secret Service agents who were under oath, and the Commission refused to place those FBI agents so accused on the stand to confirm or deny, then the assumption must be that those FBI agents did commit perjury. Under the "basic principles of American justice" perjury cannot be used to convict a person accused of any crime.

In addition to deliberately overlooking the involvement of various members of the Dallas police, the Warren Commission also benignly overlooked the conduct of the nonpolice executives employed by or elected in the city of Dallas! For example, what Dallas city official or officials ordered the condition [of] the area around Dealey Plaza to be remodeled so that authentic reenactment could be made? By remodeling that area, the Dallas City fathers effectively prevented witnesses and charts from giving proper identification of locations relating to the murder at the time the murder occurred.

To close this chapter, a short summary is made of the conduct of the Commission and its aides [and] of the evidence that proved the Commission deliberately and willfully:

– Manipulated and distorted the facts presented to them.
– Issued false and misleading statements.
– Refused to accept testimony contrary to their preconceived theory.
– Accepted false photographs.
– Accepted perjured testimony with the knowledge it was perjury.
– Permitted in excess of 200 "off the record" interviews between the witness and the Commission aide in violation of the Commission's rules.
– Accepted perjured testimony identifying Oswald as the Tippit murderer.
– Accepted false testimony which identified Oswald as the Kennedy killer.
– Accepted, with full knowledge, the perjury of Mrs. Marina Oswald.
– Refused to investigate the activity of the Dallas police prior, during, and after the murder of President Kennedy.
– Refused to subpoena the Zapruder films from "Life."
– Refused to subpoena the X-Rays from the U.S. Secret Service.
– Refused to interrogate the FBI agents who were accused by witnesses and agents of the Secret Service of deliberately perverting statements made by witnesses and given to the FBI.
– Issued statements that the Commission had read vital documents when, in fact, they never read those statements, thus lying to the people.
– Refused to purchase the TV films and radio tapes taken by that media relating to the activity prior, during, and immediately after the shots struck the president. These tapes showed (1) the grassy knoll; (2) the persons on the steps of the Book Depository; (3) persons on the fire escape of the Dal-Tex Building; and (4) persons on the roofs of the Book Depository,

the Dal-Tex Building, and the Dallas County Building.

– Accepted from the CIA and the FBI those agencies' own self-serving statements when the truth of the statements made by those agencies was under attack.

– Suppressed the Hughes photograph proving Oswald's innocence.

– Refused to investigate the infamous "double detour."

– Suppressed the Allman affidavit, which upheld Oswald's statement that he directed a man to a phone booth at the Depository entrance.

– Suppressed Inspector Sorrels' testimony.

– Suppressed the FBI reports in both the "Report" and "Hearings."

– Suppressed the official U.S. Secret Service Survey proving Oswald innocent.

– Suppressed the fight in Parkland Hospital between a "CIA" agent, FBI agent, and Secret Service agents.[39]

– Suppressed the finding of the curtain rods by its own aide.

– Suppressed the affidavits of policeman Davenport that revealed Oswald, legally, was murdered by an unidentified 21-year-old "physician" and an "unknown" Dallas detective.[40]

– Suppressed the Price Exhibit revealing Parkland Hospital prepared the autopsy room for Oswald 30 minutes before being shot by Ruby.

---

[39] Secret Service Agent Andrew E. Berger (stationed with Agent Richard E. Johnsen right outside Trauma Room One) reported that he encountered the following four figures at Parkland Memorial Hospital, who each attempted to gain entry to the room: FBI Agent Drain, accompanied by a "doctor friend." An "unidentified CIA agent," who possessed credentials. And an "unidentified FBI agent," who did not possess credentials. See Vincent Palamara, *Survivor's Guilt*, pp. 271-272. Palamara concludes: "Berger's report was totally ignored by just about everyone." Author Gerald McKnight adds that the unidentified FBI agent who attempted to push his way past the Secret Service "was instantly slammed to the wall and fell to the floor after receiving a haymaker from one of the Secret Service agents. The FBI agent was later identified as J. Doyle Williams." See McKnight, *Breach of Trust*, pp. 272-273.

[40] See chapter seven for additional details.

– Suppressed the official letters signed by J. Edgar Hoover proving that: (1) Lovelady was lying; (2) the deformed cartridge from the 6th floor; (3) the proof that the police gave the FBI planted shells relating to the Tippit murder; (4) that Bullet 399 was planted in Parkland Hospital; (5) that the Italian rifle was a nonlethal weapon, and many other items and evidence proving Oswald was innocent.

– Suppressed the devastating affidavit by Deputy Sheriff Buddy Walthers proving McDonald a perjurer and also implicating Mrs. Paine.

– Refused to read the FBI dossier on Oswald.

– Refused to investigate the Hudkins report to the Secret Service by refusing to obtain testimony from Chief Sweatt of Dallas.

– Refused to investigate the Secret Service testimony that "Oswald was not the man."

– "Lost" the Lt. Day memo relating to the actual rifle found on the 6th floor.

– Refused to investigate the official Dallas police report that 3 cartridges were also found on the 3rd floor at 12:45 p.m.

– Refused to investigate the rifleman [who was] captured with a rifle by deputy sheriffs "on the grassy knoll"; or the man fleeing from the Dal-Tex Building!

– Refused to investigate the man captured in the Dal-Tex Building, who was later mysteriously released by Dallas police agencies.

– Refused to investigate the "brown paper bag" found in the Irving, Texas Post Office.

– Refused to investigate Sheriff Decker's 12:25 p.m. announcement to his department, via his radio, that the president was shot.

– Refused to investigate the police statements in Com. Exh. No. 2003, Nos. 78-85.

– Refused to publish the autopsy report on officer Tippit.

– Suppressed the proof that the Dallas police knew Oswald's secret hideaway on Elsbeth Street and sent a police squad to arrest him there!

In brief, the "Report" was written more than twenty times in an attempt to negate the truth.

The subtitle to the Warren Commission's "Report" should read:

Here "Truth" Lies.

PART TWO

CHAPTER VII

THE GUTS OF THE CONSPIRACY

"If they've found another assassin, let them name names and produce their evidence."—Allen Dulles, ex-CIA Director to "Look" magazine.

What a declamatory statement! What a rending of the clothes! What nonsense!

Allen Dulles, a member of the Warren Commission, which had full power of the federal government to subpoena witnesses, records, books, photographs, television tapes, motion-picture camera films, radio tapes, X-rays, charts, surveys, beating his breast while mouthing outraged words at the "critics" who refuse to accept the "Report" issued by those "honorable" citizens.

Let the reply to Mr. Dulles be that it is not necessary for the critics to besmirch the "honor" of those seven commissioners: that they did themselves.

Mr. Dulles forgot that it was he and his six cohorts who gave their "bond and honor" that they would "evaluate the facts to ascertain the truth." Once they accepted the duty and responsibility of investigating the assassination, then the citizens of the nation to whom they gave their "word" had the right to assume that the commissioners would conduct a proper investigation and "let the chips fall where they may."

It was not the critics of the Commission that accepted perjury, manufactured evidence, and planted evidence. Nor did any citizen assist in writing the "Report" that was contradicted by the testimony in the "Hearings." Nor did any citizen suppress affidavits, documents, and letters from the FBI that proved Oswald innocent and, with that proof, revealed a conspiracy.

To assist the six living members of the Warren Commission and their 26 aides, the following pages will reveal how the conspiracy was proved by testimony now in the "Hearings" or in the National Archives. From those identical places, a few of the conspirators will also be named and their part in the conspiracy revealed.

The reader will probably recall the spate of news columns and television programs analyzing the "Report" after the critics began receiving some attention. The main thrust of the press and television media was an attempt to denounce the critics as money-mad vultures not permitting the president's soul to rest in peace. In all three national television programs there was no attempt to discuss the merits of the critics' case against the Commission. One system went so far as to state that the critics always saw "conspiracy" whenever a national figure was murdered.

For some reason known only to themselves, the critics of the critics have carefully overlooked the statements of J. Edgar Hoover in the murder of President Kennedy and Martin Luther King, that the Bureau has not ceased its activity in those two cases. If the cases have been solved, then why is the FBI still active?

Before exposing the conspiracy that murdered President Kennedy, which, in turn, led to a coup d'état in this nation, the legal meaning of a conspiracy should be defined.

A conspiracy is a criminal act committed by two or more persons. An act by two or more persons to commit a felony—a crime—which is not carried to its fruition is a conspiracy to commit a crime. Thus, where A and B plan to rob a store, or plan to bomb a home or school, the fact that they purchase a gun or manufacture the bomb but go no further is a conspiracy to commit a crime. If, however, they actually proceed and consummate the crime, then the conspiracy charge is merged into the completed criminal act. The penalty for conspiring to commit a felony is generally less than the [penalty for the] commission of the actual crime. Where the crime is completed, then all the persons involved in the crime are as guilty as the person or persons who did the actual criminal act. For example, four men conspire to murder the president of the United States, but one man only supplies the funds for the execution of the crime. He purchases the weapons and provides the "getaway" automobile and the hiding places for the other three men. The three men do the actual shooting of the president. All four men are guilty of murder. This is what occurred in the murder of President Kennedy. However, as the suppressed testimony revealed, more than four men were actually involved.

Many persons believe that only the so-called criminal elements would commit murder through a conspiracy. But history has revealed that it is not the criminal elements that do the conspiring to eliminate the leaders of a nation. The mainspring of any conspiracy, as shown throughout the ages, has always been the "honorable" men. The men who threw the knife, the bomb, or pulled the trigger have always been backed by "honorable" men. The five attempts on the life of General De Gaulle have been the result of conspiracies organized by "honorable men," but the men who did the actual "dirty" work were not from the ranks of those persons of "honor." Caesar was not murdered by the "criminal class."

"Honorable" men planned, organized, and paid for the murder President Kennedy.

Before exposing the conspiracy, two other legal explanations are necessary. Those are: "accessories before the fact," and "accessories after the fact." The "fact," of course, is the crime that has been consummated. An accessory before the fact is any person who knowingly contributes in any manner to the commission of an act that is defined by law to be a crime. An accessory after the fact is any person who gives aid or shelter to any person after the crime has been completed with the intent to defeat the law.

The above generally applies to the everyday citizen. However, how does the law regard persons who have knowingly and willingly accepted a position which gives to those persons the knowledge and power to negate the commission of a crime?

For example, if a police agency has knowledge that a crime is to be committed, as one of murder, does the police agency have the responsibility of forestalling that murder, or can it wait until the murder is consummated and then arrest the murderer with no punishment being given to the police?

Substituting the above for the "Dallas Police Department," the U.S. "Secret Service," the "Federal Bureau of Investigation," and the "Central Intelligence Agency," the citizen has the right to know if any of those four agencies, alone or in conjunction with each other, had prior knowledge that President Kennedy [was] to be murdered in Dallas, Texas on November 22, 1963. The next question would be that if any of those agencies did have prior knowledge [of] the Dallas murder, did the agency that had that knowledge have the legal responsibility, as distinguished from the moral, to prevent that murder?

Although the U.S. Secret Service has the legal responsibility of protecting the president of the United States, it can be legally stated that any police agency of the state, county, city, or federal governments that had foreknowledge of an attempt to murder the president and failed to act was guilty of "nonfeasance" and probably guilty of being an "accessory before the fact." The word "nonfeasance" is the failure by a person to do something which ought to have been done. The job of a policeman or agency is to prevent the commission of a crime where he has the knowledge that a crime is to be committed.

Where a police department acts in such a manner after the completion of a crime that aids or abets the criminals to escape from the processes of the law, such an act is "aiding or abetting" and places the police department as being "accessories after the act"—a criminal offense. At the same time, if those acts reveal that the police department had encouraged the crime and then committed acts after the crime to prevent capture and trial of the participants, that department could be considered participants to the conspiracy and also actors in the criminal act itself.

A good example of this has occurred in the various police departments around the nation where the police have "fingered" various businesses to be burglarized, have acted as "lookout" men, have carted away the proceeds of the burglarized business, and then have divided the proceeds of the burglary. Where the policemen involved have been captured and tried, they have been found equally guilty with the "patsies" that did the actual burglary.

As will be revealed, there is now no question that the Warren Commission knew that a conspiracy in fact and in law murdered President Kennedy. That Commission knew beyond a reasonable doubt that members of the Dallas police and members of the FBI manufactured evidence that supported the "guilt" of Lee Harvey Oswald. There is prime evidence that the FBI, the U.S. Secret Service, and the Dallas police had prior knowledge that President Kennedy would be shot from ambush. The Warren Commission had full knowledge that those agents had not only manufactured, planted, and switched evidence but that various affidavits had been altered to change the context of those affidavits.

An interesting hypothetical problem arose when some critics raised the question of whether or not there was any legal responsibility of the Commission in the manner of its conduct of the investigation. Law does not punish for the violation of a moral responsibility. Thus, a man on a bank of a river need not plunge into that river to save a person from drowning. This, in spite of the fact that the man on the bank may be a champion swimmer, [an] expert in life-saving procedures. But a man accepting pay to act as a lifeguard, who refuses to act to save a drowning person, can be charged with "nonfeasance" but not manslaughter or murder.

The Commission was responsible for the conduct of its 26 aides and, as President Truman once said: "The buck stops here!" Whether that conduct of the aides abetted in the escape of the conspirators cannot be evaluated on the testimony in the "Hearings." What is found in analyzing the conduct of the aides, as lawyers, is that far too many of those aides deliberately acted in violation of the lawyer's code of ethics. According to a statement by Chief Justice Warren, the Chairman of the Commission, the aides had no right to ask questions "off the record." But a reading of the "Hearings" reveals that more than 200 "off the record" hearings were made by the aides, and many of those "off the record" hearings permitted the aides to conceal the actual evidence that proved a conspiracy. Thus, where a Secret Service agent openly stated that he had received a telephone call on November 24 that "Oswald was not the man (the killer)," the aide immediately called for an "off the record" interview with the agent. The "Hearings" remain a total blank as to what the agent told the aide. The improper conduct of the aides as attorneys abounds [in] the "Hearings." Deliberate misrepresentations of the witnesses' statements were made by the aide[s]; deliberate misrepresentations of evidence were given to various witnesses, and based on those misrepresentations the witness gave an answer that upheld the Commission's theory.

One or two misrepresentations can be said to be human errors; a dozen or so "off the record" interviews may be held; but when the misrepresentations, when the conduct is deliberate confusion, when more than 200 "off the record" interviews are held, then it cannot be considered human error but calculated, deliberate, willful conduct used to conceal the conspiracy. Whether or not such conduct can be considered an "accessory after the fact" has never been considered by a law court where such conduct is done by a government investigating body.

The atmosphere in Dallas on November 22, 1963 was such that District Attorney Wade on that night attended a social function—dancing, drinking and laughter—which turned into a celebration during which cheer after cheer rang out for a Texan now president the United States. The elite of Texas industry attended—with no tears for President Kennedy.

The conspiracy that murdered President Kennedy was actually a conspiracy within a conspiracy. The evidence will prove this beyond a doubt.

The foundation for the murder of President Kennedy was laid out immediately after the disastrous "Bay of Pigs" defeat inflicted upon the nation by a CIA plot, approved by President Eisenhower, and supported by the Department of Defense, which went sour.

It is true that in all probability a second air strike would have secured the beachhead, but whether that would have been sufficient to overthrow Castro and replace him with Batista, or a Batista-appointed dictator is, as history has shown, extremely doubtful. But what historians have not published is the reason behind that second air strike refused by President Kennedy. The main reason was the discovery by President Kennedy of a CIA "death list" comprising some 10,000 Castro leaders and functionaries.[41] This list was known and approved by Allen Dulles, then the director of the CIA.

This "death list" came to the president's attention during the second day of the invasion, when he was informed that the CIA had imprisoned every moderate or liberal Cuban living in the United States or with the Cuban Army in Guatemala several days before the invasion. However, not only were they imprisoned but those men and women were also marked for execution. The CIA plan called for those Cubans to be flown to Cuba and given to the new Batista government. The reader must not forget that those moderate and liberal Cubans had defeated Batista, in violation of Cuban laws of 1957-59. With this horrifying prospect in store for those people, many of them who were personally acquainted with the president and had "broken bread" with him, the president had second thoughts concerning, not the second strike, but the idea that he, personally, would be labelled a butcher in the eyes of history. It is one thing to

---

[41] Marks is probably referring to the machinations of a clandestine CIA-controlled group called Operation 40. In a June 9, 1961 memo to Richard Goodwin, and citing as his source *New York Times* correspondent Sam Halpern, Arthur Schlesinger writes: "Halpern ... has excellent contacts among the Cuban exiles... Halpern says that CIA set up something called Operation 40 under the direction of a man named (as he recalled) Captain Luis Sanjenis, who was also chief of intelligence.... The ostensible purpose of Operation 40 was to administer liberated territories in Cuba. But the CIA agent in charge, a man known as Felix, trained the members of the group in methods of third-degree interrogation, torture, and general terrorism. The liberal Cuban exiles believe that the real purpose of Operation 40 was to 'kill communists' and, after eliminating hardcore Fidelistas, to go on to eliminate first the followers of [Manolo] Ray, then the followers of [Manuel "Tony"] Varona, and finally to set up a right-wing dictatorship, presumably under [Manuel] Artime." As reproduced in Larry Hancock, *Someone Would Have Talked* (Southlake, TX: JFK Lancer Productions, 2006), p. 522, n. 14. For an extended discussion on the Cuban Revolutionary Council (composed of exiled Cuban political leaders) and Operation 40, see James DiEugenio, *Destiny Betrayed* (New York: Skyhorse, 2012), chapter three.

practice Machiavellian politics; it is another to produce a Lidice.[42]

The CIA plan also included the complete destruction of the oil refineries, power plants, bridges, and all communications systems. However, not only was the CIA prepared to destroy Havana, but their plan included the complete destruction of all Havana civilians by destroying that city's only water supply: the water reservoir in the Marianao suburb of Havana. No city can exist if its people be denied water. This is the reason why Goldwater's, Reagan's, and Murphy's appeal for the destruction of the dikes in North Vietnam is so barbaric and un-Christian, for their plan calls for nothing less than the complete genocide of twelve million women, men, and children—all in the name of Christianity! Of course, the air pilots who will have to complete the destruction will not have as one of their co-pilots the two sons of Goldwater or his son-in-law. Goldwater is very patriotic with the lives of sons of other fathers! However, Reagan's plan to make North Vietnam an asphalt parking lot would include the use of the blood, bones, and marrow of the North Vietnamese women and children.

There was far more to the president's thoughts concerning the dismemberment of the CIA, for he now had received a firsthand glimpse of the feeling for democracy that existed within the 4th arm of the federal government—the CIA. However, President Kennedy's failure to remove the operating heads of that organization would be one of the causes of his assassination. The first executive under Dulles was Richard Helms (1961-1964), who was appointed at the insistence of Vice President Johnson. Within a year after the murder of President Kennedy, Mr. Helms was appointed to be director of the CIA. They are both Texans.

Although President Kennedy was an avid student and writer of history, he overlooked three great Americans who knew what a 4th arm of government would do to the fabric of this nation.

George Washington, in his second term of office, said: "Let there be no change by usurpation; for though this, in one

---

[42] A reference to the June 1942 annihilation of the village of Lidice, a massacre ordered by Adolf Hitler and Heinrich Himmler.

instance, may be an instrument of good, it is the customary weapon by which free governments are destroyed." (The TV chains should remind Congress and Vice President Agnew!)

Nearly a decade and a half later, President Thomas Jefferson said: "Whatever power in any government is independent, is absolute also."

And nearly one hundred and seventy-five years later, President Truman said this about the CIA: "It has become an operational and, at times, a policy-making arm of the government." In other words, the CIA is the 4th branch of this nation; with no restrictions upon its activity and, at times, higher than God Himself.

Mr. Nixon has not studied the writings of Washington or Jefferson. For it is Mr. Nixon's attorney general who advocates "preventive arrest"—an offshoot of Hitler's 1933 criminal law. The hidden key to Mitchell's Hitlerian proposal is the fact that, under "protective arrest," the alleged criminal need not be brought trial at all! The government, under that law, need only seek delay, delay, delay, and delay on any ground—crowded courts, insufficient judges, seeking to locate witnesses, and so forth! With Sec. IV of the McCarren Act—where the president may declare by presidential executive order a "national state of emergency" and order the arrest and imprisonment for any length of time of any person without trial—the "preventive-protective arrest" law, plus the McCarren Act, would mean the total collapse of the American philosophy and government.

The gods that were the CIA were not going to permit any mere U.S. president to "break the CIA into little pieces"—not if the gods could prevent it. And the gods did prevent the making of little pieces with the final result being enacted when pieces of the president's skull went hurtling to the dirty street in Dallas, Texas. For running like a thread over and under a blanket is the mysterious name of G. De Mohrenschildt, a CIA agent, who was in Guantanamo at the time of the invasion of Cuba; who befriended an alleged "traitor," Lee Harvey Oswald; who wrote a bereavement letter to the stepmother-in-law of President Kennedy; and who skips in and out of the testimony in the "Hearings" like a wraith. Did this White Russian CIA agent know that Oswald was a CIA agent in the Soviet Union and was still an agent in United States? Why would Mr. G. write to the FBI to see if Oswald was "in the clear" or was "clean" as a citizen?

The Bay of Pigs and President Kennedy's threat to break the CIA into small pieces was the initial starting point of a slow-burning fuse that led to a keg of dynamite blowing up in Dallas, Texas. The evidence is beyond dispute that the CIA, time and time again, deliberately violated President Kennedy's orders to cease arming the Batista forces in the United States. Arms caches were being turned up all over the southern section of the United States. In fact, on a CBS program in 1969 (!), it was revealed in actual films taken in Louisiana that the CIA was still training sabotage and assassin groups (see Hoover letter to Rankin re: CIA training film in illustrated section), with weapons that could only be secured from the latest weapons arsenal—weapons that had not yet been given to our troops in Vietnam! The fact that many of these weapons were also being siphoned off by our "friendly" Batista forces and sold to illegal arms dealers for sale in the Mideast, or South America, or through various means into Red China and North Vietnam, raised no qualms.

While President Kennedy was attempting to bring the CIA to heel, he was also trying to secure some detente with the Soviet Union, Red China, and Cuba. Wheat sales were being made to the Soviet Union, while cautious inquiries were being made through various diplomatic channels to secure some sort of relaxation with Castro. The CIA also attempted to interfere in this operation, for that bureau proposed to President Kennedy that all the wheat shipments be sprayed with a delayed poison! The president rejected the proposal. However, the CIA was successful in pouring several tons of ground glass in Canadian wheat shipments before being caught by the Canadian government. What an example of Christianity in action! "Suffer, little children, suffer"!

The move that finally led to the conspiracy was the president's determination to compel those Texas millionaires and billionaires to pay some tax on their wealth. One Texas oil man was bragging that on his million-dollar-a-DAY income he was paying less tax than what his own chauffeur was paying.

The president had informed various news media columnists that in 1964 he was going to go "all out" on those types of persons and strike at the oil depletion allowance "racket."

With that knowledge, the president's enemies were waiting to strike, and only by a fortuitous circumstance were they able to complete their act.

In an attempt to find some evidence regarding the involvement of the CIA—Batista arm that was involved in the murder of President Kennedy, one must search diligently the newspapers and books that have written and painted a picture of the background showing the involvement of the CIA.

Thus, a book written by the U.S. advisor to our African Affairs Mission at the United Nations painted a few of the strokes that composed the picture. Mr. William Attwood wrote a book, "The Reds and the Blacks," which was published in 1967. In that book he related his efforts on behalf of President Kennedy immediately prior to the assassination, when Mr. Attwood was approached by the Guinea Ambassador to Cuba to sound out the United States for a detente between Cuba and the United States. That cautious approach was first made to Mr. Attwood in the middle of September 1963.

Mr. Attwood informed UN Ambassador Adlai Stevenson and Averell Harriman, who then advised Mr. Attwood to contact Robert Kennedy, the attorney general. The attorney general then informed President Kennedy, who authorized further inquiry between Mr. Attwood and the Cuban UN Delegate, Sr. Lechuga. Now, one of TV's brightest women news commentators, Lisa Howard, learned of the discussions, and she contacted Castro's aide, a Major Vallejo, via telephone. By October 31st Castro had approved negotiations, provided such preliminary talks were unpublicized. Five days later, Maj. Vallejo had again conversed with Miss Howard and informed her that Castro would personally discuss the negotiations, alone, and without any aides. By November 15th the preliminary discussions had been concluded, with McGeorge Bundy of the White House staff informing Mr. Attwood that the president would see Sr. Lechunga after the president's trip to Dallas. After the assassination, Mr. Attwood had been informed by Sr. Lechunga that Castro had approved the formal entry into discussions with Mr. Attwood as the president's go-between. Of course, with a new president, and with a new CIA Director, R. Helms, who was also a longtime fellow Texan, the talks were abandoned.

On March 10, 1967 the events outlined in Mr. Attwood's book were confirmed by Robert Kennedy in the New York "Times." Miss Lisa Howard's role in creating the preliminary atmosphere and in arranging a secret meeting between Robert Kennedy and a special Cuban envoy was to lead to her murder on July 4, 1965. She knew too much.

Three days prior to this story by the New York "Times," there appeared a column of the nationally syndicated columnist, Drew Pearson. In that column Pearson wrote that President Johnson was sitting on a "time bomb" in that he had been informed by the CIA that Robert Kennedy had plotted with CIA executives to assassinate Castro; that Castro had foiled the plot and that the CIA then turned around and used the identical modus operandi to murder President Kennedy—without the knowledge, naturally, of Robert Kennedy. Pearson implied that this was President Johnson's method of containing Robert Kennedy's political attacks on the president's policies. Pearson concluded his column with the following sentence: "There have been times when the CIA has been forced to resort to the most extreme measures to protect the national security." Although Pearson's words seem to have been directed at the "enemies" of the United States, one should not forget that, in the modern world of politics, the phrase "to protect the national security" has now been broadened to mean those persons whom the CIA interprets to be "internal" as well as external enemies.

There has never been any denial that the CIA violated President Kennedy's direct order to the agency to disband all activity directed against sabotage and murder in Cuba. Jim Garrison's excellent profile and interview published in the October 1967 issue of "Playboy" should dispel any naive idea that the CIA is under the direct command of the president of the United States, or the National Security Council, or the Senate Committee that is supposed to oversee and control that agency's activities. The CIA does what it wants and controls the methods of accomplishing its objectives. The CIA has interfered directly in Army operations in Vietnam via the Green Berets, and that agency controls Kỳ and Thiệu.[43]

Martin Luther King was murdered on the direct orders of the CIA, which operated through the various right-wing organizations receiving funds from that agency. The "tip-off" that Rev. King was to be murdered came when Mr. Hoover called him a "communist" and an "un-American"—which, in Hoover's terms, means a "traitor." Within 120 days King was dead, murdered in the exact duplicate modus operandi used to murder President Kennedy. Is that why the CIA requested the Zapruder films from the FBI for "training purposes"? (See illustrated section, affidavit #2.) The CIA had Rev. King murdered because the "traitor" had to be murdered to "protect the national interests." After all, 75,000 unarmed persons congregating in Washington, D.C. might overthrow the government, which had 155 tanks, thousands of tons of mace, and 25,000 troops armed with submachine guns surrounding the parade route and [the] Washington Monument assembly area.

There may have been some truth in the Drew Pearson column outlining the CIA—Robert Kennedy attempt to assassinate Castro.[44] The "Hearings" did bring out the fact that Oswald made an attempt to obtain an entry into Cuba. The Commission deemed it necessary to suppress, until the year 2038, a CIA document entitled: "Role of Cuban Intelligence Service in processing Oswald's visa application."[45] What is important is

---

[43] Nguyễn Cao Kỳ was prime minister of South Vietnam from 1965 to 1967. He served as vice president from 1967 to 1971. Nguyễn Văn Thiệu was the president of South Vietnam from 1967 to 1975.

[44] Although this was a reasonable speculation to make in 1970, it has since been disproven. Pearson was being manipulated by the intelligence agencies.

[45] The July 1, 1967 *New Orleans Statesman* headline reads: "DA Aide Cites Hidden CIA Data on Oswald." The lead story, under the byline of Ross Yockey, said that Jim Garrison's aide Tom Bethell "charged today that the Central Intelligence Agency has concealed at least 31 official documents vital to an investigation of President John F. Kennedy's assassination." Commission Document 935, which features the title "Role of Cuban Intelligence Service in processing visa application," was classified as Top Secret and is one of the files

the radio address by Premier Castro two days after the murder of President Kennedy. In that long speech discussing the murder, the premier brought up the speech made by Sergio Carbo to the Executive Council of the Inter-American Press Association—a CIA affiliate. In that speech delivered on November 18, 1963, Carbo said: "I believe that a coming serious event will oblige Washington to change its policy of peaceful co-existence." This Carbo speech was given four days prior to the murder of the president, and the Warren Commission never summoned Carbo to question him regarding the speech's implication—that Carbo knew of the plot through his association with the CIA.

Thus, when the CIA accomplished its objective, that organization knew that the new power in Washington, President Johnson, would reverse the attempt of a detente between Cuba and the United States. To say that the murder of President Kennedy did not change the course of History is to deny the truth. Five days after the Dallas murder, President Johnson's favorite news columnist, William S. White, was to write that the new President would definitely increase this nation's war

---

noted in the article. Fifty years after it was declassified by the CIA, the Mary Ferrell Foundation obtained a copy of CD 935 and included it in their online archive, under the title "Commission Document 935—CIA Helms Memorandum of 15 May 1964 re: Cuban Intelligence Service." The file consists of a two-page memo from CIA Director Richard Helms to Lee Rankin: "Role of Cuban Intelligence Service in Processing Visa Applicants; Reaction of that Service to the Assassination of President Kennedy." Attached to this memo is a two-page report, "Subject: Lee Harvey Oswald," summarizing information obtained from a source that had regular contact with Cuban intelligence agents. One of the agents reported that Oswald had gone to the Cuban Consulate in Mexico City "two or three times in connection with a visa application." Helms informs Rankin that the source was questioned "in detail" concerning possible connections between Oswald and Cuban intelligence," but the attachment makes it clear that nothing was uncovered and that the source had never heard of Oswald until after the assassination. Since Helms would have known that Oswald's true ties were with the American intel community, the entire memo reads like a red herring.

efforts—including the increment of many GIs—to militarily defeat the North Vietnamese. Mr. White, knowing his subject well, also wrote that the "conservatives," i.e., Texas oil interests, "have less to fear, domestically, from Johnson than from any of the other Democratic candidates." The events from the day President Johnson took the oath of office until he retired to his Texas ranch bore out Mr. White's column which was published on November 27, 1963.

Jim Garrison, the district attorney who prosecuted Clay Shaw, was one of the few public figures who did have the courage to fight the CIA and the federal government. Nor did he hide behind innuendos, for he submitted to long press interviews published in Playboy"—October 1967, "Ramparts"—January 1968, "Issues and Answers"—ABC interview, May 25, 1967, WWL-TV in New Orleans, May 20, 1967.

A statement by Mr. Garrison, published by CBS News and the "AP" on December 26, 1967, brought forth no denial by the Director of the FBI, J. Edgar Hoover. The statement, never denied: "On that day (September 17, 1963) Lee Harvey Oswald tipped the FBI that an assassination was being plotted. On that day the FBI sent out TWXs, the telegrams within the Bureau circuit, to a number of its offices announcing—this is Sunday, the Seventeenth of November 1963—announcing that on the twenty-second of November an attempt would be made to assassinate John F. Kennedy in Dallas, Texas. This went up to J. Edgar Hoover. What came down to John Kennedy and the men who were assigned to guard him, and other law enforcement personnel, you can judge for yourself by the fact that the president was allowed to ride in the parade without a bubble top, without any real protection—when the specific information had been received that there would be an attempt to assassinate him."[46]

---

[46] Remarking on this same turn of events, Paris Flammonde adds: "The possibility that the original tip for the FBI may have come from Lee Harvey Oswald is not discarded by the district attorney. See Flammonde, *The Kennedy Conspiracy* (New York: Meredith Press, 1969), pp. 273-74. Marks would have known of this through his careful reading of Flammonde's work.

Mr. Garrison has in his possession an affidavit signed by W. S. Walter, an FBI security clerk in the New Orleans office during the year 1963. Mr. Walter swore that on November 17, 1963 he had in his hands a TWX message from Mr. Hoover's Washington office stating that "an attempt to assassinate President Kennedy would be made in Dallas on November 22, 1963." Mr. Walter immediately contacted the New Orleans Agent in Charge, Mr. Maynard, who ordered Mr. Walter to contact local FBI agents, whom he was to instruct to contact their various Cuban informers.

What is more damaging is Mr. Walter's information that the FBI New Orleans Bureau was instructed by this same TWX message to destroy all the old files containing information regarding a conspiracy to murder President Kennedy and to prepare "new" files—in other words, to forge reports. Since Oswald was in New Orleans in September 1963, and since he did have contact with the New Orleans FBI Bureau as published in the "Hearings," and since Oswald did know both Ferrie and Shaw, then it can be logically assumed that Oswald was probably the "tipster" who informed the FBI that a conspiracy was underway to murder the president in Dallas on November 22.[47]

In my previous book, "MURDER MOST FOUL!," published three months (Sept. 1967) prior to Mr. Garrison's various public announcements concerning the involvement of the CIA and FBI involvement in the murder, I also pointed out the various pieces of evidence that revealed that involvement.

Many persons are now perplexed as to why Mr. Garrison, as

---

[47] Author James Douglass has concluded that Oswald was an "admirer of President Kennedy" as well as "an FBI informant trying to stop the CIA plot to kill the president. In late July [1963], in the notes he wrote for his speech to the Jesuits, Oswald warned of a coup d'état against the U. S. government.... In August, according to New Orleans FBI employee William Walter and other witnesses, Oswald was acting as an FBI informant.... it is reasonable to suppose Oswald at this point in his FBI contacts was trying to save Kennedy's life—and in the process, risking his own." See James Douglass, *JFK and the Unspeakable* (New York: Simon and Schuster, 2008), p. 362.

the district attorney in the Shaw trial, failed to reveal the matters discussed above. He could not, for the Department of Justice prevented all FBI agents, including Mr. Hoover, from testifying under the rule of "executive privilege." That is, under our Constitution, the president of the United States may prevent any employee, officer, or executive in the executive branch of the government from testifying in any trial—state or federal. The use of that "privilege" by President Johnson clearly supported the charges uttered by Mr. Garrison. By invoking that "privilege," the president was also preventing any criminal trial in a federal court of any FBI agent for criminal negligence in permitting the president to be assassinated. As previously stated in this book, where a police agency has prior knowledge of a crime and that agency does nothing to prevent the execution of that crime, then the agents of that police bureau who had that prior knowledge are guilty of being "accessories before the fact," which, in turn, is a felony.

Since Mr. Garrison was a district attorney of a STATE, he had no power to indict any federal employee; for the murder took place in Texas, an area outside of Mr. Garrison's jurisdiction. When he attempted to examine or summon federal employees within his jurisdiction, his efforts were thwarted by the Department of Justice and President Johnson, who could have compelled his own Attorney General, Mr. Ramsey Clark, not to claim "executive privilege" for members of the FBI and CIA agencies.

The above are the reasons why Mr. Garrison failed to present the necessary evidence in the Clay Shaw trial. In November 1969, in spite of the two New Orleans newspapers and the other powers in that city, the people of New Orleans voted to have Mr. Garrison run on the Democratic ticket for another term of office. Later in the year, Mr. Garrison was reelected [when] his conduct in the Shaw trial was the main campaign issue.

Thus, the "guts" of the conspiracy involved elements of the CIA, the FBI, and the Mafia! The Dallas police were deeply involved in both the murder of the president and their own fellow officer, Tippit. The role of the Secret Service, especially the Protective Research Section, is a little murky, for no Secret Service executive disputed the testimony of Chief Curry that an agent of that bureau did not desire to have the president's cavalcade go through that ambush area; yet someone overruled the Secret Service, who had the final authority regarding the route. The "beer bust" party held on the night prior to the assassination, and the mysterious imprisonment of the Negro Secret Service Agent, A. Bolden, by the federal government on perjured testimony is an indication of the involvement of some Secret Service agents. In the files of the National Archives are two interesting documents, No. 197 and 404. The author of those two documents is a former CIA agent being held without trial in various federal penitentiaries.

Thus, a plot within a plot was functioning, and each plot was independent of the other, with none of the plotters in the separate plots knowing about the other.[48]

The plotters that desired the death of President Kennedy had obtained notice that when he visited Dallas, Texas an attempt would be made upon the life of Governor Connally. This statement is supported by testimony in the "Hearings" and was suppressed by the Warren Commission.

Two conspiracies existed on November 22, 1963—one by the Texas industrialists, through their contacts with the groups outlined in the Miami, Florida police tapes,[49] to murder

---

[48] In the early days of JFK assassination research the notion of an overlapping of two separate and distinct plots was hypothesized by a number of researchers, although with the passage of time this possibility seems far less likely. Even Marks himself seems to have eventually abandoned this idea, for the 1992 publication of his last assassination-related title (*Yes, Americans, A Conspiracy Murdered JFK!*) contains no reference to this subject. Although the notion of overlapping conspiracies is probably erroneous, there may have been overlapping or conflicting agendas at work within the intelligence community and overall power elite, and in this broader sense Marks may have been onto something. That is, we may be examining the fragmentary evidence of multilayered operations, one buried within another.

[49] A reference to the taped surveillance of right-wing extremist Joseph Milteer by Miami police informant William Somersett, who successfully infiltrated the States' Rights Party. More about the Milteer—Somersett conversation to follow.

President Kennedy; the other initiated by the Mafia. The Mafia's victim was not President Kennedy but the governor of the state of Texas, who had refused to "open" the state to the "Cosa Nostra" of the United States. With Texas being one of the wealthiest States in government contracts, Army and Air Force bases, and with the space program developing rapidly, the Mafia wanted some of that wealth. However, with the governor standing fast against them, the Mafia could do nothing—until the White House, in September 1963, announced that the president would visit Dallas, Texas in November, accompanied by the governor.

Now, into the Mafia conspiracy to murder Governor Connally strode a minor underling of that organization—Jack Ruby—and it was he who was instructed to obtain the would-be assassin of the governor.[50] Ruby, as seen from the testimony and affidavits

---

[50] In her largely bogus and coerced testimony to the Warren Commission, Marina Oswald claimed that her husband's actual target was Connally and not Kennedy. But she also said that Lee was plotting to kill Richard Nixon—a statement so absurd that it was never taken seriously by investigators. She repeated the story about Connally in her testimony to the U.S. House Select Committee on Assassinations in 1978. Shortly after the assassination, Secret Service Agent James F. "Mike" Howard was assigned to keep Marina in so-called protective custody. (The other two agents assigned to this task were Leon L. Gopadze and Charles E. Kunkel.) Howard, who was known to spread disinformation (he once planted a story that features a janitor watching Oswald shoot Kennedy) was perhaps the earliest official source of the "Oswald targeted Connally" fabrication. In his book *Survivor's Guilt*, Vincent Palamara says that Howard and the other agents, "serving as both her interpreters and her captors ... threatened Marina with deportation in subtle (and not-so-subtle) ways if she didn't tow the 'official' line that her husband ... was the lone-nut assassin of JFK." In a May 12, 1964 FBI memo contained in Warren Commission Document 1066, p. 533, Oswald's mother, Marguerite, testified that she was "deathly afraid" of Agent Kunkel and was "afraid that he will harm her," adding that she refused to have any further contact with him. An FBI memo from May 19 adds: "Mrs. [Marguerite] Oswald said that she is actually 'afraid' of Howard and Kunkel and does not want anything to do with either person" (CD 1066, p. 539). Palamara adds that "... just moments before he died ...

in the 'Hearings" and the National Archives, was a completely amoral person, a gunrunner to Cuban sabotage groups, a pimp, a whorehouse owner, swindler, dope peddler. He was "in" with both the Dallas police and with various functionaries in the office of District Attorney Wade—the man who was so affected by the murder of President Kennedy that he dined and danced on that night. Ruby, as the evidence revealed in the "Hearings, was very well known to the vast majority of Dallas cops. And regardless of the "Report" he was a close friend of officer Tippit—the Tippit that was murdered. The person who substantiated that statement, under oath, was Mrs. Eva Grant, the sister of Jack Ruby. And where was Tippit murdered? Three blocks away from Ruby's apartment!

Jack Ruby was also very well known among the wealthiest Texas oil family—the H. L. Hunts. "Popsie" Hunt believes that he discovered God, and for that discovery God repaid him by revealing to him oil in Texas. Of course, the fact that "Popsie" sponsored some of the most despicable anti-Mexican, anti-Semite, anti-Negro, and anti-Catholic filth with the money he does not pay in taxes—the same money used by his family to supply the infamous "The President is a Traitor" advertisement in the Dallas press, and the same money used to supply funds for the White Citizens' Council, the KKK, the John Birch Society, and even branches of the American Nazi Party—failed to give the Commission any hint that any of those organizations were involved.

The testimony in the "Hearings" revealed the fact that Jack Ruby was so well acquainted with some members of the H. L. Hunt organization that he drove a woman seeking employment to the executive offices. Whom did he know that well among the Hunt family to personally seek employment for a person he knew not too well?[51] There is also evidence that Ruby was the

---

former President Johnson asked that Agent Mike Howard come to his room 'immediately.'" (Sourced from Irwin Unger's book, *LBJ: A Life*.)

[51] "On November 21, Ruby drove Connie Trammel, a young college graduate whom he had met some months previously, to the office of Lamar Hunt, the son of H.L. Hunt, for a job interview. Although

"bookie" for some members of the Hunt family.

Immediately after the murder of President Kennedy, agents for the FBI Dallas Office spirited an "unknown" oilman out of Dallas by driving him, in an FBI automobile, to American Airlines. Why should the FBI conduct itself in that manner unless the Dallas FBI Bureau had reason to believe, or know, that the best place for that man was at an unknown hideout—for seven days? Why this protection?[52] Did not Jack Ruby give the hint in his confession that was smuggled out of prison several days prior to his removal from the eyes of the Dallas police and the district attorney's office to the hospital—where he died of induced cancer?

The concern the FBI showed for that Texas multimillionaire was not extended to the President of the United States—John F. Kennedy. Instead, that bureau, after receiving twelve days' prior notice (November 10, 1963) of an assassination attempt in

---

Ruby stated that he would like to meet Hunt, seemingly to establish a business connection, he did not enter Hunt's office with her." Warren Commission Report, chapter six, p. 368. Seth Kantor reports that "[Harry] Hall and Ruby won a large amount of money from oil magnate H. L. Hunt on the Cotton Bowl and Rose Bowl football games, after Ruby arranged a meeting between the two." And "Ruby was reported to be in or near the Hunt offices the day before the Kennedy assassination, and had two of Hunt's politically conservative "Life Line" radio scripts in his car the day he shot Oswald…" See Seth Kantor, *The Ruby Cover-up* (New York: Kensington Publishing Group, 1978), p. 219.

[52] According to *Farewell America*, a book purportedly written by French intelligence agents and first published in 1968, at the moment of the assassination ex-General Edwin A. Walker "was in a plane between New Orleans and Shreveport. He joined Mr. Hunt in one of his secret hideaways across the Mexican border. There they remained for a month, protected by personal guards, under the impassive eyes of the FBI." Since *Farewell America* lacks documentation and originates from a dubious source, the story about Hunt and Walker must be taken with a grain of salt. See James Hepburn, *Farewell America* (Roseville, CA: Penmarin, 2002), p. 244. However, it has been confirmed that Walker was in Louisiana on the weekend of the assassination. There are also rumors that Hunt was escorted to Washington D.C. and not to Mexico.

Dallas, waited five days after the murder to interview the tipster who had correctly informed the Miami, Florida, Police Department that an attempt was to be made upon the president's life when he visited Miami, Florida on November 18, 1963; or, if that attempt aborted, in "the next Southern city" he visited!

The story of the Miami, Florida police tapes was revealed on February 2, 1967 by Bill Barry, reporter for the Miami "News." The full story is based entirely upon a tape recording taken by the Miami, Florida, Police Department on November 9, 1963 between an informer and an unidentified person who was an active member of a racist States' Rights Party—which has received thousands of dollars from various Texas industrialists who disapproved of President Kennedy's moves to reform the oil depletion income tax laws, civil rights, and easing of tensions vis-a-vis the United States and the Red Bloc.

That the story and investigation by Bill Barry was true can be substantiated by the fact that both the FBI and Secret Service "Protective Research Section" had received the tape recordings, [as] substantiated by the Miami, Florida Police Department's files, which revealed that department forwarded a duplicate of the tape the following day to the Bureau. Thus, by not later than November 10, twelve days prior to the assassination, the agency responsible for the protection of the president had complete knowledge of where and when the attempt would be made and from what type of ambush site. The same police department also forwarded a complete copy of the tape to the FBI on the same day—November 10, 1963.

When the Barry story was published in 1967, both federal agencies stated, to questions as to whether or not they had received those tapes, "no comment." The agencies did not at any time, and up to this day, say they had not received the tapes. But it should be noted that the Miami, Florida police took the information so seriously that they refused to permit President Kennedy to drive from the Dade Airport to downtown Miami, and instead they helicoptered him from the airport to downtown Miami.

The FBI, when questioned by the Warren Commission concerning presidential protection and safety, kept its mouth shut in spite of the fact that five days after the murder they had detained and questioned the unidentified man who gave the information to the informer. Nor did the Secret Service head of the Protective Research Section open his mouth to inform the Commission that they too had 12 days' prior information that an attempt would be made in Dallas upon the life of the president. The name of that informer is secret, but whether he is alive today is doubtful, since many FBI agents sincerely believe in the causes espoused by Birchers, Wallacites, White Citizens' Council, and other "100% Americans." (See "Wall Street Journal," Sept. 1968.)

The reader is advised to remember that the president "would be shot with a high-powered rifle from an office building; and he said that the gun would be disassembled, taken into the building, assembled, and then used for murder. They will pick up somebody within hours afterward just to throw the public off ..."

The above is exactly what occurred in Dallas, Texas.

The prime responsibility for the murder of President Kennedy must be laid directly upon the doorstep of the U.S. Secret Service and the Federal Bureau of Investigation. Both agencies had full knowledge that an attempt would be made, and they did absolutely nothing. As will be seen, testimony revealed that the Secret Service not only had direct knowledge but protested the use of the Dallas downtown area as a parade route. However, in spite of their protest, someone very powerful in the U.S. government who knew of the conspiracy to murder the president overruled the agency and permitted the assassination to proceed.

The FBI has the blood of the president upon its hands, for not only did it refuse to act, but, after the murder, became an accessory after the fact when it deliberately concealed from the Warren Commission that it not only had prior knowledge but also had interviewed the "unidentified" man—but have thus far refused to permit the release of their interrogation of that man. For what reason? The man gave the Bureau the names of the men involved, not only in the assassination but also those who planned and executed the bombings of various churches and synagogues and killings of civil rights workers. Those men who were named involve the political and economic structure of this nation. Of course, Mr. Hoover's "carte blanche" approval of members of the John Birch Society permits those members, as "100% Americans," to remove, by any means, a person they deem "un-American." The refusal to identify and discuss the facts on the Miami, Florida tapes was to lead to the direct path linking the murder of President Kennedy, Martin Luther King, and Senator Robert F. Kennedy. As will be revealed later, one of the assassins of President Kennedy was arrested by the Dallas police, taken to the police station, and released. This same man, who was arrested with a discharged rifle in his hands on the "grassy knoll," was also to murder Martin Luther King in Memphis, Tennessee in 1968. The FBI knew of him in 1963, 1964, and 1967, and he was not James Earl Ray, the "patsy" now serving a life sentence for that murder.[53]

---

[53] A transcript of the Milteer conversations has since been published, and some of the tapes can now be listened to online. The names mentioned on the transcript are as follows: Kenneth Adams, a Mr. Brown, Jack Caulk (phonetic spelling), Lee McCloud, and Connor McGintis (phonetic spelling) of Union, New Jersey Milteer adds: "He is the one that puts out that *Common Sense*." "Connor McGintis" was actually Michael Conde McGinley, who died in his home at the age of seventy-two on July 2, 1963. McGinley's online Wikipedia entry describes *Common Sense* as an "anti-Communist" and "anti-Semitic broadsheet," but oddly enough it makes no mention of McGinley's name being mentioned on the Milteer tapes. Milteer was recorded by FBI informant William Somersett on November 9, 1963: just 13 days before the assassination. Several of his remarks closely parallel what actually occurred in Dallas. When asked, "Well, how in the hell do you figure would be the best way to get him?" Milteer replies: "From an office building with a high-powered rifle." He also confirms that the plan was already set in motion: "SOMERSETT: They are really going to try to kill him? MILTEER: Oh, yeah, it is in the working." And he describes how a weapon could be slipped into a building: "... disassemble a gun, you don't have to take a gun up there, you can take it up in pieces, all those guns come knock down, you can take them apart." Then comes the most chilling remark: "They will pick up somebody within hours afterwards ... just to throw the public off." In a subsequent meeting between Somersett and Milteer that occurred on November 23, Milteer said: "Well, I told you so. It happened like

The original plan by Jack Ruby was to murder Governor Connally for the reasons outlined on the previous pages. In the National Archives is a document suppressed by the Commission with a code number, 2821. The conduct of the Warren Commission investigating the material in that document, and the manner in which it condoned the spurious investigation conducted by District Attorney Wade, can only lead to the conclusion that the Commission willfully suppressed that document because of its truthfulness and accuracy. In an attempt to discredit the accuracy of the document the district attorney was to commit perjury; but he was be one of several, and the Warren Commission could not indict all those Dallas officials as perjurers.

Commission Exhibit No. 2821 also contains another document with the official FBI Code: DL 44-1639, dated December 5, 1963. The document is signed by Carroll Jarnagin, an attorney in practice in Dallas, Texas for many years and a member of the same legal fraternity as District Attorney Wade.

On December 5, 1963, Attorney Jarnagin mailed an 8-page letter describing a conversation he had overheard on October 4,

---

I told you, didn't it? It happened from a widow with a high-powered rifle." According to author Michael Newton, "Brown" was Jack William Brown, co-founder of the Dixie Klans, who died of a heart attack in October 1965. Lee McCloud was a racist from Atlanta; and "Jack Caulk" "remains unidentified." See Michael Newton, *The National States Rights Party: A History* (Jefferson, NC: McFarland & Company, 2017), p. 107. See also the book authored by the FBI agent in charge of interviewing Milteer: Don Adams' *From an Office Building with a High-Powered Rifle* (Walterville, OR: Trine Day, 2012). Milteer was not the only one to go on record with an advance knowledge—in one form or another—of the JFK assassination plots. Other members of this group include figures such as Sergio Carbo, Rose Cheramie, U.S. Air Force Sergeant David Christensen, Eugene Barry Dinkin, Adele Edisen, John Martino, Silvia Odio, and Richard Case Nagell. Researcher Paul Bleau has investigated and documented evidence of plots arranged in at least three other U.S. cities: Chicago, Los Angeles, and Tampa. See Paul Bleau, "The Three Failed Plots to Kill JFK: The Historians' Guide on How to Research His Assassination," November 18, 2016, Kennedys and King website.

1963 in the Dallas Carousel Club between Jack Ruby and a man "using the name of [H.] L. Lee." During that conversation between those two men, the attorney heard them discussing plans to kill the Governor of Texas, [John] Connally.[54] In the same letter is a request by Jarnagin that FBI Director Hoover forward copies to the district attorney of Dallas County and to the attorney general of Texas. Mr. Hoover complied.

On the same day he received this letter Mr. Hoover forwarded it to the Warren Commission in Washington, D.C., which had commenced its investigation. How did the Commission react to Mr. Hoover's covering letter containing the Jarnagin sworn statements? The Commission did nothing. The Commission desired no testimony that could prove that not only did a conspiracy commit the President Kennedy murder but that another conspiracy attempted to murder Governor Connally. Mr. Jarnagin's testimony would have proved so devastating that the Commission not only refused to summon him for examination but also refused to place his name on the official list of witnesses, of which there are 552 names.

The facts in the Jarnagin 8-page letter to Mr. Hoover have never been denied; and as the story unfolds on these pages the

---

[54] CE 2821: "FBI report of investigation of claim that Jack Ruby and Lee Harvey Oswald were seen together at Carousel Club," which includes a "copy of a letter and an eight-page statement received at the Bureau on December 5, 1963, from MR. CARROLL JARNAGIN ..." The letter states: "I heard Jack Ruby talking to a man using the name of H. L. Lee. These men were taking about plans to kill the governor of Texas." Unfortunately, Jarnagin's testimony is highly problematic. Besides admitting that he was drunk on the night in question, Jarnagin also failed a lie-detector test. And his companion that evening, Shirley Mauldin, told the FBI there had been no such conversation at the club. (Mauldin was a professional stripper, aka "Robin S. Hood," who had worked for Ruby.) See Seth Kantor, *The Ruby Cover-up*, pp. 391-92. The results of Jarnagin's polygraph test are actually quite amusing. Of the eleven "pertinent questions" asked, he responded truthfully to only two: "Were you drinking that night?" (Yes.) "Were you drunk that night?" (Yes.) For a photo of this document, see texashistory.unt.edu, "Polygraph Transcript of Carroll Jarnagin #1," dated March 2, 1964.

outline of two conspiracies emerges, or a conspiracy within a conspiracy. For several years, the best-kept story has been the number of "Oswalds" seen in Dallas several months prior to the assassination.[55] By using words, the Warren Commission successfully concealed the number of "Oswalds" in its "Report," but when the testimony in the "Hearings" and in the documents in the National Archives are examined, the proof of more than one "Oswald" clearly emerged.

The key to Mr. Jarnagin's statement in the body of that letter is the one stating that the "picture of Lee Harvey Oswald published in the 'Times-Herald' of November 23, 1963 was a picture of a man using the name of H. L. Lee" when he saw Ruby and "Lee" discussing plans to murder Governor Connally.

The conversation of October 4, 1963 in the Carousel Club related only to facts concerning the murder of the governor, not the president of the United States. Jack Ruby[56] had no intention or desire to harm or injure President Kennedy in any manner.

---

[55] Marks was familiar with Richard Popkin's 1966 study, *The Second Oswald* (New York: Avon, 1966), and cites it in his first JFK assassination title, *Murder Most Foul!* as well as in his subsequent title, *Two Days of Infamy*.

[56] In her May 28, 1964 Warren Commission testimony Jack Ruby's sister, Eva Grant, did all she could to promote the legend that Ruby was a JFK lover and would never have wished for harm to come to the president. Her ludicrous testimony also neatly dovetails with Ruby's claim that he killed Lee Oswald so that Jacqueline Kennedy could be spared the stress of testifying at Oswald's trial. Grant told the Commissioners: "… my brother had such a great admiration for this man, it's unbelievable." Indeed. "… he had a little picture and on one side is the late President's picture in color. It is the most beautiful picture of him that I have seen.… He had kissed the President's picture in front of me—right in front of me like a baby …" When asked, "He was very respectful of President Kennedy as a man and as a President?" she replied: "Oh, he admired him—he thought this man was a great man of courage. If I said anything, like I said there something about his brother and integration, he said, 'This man is greater than Lincoln'.…" Even in the most remote realm of fantasy, it remains difficult to imagine Jack Ruby kissing a photo of President Kennedy.

He was only interested in eliminating Governor Connally. During the conversation between Ruby and the man, the latter expressly stated that he was using the name of H. L. Lee and repeated to Ruby that "H. L. Lee" had been arrested in a New Orleans street fight. This man also informed Ruby that Lee's family resided in Irving, Texas and that "Lee" had returned to Dallas from Mexico City. This latter statement was to trip up one conspirator; for the Commission, through Mrs. Paine, the FBI informant on Oswald's affairs, proved that Oswald had returned from Mexico City, not New Orleans.

Thus, for the first time, a man who is "lookalike" for Oswald appears in the National Archives, and [that] is where the Commission hoped it would remain.

Backtracking further from Jarnagin's FBI letter is the fact that everyone who desired the information knew that President Kennedy was to visit Dallas on either November 21 or 22, since that information was announced in the September 13, 1963 issue of the Dallas "Times-Herald." As early as June 5, 1963 an agreement had been reached by President Kennedy, Governor Connally, Vice President Johnson, and Presidential Secretary Ken O'Donnell that the president would visit Dallas on November 22, 1963 and travel with Governor Connally in the same automobile during the Dallas visit. At no time was the route used on November 22 ever discussed by either the president or the governor, nor were they ever informed by the FBI or Secret Service prior to that day that the president was to be subjected to rifle fire.

When a person attempts to put together pieces of a jigsaw puzzle, those pieces are not picked up in sequence. A conspiracy is a jigsaw puzzle which is practically unsolvable when the pieces of that jigsaw are not only withheld from the investigator but are also never shown. The Warren Commission deliberately withheld the Jarnagin statement in spite of the fact that Mr. Hoover thought it of such great importance that he delivered copies of it to the Commission on the same day he received it.

District Attorney Wade, however, did admit to the Commission that "some 8 or 10 witnesses have said that they had seen Ruby and 'Oswald' together." In another question put to him he was asked if Ruby was ever involved with anyone else in the killing of Oswald and he said "no." In an attempt to deprecate the Jarnagin statements, the Commission said that Wade had given a private polygraph test to his fraternity brother, Mr. Jarnagin, although he also admitted that he knew nothing about the operation of that machine to bring forth the truth. Wade's testimony brought forth contradiction upon contradiction of his "investigation" of the facts in the Jarnagin letter.

District Attorney Wade's conduct as an attorney and prosecutor was so poor that, in an unanimous opinion, the Warren Commission said that Wade "lacked a thorough grasp of evidence and made a number of errors." In other words, this man was unfit to act as prosecutor to send human beings to the electric chair or prison.

However, that opinion did not deter the same Commission from accepting Wade's self-serving statement that Jarnagin was "imagining things" when he wrote his 8-page letter to FBI Director Hoover. The Commission was compelled to accept Wade in spite its collective knowledge that Wade was a poor specimen of an attorney and a district attorney, because without Wade they had no weapon with which to discredit Jarnagin, who established the identity of one "Oswald" double.

Again, the commissioner who revealed Wade's lack of candor, if not outright deceit, was Allen Dulles, former head of the CIA. He asked Wade if the district attorney had received any evidence to corroborate the facts outlined in the Jarnagin statement. Wade replied that he had seen an FBI report relating to Jarnagin's woman companion when he [Jarnagin] overheard the Ruby—"Oswald" plot, and that FBI report said the woman corroborated some of Jarnagin's facts. This admission by Wade, however, did not compel Mr. Dulles or any other commissioner to examine the woman witness, for there is no mention of her name in the official witness list or in the National Archives. Whether she is alive or dead is not known. The main fact given by Wade was that she did substantiate some of Mr. Jarnagin's facts.

Thus, the Commission had full knowledge that Ruby had employed a killer whose objective was to murder Governor

Connally. Was this killer a former Army marksman who was using the background of Lee Harvey Oswald as a smokescreen? The Commission admitted that Oswald was not in the Carousel on the night of October 4, 1963, but there was a man who was so similar in physical and facial features that witnesses who saw Ruby's companion thought he was "Lee Harvey Oswald." In other words, he was a "double."

Can one of the murderers be named? Can he be found by reading the testimony in the "Hearings" or in the Archives' files? Is he one of the murderers of President Kennedy? District Attorney Wade had admitted to the Commission, under oath, that he knew 8 or 10 witnesses who said they had seen Ruby and "Oswald" together. The question now remained as to the identity of that "double" Oswald.

To unravel the answer to the identity, one must be reminded that at no time did Mr. Jarnagin state that the man with Jack Ruby was, in fact and in law, Lee Harvey Oswald. He saw a man who had brown hair, was about 5'9" tall, age about 25, who was "a picture of the man using the name H. L. Lee." The attorney saw a picture of the real Oswald in the newspaper and associated that photograph with the man he saw on October 4, 1963 in Ruby's Carousel Club. He never stated that the man he saw in the flesh was the identical man he saw in the newspaper photograph.

Thus, Attorney Jarnagin, with a woman companion, saw a man who resembled Lee Harvey Oswald at a time when Oswald was not in Dallas, Texas. But other witnesses were also to see that same man, and those witnesses saw this "Oswald" when they were not in the company of each other. Nor was the Commission able to discredit their eyesight. An analysis of those witnesses' testimony revealed that none of them testified that the man they saw was Oswald; they stated that the man they saw resembled Oswald.

One of the witnesses was Bill DeMar, the master of ceremonies in the Ruby-owned nightclub. He had seen a man resembling Oswald "a night or so before the assassination." What happened to this witness? He became so harassed by the

Dallas police that he fled the city; and his union, the AGVA,[57] refused to divulge his new address to anyone, because, in view of the many injuries and deaths of witnesses unfavorable to the Commission's theory, he thought he would become one of them.

The Commission also had a photograph of this second "Oswald," for Ruby's nightclub photographer had taken a picture of that man. The Warren Commission has refused to publish that photograph for fear the public would have instantly seen the remarkable resemblance between the photographed man and Oswald. The picture, including the negative, was confiscated and cannot be located in the National Archives.

In the files of the National Archives are affidavits which supported the "double Oswald" testimony. A Mr. Litchfield saw a man "resembling" Oswald in late October or early November 1963. Billy Joe Willis and Karen Carlin also testified under oath that they saw "Oswald" in the Ruby nightclub. More shocking is a statement in chapter IV of the "Hearings" by a waitress in the B&B Cafe that at 2:30 on the morning of the murder she saw Jack Ruby having food with a man who "resembled" Lee Harvey Oswald. Was Ruby going over his final instructions to this "double" and informing the double of

---

[57] The American Guild of Variety Artists (AGVA), an AFL-CIO affiliated labor union. "Bill DeMar" was the stage name of William D. Crowe, Jr., a ventriloquist and mentalist (or "mind reader") who worked at the club. During his June 2, 1964 Warren Commission testimony DeMar refused to make a definite, positive identification of Oswald; instead, he stated "it seemed to me that his face was familiar, and I had possibly seen him in the club the week before." In an interview with the FBI on November 24, 1963, Wally Weston, a master of ceremonies who also worked at the Carousel Club, said that DeMar had invented the story about Ruby and Oswald in an attempt to garner publicity. But thirteen years later, in an interview Weston gave to the *New York Daily News*, he claimed that Oswald had been in the club "at least twice" before Kennedy's murder; he also said that he'd been heckled by Oswald during an appearance on stage. As Seth Kantor points out, Weston had neglected to share any of these obviously concocted fables with the FBI during his 1963 interview. See Kantor, *The Ruby Cover-up*, p. 390-91.

the "double detour" route known only by the Dallas police and their conspirators engaged in the conspiracy to murder President Kennedy? Yet, at 2:30 a.m. of that morning, Oswald was sleeping in the same bed with his wife in Irving, Texas. The waitress' statement to the FBI has been removed from the files of the National Archives.

On November 1, 1963 Jack Ruby was seen by an electronics equipment salesman, R. K. Patterson,[58] to be in the company of a man who "resembled" Oswald, when Ruby purchased equipment in the radio store. Two other men in the store at that time also testified the man with Ruby "resembled" Oswald.

The Commission, in an attempt to discredit all of those witnesses, published a statement that the man with Ruby was not Lee Harvey Oswald. It was a shrewd maneuver; for, by a sleight-of-hand use of the language, the Commission perverted the testimony, for not a single witness ever testified that the person they saw with Jack Ruby was Oswald—they testified that the man "resembled" Oswald to such an extent that, when they saw pictures of Oswald, they thought that Oswald was the identical man they had seen with Ruby.

The Commission also had testimony from the FBI informant, Mrs. Paine, that the man who "resembled" Oswald was a man in the employ of Jack Ruby—Larry Crafard. Was this man hired by Jack Ruby to murder Governor Connally? Did a bullet come from a rifle, miss the governor, and strike the president in the head, leading to the death of John F. Kennedy? Mrs. Paine, who knew Oswald very well, was more emphatic and testified that Crafard "strongly" resembled Lee Harvey Oswald! He was a double for Oswald.

Who was, or is, Larry Crafard? According to the FBI report of November 29, 1963, Curtis LaVerne Crafard, also known as Larry Crafard, "C. L.," and "Smoky," was 22 years old, 5' 8" in height, brown hair, brown eyes, 150 pounds in weight. He served in the U.S. Army and was honorably discharged, but then the Bureau added this cryptic statement: "honorable discharge but not subject to reenlistment." The FBI description

---

[58] Robert K. Patterson, a Dallas electronics salesman, cited in the Warren Report, chapter six, pp. 255-56.

of Larry Crafard, with no photograph, is an exact duplicate of the physical features belonging to Lee Harvey Oswald.

What is important in this FBI report is the fact that the agents conducting the inquiry of Crafard made not a single reference to his "strong resemblance" to Lee Harvey Oswald. Every person who knew Crafard had remarked on the extraordinary resemblance between the two, but the experienced FBI agents made no comment. Why? Nor did the FBI take any photographs of Crafard after they had tracked him down in his hometown in Michigan. Why? After the receipt of the Jarnagin statement, the FBI never thought of returning to Crafard and snapping a few facial photographs of this former employee of Jack Ruby. Why? They knew from their FBI informant, Mrs. Paine, that Crafard had a strong resemblance to Oswald, but no pictures were taken. Why? Because Oswald was dead, and the powers-that-be in Washington had no desire to reveal the existence of a conspiracy.

Larry Crafard in his various statements to the FBI committed perjury. He stated that he became a handyman in Ruby's nightclub on or about October 21, 1963 but did not commence work until October 31. The "Report" clearly stated that he commenced work in the club in mid-October, not on October 31. But Mr. Jarnagin's statement revealed that Ruby and Crafard had met prior to October 4, when the plot to murder the governor was discussed.

The Warren Commission admitted that the person in the company of Jack Ruby at 2:30 a.m. on the morning of the murder was Larry Crafard, the man who resembled Oswald "strongly." The Commission was to say that this "double" had no relationship to the murder. However, in the Commission's files was an FBI report given to the Bureau by Larry Crafard which was political dynamite. In the August 1964 statement, Crafard informed the FBI that, while he was in the presence of Jack Ruby, the news came over the radio relating to the deaths of President Kennedy and officer Tippit, [and that] Ruby informed him that he "knew him (Tippit) quite well!" The FBI agents then added a comment to their report that Crafard was definite that Ruby referred to the murdered officer.

To further their concealment of a conspiracy, the Commission calmly accepted Crafard's unsupported statement that, at the time of the assassination, 12:30 p.m., he was asleep in the Carousel Club. Crafard swore that he was informed of the murder "shortly after noon"—not in the afternoon, but shortly after 12:00 noon, by another now missing ex-convict employee of Jack Ruby, Andy Armstrong. The announcement over television and radio of the president's death was made at 1:30 p.m., not shortly "after noon." It should be [noted] that Crafard mentioned nothing about the shooting but of the murder. The first announcements by both media were the shooting of the president and the governor—and no mention of the death was made until 1:30 p.m. How did Armstrong notify Crafard of the murder "after noon" time when the public was not informed until 1:30 p.m.?

The Warren Commission accepted Crafard's statement that he had made preparation to leave Dallas prior to November 22, and the FBI produced a letter he had allegedly left behind in his bedroom at the Carousel Club to prove his statement. The only thing wrong with that letter was that it was undated and unmailed. Furthermore, no employee of the club, including Ruby, could recall that Crafard had ever informed them that he was leaving to go home to Michigan.

The testimony did reveal that, on the spur of the moment, Larry Crafard fled Dallas in fear of his life! He not only fled from Ruby's Mafia members, but, in his haste, he left all his clothes at the Carousel Club and, with only $7.00 in his pocket, commenced hitchhiking to his Michigan home more than 1,000 miles away from Dallas. He hitchhiked because it gave him a greater opportunity not to be discovered, for he did not arrive until November 28. Even though the FBI sought him, that Bureau never issued a "wanted" bulletin for him, either in public or secretly, to the various police agencies along that route to Michigan. Nor did the Bureau publish or release any photograph of Crafard despite the fact that it had photographs of him in its possession. Why? Because the public would have quickly grasped the fact that Crafard and Oswald "strongly" resembled each other.

The Warren Commission had many opportunities to confront Crafard with witnesses who could have determined whether they saw Crafard or Oswald. For example, there was Dr. Wood and his son, Sterling, who saw a man "resembling" Oswald at a rifle range in November. Mr. Price, the rifle range owner,[59] saw "Oswald" receiving a wrapped up rifle from the hands of a stranger. The Commission did not see fit to summon automobile salesman Al Bogard and confront him with Crafard to see if Bogard would recognize Crafard as the man who had the salesman drive him around in an attempt to purchase an automobile. Mr. Bogard's testimony regarding "Oswald" was confirmed by two other salesmen in the automobile showroom on November 9. But as the Commission knew, Oswald not only could not drive an automobile but on that day the Commission proved Oswald was not in that area, just as Oswald was somewhere else when the other witnesses saw an "Oswald" at the rifle range.

Thus, the Commission had a minimum of 15 witnesses who, when seeing Oswald's picture on television or in the newspapers, believed that he was the one they had seen personally. Yet, on all those occasions, the evidence proved that Oswald was in another place.

---

[59] Virginia and Floyd Guy Davis owned and operated the Sports Drome Rifle Range. Malcolm Howard Price, who occasionally volunteered to help the Davises at the range, reported that they were "close friends of mine, and I have helped them get the things set up and get it started." Price said the man who resembled Oswald appeared at the range on three separate occasions and that he was equipped with what Price believed was a sporterized German Mauser. "I thought it was a Mauser, because there's a friend of mine in Grand Prairie that has an Argentine Mauser that was 7.6 and it looked very familiar—they looked a whole lot alike." He added: "The gun wasn't blued at the time—it had a bright finish on the barrel. It looked like it had been placed in a lathe and turned down, as far as—well, in an attempt to sporterize the gun." He also reported that "Oswald" had arrived at the range while driving a car, unaccompanied by anyone else, even though "Oswald" was reportedly unable to drive an automobile. "He was by himself, and I have heard that he couldn't drive, but he was driving that day because he was the only one in the car …" Price's testimony was taken on April 2, 1964 and is contained in Warren Commission Hearings, volume X, pp. 369-78.

To say that there was no Oswald "double," to deny Attorney Jarnagin's 8-page report to the FBI, is to deny the truth under the "basic principles of American justice." Oswald had several doubles, and one of those doubles was one of the murderers of President Kennedy. Was one of those "doubles" Larry Crafard? But was it Larry Crafard, and was he also a "patsy?" He was involved—but how? The fact remains that the Warren Commission refused to have any one of those 15 witnesses who saw an "Oswald double" confront Larry Crafard.

Jack Ruby talked, and as he talked he bragged. One of his brags was that he was "going to get Connally." He was heard, and one of the hearers in late September reported to someone in the Hunt organization who, in turn, passed the information to the powers-that-be—the powers that wanted President Kennedy dead: the KKK, the White Citizens' Council, members and executives of the John Birch Society, and the CIA Batista group. A great many wanted him dead, and that is how the plot within a plot was hatched—not in November, but in September, when the plans were formulated for the president's visit. The Miami plan was frustrated by that police department, which obtained the "tip"; and they helicoptered the president into Miami. But Dallas? That was a city of another color.

CHAPTER VIII

THE TWO CONSPIRACIES IN OPERATION

To conceal the conspiracy the Commission used every possible tactic to obstruct two vital questions: (1) What agency—city, state, or federal —approved the "double detour" route, which brought the president directly under the gunfire of four assassins? (2) What time was the president shot? These essential questions were never answered, and the reason is the undeniable fact that the answers would have exposed the conspiracy.

In an attempt to obtain the answer to the selection of the route that led the president's automobile into two turns that slowed the pace of the automobile below the speed requirements set forth by Secret Service regulations—not less than 25 miles per hour, to between 8 to 10 miles per hour on Elm Street—there is an admission by the Commission.

"Seek and ye shall find." The Commission admitted in its "Report" that the route "... eventually selected ... passed through a portion of the downtown area along MAIN STREET and then to the Trade Mart via STEMMONS FREEWAY."

The Commission published no evidence, nor is there any in the "Hearings" or in the files of the National Archives, that the president's motorcade was to turn onto Houston Street, travel the short half block to Elm Street, come to a complete stop to make the abrupt left turn onto Elm Street, and then proceed on that street for several hundred yards and then onto Stemmons Freeway.

Attempting to confuse the reader of its "Report," the Warren Commission published the only route that had appeared on the morning of November 22, 1963 in the Dallas "Morning News". However, this published map was so reduced in size in the "Report" that no clear definition of the route can be seen. When an investigator obtains the actual map as published (the map can be seen in the illustrated section), then one can see there is no detour but that the cavalcade proceeds directly down Main Street onto Stemmons Freeway.

Governor Connally and the various White House aides testified that at no time did they have any information regarding the route that was to be used by the presidential motorcade. The selection of that route was left entirely to the control of the Dallas Police Department, subject to approval by the Secret Service. Thus, the mystery of the selection of that "double detour" is placed upon the specific shoulders of the police department and the Secret Service.

The Commission has admitted that, on the day of the murder, Lee Harvey Oswald had no knowledge that the president's automobile would pass directly by and under the 6th-floor window. The Commission further admitted that the police statement that he had a map in his possession showing the route was a deliberate lie given to the press. Thus, the Commission was indirectly admitting that their concoction that Oswald visited his Irving, Texas home on November 21 to obtain his rifle for the purpose of murdering the president the following day was a fabrication obtained by the use of words. Or, the converse would have to be true: that some person in the Dallas Police Department or the Secret Service, or the FBI, or the CIA, informed Oswald that on the 22nd of November he should take his rifle and shoot the president because the president would pass under the 6th-floor window. If this be true, then a conspiracy existed! The Warren Commission cannot eat its cake and have it too.

What is now known to everyone is that on November 10, 1963 the federal agencies—FBI and Secret Service—had full knowledge from the Miami, Florida Police Department that an attempt would be made upon the life of the president of the United States in the next Southern city he visited. Both agencies knew the method and the type of weapon that was to be used. BOTH AGENCIES DID ABSOLUTELY NOTHING TO PROTECT THE PRESIDENT. The Secret Service admitted to the Commission that they made NO attempt to guard any of the buildings which applied to the information on those Miami, Florida police tapes. The FBI did nothing. Why? Why? Why?

The city of Dallas, or rather, the people who controlled that city, the "21" as called by "Fortune,"[60] had an overwhelming hatred of the president. The newspapers, radio, and television stations had for more than two years poured out a steady stream of vituperation and hatred against the president and other leaders in national life who believed as he did. One month prior to the president's visit, the police chief admitted that if they had not protected Ambassador Stevenson during his visit to Dallas he would have been lynched! Yet, the FBI and the Secret Service calmly permitted the president to go into Dallas with the full knowledge that, 12 days prior to its occurrence, an attempt would be made to murder him. Yet, they did nothing! Why? The Warren Commission knew that the "double detour" could only have been planned by either the Secret Service or the Dallas police. Granted that the FBI and the Secret Service did not give [the Commission] the information they had of an attempt upon the president's life, but that failure does not excuse the Commission from investigating the reason why the published map route was not complied with by the Dallas police and the Secret Service. The only reason why the Commission refused to investigate is the fact they knew that a conspiracy existed, and they knew the interests who were behind the conspiracy.

Dallas, on the day of the murder, as it is today, was completely controlled by a hierarchy that selects every public official, including the police power in the city and country. Dallas is a city that has retrogressed to the machinations of a feudal state. It neither believes in democracy nor practices it.

The day following the murder, the Chief of Police, Curry, gave a statement to the press that the Commission quickly overlooked. The chief said: "THEY had to bring him through town.... A Secret Service man told me they didn't want that either." Although this statement was published in every major newspaper, including the two papers in Washington, D.C., the Commission showed no desire to ask the chief to answer several questions: (1) Who were "THEY"? (2) What was the name of the Secret Service man who did not want the president driven

---

[60] A reference to *Fortune* magazine.

through Dallas? (3) Why did the Secret Service agent express such an intense dislike for the "double detour" route? (4) Since it was evident that the Secret Service man did not want the president to travel that route through downtown Dallas, who overruled the Secret Service? (5) In addition, why did the Secret Service violate every safety precaution as outlined in its regulations regarding the speed and safety of the president's car [when] the Secret Service had prior knowledge for 12 days that an attempt would be made upon the president's life by a rifleman shooting "from a tall building?"

Nor did the Secret Service give any reason why, under those circumstances, the car's steps located behind the automobile were not used by its agents. The Secret Service testified that President Kennedy refused to use the canopy that would have protected him from shots fired at his back. What that Bureau failed to say was that they did not inform the president that they had information that an attempt would be made to murder him during that motorcade through Dallas! Nor should the FBI be overlooked, for the director of that Bureau never informed his immediate superior, Attorney General Robert F. Kennedy, the president's brother, that the FBI had received information that his brother was in danger from a rifleman firing from a tall building. J. Edgar Hoover considers himself above and beyond the stupid mortals who put him in power. When a man believes he is God and at the same time holds absolute police power, beware!

The Commission casually mentions the fact that the driver of the lead automobile which guided the president's automobile was none other than Chief Curry! Chief Curry, the Judas Goat! Why did the chief violate the published route?

The only people in the city of Dallas that knew of the "double detour" were members of the conspiracy. But an "Oswald double" was instructed and hired only to murder the governor; therefore, there had to be other members; for where did an "Oswald double" know where to station himself unless he had prior knowledge that the president was to go past the Dal-Tex Building, the Book Depository, and the fence on the grassy knoll? Jack Ruby also knew the double detour, as did various members of the Dallas police, and as did the other three assassins who were directed to murder the president.

The Commission sought to absolve Chief Curry by stating that the road dividers near Stemmons Freeway and Elm Street prevent any automobile from crossing over from Main Street onto the Freeway. Balderdash! In the National Archives is a statement by the policeman who was always stationed at that point, and he testified that the alleged "cement divider" was less than one inch high. The Commission gave the impression that the cement divider would have stopped the president's automobile from crossing over. The Commission simply desired to protect the chief from any inquiry; for, prior to the president's motorcade, the Dallas police had used Main Street and the crossover onto Stemmons Freeway many times for other occasions.

Chief Curry was to expose another portion of the conspiracy in volume 4, page 150 of the "Hearings." The chief was being examined by J. Lee Rankin, General Counsel for the Commission.

RANKIN: "When did you hear of the arrest of Lee Harvey Oswald?"

CURRY: "When I was out at Parkland Hospital."

RANKIN: "Do you know about what time that was, the day?"

CURRY: "It was on the 22nd and the best I recall it was around 1 o'clock or a little after 1 o'clock."

RANKIN: "How did it [the knowledge of the arrest] come to your attention?"

CURRY: "Some of my officers came to me and said that they had a suspect in the shooting of our officer Tippit."

RANKIN: "What else did they say?"

CURRY: "They also told me a little later, I believe, that he was [a] suspect in the assassination of the president."

RANKIN: "What did you do then?"

CURRY: "I didn't do anything at the time. I was at the hospital, and I remained at the hospital until some of the Secret Service asked me to prepare two cars, that we were informed that President Kennedy had expired, and we were requested to furnish two cars for President Johnson and some of his staff to return to Love Field."

RANKIN: "Did you do that?"
CURRY: "Yes, I did."
RANKIN: "What else? What did you do after that?"
CURRY: "After the planes departed ... after the planes departed ... I remained there I guess for an hour."

Thus ended the portion of the chief's testimony which proved the existence of the conspiracy and the sworn testimony that Oswald was the "patsy" selected by the conspirators. When Oswald became frightened and realized that he was doomed to die, he wanted to talk to an attorney of his choice, but the police saw that he did not; for they instructed Ruby and two other members of the conspiracy to shut Oswald's mouth. They did!

Properly analyzed, the chief exposed the conspiracy and at the same time used the nails he desired to crucify Oswald by driving those nails into his own cross.

(1) Chief Curry was notified of the arrest of a suspect for the murder of officer Tippit between 1:00 p.m. or "a little after." It was not 1:15 p.m. or 1:30 p.m., for then common sense would have permitted the chief to mention that time. But a "little after" is subject to a common sense interpretation.

(2) The shooting of officer Tippit was not logged in the police records until Mr. Bowley notified them at 1:16 p.m.

(3) The first police flash that Tippit was shot and the description of his killer was not given over the police radio band until 1 p.m.

(4) Oswald was not captured until 1:50 p.m., but his arrest as a suspect was not broadcasted by the police at the Texas Theatre until he was on the way to the police station in a police squad car, and that time was 2:05p.m.!

(5) Curry, testifying under oath and in capacity as chief of police, swore that "some (unidentified) police officers" notified him between 1:05 and 1:15 p.m. that "an arrest had been made of the suspect in the Tippit murder." He lied! Tippit had not even been shot according to the police radio tapes.

(6) How did those "(unidentified) police officers" know (a) officer Tippit had been shot at the time "they" notified Curry; and (b) how did "they" know that a suspect had been arrested prior to 1:30 p.m., when Oswald had yet to arrive at and enter

the Texas Theatre?

(7) Why did Chief Curry refuse to name those police officers who allegedly gave him that news?

(8) How did those same (unidentified) police officers notify him at the Parkland Hospital that the same suspect was also involved in the murder of the president prior to 2:00 p.m., when Oswald was still riding in the squad car and was not interrogated until 2:30 p.m.? Nor did Oswald admit his name was Lee Harvey Oswald until some fifteen or twenty minutes had passed in the police station, which meant it was not until 2:30 p.m. that the police knew his name.

As can be seen from his sworn testimony, Curry stated he was informed that the suspect captured in the Texas Theatre was a suspect in both murders, and this was given to Curry prior to 1:30 p.m.

In fairness to Chief Curry, could it be possible that he was grossly mistaken regarding his time elements? Absolutely not! The reason being that the chief's time schedule proved he was on his way to Love Field prior to 2 p.m. Therefore, according to his own sworn statements, he did receive the information while he was in the hospital. He was also positive that he had been notified during that time that the same man arrested as a suspect in the Tippit murder was also the suspect in the murder of the president.

The chief was extremely careful during his testimony to constantly refer to "unidentified" police officers who did the notifying. The chief did not explain how those unidentified police officers knew between 1:15 and 1:30 p.m. that not only was a suspect being followed but the same suspect was also the one sought for the president's murder.

Nor did the chief explain how those unidentified police officers of his own department knew that Oswald was the one unless the chief also knew that his "unidentified" police officers were involved in the conspiracy.

The Warren Commission had no desire to question Chief Curry regarding the "knowledge" possessed by his unidentified police officers. But, as shown, they did know that the chief was perjuring himself.

Five years and seventeen days after the murder, Chief Curry

was to admit Oswald was innocent.

The Commission was also placed in an unenviable position—on the horns of a dilemma—when they published a statement that the time the president was shot was at exactly 12:30 p.m. The time, according to them, was established by a photograph of the clock on the building which revealed it was 12:30 p.m.

The clock was to be witness to (1) involve the complicity of the Dallas police; or (2) the Sheriff's Department of Dallas County and Sheriff Decker. If the time element be true and the clock be accurate, then one or the other, or both, were involved in the conspiracy. Of course, [due to] the manner in which the Commission handled the evidence, it could be possible that they selected any photograph which showed the 12:30 p.m. time on the clock.

However, two vital pieces of evidence more than proved the time to be 12:25 p.m., not 12:30 p.m.! If that evidence proved the shooting to be at 12:25 p.m., then Oswald was never at the window at the time the Commission said he was. (As has been shown, Oswald was on the front steps of the Book Depository, but it can now be shown by the following evidence that he could not have been at the window.)

The Dallas "Times-Herald" published the statement that Sheriff Decker said the shooting took place at exactly 12:25 p.m. The Dallas "Morning News" stated the murder occurred at 12:20 p.m. Both newspapers repeated the time they had published in all subsequent issues on November 22 and November 23. To this day, neither newspaper had corrected the time to match that published by the "Report." Why? One reason was that on both the police and sheriff's radio tapes are the words of the sheriff instructing all his men to go to the railroad tracks to investigate the source of the shots! The time he uttered those instructions was recorded in the Dallas police radio room and entered into the official police records as 12:25 p.m.

Furthermore, a police reporter who was stationed at the police radio room heard Sheriff Decker's voice announcing the shooting, and he immediately telephoned to his city editor. The city editor entered on his record the reporter's excited announcement at 12:28 p.m.!

Thus, the evidence, not the words used by the Commission,

proved that the president was shot a minimum of five minutes prior to 12:30 p.m. And the reason they made this five-minute adjustment was due to the fact that the Commission had to give Oswald time to do the things they theorized he had done on the 6th floor. That is, the six minutes to reassemble the rifle, to run up 5 flights of stairs, and to construct a 1,500-pound shield of cartons. Since Bonnie Ray Williams had testified he did not leave the area near that window until 12:22, then Oswald could not have been convicted by the Commission as being there at 12:19 p.m. Six minutes from 12:25 leaves the time at 12:19 p.m. The Commission simply juggled the time in an attempt to persuade its readers of the "Report" that Oswald had sufficient time to do all the things they wanted him to do.

The Commission, although knowing that the sheriff's announcement could not be eliminated because of his voice being on the police records and the reporter being in the radio room when he recorded the announcement, simply passed over it with no comment in the "Report." If Sheriff Decker was correct, then the Commission's time of 12:30 was false and proved Oswald innocent. If the sheriff was incorrect then the Commission had to demand of him why he broadcast the announcement the president was being shot at five minutes prior to the time the shooting commenced! That was the dilemma. If the sheriff was lying, then why did he lie? Was the sheriff so overcome with emotion that the president was to be shot that he could not withhold those emotions, and it burst forth from him unintentionally? If that be the case, then the sheriff also had prior knowledge of the murder.

Thus, two vital questions would have been asked by any intelligent, impartial body investigating a murder. When it is considered that the murder was that of the president of the United States, it is inconceivable and reprehensible that those two questions not be asked and not be answered.

Two pieces of the jigsaw puzzle have now been replaced in the box containing that jigsaw. The Commission had exposed the piece that revealed the evidence that the "double detour" was not the route known to any person except the conspirators. The same evidence proved that the Dallas Police Department was involved in driving the president into an ambush, and the

"Judas Goat" was none other than Chief Curry.

Chief Curry was to expose another piece when he testified that prior to the capture of Oswald, and prior to the time his department flashed the news of Tippit's death, the chief was informed that a "suspect" had been arrested for both murders.

The actual time of the president's murder is also proved to have been juggled by five minutes—if the testimony of Sheriff Decker is to be trusted. There now can be no question that Oswald was the "patsy" selected by the conspirators, in conjunction with their police associates, as the "killer" of the president.

The police officer who clearly established the conspiracy and provided the final piece of the jigsaw was none other than Captain Fritz, head of the police homicide department. He was also to prove himself to be an "accessory before and after the fact."

The captain was to give the first clear indication that the police were definitely involved in the conspiracy. The Commission's deathly silence regarding the testimony of Deputy Sheriff Craig was a clear indication that the Commission knew a conspiracy existed. The deputy was the first person to see "Oswald" from the time he left the Depository until 1 p.m., when he was seen by his landlady, Mrs. Roberts, at the Berkley Street rooming house.

On November 23, 1963 Deputy Craig signed an affidavit in the sheriff's department that swore that at 12:45 p.m. he saw a "white male running down the hill from the Texas Book Depository, and I saw what I think was a light-colored Rambler station wagon with luggage rack on top pull over to the curb, and this subject who had come running down the hill got into the car. The man driving this station wagon was a dark-complected white man.... I reported this incident at once to a Secret Service officer whose name I did not know.... (Author's Note: This "officer" was one of the conspirators, as will be proved later by the U.S. Secret Service).... Later I heard the city (police) had a suspect in custody, and I called in I had reported the information about the suspect ... to Capt. Fritz ... and was requested to come at once to the City Hall.... I went to the City Hall and identified the subject (Lee Harvey Oswald) as being the same person I saw running down the hill and get into the station wagon and leave the scene." One need not now wonder why the Commission deliberately buried this affidavit nineteen volumes, and one million words, away from their 888-page "Report!"

As previously stated, in a law trial a lawyer is in clover when he can find a witness who can substantiate the testimony of another witness. But the Commission, knowing that there was another witness to Deputy Sheriff Craig's affidavit buried in the 19th volume of the "Hearings," suppressed the corroborating witness's testimony not in the "Hearings" but in the National Archives, Washington, D.C.! Substantiating the deputy's affidavit is one under File Code No. "CD-5," where a Mr. M. C. Robinson testified to the FBI that between 12:30 p.m. and 1 p.m., [when] "he was in front of the Texas School Book Depository building, a light-colored Nash station wagon suddenly appeared before him ... stopped ... and a white male came down the grass-covered incline between the building and street and entered the station wagon after which it drove away in the direction of the Oak Cliff section (Oswald lived near that section) of Dallas."

Craig's description of the white man he saw get into that station wagon was a man "in his twenties, five-feet eight, about 140 or 150 pounds, with blue trousers and a light-tan shirt." An exact description of the clothes worn by Oswald. After Craig had reported to Captain Fritz and identified Oswald as the man getting into the Nash station wagon, Oswald's first words were: "Don't Involve her. She knows nothing!" The "she" was none other than Mrs. Paine, the FBI informant! Oswald, according to the inestimable Captain Fritz and Deputy Sheriff Craig, never denied getting into a station wagon and never denied that the station wagon was owned by Mrs. Paine. Nor did Capt. Fritz, that paragon of police efficiency, ever question Mrs. Paine to elucidate (1) was that station wagon her station wagon; (2) who was the driver; (3) where did that "dark complected white man" take Oswald?

In his testimony before the Commission the captain swore that "he (Craig) was telling me things (at 5:30 p.m. on November 22nd) I knew would not help us ... his (Craig's) story didn't fit in with what we knew to be true."

With that testimony, the captain was candidly admitting the existence of a conspiracy!

The captain opened the door to the hallway leading to the conspiracy, for the Warren Commission knew:

1. Captain Fritz testified that he was at Parkland Hospital from 12:45 p.m. and returned at 12:58 p.m. to the Book Depository.

2. The 7.65 German Mauser rifle was not found until 1:22 p.m.

3. No palm print of Oswald's was ever found on the switched Italian rifle.

4. No fingerprints of Oswald's were ever found on the same rifle.

5. At the 4 p.m. identification lineup, Brennan did not identify Oswald.

6. At the 4:30 national TV and radio broadcast, Police Chief Curry admitted the police had no eyewitness to the identity of the rifleman.

7. Oswald denied killing President Kennedy. Since the police had absolutely no evidence of any kind at 5:30 p.m. in their possession as seen in 3, 4, 5, and 6, Oswald was legally and morally innocent. Thus, in view of those elements, how did Capt. Fritz "know" Oswald was "guilty?"

8. Therefore, at 5:30 p.m., when Deputy Craig made his identification of Oswald, how did Capt. Fritz, in spite of the above six elements, know that what Craig was telling him "would not help us" and "didn't fit in with what we knew to be true"?

Captain Fritz's standard of Christian morality was subject to doubt when he testified before the Commission. At that time he used a shroud of silence to conceal Oswald's statement that Oswald had talked to "a man or Secret Service agent" who sought directions to a telephone booth while Oswald was near the front entrance of the Book Depository when the shots rang out. If the dead cannot speak, should not the living?

What did police Captain Fritz know that no one, including 197,000,000 Americans, know? What did Captain Fritz "know," and why did the Warren Commission refuse to demand that he inform the American People? Why did the Warren Commission refuse to ask Captain Fritz why he failed to question Mrs. Paine? Why did the Commission fail to ask her when she appeared before them? Or did the Commission know that she was an FBI informant and that the driver of that station wagon was also a person in the position? Of course they did.

In an attempt to overcome the Robinson and Craig affidavits, and to draw the public's eyes from the conspiracy testimony given by Captain Fritz, the Commission invented a "cock and bull" story of Oswald's alleged movements. In that episode the Commission denied the sworn testimony of one witness, suppressed further evidence of a conspiracy, and accepted the "identification" of two witnesses who collapsed under a friendly cross-examination by an aide.

It is interesting to note that when Captain Fritz was undergoing this friendly examination by the Commission aide, the captain had extraordinary lapses of memory or committed downright perjury. The captain testified that he could recall speaking to the deputy, but a few moments later he said he had turned him over to a Lt. Baker, who was to take an affidavit from Deputy Craig. There is Lt. Baker, but the Commission refused to summon that officer to substantiate the captain's testimony. Craig's affidavit is published in the illustrated section and properly notarized. As has been seen, the deputy's testimony was substantiated by Mr. Robinson. The evasiveness of Captain Fritz, his lapses of memory, and his perjury is sufficient to support the deputy's affidavit.

What is certain is that the Commission accepted the "word" of a perjurer in spite of the fact that Fritz was at Parkland Hospital when Deputy Craig's substantiated testimony (1) proved he personally saw Oswald at 12:45 p.m. getting into a station wagon; (2) that Lee Harvey Oswald was the same man who shouted to him at the police station that the police should not involve Mrs. Paine!

Historians will never know what Captain Fritz meant when he informed the Commission that at 5:30 p.m. he knew that what Deputy Craig told him was not correct. But that should not protect the Commission from being accused of being negligent in its conduct. Nor should the Commission be permitted to escape the right of a historian to apply reasons why the Commission was so willingly neglectful.

In addition to the evidence produced by Chief Curry and Capt. Fritz, there is a great deal of additional evidence in the "Hearings" that proved a conspiracy.

The chief of the United States Secret Service not only informed the Commission of a conspiracy but also proved it was a conspiracy. What happened to the men who identified themselves as "Secret Service" agents to the various witnesses, and collected evidence from those witnesses, and then those "agents" disappeared with the evidence? The chief of the Secret Service admitted that every Secret Service agent went either to Parkland Hospital or went to guard Vice President Johnson immediately after the rifle ceased to fire. Then, who were those "agents" seen near and behind the "grassy knolls" when policemen and deputy sheriffs approached them and those "agents" flashed "credentials?" Uncle Remus and his friends? Or members of the conspiracy?

There is now positive photographic evidence that an assassin was dressed as a Dallas city motorcycle cop and stationed behind the fence on the grassy knoll. In a suppressed statement signed by Assistant Chief of the Dallas Motorcycle Division, C. Batchelor, the chief stated that he had no cyclists stationed either behind, in front, or near that area at any time. But Deputy Sheriff Mabra testified he saw a Dallas motorcycle cop wearing a white helmet and dark glasses in that area. Testimony of Dallas patrolman Smith stated that he saw a Secret Service agent in that area immediately after the shooting.[61]

---

[61] Joe Marshall Smith's testimony, as given on July 23, 1964 to Wesley J. Liebeler, assistant counsel of the Commission, reads as follows: SMITH: "... this woman came up to me and she was just in hysterics. She told me: 'They are shooting the president from the bushes.' So I immediately proceeded up there[....]" "Mr. LIEBELER: There is a parking lot in behind this grassy area back from Elm Street toward the railroad tracks, and you went down to the parking lot and looked around? Mr. SMITH: Yes, sir; I checked all the cars. I looked into all the cars and checked around the bushes. Of

Furthermore, this "Secret Service agent" was seen at the same time by Deputy Sheriff Weitzman. But the official records of the U.S. Secret Service revealed the time and whereabouts off every agent, and none of them were in that area, or in the Book Depository, or engaged in any activity surrounding the Tippit murder. According to the testimony in the "Hearings," there were a minimum of eight "Secret Service" agents collecting the evidence.

However, at no time, and there exists no testimony in the "Hearings," did the FBI or the U.S. Secret Service use its own agents to ferret out those spurious "agents." [Neither] the FBI nor the Secret Service [ever] asked any of the persons who had seen or talked to those imposters to describe those "agents" in an effort to apprehend them. Why?

Nor did those two federal agencies show any interest in the suppressed Nix photographs, which were published by "Esquire" in December 1966 and by the "Saturday Evening Post" in January 1967. The Nix photographs were in the possession of the Dallas police, the FBI, and the Secret Service as early as November 26, 1963. Those photographs reveal the existence of a jeep at the south end of the arcade behind the fence prior to and immediately after the assassination. A postal employee, J. C. Price, testified that he saw a white man, about 25, wearing a white shirt, running from that area to the railroad tracks.[62] The value of the Nix film is that it shows the activity

---

course, I wasn't alone. There was some deputy sheriff with me, and I believe one Secret Service man when I got there. I got to make this statement, too. I felt awfully silly, but after the shot and this woman, I pulled my pistol from my holster, and I thought, this is silly, I don't know who I am looking for, and I put it back. Just as I did, he showed me that he was a Secret Service agent. Mr. LIEBELER: Did you accost this man? Mr. SMITH: Well, he saw me coming with my pistol and right away he showed me who he was. Mr. LIEBELER: Do you remember who it was? Mr. SMITH: No, sir; I don't—because then we started checking the cars. In fact, I was checking the bushes, and I went through the cars, and I started over here in this particular section."

[62] Price's affidavit was taken on November 22, 1963: "I was on the roof of the Terminal Annex Bldg. on the NE corner when the

in the opposite direction of that shown in the Zapruder films. But the Warren Commission suppressed all evidence regarding the conspirators and the assassins revealed in the Nix and Moorman film and photographs.

The Commission's method of operation concerning evidence proving a conspiracy was to bury the proof in either the "Hearings" or the National Archives. There is uncontradicted evidence that witnesses also heard shots fired from the Dal-Tex Building, from the County Records Building, or the County Jail Buildings, which abut each other. A Mr. Mudd testified that he heard shots from the Dal-Tex Building, as did Miss Dorman, while Mr. Williams testified that some of the shots came from the County Building. The lead article in the Dallas "Morning News" after the murder of the president stated that the shots "came from a building beyond the Book Depository." That building is none other than the Dal-Tex Building, in which Dallas deputy sheriffs arrested a man and took him to the jail for investigation. To this day no record exists of the name of that man and the questions and answers given and taken in the "Hearings," the records of the Dallas Sheriff's Office, or in the National Archives. Why? He is mentioned as an unknown. This man had a rifle in his hands when arrested. Another man, within 15 minutes after the shooting, was arrested by a Patrolman Barker. He was held, incommunicado, from November 22, 1963 until December 10, 1963, and then mysteriously released. His fingerprints are not on file, and why he was held after the murder of Oswald on November 24th until December 10th is

---

presidential motorcade came down Main to Houston, North on Houston and then west on Elm. The cars had proceeded west on Elm and was [sic] just a short distance from the Tripple [sic] underpass, when I saw Gov. Connelly [sic] slump over. I did not see the president as his car had gotten out of my view under the underpass. There was a volley of shots, and then much later, maybe as much as five minutes [sic!] later, another one. I saw one man run towards the passenger cars on the railroad siding after the volley of shots. This man had a white dress shirt, no tie and kahki [sic] colored trousers. His hair appeared to be long and dark and his agility running could be about 35 yrs [sic] of age. He had something in his hand. I couldn't be sure but it may have been a head piece."

not known.

If two men, both carrying rifles, were not suspicious to the Commission, then the arrest by the sheriff's deputies of a man on the "grassy knoll" who was identified by two witnesses to the shooting as the man seen firing at the president should have created a little concern by at least one commissioner: Mr. Dulles. Yet, what happened to this man? Sheriff Decker? (See illustrated section.)

The testimony in the "Hearings" is overloaded with proof that Oswald was "wanted" by the Dallas police prior to the murder of officer Tippit. On a police radio tape, timed at 12:45 p.m., is the police announcement that Lee Harvey Oswald was wanted for the murder of President Kennedy! Why does all testimony and affidavits by the Dallas policemen taking part in the arrest of Oswald at the Texas Theatre reveal the fact that every one of those policemen swear that the "tip" said Oswald was in the balcony, not on the first floor? How did McDonald, the last patrolman to arrive, know [that] Oswald—who was not wearing the clothes broadcast by the police—was on the first floor and know Oswald to be the suspect? Why did one of the Commission's three witnesses testify that one of the cops hit Oswald and said: "Kill the president, will you, you son of a bitch!" How did those cops know Oswald was the killer?

Another fraudulent statement by the Commission is one that Oswald was unknown to the Dallas police. That is a lie, for the testimony in the "Hearings" revealed that not only did the Dallas police know Oswald's address on Berkley Street but [they also] knew his secret address on Elsbeth Street, which Oswald kept secret from the Paines and his wife, Marina. The Dallas police had Oswald's secret address on Elsbeth Street, and the Dallas police sent a party of policemen to arrest him there. This testimony is suppressed from the "Report," but in the "Hearings" Detectives Carroll and Taylor made that statement, and it was substantiated by Detectives Westphal and Parks.

It is abundantly clear from the testimony in the "Hearings" or in the National Archive's files that some of the Dallas police were involved in the Tippit murder. In an effort to solve this "mystery" the Commission had the police submit their radio tapes to the FBI because of the deliberate lies made by the police in their transcription of those radio logs. The logs reveal that only 2 squad cars in the entire city of Dallas were instructed to move into the Oak Cliff area. One of the squad cars, however, went to the Book Depository; the other was driven by officer Tippit, who immediately violated the instructions. At the time he was murdered, the radio logs revealed that Tippit was not in the district where he was ordered to patrol, but in District No. 109. Why? That Tippit was scheduled to die was revealed in the tape recordings, for when Mr. Bowley saw Tippit's body at 1:10 p.m. on the street and he called in the report over Tippit's squad car radio, the police dispatcher immediately called Tippit's squad car number, not the squad car code number of the officer who was supposed to be on regular duty in that Oak Cliff area. How did the dispatcher know to call Tippit's code number in an area where Tippit was never instructed to patrol? The radio tapes revealed that when Mr. Bowley spoke to the police dispatcher, Mr. Bowley never gave the dispatcher Tippit's badge number or his squad car number—No. 10.

The same Dallas police also testified that although Tippit's clipboard was attached to his dashboard, they never looked at it or read it! Would any police department fail to read a fellow officer's clipboard which would reveal where he had been, and who he had seen, in their efforts to locate and capture the murderer of a fellow officer unless the police themselves were involved in his death? Of course, the police would have had to come up with the answers to such questions as: "Why did Tippit leave his district and go home two hours before he was murdered? What was so important that while on duty he had to visit his family? Why was a police squad car missing from 12:45 p.m. in front of the Book Depository until 3:45 p.m., when it was mysteriously returned? Could the answer to the last question be that it was that car that went to Oswald's Berkley Street address and, at 1:02 p.m., "tooted twice," and Oswald then rushed out of his rooming house?

The willful and deliberate acts of the Dallas police, their deliberate commission of perjury, and their deliberate refusal to investigate the murder of officer Tippit can only lead to the conclusion that some of those Dallas police were deeply involved not only *in his murder but also as participants of the conspiracy that murdered President John F. Kennedy.

Other evidence of the "conspiracy" is seen in the Illustrated section of this book, where one can read the "arrest report." Oswald was arrested, according to that report, at 1:40 p.m. by four police officers, none of whom filed the charge! He was arrested but never charged. However, at the time he was "booked," not arraigned, the invisible officer wrote in the section: "Other details of the arrest—This man shot and killed President John F. Kennedy and police officer J. D. Tippit. He also wounded Governor John Connally." The reader is advised to note (1) the time of arrest; (2) no policeman signed the "charge filed" section; (3) the sections below the arresting officer section; (4) the "other details of arrest" section. (5) Notice that when this charge was filed, the police did not charge Oswald with fighting or resisting arrest, and (6) there is no charge of a revolver taken from Oswald! Was the revolver in the possession of the police prior to Oswald's arrest?

According to the police, Oswald arrived at the police station at approximately 2:20 p.m. He was immediately booked by an officer who completed the "arrest report." That would be approximately 2:30 p.m. Oswald was not notified of any charges against him until after 6 p.m. The Commission and the police admitted no charge was ever filed against him relating to the President Kennedy murder until 1:30 a.m. on November 23, 1963. That, as will be shown, is another Commission falsehood.

The Commission stated that, at the time of Oswald's arrest, none of the police knew he was wanted or suspected in the murder of President Kennedy, although one witness testified that during the struggle (?) to capture Oswald a policeman did say he was the killer of President Kennedy. Thus, the vital question never answered by the Warren Commission is that, at the time the charge sheet was completed at 2:30 p.m., how did the policeman writing up the "arrest report" know that Oswald had "killed" President Kennedy and "wounded" Governor Connally?

Why did the officer use the word "killed" instead of "arrested for suspicion of murder?" How did the Dallas police know that Oswald had killed President Kennedy at 2:30 p.m.? There was no fingerprint or palm print evidence, for Lt. Day "discovered" no prints on that rifle until 8 p.m.! The FBI never traced that Italian rifle from Klein's of Chicago to "Hidell" until late in the day of November 23rd. The police chief of Dallas went on a national television and radio broadcast and admitted on November 22nd at 5:30 p.m. that they had no eyewitness to the rifleman. Mr. Brennan admitted he could not identify the rifleman he saw. How did the Dallas police know at 2:30 p.m. that Oswald had "killed" President Kennedy and "wounded" Governor Connally? Now the reason is found why no Dallas police officer signed the "arrest sheet." No one wanted to be responsible for the lie.

Another revealing example of the Commission's method in interpreting "the basic principles of American justice" is its reliance upon Captain Fritz's memory to "convict" Oswald. It will be recalled that the "Report" stated that the captain "kept no notes" and relied upon his memory to recall the questions and answers made by Oswald during his various hours of illegal interrogation in the Dallas police station. However, the "Report" published a 13-page memorandum signed by the captain and accepted by the Commission as being truthful. The captain testified he made that memo from "rough notes and memory." After writing his 13-page memo, the captain conveniently destroyed his "rough notes," which, as a police executive, he knew was illegal.

It is revealing to read the captain's memo and see how badly his "rough notes and memory" served him. On Page 4 of this memorandum is the startling statement: "At 7:06 p.m. I signed a complaint before Bill Alexander of the district attorney's office charging Oswald with the Tippit murder. At 7:10 p.m. Tippit was arraigned before Judge Johnston." No, the last sentence is not a printer's error. Tippit was being arraigned for his own murder! When it is considered that this memorandum was written several days after the murder of Oswald, when the captain had plenty of time to fabricate the questions and answers of the various "interrogation" sessions, the captain's subconscious prevented him from writing the truth! Furthermore, the Alexander "affidavit" is published in the illustrated section of this book and it is an outright fake!

Conclusive proof that Oswald never was legally arraigned for the murder of President Kennedy prior to his own murder by another conspirator can also be seen in the illustrated section of this book. This "Alexander" affidavit was published in the "Report" as a true copy for the "arraignment" of Lee Harvey Oswald in the murder of President Kennedy. The background relating to this photograph was revealed in the testimony that on the night of November 22, 1963, Alexander showed this "affidavit" at the press conference as proof to the news media that Oswald had been legally arraigned for both murders. Minutes prior to this showing, Oswald cried out that he was not charged with the murder of President Kennedy, only with that of officer Tippit; then [he] exclaimed that he was being used as a "patsy." He also stated that he was innocent of both charges and he wanted a lawyer.

Photographers and reporters are not lawyers so they accepted, as true, Alexander's statement that Oswald had been arraigned. What those members of the press media did not understand was that, in criminal law, the Alexander "affidavit" was a fake, since no person, either as the "affiant" or as a justice of the peace, had signed that "affidavit." Oswald was thus, according to the Alexander "affidavit," being accused by an unknown person; for not even a Dallas policeman, a justice of the peace, or a member of the D.A.'s office had signed that affidavit. That "affidavit" was a worthless piece of paper in any court of criminal law in any state of the United States. The Commission and its 26 lawyers knew that "affidavit" was absolutely worthless, but they published it under "the basic principles of American justice."

Attempting to corroborate this fake Alexander "affidavit" the Commission then proceeded to pour additional oil on the fire by publishing another photograph in the "Report" titled: "Johnston Exhibit No. 4." This can be seen in the illustrated section of this book. This photograph is another fraudulent example of manufactured evidence. As the reader can see, this "affidavit" is torn in half, and the two torn portions do not match! The Warren Commission gave the Alexander "affidavit" a full page; the Johnston exhibit an eighth of a page. Since when is a torn affidavit admissible in any court of law, especially in view of the evidence that the two torn parts do not match each other? It can be noticed that printing on both the Alexander "affidavit" and the Johnston "exhibit" are one and the same, yet no one knows whose handwriting it represents. The reader should also compare the Alexander "affidavit" to the Johnston "exhibit," for both of them revealed a blank space under the word "affiant"! This could only mean that both "affidavits" are one and the same and that Mr. Wade's and Captain Fritz's signatures were simply added to the photograph of the Johnston exhibit. That is why the Johnston exhibit is torn! What is another problem is that on the side of that Johnston "affidavit" is the strange writing that appears. A word "June" or "Jan." 26, 1964 appears, with "2 of 4" also written. What the meaning of those written words is was not explained by the Commission. It could mean that Oswald was posthumously "arraigned" after his murder to satisfy the Commission!

Thus, from a reading of the testimony in the "Hearings," the legal fact is that Lee Harvey Oswald, while alive, was never legally arraigned for the murder of President Kennedy. The next question that must be answered is whether or not that statement can be supported by testimony.

Oswald, according to the Commission, was charged with the murder of President Kennedy at 1:30 a.m. on November 23, 1963 by Capt. Fritz of the Dallas Police Department before Texas Justice of the Peace Johnston. The Commission said that, but the testimony in the "Hearings" informed the reader the Commission lied. Police officer Hider testified that he was the duty officer in charge of the identification bureau where arraignments are made of accused persons. Officer Hider swore that he was on duty until 2:15 a.m. on November 23, 1963. He further testified that at 1:30 a.m. of the same day he never saw Capt. Fritz or J. P. Johnston make any arraignment of Oswald for the murder of President Kennedy!

On the basis of the testimony in the "Hearings," Lee Harvey Oswald was never charged by any legal body in the state of Texas with the murder of President Kennedy or the wounding of Governor Connally. In a legal sense, Oswald died innocent of any charge of being involved in the murder of President Kennedy.

After the arrest of Oswald, he kept shouting, "I'm not resisting arrest; I'm not resisting arrest!" According to the various affidavits in the "Hearings," namely Com. Exh. No. 2003, Oswald's "gun" was in the possession of several policemen and "marked" by several other policemen with six live bullets, but when given to Capt. Fritz by Sgt. Hill the captain announced that the revolver now had 4 live bullets and 2 spent ones (CBS and NBC broadcasts: Nov. 22, 1963). Since the captain received the revolver directly from the hands of Sgt. Hill and he signed for it, how did 6 live bullets become reduced to 4 live bullets and 2 spent ones? Was the "Oswald" gun the weapon taken from him, or was it planted?

On the Oswald "arrest charge sheet" no policeman desired to accept credit for the capture of the 20th century's Number One Killer. With the FBI bluntly stating that the bullets given to them by the police did not match the Oswald revolver, the Commission's case, under the "basic principles of American justice," collapsed completely. Thus, the Commission was presented with a solution given to them by the same police department: namely, Jack Ruby shot Oswald to protect the president's wife and their children.

But the evidence suppressed by the Commission revealed that Jack Ruby was directed by the police executives to murder Oswald. To make sure that Oswald died before he could talk, the same police had two back-up assassins: one an unidentified Dallas policeman and another an unknown "doctor."

The evidence revealed that Oswald was scheduled to die as he ran from the Texas Theatre through the rear door. Oswald must have had some inkling or premonition that something went wrong when McDonald pulled out a pistol as he approached Oswald. But whether that pistol was McDonald's is now subject to great doubt, for the activity around the McDonald—Oswald "struggle" as related by the other patrolmen suggests that McDonald planted that revolver with a dented firing pin during the struggle, and that is why Detective Carroll testified that he did not know from whom he jerked the revolver. The Commission never asked McDonald if he had his revolver with him. No witnesses testified that they saw McDonald with a pistol or revolver in his hand, neither did any policeman. That McDonald would leave the scene of the Book Depository, in direct violation of his captain's order to assist his fellow police at the Depository, to capture a man sneaking into a theater is more than incredible—it is a downright lie.

What everyone has overlooked, and the Commission did not emphasize, was that McDonald said he had drawn his gun from his holster and approached Oswald with the weapon in his right hand. Therefore, if Oswald has a revolver in his hand during his "struggle" with McDonald, the police and the witnesses should have seen TWO weapons. But everyone involved in that capture testified they saw only one gun! Detective Carroll testified he "jerked" a gun from someone and took that gun to Sgt. Hill. At no time did he see two guns, only one. He never saw Oswald with a gun in his hand, nor did the FBI testify that the Oswald revolver had any person's—including Oswald's—fingerprints or fingerprint smears on the revolver! Was that gun planted by McDonald, and did he go to the theater to plant the weapon?

At first blush the killing of Oswald by the Dallas police in their "100% security" police station would seem to be a separate and distinct murder from that involving the assassination of President Kennedy. But a deeper look into the "Hearings" and affidavits in the National Archives reveals that both of the murders were part and parcel of the conspiracy that murdered President Kennedy.

During the trial of Jack Ruby, his attorney repeatedly asked that a policeman and his girlfriend be summoned as a key witness for his client. The attorney was informed that the district attorney's office only knew the wanted policeman had resigned and disappeared from Dallas. That policeman did not disappear on his own volition; he left Dallas to save his life, and he resurfaced in the sunny state of California.

This policeman's name was Harry Olsen and the girlfriend had married him.[63] They were so much in love that when Olsen

---

[63] Olsen's companion was Kay Helen Coleman, who worked as a stripper at Jack Ruby's Carousel Club under the name of "Kathy Kay." See Seth Kantor, *The Ruby Cover-up*, pp. 28, 30, 103-05, 411.

was finally questioned by the Commission (they were able to locate Mr. and Mrs. Olsen AFTER Ruby was convicted) he did not know whether he had been married in December 1963 or January 1964! Their marriage was more on the order of a "let us save each other's life" campaign; for the testimony revealed that they knew too much, and a wife or husband cannot testify against each other in a criminal trial.

Was policeman Olsen, a mysterious messenger for Chief Curry, the conduit used to inform Ruby of the time Oswald was to be transferred from the city jail to the county jail? This same policeman was also to figure in the Tippit murder; for, at the time of that murder, Olsen, in violation of Dallas police regulations against "moonlighting," was "protecting" the estate of a multimillionaire Dallas oilman. By a strange coincidence, between 12:45 p.m. and 1:00 p.m., Tippit was supposed to have cruised by the exact corner where Olsen had stationed himself in guarding this oilman's estate. But Olsen did not see Tippit go past him, although the police radio logs—which were faked by the police—stated that Tippit should have been seen by Olsen. Olsen is also the only Dallas cop that could not remember the name of the oilman who was paying him to guard the estate, nor could he remember the exact location—and the Warren Commission believed him!

This policeman also had a most remarkable loss of memory when he could not remember one single sentence of his two- to three-hour conversation held with Jack Ruby at 2:30 a.m. on November 23, 1963. And who was with them at that time of the morning, nearly 12 hours after the death of President Kennedy? Why, none other than Kay Coleman, a Ruby employee in his striptease club. If she remembered anything, she said nothing incriminating to the Commission, but she did remember to become married to Olsen sometime in 1963 or 1964. And then both of them fled Dallas.

Yet this innocuous patrolman, a good friend of Chief Curry, saw more of Jack Ruby than what the Commission told the general public. The "Hearings" revealed that on the night prior to the murder of President Kennedy both Ruby and Olsen met for another conversation, which Olsen also forgot of what was spoken; and on Saturday, November 23, they met again between 10 and 11 p.m.

Buried in the "Hearings" and the "Report" is the testimony of a witness who informed the Commission that on November 23 he heard Jack Ruby mention Chief Curry's name, and Ruby informed the person to whom he was speaking of the whereabouts of Chief Curry. But the FBI and the Secret Service could not locate the chief of police when they desired to inform him that they had obtained tips that Oswald was to be shot when he was to be moved from one jail to another.

As Jack Ruby informed Chief Justice Earl Warren during the chief's interrogation of Ruby in the Dallas jail, Ruby had to have "inside" information as to the exact time when Oswald was to be brought down to the jail basement; for Ruby's activity prior to the time of the Oswald shooting proved Ruby knew the exact time—11 a.m.! Ruby could only obtain that time schedule from some officer high in the confidence of the Dallas police. As the evidence below will reveal, Ruby did not just "wander in" from the street; he came in at the proper time to do the job he was instructed to do—murder Oswald. But the conspirators, knowing that a bullet may not necessarily be fatal in all occasions, had two "back up" assassins who completed the actual murder of Oswald.

With Oswald's refusal to run and be gunned down near the theater with several dozen witnesses looking on, the Dallas police now had a live "patsy" on their hands. It would take all of the 23rd to make the preparations that would lead to Oswald's murder on the 24th of November. The "Report" has admitted that the Dallas police were warned several times that Oswald would be murdered. Mr. Hoover tried several times to contact Police Chief Curry and personally warn the chief that Oswald was going to be murdered. However, the police chief testified that on the night of the 23rd he went to bed with the telephone receiver "off the hook." As one can see, that is a new method in running a police department. It is more probable that the chief desired no official notice of the prospective Oswald murder.

Jack Ruby—the alleged murderer of Oswald who was a fringe member of the conspiracy that murdered President John F. Kennedy—now became the leading character actor in the conspiracy. Jack Ruby was well known by the Dallas police and the district attorney's office. In fact, there is a suppressed document in the National Archives, Com. Exh. No. 1467, which proved Ruby knew, by sight or personally, more than 70% of the Dallas Police Department. Jack Ruby was also well known by members of the staff of the Dallas district attorney. Ruby was even well known among the legal profession; for at the Texas State Bar Association meeting in 1963 Ruby was a nonparticipating member and introduced to many members of the Texas Bar.

Jack Ruby, on the day prior to the murder of Oswald, visited several high police executives and their offices on the 3rd floor of the police station. When Chief Curry announced on the 23rd that Oswald would be transferred the next day at 10:00 a.m. (to cooperate with the press or ...?), Ruby continued his exploration of the police building. Although the Commission attempted to prove that Ruby acted spontaneously in shooting Oswald, the testimony proved the contrary. On the afternoon prior to Oswald's murder, the police issued a statement that Oswald would be moved from the Dallas police station to the county jail at 10 a.m. That time was published by the two Dallas newspapers, the radio, and TV stations. But where was Jack Ruby at 10 a.m. the day he shot Oswald? Not at the jail but walking around the Dallas downtown area on various chores. Thus, as the evidence showed, Oswald should have been out of the jail and Ruby admitted he knew Oswald was to be removed at 10 a.m.

In spite of the fact that the Commission said Jack Ruby acted emotionally in his murder of Oswald, the testimony revealed that it was beyond doubt a premeditated act. For in the presence of his own attorney, Ruby, prior to taking a "lie" test, and in the presence of Assistant D. A. Alexander, admitted that he had on the morning of November 24 informed his roommate, George Senator, that he was going to murder Oswald in the police station. Ruby's smuggled confession, which was reprinted in full in "Ramparts," revealed the fact that he was ordered to murder Oswald.

The Commission, in its attempt to prove that no one assisted Ruby in his plan to murder Oswald, conveniently overlooked positive testimony that proved Ruby was given assistance by some members of the Dallas police. The Commission contended that Ruby entered the Dallas police station's basement via the ramp on Main Street approximately five minutes prior to the shooting of Oswald. However, patrolman Vaughn, the guardian of the entrance, testified he never saw Ruby at any time prior to the shooting of Oswald. To substantiate patrolman Vaughn were [Lt.] Pierce and Police Sgts. Maxey and Putman. However, since some of the police are involved, the investigator must seek impartial testimony to solve this entry problem.

Buried in the National Archives is an affidavit given to the FBI by a UPI reporter, Mr. T. McGarry, who testified that 15 minutes prior to the shooting of Oswald by Ruby the reporter was standing in the middle of the basement looking at the Main Street ramp entrance. He did not see Jack Ruby enter from the ramp entrance at the time stipulated by the Warren Commission. The reporter's sworn testimony was, in turn, upheld by Mr. Tasker, a taxicab driver who was stationed at the Main Street ramp entrance across the street. He testified that, while he was at the entrance during a time period which was about fifteen minutes prior to the shooting, he did not see Jack Ruby enter the building through that ramp entrance.

The Warren Commission emphatically states that Jack Ruby could only enter the Dallas police station basement by using the "down ramp." As per their custom, the testimony revealed they lied. Not only is there a "down entrance," there is also, naturally, an "up" entrance. Furthermore, there is also an elevator and stairway leading from inside the station down to the basement. In addition, many of the news media reporters, and the police, admitted that many of them walked into that basement without having their credentials checked by any policeman in that area. The evidence also proved that Ruby was so well known that he was "persona grata" to the district attorney's office, to Chief Curry's office, and to Capt. Fritz's office, where he visited all of them on November 22 and 23. Jack Ruby simply followed police instructions and came into the basement two to three minutes prior to the time he was informed that Oswald would be in the basement and walked directly toward Ruby.

Of course, no policeman or civilian saw Jack Ruby enter the police building for the reason he was already in the building! By strange coincidence, he stationed himself in the exact spot where Oswald had to walk to the truck which was to take him out of that building. With an inaudible sigh of resignation, the Commission "accepted" the "testimony" of the police that by "accident" the police ordered a truck that could not fit the space within the platform from which Oswald was to step off and into that truck. It was also a "coincidence" that the police walked Oswald with no police in front of him, just to the side, so that Ruby had a perfect shot at Oswald. It was an "accident" that the police walked Oswald directly in front of Ruby. It was a "coincidence" that the police failed to check all the credentials of the civilians in the basement. It was a "coincidence" that Chief Curry did not talk to the FBI and Secret Service bureau, who desired to inform him that they suspected Oswald would be murdered at the time he was to be transferred.

If any person with common sense can accept those "accidents" and "coincidences," they can accept the infallibility of the Commission's "Report"!

In an attempt to discredit the testimony of the four police officers, three of whom knew Jack Ruby personally, and the two civilian witnesses who upheld the testimony of those four policemen, the Commission summoned three other police officers whose testimony revealed flagrant perjury. When Ruby was interrogated after the shooting of Oswald, FBI Agent Hall testified that Ruby made no mention of entering the police building at the ramp entrance. The official report of those three officers revealed that none of them made any statement that Ruby informed them he had entered through the ramp entrance. They "remembered" it after days or months had passed, but not in their official report.

In two of the most remarkable documents ever written and given under oath is the positive proof of the existence of a conspiracy that murdered President Kennedy and Lee Harvey Oswald. Both documents are suppressed from the "Report" and buried in the 19th and 21st volumes of the "Hearings." To prevent an investigator from exposing the conspiracy, the

Commission deliberately buried the evidence that Oswald was to be murdered by conspirators by scattering that evidence in the National Archives or in the 26 volumes of the "Hearings."

Volume 21 contains the famous "Price" exhibit,[64] which refers to the activities of the various members of Parkland Hospital from November 22 to and including November 24, 1963—the Oswald murder. This exhibit contains testimony so inflammable that the Commission buried it deep in the "Hearings."

The evidence contained in the "Price" exhibit revealed that, approximately one-half hour prior to the shooting of Lee Harvey Oswald, the staff of that hospital was instructed to prepare the operating room to receive the body of Lee Harvey Oswald!

Did Ruby murder Oswald, or did he merely shoot him? The autopsy report relating to Lee Harvey Oswald revealed that Oswald was struck down by a bullet that entered his stomach area. In view of modern medical practice, that wound is not a fatal wound if treatment is made promptly. The autopsy report also stated that Oswald's death was hastened by the loss of blood. Where certain acts occur which promote the original nonfatal wound into a fatal wound, the law presumes that the person who caused the nonfatal wound is not guilty of murder where he did nothing to convert that wound from the nonfatal to the fatal. For example, if a doctor operates on a patient for the removal of the appendix, and his assistant deliberately leaves in the wound an instrument which infects the wound after the operation, the second doctor could be found guilty of murder, since he did his act deliberately, not negligently. This example is applicable to the shooting; thus also to the murder of Lee Harvey Oswald. Ruby, in law, shot Oswald; Oswald was murdered by another person. On November 1, 1969 a Los

---

[64] Marks is referring to an affidavit featured in Price Exhibit Number 7 (*Warren Commission Hearings and Exhibits*, volume 21), dated November 24, 1963. Charles Jack Price was administrator, Dallas County hospital district, which included Parkland Memorial Hospital and Woodlawn Hospital.

Angeles police officer was shot in the identical area where Oswald was shot. In addition, the officer was also wounded in the shoulder. This officer was rushed to the hospital and today is alive and well and on active duty. He lived because his police buddies knew that no one should attempt to give artificial respiration to a person hit by a bullet entering the stomach region.

In volume 19, pages 410-413, is a statement by a Dallas policeman, [Cutchshaw],[65] who gave a sworn affidavit to the events that occurred prior to and after the shooting of Oswald. This policeman testified that he saw a man assist television technicians move their equipment into the basement on the morning of the shooting. This "assistant" was dressed in a physician's standard white uniform with a stethoscope hung around his neck. How he could be an "assistant" and a "physician" at the same time was not explained. Nor did the Commission explain its statement that "all" persons who entered the basement had their credentials checked. The policemen neither checked the credentials of the television crew

---

[65] In the original edition of *Coup d'État!* Stanley confused Cutchshaw with officer R. A. Davenport, who was involved in the Tippit case. This has been corrected in the present edition. Dallas Detective Wilbur Jay Cutchshaw's testimony regarding Oswald's transfer and the appearance of the anonymous "doctor" is recorded on pages 410-413 of volume XIX, in an FBI affidavit from December 2, 1963, and labelled "Cutchshaw Exhibit," Nos. 5042-5043. Pages 411-12 include the following testimony: "Cutchshaw stated that after marching through the jail office door he immediately closed this door to prevent anyone from following, after which he opened the door to admit Oswald, who was being carried on a stretcher. He said he was still at this door when a young man, approximately 24 or 25 years of age, wearing a dark-colored sport coat, came to the door and said he was a doctor stationed there. Cutchshaw said he admitted this man when he noticed a stethoscope in the right-hand pocket of the individual." It's also interesting to note that "Cutchshaw estimated that there were approximately 76 officers on the Security Detail who were practically standing shoulder to shoulder in the pertinent area." Yet no one thought of asking Jack Ruby what he was doing there. (See "Cutchshaw Exhibit No. 5044," page 414.)

nor the "physician." This "doctor" looked to be about 22 to 23 years old, which made this "doctor" the youngest "doctor" in the United States!

When Oswald fell to the basement floor after receiving the Ruby bullet in his gut, this "doctor" rushed to Oswald's side and pressed down, not once but several times, while the blood rushed out of Oswald's wound. After a short time, this "doctor" did not wait for any ambulance but simply rose from Oswald's body and vanished into the crowd. But while this "doctor" was assisting Oswald to Death's Door, an unknown Dallas police officer was also pumping out Oswald's blood by giving him artificial respiration! In other words, the "doctor" and the "plainclothes policeman" were pumping out Oswald's blood on the basement floor! There is no policeman in any police force in the United States that is ever instructed to handle the body of a living person who has just been shot. The Dallas police regulations so instruct their policemen. Why was that disregarded?

Thus, the only evidence in the Oswald—Ruby affair is that Ruby shot Oswald; he did not murder him. The actual cause of death was "lack of blood," which was pumped out of Oswald by two unknown persons.

Thus ends the official record of Lee Harvey Oswald. A young man of 24 involved in a matter far over his head. A man selected to enact the role of a "patsy," but when he was engaged to play that role the producer failed to inform him that the final scene was to be enacted on a dirty, damp, oil-stained floor in a police station basement with the spotlight slowly being dimmed on his own red blood gushing out of a wound given to him by a fellow conspirator.

CHAPTER *IX*

MORE PIECES OF THE CONSPIRACY

Although the Warren "Report" is considered by the government to be the "official" record, too much is coming to the surface to be disregarded by any investigator of the Commission's activities. It is true that time cannot be reversed—that John F. Kennedy cannot be returned to life—but it is also true that no nation can continue to live a lie. One way to affirm the "basic principles of American justice" is to attempt to reveal history as it was—not as it is written by people who have an interest in seeing that the lie is perpetuated.

Scattered throughout the 26 volumes of the "Hearings" are little gems, or pieces of the jigsaw puzzle that revealed parts of the conspiracy that murdered President John F. Kennedy.

The aides adopted and perfected the Commission's theory that any testimony that revealed a path to the conspirators or the conspiracy must be confronted with obstacles so that no progress could be maintained.[66] The aides deliberately confused the witnesses as revealed by Specter's examination of Mr. Tomlinson, the man who discovered the planted Bullet 399; or Liebeler's examination of Mr. Altgens, the photographer; or the examination of Capt. Westbrook and Lt. Cunningham on the

---

[66] In many ways the performance of the FBI was no better. As noted by researcher Malcolm Blunt, many of the Bureau's investigative files on the JFK case have the phrase *No lead* "scrawled in the bottom left-hand corner." As Blunt explains, this was a thinly veiled instruction not to follow up on witness "statements which didn't fit with the 'Oswald did it' theory." "In other words, do not pursue." Accompanying the phrase "no lead" one frequently finds the acronym *UACB*, meaning: "Unless Authority Communicated from Bureau." Blunt regards this as a form of "self-censoring" on the part of Hoover's FBI. See Alan Dale and Malcolm Blunt, *The Devil is in the Details*, chapters four and six.

Tippit murder; or the moral cowardice in the aides' refusal to continue the examination of Dallas Police Captain Martin.

Where any key witness testified regarding Oswald's association with the CIA, the FBI, or any other federal agency [such as] the State Department or the U.S. Marine Corps, or if the witness testified to events that, if developed, revealed a conspiracy, the aide deliberately changed the subject or held "off-the-record" conversation with the witness. With more than 200 of those types of conversations dotted throughout the "Hearings," no court of law would permit that type of conduct by any attorney.

Some of the fascinating examinations by aides of witnesses who sought to reveal the conspiracy should be an inspiration for the next government body that will seek to find the assassins of the next president of the United States. The Warren Commission has set many a precedent for its successor to avoid the disturbance of the new president and the powers-to-be. The President is dead—long live the president!

Many witnesses gave evidence that a conspiracy existed. Capt. Martin of the Dallas Police Department requested an opportunity to expand on his accusation that he knew facts concerning the assassination. For example, he was examined by Commission aide Hubert: "Now, Captain Martin, is there anything else you would like to say concerning any aspect of this matter at all?" Captain Martin: "I ... don't take this down!" Hubert: "Well, if you don't want to say it on the record, you'd better not say it at all." Captain Martin: "There is a LOT TO BE SAID, but probably be better if I don't say it."

Captain Martin, the record revealed, worked his way up to that rank over a 23-year period. On May 25, 1966 he had to take a leave of absence and three weeks later, on June 16, 1966, he died of what was "apparent cancer"! Ruby died from a cold that developed into galloping cancer within three weeks after he was removed from the hospitality of the Dallas jail. Captain Martin was murdered, for there is no such illness as "apparent cancer."

The flagrant refusal of aide Hubert to examine Captain Martin after he had offered to furnish additional information regarding murder of President Kennedy and officer Tippit reveals the methods used by the Commission. Furthermore, why did the aide refuse to go into an "off the cuff" interview with the captain? After all, aide Hubert had conducted that type of interview many times; now, why the exception? The reason is that aide Hubert did not want to become involved [in] having knowledge of that additional information. After all, if he had become a recipient, he might also die of "galloping cancer!" So Captain Martin, like Jack Ruby who offered to talk and confess to Chief Justice Warren if the chief justice removed Ruby to Washington away from the guns and stranglers in the Dallas Police Department, was to die with his information securely locked within his brain.

In the testimony of Gary E. Taylor there is no hesitancy by Mr. Taylor to openly assert that there was a conspiracy; but he went further and proceeded to name one of the conspirators! His testimony: "Well, the only thing that occurred to me was that ... uh ... and I guess it was from the beginning ... that if there was any assistance or plotters in the assassination, that it was, in my opinion, most probably the De Mohrenschildts!"

Mr. Taylor was none other than the son-in-law of the man he accused! There is nothing in the "Hearings" that revealed that the aide attempted to develop Mr. Taylor's accusation. After all, one would believe that the aide, as an investigator and attorney with some pride in his profession, would have extended his examination of Mr. Taylor. But he did nothing.

When De Mohrenschildt and his wife were on the witness stand, there was not one single question asked of them regarding their son-in-law's charge of murder and conspiracy! Yet the evidence revealed that this man and woman had gone out of their way to "befriend" the Oswalds. Why? No one knows, for he was never examined on this point. The De Mohrenschildts were sophisticated people, deeply involved in the oil industry, and seemingly very wealthy. By a strange coincidence, he was paid by Texas oil interests that were also interested in securing mineral rights in various "red-leaning" nations. More strange are the various newspapers in foreign nations publishing statements that he was involved with the CIA and with various anti-Cuban Castro groups. But strangest of all "coincidences" is the revelation that he knew Betty MacDonald, the striptease artist who was later murdered in the

Dallas police station (Mrs. Paine and Mr. and Mrs. Lee Harvey Oswald all having attended parties given by Betty). But the Commission was not interested in the De Mohrenschildts, nor in the accusation by their son-in-law that they were "in assistance" or "plotters" in the assassination. What a mockery of the "basic principles of American justice"!

Another person the Commission shied away from was none other than Assistant District Attorney Alexander—he who wanted war with the Soviet Union; he whose background reeks with association with the extreme right-wing un-American groups in this country.

The assistant district attorney was a power in himself. He was so powerful that he was never called before the Warren Commission and asked to give a detailed account of his activity prior to, during, and after the murder of President Kennedy and officer Tippit. Jack Ruby informed the Commission that he and Alexander were very good friends—in fact, they had been for some eight years. They were so friendly that the testimony of Ruby reveals that Ruby relied greatly upon that friendship. In fact, Alexander could have thrown Ruby into prison on several occasions prior to November 24, 1963. As the testimony revealed, Jack Ruby even agreed to everything Alexander told him to do, going so far as to disregard his own attorney representing him prior to the commencement of Ruby's trial.

But Mr. Alexander's activities are more intriguing when analyzed. When Ruby visited the Dallas "Morning News" on the morning of the assassination, who was on the front steps of that building? None other than Assistant District Attorney Alexander. From there, Ruby was seen at Parkland Hospital, and he conversed with Seth Kantor. When Tippit was murdered, who arrived at the Tippit murder scene? Mr. Alexander. And he was in the first police squad car!

When Oswald was arrested in the Texas Theatre, who was at the "back door" of that theater, waiting for Oswald to flee through that door into the guns of the police? None other than Assistant District Attorney Alexander, though he had never in his career as a member of the staff of the district attorney's office sought to assist in the arrest of a man who had refused to pay the price of a 75-cent ticket to enter a second-rate theater.

But somehow, despite the fact [that] he was supposed to be investigating the murder of the president, this assistant D.A. thought so much of upholding "law and order" [that he] found time to assist in the capture of a sneak thief.

Of course, that is one way to look at those facts. A more ominous way would be supported by the testimony; for at no time was the description of Oswald or of Oswald's clothes ever used by the Dallas police [for identifying him] as either a suspect in the murder of President Kennedy or officer Tippit.

But if Alexander knew that Oswald was the "patsy" and knew that Ruby had hired a killer who missed the governor and struck the president, and knew that Tippit was to be shot, and then knew that Oswald was supposed to go to the Texas Theatre, then that would have been the reason why he stationed himself [outside] the back door of that theater, waiting with six other cops to gun down the unknown man who was instructed to run out the rear door. The Commission admitted that Oswald did not match the description of the man sent over the police radio as the Tippit killer. Thus, Alexander could not say he went to that theater to arrest the Tippit murderer. Then why did he go there in a speeding police automobile? To arrest Oswald as the murderer of President Kennedy? No, for no one knew Oswald was wanted. It is incredible that an assistant district attorney would go to arrest a man who "snuck" into the theater, and then hang around the rear door of that theater, unless he had a motive that had absolutely nothing to do with the capture of the sneak thief.

This assistant district attorney was also present when the police illegally searched Oswald's room and gleefully "found" a gun holster which was never seen by Mrs. Roberts at any time. The police knew how to take care of witnesses who called them perjurers. Within a year, Mrs. Roberts was found dead, murdered, and the subservient coroner's office issued a death certificate saying she died of "acute alcoholism." Mrs. Roberts had lived for years as a diabetic, had never drank the smallest amount of liquor according to all those who knew her, and knew that drinking liquor would have killed her. She did not touch it, but some Dallas killer-cop forced a bottle between her lips while she was in the police station after being framed on a "driving while drunk" charge, and she collapsed.

Alexander, playing out his mysterious role in both murders, was to be present at all of Jack Ruby's press conferences. He was present at all press conferences, watching to see that the medical profession kept within bounds regarding the condition of Ruby's "health." He was also at the final press conference when the physicians gave their "honest" report as to the cause of death—"cancer"—but those doctors refused to answer questions of the reporters who demanded to know how Captain Fritz kept Ruby away from all medical attention for two years and how the jail physicians never discovered Ruby's "cancer" until three weeks before his death. Bill Alexander was there for a purpose.

And Bill Alexander, in violation of all the directives of the Warren Commission, was right at the elbows of Commission Chief Earl Warren and Congressman Ford when they examined Jack Ruby in the Dallas jail. And Alexander was there, where Betty MacDonald had been murdered in the same jail, when Ruby pleaded with both of those courageous, upstanding, fearless Americans to take him out of that jail, out of Alexander's sight and reach, so that he could talk to them in Washington, D.C. But that Fearless Twosome had no desire to know; for they knew that the conspirators would kill them if they had any, or accepted any, knowledge of the conspiracy that murdered President Kennedy. And Bill Alexander knew they knew, and so they crept away; and [vanishing] with them [was] the only opportunity for the American people to know who the conspirators were.

And how did all this information reach the eyes and ears of the public? Why, Bill Alexander boasted of his activities of that day on a TV interview with Penn Jones, Jr., the famous investigating editor of "Forgive My Grief." Perhaps if the Commission had the courage of Mr. Jones, Alexander would have boasted to it too.[67]

If ever a person made a mockery of the words "friend" and

---

[67] A brave independent journalist, after Jones received the Elijah Parish Lovejoy Award for Courage in Journalism, President Kennedy sent him a message of congratulations.

"friendship," Mrs. Ruth Paine would head the list. Her activities were carefully researched by the Commission so that her testimony would reveal as little as possible. Through dribs and drabs of testimony came a picture of Mrs. Paine that was a little nauseating to the soul. She set up Oswald to be the perfect "patsy," and she was as friendly to Oswald as another Judas who kissed his friend. Both kisses were to lead to death.

When the Oswald family returned to Irving, Texas they rented a room from Mrs. Ruth Paine. He needed a job, so on the morning of October 14th, 1963 Mrs. Paine contacted Mr. Truly, the Superintendent of the Texas Book Depository. According to him, Mrs. Paine made such an appeal to secure Oswald a job that he consented; and the next day, October 15th, Oswald reported for work at $1.25 per hour. Everyone would say that it was very nice of her to go out of her way for her tenants. That is, unless they knew the truth.

But on the same day he accepted the position from Mr. Truly, Mrs. Paine concealed from Lee Oswald that on the same morning he was being interviewed by Mr. Truly she accepted a phone call from the Texas Employment Commission offering Oswald a job with the airlines as a cargo handler at $25.00 per week higher than what he was offered by Mr. Truly. The Commission "Report" admitted that Oswald did not learn of this higher paying job. Why? Because Mrs. Paine kept silent. And why did she keep silent? Oswald was the "little-bitty" bait for something larger. Oswald never was listed at the Berkley Street rooming house under the name of Lee Harvey Oswald, and at the State Unemployment Commission he had listed his true name, his place of residence as the Paine home, and the Paine's telephone number. Thus, he could only have been called by the State Commission at the Paine home. But Mrs. Paine, that good friend of the Oswalds who felt so sorry for her poor tenants, kept the news from Oswald that he could have a job paying him $25.00 higher than what was offered to him by Mr. Truly of the Book Depository. That is friendship!

Mrs. Paine was to drive many nails into Oswald's body with the hammer she held in her hand.

Mrs. Paine testified that although she had assisted Oswald in obtaining employment at the Book Depository, she believed that he was to work in the warehouse and that she never knew where Mr. Truly's office was located. What she could not have forgotten was that she also testified that she gave Mr. Truly's office address to Oswald when she informed her "patsy" to go for an interview. That office address was not the warehouse, which is located several blocks away from the Depository, but in the Depository itself. Furthermore, Mrs. Paine was well acquainted with that location, for her home in Irving, Texas must pass that building when one drives from Irving to Dallas. The Commission calmly accepted her "explanation."

To corroborate her "friendship," Mrs. Paine admitted that the map found in Oswald's rooming house had been made with her assistance to guide Oswald in his search for employment when he moved from New Orleans—with the help of Mr. and Mrs. Paine, who used their green-[and-]white station wagon—to Irving, Texas. But Mrs. Paine kept her sympathy to herself when she kept her mouth shut as the Dallas police, under Captain Fritz, Chief Curry, and District Attorney Wade proclaimed in three consecutive news conferences that the map "convicted" Oswald of the premeditated murder of President Kennedy.

Mrs. Paine was more than a friend, for from the day she gave her "friendship" to Oswald she was also furnishing reports to the Federal Bureau of Investigation—as both she and the Commission admitted. The FBI's weak, lame excuse that they kept no watch on Oswald as a "subversive" is denied by Mrs. Paine and by their own Agent Hosty, who was vividly accused by Oswald [of] "accosting" his wife, Marina. And "accosting" as used by Oswald when he saw Hosty in the Dallas police station did not mean saying "hello."

Far more damaging than all of Mrs. Paine's testimony was that given to the Commission by Deputy Sheriff Walthers—so damaging that it is reprinted here:

WALTHERS: (Examined by aide W. Liebeler.) "... at this address in Irving and when we went to the door, what turned out to be Mrs. Paine—JUST AS SOON AS WE STEPPED ON THE PORCH SHE SAID, 'Come on in, we've been expecting you,' and we didn't have any trouble at all—we just went right on in and started asking her—at that time it didn't appear that her or Mrs. Oswald, or Marina, who came up carrying one of the babies in the living room—it didn't appear that they knew that Oswald had been arrested at all—the way they talked."

LIEBELER: "How do you account for the fact that Mrs. Paine said, 'Come on in, we've been expecting you'?"

WALTHERS: "I don't know—to this day, I don't know."

LIEBELER: "Are you sure that's what she said?"

WALTHERS: "I know that's what she said."

LIEBELER: "Mrs. Paine said that?"

WALTHERS: "Yes, sir, she said: 'Come on in, we've been expecting you.'"

But Mr. Liebeler—who was to rise from attorney, to assistant professor of law, to professor of law in a leading law school, and who was to challenge all the critics of the "Report" as idiots and scavengers, and who in 1967 was to publicly state that he was going to use the services of his 22 law students to prove the critics phonies—never thought of examining Mrs. Paine regarding her statement that clearly implied she knew that Oswald was to be involved as a suspect in the murder of President Kennedy. Liebeler tried his best to shake the deputy, but he only succeeded in emphasizing the fact that Mrs. Paine had foreknowledge of Oswald's "involvement." He did not desire to become involved in obtaining facts, in the same manner as Justice Warren and Congressman Ford [had] turned their backs on information offered to them by Jack Ruby.

Still the testimony in the "Hearings" keeps pointing to a conspiracy, but the aides and the commissioners wanted no part of it.

The Commission also had the testimony of a fellow worker of Mrs. Paine's husband, Michael. Mike was the same witness who informed the Commission that he believed that the "curtain rods" found in his garage could have been purchased by Oswald. While at work, Mike and a fellow employee, Ray Krystinik, during their lunch hour, were informed by a waitress that both President Kennedy and officer Tippit had been shot and Oswald captured. From the mouth of Mike Paine came the surprised words to the ears of Ray: "He is not even supposed to have a gun!" Ray's testimony stated: "And that I can quote, 'He is not even supposed to have a gun' or 'Not even supposed to own a gun,' I have forgotten." Ray also said that Mike said Oswald was a "stupid something, I have forgotten. It was not a complimentary thing."

Again, there is no further discussion of the matter by the aide nor, in the examination of Mike Paine's testimony, is there any discussion of him concerning those expressions. Thus, Mr. and Mrs. Paine knew more than what they said to the aide; but the aide, despite the fact that both Paines were implicated in some manner in the plot by independent witnesses, had no desire to have any formal knowledge of the conspiracy. The Paine station wagon, the exact duplicate of the one seen by both Deputy Sheriff Craig and Mr. Robinson, was not in the garage at 3 p.m. when she was visited on the afternoon of the murder by Deputy Walthers. But that did not concern the Commission; they wanted Oswald, and get him they would.

Why would Mrs. Paine, unless she forgot during the excitement of knowing that the president had been murdered, inform a deputy sheriff to "come right in, we're expecting you" unless she knew that Oswald would be traced to the Irving address? Why did she expect to see the police when, at the time the deputy appeared at her home, Oswald's name was yet to be given to the mass communication media at approximately 3 p.m. as a suspect in the murder of the president? Why would her husband call Oswald a "stupid son of a bitch," and why would he say "he was not even supposed to have a gun"? There was no mention on the public TV or radio system that Oswald had a gun when captured. How did Mike Paine know he had no gun?

All these are little pieces of "flotsam and jetsam," but added together they slowly fit within the jigsaw puzzle. Mrs. Paine turns out not to be a friend but rather a sinister person who carefully pulled several strings guiding friend Oswald toward a certain goal.

Bill Alexander hovers around in places a man in his high position as the senior assistant district attorney would never be watching, and directing traffic leading to the conspiracy. The aides refused to permit Captain Martin to talk, and he dies of "apparent cancer"! The Dallas coroner's office, faking the autopsy report on officer Tippit, continued to produce fraudulent reports regarding the murder of Betty MacDonald, who supposedly hung herself in the city jail within thirty minutes after being placed in a cell. And how did she hang herself? By taking one leg of her toreador pants, wrapping it around the jail window bar, and wrapping the other one around her neck. Betty was so small that it was impossible for the length of the pants to go around her neck and around the jail bars! She was strangled to death.[68]

This is the same Betty MacDonald who was the witness to place the Paines, the De Mohrenschildts, and the Oswalds as social equals at the same social functions; the De Mohrenschildts who were accused by their own son-in-law [of] being in the conspiracy. The U.S. Secret Service informed the Commission that persons were impersonating themselves as agents of that agency. Yet, the commissioners and their 26 aides, so lacking in courage, so weak in spite of their power to protect themselves with the full weight of the federal government, were to proclaim no conspiracy.

The activity of the Warren Commissioners and their 26 aides violated every concept of the "basic principles of American justice." Not only did they deliberately conceal the conspiracy but they committed a rape of the American conscience. There can be no forgiving when that rape destroyed the soul of the nation.

The Warren Commissioners not only knew from the very first meeting that a conspiracy murdered President Kennedy, but they had in their possession fully substantiated evidence given to them by the Federal Bureau of Investigation and the U.S. Secret Service that Lee Harvey Oswald was not the "sole and exclusive killer of President Kennedy." Within three months they had been given overwhelming evidence not only of the nature of the conspiracy but the names of a few of the actual conspirators. The contempt and cynicism of the commissioners

---

[68] Nancy Jane Mooney, aka Betty MacDonald, was found dead in her jail cell on February 13, 1964.

and their aides is evidenced by the Willens[69] memo to J. Lee Rankin, the Commission's general counsel, that the "Report" was being written three months prior to the examination of all the evidence and witnesses being completed.

The testimony, the documents, the exhibits, are not rumors or speculations. They were obtained under oath and the plain use of the English language reveals the conspiracy.

Every dictator proclaims the establishment of his dictatorship under the guise of "in the interests of national security." Every democracy in history has been overthrown under that phrase. In the United States, a nibbling of the democratic process has been under way—in other words, the enemies are using the "salami" tactics of both the Right and the Left. But then, that can be expected when a nation throws away the youth in a stupid war some seven thousand miles away from its shorelines to "protect" the "democracy" of another nation whose dictator openly throws its political opponents in prison or silently executes them with the tacit approval of the nation offering its youth in a blood bath on behalf of the dictators.

History has proven that once assassination has become the weapon by which to change the government, that style and form of government preceding the assassination falls beneath the hard-nailed boots of the assassins. Both Right and Left favor no democratic spirit in the people. The cold of Siberia and the heat ovens of the concentration camps proved it.

The tragedy of the Warren Commission is that it helped set those boots on the road to the destruction of American democracy.

---

[69] Although he was a Commission defender until the very end, in a 2019 email interview conducted with author Jefferson Morley, Howard Willens stated: "I agree that my journal comments about the CIA were naive, to say the least. As you probably know, the CIA officials who were designated to work closely with the Warren Commission later testified that they personally did not know about the assassination plots being considered by the agency during the 1960-63 period. Deputy Director for Plans Richard Helms, of course, did know about the plots and did not tell the truth to the Warren Commission when he testified. It is clear that the CIA 'did have an axe to grind' during our investigation." See jfkfacts.org.

It would not be fair to Mr. Dulles not to accept his challenge flung to the American people to prove a conspiracy and name the assassins. To "name the assassins" cannot be done, either by the author or the "general public." A conspiracy has been proven beyond a reasonable doubt. But what was the purpose of the conspiracy?

History has shown that an invisible coup d'état occurred when President Kennedy was murdered. It is the belief of the author that more than the murder of a head of state was involved. This belief is based on two events that occurred during the three years President Kennedy occupied the White House: (1) The Bay of Pigs, and (2) The Cuban Missile Crisis.

The citizens of the United States, living in a dream world concocted by the mass communication systems, have been constantly told that a conspiracy to murder any president would be impossible, since that kind of secret could not be kept. Overlooked, or rather not brought to their attention, is the fact that all political assassinations involve a conspiracy. Some are exposed; some are successful. President De Gaulle of France was the target of five conspiracies, each a failure. Between 200 and 400 persons were involved in the conspiracies, with the leaders of those attacks being in the highest places of the French government. Yet, outside of those persons involved, the French general public never learned of the conspiracies until the failure, capture, and imprisonment of the conspirators. So, as history has shown, conspirators do keep their mouths shut.

The involvement of various executives and police officers of the Dallas Police Department has been proven beyond a reasonable doubt. With the police department riddled by members of the Birch Society and the KKK (a lieutenant of the Dallas police department was a "Grand Dragon" in 1963), it was an easy task for the Texas oil and steel industry to organize the "task force" that murdered President Kennedy. These men operated on the philosophy of supplying the money but left the details with others.

The Warren Commission not only revealed a strange reluctance to question members and leaders of the KKK but a downright fear of questioning the leaders of the John Birch Society in Texas, although their names were brought into the testimony. The Commission, for example, showed a blind eye to the fact that the FBI could not locate a member of the H. L. Hunt family, who gave some of the immoral advertisement money calling for the death of a "Red" President Kennedy. But Jack Ruby knew where to locate the H. L. Hunt family!

Is it more than a mere coincidence that the private secretary to the president of the Lone Star Steel Company was appointed to be the right-hand confidential secretary to the President of the United States, Lyndon B. Johnson, and then promoted to be the postmaster general of the United States when the Lone Star Steel Company's president is on the executive board of the John Birch Society of Texas?[70]

The life of President Kennedy was only an incident to bring into operation the main purpose of the conspiracy. The conspiracy was a four-pronged affair: (1) the murder of President Kennedy; (2) the invasion and overthrow of the Castro regime in Cuba, with the installation of a right-wing dictatorship under the direct control of the CIA, which is, in turn, controlled by the fascist forces in the United States; (3) involvement with a war with the Soviet Union; but, if that not be possible, a complete diplomatic break with the Soviet Union, isolating that nation by the new government in the United States by exerting economic pressure upon NATO and nations receiving our foreign aid; and (4) a "coup d'état."

The testimony in the "Hearings" has given some glimmering that the four-prong conspiracy is not speculation. The background of Lee Harvey Oswald supports the thesis; for he did everything that would cast suspicion on the Soviet Union as being involved. The willingness of all agencies of the federal government, State, Navy, Army, Marine, Secret Service, Bureau of Immigration and Naturalization, Office of Naval Intelligence, the CIA, and the FBI, to assist Oswald in maintaining his fiction that he was a loyal and willing servant

---

[70] W. Marvin Watson, Jr. was actually the executive assistant to the president of the Lone Star Steel Company in Dallas. President Johnson tapped him to serve as "appointments secretary" in January 1965. According to Watson's *Washington Post* obit, he was LBJ's "chief of staff in all but name." He also served as postmaster general.

of Communism. Oswald's ease in obtaining passports was not due to his good looks; nor would an intelligence agent acting on behalf of the Soviet Union openly appear on the steps of the Mexican, Cuban, or Soviet Consulates so that "hidden" FBI and CIA agents could snap his picture. Hitler, to convince his people that the Polish soldiers had invaded Germany in September 1939 simply had prisoners shot who were dressed in Polish Army uniforms, placed their bodies near the German— Polish border, and took their pictures.

The research done by Popkin in his "The Second Oswald;" by Mark Lane in his two excellent books; by Weisberg in his four-volumes of "Whitewash," and by Meagher in her "Accessories After the Fact" prove beyond a reasonable doubt that Lee Harvey Oswald had more than one double traveling around the southern part of the United States. The evidence published on the previous pages of this book also proved the existence of Oswald "doubles."

In Popkin's book he uncovered the evidence that, three days prior to the murder, two men and a woman appeared at the Red Bird Airport outside of Dallas and attempted to hire an airplane that had a long-range capacity.[71] The plane was to be hired for a flight on the day of November 22, 1963 for an unknown destination. The owner of the airport refused the request, and he stated one of men "looked" like Oswald. He was never shown a picture of Mr. Ferrie, the man charged by Mr. Garrison, the D..A. of New Orleans, as being one of the conspirators. Nor did the Warren Commission deem it fit and proper to investigate Professor Popkin's facts. Why did the FBI inform the Dallas Police Intelligence Division that Oswald was "all right," according to that division's memo dated February [17], 1964? Oswald was known by the FBI to be on the payroll of the CIA; and, in turn, Oswald was a paid informer for the FBI!

After the murder of President Kennedy, members of the conspiracy were to take off from the Dallas independent airport

---

[71] The Red Bird Airfield event, which was already being commented on in the early days of research, was later explored in depth by Matthew Smith in *The Second Plot* (Edinburgh, UK: Mainstream Publishing, 1992).

and fly direct to Cuba. Upon landing they were to proclaim the fact that they had murdered the president of the United States and were seeking political asylum. With Oswald's background secure in the smokescreen that he was an outstanding "communist"," the reader can well imagine what would have happened in the United States. Bismarck, by changing a word in a telegram prior to the French—German War in the 1870's, brought about the defeat of France. The mass communication media, backed by the right-wing forces in Congress and among the public, would have whipped the public into a frenzy to invade Cuba. And that would have happened. "Remember the Maine!" In 1963: "Remember Kennedy!"

But, the reader may ask, "Where did the Soviet Union come into the picture?"

In Manchester's book[72] is a single paragraph which far too many people who have read the book have overlooked. The author claims that on the afternoon after the death of President Kennedy, Assistant District Attorney Alexander sought to present to the press and television media an affidavit charging

---

[72] Dallas "brooded about its image, unaware that the watching country would regard that very anxiety as suspect. In the Baker Hotel's Club Imperial and in the Republic and Mercantile Bank buildings there was a deepening worry that the bad publicity might get worse. Civic leaders were glum. The Dallas Chamber of Commerce issued a statement of regret over the president's death. Late Friday afternoon District Attorney Henry M. Wade, the man responsible for the assassin's prosecution, departed his office for a social function and failed to leave a number at which he could be reached, but his second assistant, William F. 'Bill' Alexander, prepared to charge Oswald with murdering the president 'as part of an international Communist conspiracy.' Perhaps that canard would have absolved Dallas. The indictment could have had grave repercussions abroad, however, and although it had already been drawn up, when [U.S. Attorney H.] Barefoot Sanders heard of it from the FBI he phoned [U.S. Attorney General] Nick Katzenbach, who persuaded two members of the vice president's Washington staff to have their Texas contacts kill it." Manchester, *The Death of a President* (New York: Harper & Row, 1988), p 287.

the Soviet Union as being the principal agent in the murder! However, prior to the Manchester book, there appeared similar stories in the New York "Herald-Tribune" (May 16, 1964) and the Washington "Post." This method of insanity would have brought on a war, for no nation could accept such a charge that it had directed the murder of the head of another nation. That is a charge of war under international law. There is no doubt that the mass communication media would have accepted Alexander's charges, for they accepted everything that was "dished" out by the Dallas authorities. They have even accepted, as of today, the blatant lies "dished" out by the Commission, so what was a "little atomic war" to that media? They accepted, in toto, the "faked" indictment held by Alexander's pictures; why would they not accept another faked piece of paper held by Alexander for a few more pictures? Manchester stated that when the State Department heard of his proposed insane act it rushed an assistant secretary of state to plead with Alexander not to do this rash act. What other pleading was made by the State Department is [not] known. But it is significant that the Warren Commission made no comment upon Alexander's proposed act. Was their refusal to investigate Alexander's conduct due to the fact [that] they knew who was behind his psychotic behavior? That they knew the oil men who openly boasted on the night of the murder at the "social" and "victory" dinner dance—which was attended by District Attorney Wade—that "war with the communists would come within 24 hours"?

The reader should not have forgotten that, at 2 p.m. on that day, the new president of the United States ordered an immediate "red alert." This was applicable, as he explained, to all our military forces in all parts of the world, including our Polaris submarines and our bases on the fringes of the U.S.S.R. The plot was a hair's breadth from success. An itchy trigger finger on one of those bases, in one of those subs, in one of those airplanes flying toward Soviet territory, and the war would occur. If Alexander's proposed insane act had been accomplished, there would be no world today!

In this crisis, President Johnson turned not to the CIA but to the former ambassador to the Soviet Union. It was the ambassador who convinced the new president that the Soviets do not engage in the policy of murdering heads of states and never have. Messages to Moscow and other foreign capitals revealed that there were no out of the ordinary movements by either the Russian military or the citizenry; that also convinced the president that the Soviets were not involved in any adventure. Another phone call to Guantanamo Naval Base in Cuba also revealed that that sector was quiet.

It may seem like a screenplay scenario, but if one looks back into history the United States was nearly led into war by the CIA on two other occasions. The first one was the U-2 affair which destroyed, for the time, any detente between the U.S. and USSR. That affair was strictly a CIA affair designed for the long-sought war between the two countries. It must be recalled that a mysterious "red alert" was flashed to the armed services while President Eisenhower was in Paris with the premier of the Soviet Union sitting right beside the president. Why the Soviets would seek a war [while] their premier and defense minister [were] in Paris is unknown. But at the same time that "red alert" was flashed the CIA, in violation of the president's order, again sent a U-2 over the borders of the Soviet Union near the Turkish border. The CIA was then, as it is now, more powerful than the president the United States.

The other example of CIA interference with the commander in chief of the armed forces, the president, occurred during the Cuban Missile Crisis. Again, in direct violation of President Kennedy's orders, the CIA, during the negotiations on the third and fourth day of the crisis, sent a U-2 plane into Soviet Siberia. The excuse was that "the plane had strayed off its course." What was it doing there in the first place?

That was the four-pronged conspiracy. The conspiracy achieved two of its objectives—the murder of President Kennedy and the coup d'état. With that coup d'état came a new philosophy of government in the United States. It is now permissible, as long as the coup succeeds, to assassinate any future president. With the murder of President Kennedy also came a new direction in both the federal and state governments. President Johnson was to promise "no American boys" in Asiatic wars until November 4, 1964. After that he was to cynically send a half-million or more boys on behalf his friends in Texas to protect their interests in Vietnam. Mr. Nixon was to make the same promise, which he promptly forgot when he assumed the presidency.

And so, the ship of state sails on—but to where, no one knows.

The conspiracy that murdered President John F. Kennedy was well planned; it was not well kept, for both the FBI and the U.S. Secret Service knew well in advance of the murder they permitted to take place in Dallas. And thus, the conspiracy deliberately changed the course of world history.

CHAPTER X

THREE TRIALS
Clay Shaw
Sirhan B. Sirhan
James Earl Ray

Preface to "Three Trials":

The outstanding characteristic of Lee Harvey Oswald, Sirhan B. Sirhan, and James Earl Ray is the fact that all three of them, although of very poor families and earning very poor wages, could travel around the country with no visible funds. Who gave Oswald the money to travel from New Orleans, to Dallas, to Los Angeles, to Mexico, and everywhere he wanted to go? How did James Earl Ray obtain the various sums of money to travel around the United States, secure a fake passport, go to London, then [to] Portugal, and then back to London? He was supposed to have left a trail of robberies, but for some strange reason the FBI was never able to catch up to that trail. Of course, there also seemed to be no witnesses who identified Ray as the robber. As to Sirhan B. Sirhan, he also seemed to travel.

One of the strangest stories came out of Dallas, Texas after Sirhan B. Sirhan was arrested and his photograph published in the Dallas press. The two newspapers received several telephone calls that Sirhan B. Sirhan looked like the young man who shot down officer Tippit! Mrs. Markham's testimony, substantiated by D. Benavides and the Davis sisters, said the killer had "curly hair" and was "dark complected." The age of the Tippit killer was around 18 to 20 years old [according to] one witness. Sirhan, in 1963, was of that age period. A remarkable resemblance, but no one questioned Sirhan as to where he was on November 22, 1963, and no one will. Finally, the key woman witness in the London boarding house who personally knew the difference between the two "Earl Rays" arrested at the London airport has now disappeared and is believed to have been murdered. She disappeared at a very convenient time. The same "coincidence" as in the harassment and death of Mrs. Roberts, also a boarding-room keeper of an alleged murderer. The London housekeeper was also harassed by the London police, the CIA, and the Special Branch; but who committed that woman's murder is unknown. In Mrs. Roberts' case, it was the police.

A. The Clay Shaw Trial—A Conspiracy Proved

The trial of Clay Shaw for the felony of participating in a conspiracy to murder President Kennedy was one of the most bizarre trials in the history of American criminal law. Clay Shaw was found "not guilty" by a jury of his peers.

Never has a defendant in any crime been so ably defended by the full power of the federal government—from the Attorney General of the United States, Mr. Ramsey Clark, to a half dozen governors of various states. Not only was the Department of Justice used to defend Shaw, but the Central Intelligence Agency was thrown into the battle on his behalf.

Figuratively speaking, Mr. Garrison, the district attorney of New Orleans, had less chance than the proverbial snowball in hell to convict Shaw.

The previous pages of this book have clearly established the existence of a conspiracy that murdered President Kennedy. However, what is not understood by the nonlawyers of the population is the legal principle distinguishing between a "conspiracy to commit" murder and a "conspiracy that committed murder." Under the laws of Louisiana, Clay Shaw was indicted for a "conspiracy to murder" President Kennedy. He was not accused of being a member of the conspiracy that did murder President Kennedy. Unless that is understood, no one can understand the Shaw trial. Mr. Garrison did prove beyond a reasonable doubt in the Shaw trial that a conspiracy did murder the president; but, being hampered by the federal government, under President Johnson, and by various governors, Garrison did not prove that Shaw was a member of any conspiracy.

In the opinion of this author the jury's verdict of "not guilty" was proper, but that verdict, contrary to newspaper opinion, did not imply or state that no conspiracy existed. The jury's verdict simply said that Clay Shaw, based on the evidence presented to them, was not a member of any conspiracy to murder the president.

Hampering Garrison's case against Shaw was the law regarding extradition. Under the Constitution of the United States the power to return a person for an alleged criminal act to a state requesting that person's presence rests solely upon the governor of the state where the person is then residing. Many of the persons that Mr. Garrison desired to extradite to Louisiana were indicted by a legally created grand jury in the Parish of New Orleans for an alleged crime which did not involve the sought-for person in the conspiracy. Extradition can only be applied, in the vast majority of cases, to a criminal case. There has been no extradition proceeding in which the Department of Justice has ever entered the proceedings to protest the extradition of the person sought—except in the Clay Shaw case!

There have been exceedingly few extraditions not permitted by a governor, and in those proceedings where extradition has not been granted it has generally been on the issue of failure of the person to obtain a fair trial, or where the person sought has led an exemplary life in the state where he now lives. After long and arduous research of available legal records, this author could find no proceeding for extradition being dismissed by the governor of the state where the wanted person had been indicted by a grand jury for a felony and the governor had refused to grant extradition. Governor Rhodes of Ohio[73] refused to grant extradition in the Shaw case in spite of the fact that the wanted person had been indicted for a felony not connected with that case. The governor's statement limited the district attorney to

---

[73] On May 3, 1970, Governor Rhodes sent the National Guard to Kent State University after the burning of an ROTC building. During protests the following day, Guardsmen killed four students and wounded nine others, causing a national uproar.

questioning only in the felony case and not to any other alleged crimes, i.e. membership in the conspiracy to murder President Kennedy. Naturally, Mr. Garrison refused to accept that condition, for it is the first time in the history of this nation that a person, once indicted, can never be questioned or indicted for another felony in the state from whence he fled. This was the type of conduct that hampered Mr. Garrison's case against Mr. Shaw.

However, not only did the various governors fight Mr. Garrison's attempt to delve into the conspiracy, but the various federal district attorneys also refused to issue warrants against the wanted persons who could have been arrested under the federal code of "fleeing the jurisdiction and prosecution of state in a felony case." The Department of Justice, headed by President Johnson's lifelong friend, Ramsey Clark, evidently did not believe that the conspiracy warranted any investigation by a grand jury. But the Department of Justice was to thrust itself deep into the construction of Clay Shaw's defense and Jim Garrison's prosecution of Shaw.

The background of the Shaw trial is lengthy, but when the New Orleans Grand Jury on March 2, 1967 issued its indictment of Clay Shaw, David Ferrie, Lee Harvey Oswald (deceased), et al, charging them with conspiring to murder President Kennedy, the Department of Justice sprang to Shaw's defense like a greyhound bounding from the gate in pursuit of a jackrabbit. That's speed!

Mr. Ramsey Clark, the Attorney General of the United States, official head of the Department of Justice, and superior to the FBI, immediately called a press conference and stated that Mr. Shaw had been thoroughly investigated by the FBI in November and December of 1963. With that statement, Mr. Clark put in his mouth his big foot from Texas. An enterprising reporter for the New York "Times" then commenced a search of the Warren "Report" and the available public records in the National Archives and never located the name of Clay Shaw. The Department of Justice had no comment to the same reporter's question as to why Shaw's name was not mentioned in any FBI report, in the "Report," or in the National Archives files.

From March 2, 1967 until June 13, 1967, the Department of Justice kept a discreet silence. On the latter day the Department of Justice then issued a press release that Mr. Clark was "mistaken." The question then arose how did the Justice Department know, within 24 hours after Shaw had been indicted, that he had been under investigation by the FBI? Furthermore, why had Shaw been investigated by the FBI and on what facts did the FBI base their "clearance" of Shaw in the murder of President Kennedy? No answer!

An investigation of the "Report" and the "Hearings" revealed that a New Orleans attorney, Dean Andrews, had represented several homosexuals of Cuban nationality who had been sent to him to represent by a "Clay Bertrand." Mr. Andrews testified that they had in their conversations mentioned a Lee Harvey Oswald. Mr. Andrews had been seeking this "Clay Bertrand" because he had guaranteed [to pay the] legal fees in defending those homosexual friends of "Bertrand."

On March 3, 1967 the New York "Post" carried the story that its Washington. D.C. correspondent had been informed by a Department of Justice spokesman [that] he was convinced that "Mr. Bertrand and Mr. Shaw were the same man."

Leaning over backward to protect the rights of the defendant Shaw, Garrison, on his own motion, requested a preliminary hearing under a procedure that would permit a court of law to determine whether or not the district attorney (Mr. Garrison) had presented sufficient facts to the grand jury to sustain the indictment—not the guilt—of Clay Shaw. Thus, it was the mass communication system that placed the brand of "publicity seeker" upon Garrison—not his activity.

Knowing the importance of the case, Mr. Garrison then requested a trial to be conducted by three judges who would rule upon the legality of the indictment. In an attempt to have the indictment ruled invalid, Shaw immediately requested that the three judges rule (1) that the Warren "Report" be ruled legally binding upon the state of Louisiana; (2) if that "Report" be ruled a legal document, then the indictment against Shaw be dismissed, since the "Report" definitely stated that there was (a) no conspiracy, and (b) the sole and only assassin of President Kennedy was Lee Harvey Oswald, deceased. In a four-day legal battle, the three-judge panel unanimously upheld the indictment and legally stated that the "Warren Report was 'hearsay piled upon hearsay'"! In other words, that "Report" was not worth the paper it was printed upon, and the 8 conclusions of the Warren Commission were not upheld by any testimony or evidence that proved Lee Harvey Oswald was the "sole killer of President Kennedy."

With that ruling, Shaw was to fight for a reversal in the state judicial system, and he lost. He was also to lose in the federal courts: from the district [court], the appeals [court], and finally, the U.S. Supreme Court denied him the right to appeal to them for a ruling. Thus, the final decision by the U.S. Supreme court upheld the decision of the three-judge panel in Louisiana that the Warren Report was "hearsay piled upon hearsay" and, hence, the conclusions of the Warren Commission have no validity whatsoever!

With deliberate foresight, every major newspaper, radio, [and] television system refused to comment upon that legal decision rendered by the highest court of this nation. Their advertising revenues would be lost if they aggravated The Establishment, which manufactured automobiles, radios, oil, gas, and oh, so many businesses that used those facilities.

"Justice delayed is justice denied!"[74] That is the concept of justice applied to any person seeking redress in any court of this land—civil or criminal. But when it is the defendant who seeks delay after delay, then no district attorney should be held up to scorn and ridiculed by the press. Yet, that was what the press continued to do for two long years, from March 1967 to January

---

[74] "The idea is said to have first been expressed in the biblical writings of Pirkei Avot 5:8, a section of the Mishnah (1st century BCE—2nd century CE) in which it is stated 'Our Rabbis taught: ...[t]he sword comes into the world, because of justice delayed and justice denied...'; as well as in the Magna Carta of 1215, cl 40 of which reads, '[t]o no one will we sell, to no one will we refuse or delay, right or justice.' Martin Luther King Jr. also said 'justice too long delayed is justice denied' in his Letter from Birmingham Jail (August 1963)." Tania Sourdin and Naomi Burstyner, "Justice Delayed is Justice Denied," January 24, 2016, SSRN (online), ssrn.com, p. 1, n. 1.

1969. It was Clay Shaw who delayed his trial, free on bail, while the federal government, through its Department of Justice and Central Intelligence Agency scurried around, from state to state, from pillar to post, in an attempt to intimidate Mr. Garrison or subvert those witnesses needed by Garrison to prove a conspiracy existed. It was not Jim Garrison who attempted to suborn justice, it was those two federal agencies.

It was Mr. Ramsey Clark, the attorney general of the United States, who directed an FBI Agent, Mr. Regis Kennedy of the New Orleans office, to claim "executive privilege" when he was summoned before the New Orleans Grand Jury investigating the conspiracy that was organized in that city. The implication of Clark's action is that, from that time on, no federal employee may be called before any jury to discuss any criminal activity which the FBI [is] investigating. But far more damaging is the implication that Mr. Clark was protecting "interests" higher than his department! Mr. Clark was saying that NO grand jury, federal or state, can investigate the death of President Kennedy, for the FBI would be prevented from presenting any evidence that they obtained that led to a conspiracy that either was incomplete or completed. In the entire history of the Department of Justice no agent of the FBI had been forbidden to discuss his activity before a grand jury uncovering criminals or crimes. Of course, Mr. Ramsey was also protecting the FBI from testifying [about] the Miami, Florida police tapes and the FBI's TWX[75] messages received by the FBI New Orleans bureau!

One of the witnesses sought by Mr. Garrison fled to the protective cover of the CIA—the agency that openly defied President Kennedy after he commanded it to cease arming airplanes and ships for assaults on Cuba. The witness, Mr. Novel, was a little more intelligent than Miss Kilgallen, who was mysteriously murdered after she proclaimed her intention to publish her interview with Jack Ruby given to her during his trial for murdering Lee Harvey Oswald. Although Novel was

---

[75] TWX: a switched teleprinter network first developed in 1932 by AT&T. An FBI memo unearthed by Mark Lane documents the TWX message discussed here by Marks.

charged by the New Orleans Grand Jury as being a participant in the conspiracy to murder President Kennedy, the U.S. district attorney in the McLean, Va. district refused to issue a fugitive warrant. This district attorney knew the law, but he also knew that he served at the pleasure of the president of the United States. So the district attorney, under the command of Ramsey Clark, refused to issue the warrant.

To save his life, Novel resorted to the expedient of writing to his attorney that he had placed certain documents and papers with persons inside and outside the United States to be opened upon his death. Since he was a CIA agent and attached to the "Double Chek" company that supplied flyers and fighters in the anti-Castro front, Novel was in possession of certain facts concerning the anti-Kennedy faction of this Batista—CIA organization.[76] Novel, a man of no substance, was suddenly able to secure the services of various high-priced attorneys in every state he fled to escape extradition. The CIA supplied him with a $10,000 cash bond, and, mysteriously, on May 21, 1967, six shots were fired at him while he sat in a station wagon. To this day Novel has remained in the sovereign state of Ohio, fully aware that if he leaves that area he is a dead man. The CIA is satisfied even though Novel's lawyer, Mr. Plotkin, admitted that Novel was a CIA agent. Mr. Novel also admitted that he and Clay Shaw were very close friends.[77]

---

[76] Based in Miami, Double Chek was a CIA front company that supplied planes for the Bay of Pigs invasion. It also employed E. Howard Hunt, who ran a domestic propaganda operation during the invasion.

[77] "Novel's own lawyer, Stephen Plotkin, has admitted that his client is a CIA agent. On May 23, 1967, Plotkin was quoted in the New Orleans States–Item as saying that 'his client served as an intermediary between the CIA and anti–Castro Cubans in New Orleans and Miami prior to the April 1961 Bay of Pigs invasion.' And that same day, the Associated Press, which has hardly served as my press agent in this case, reported: 'When Novel first fled from New Orleans, he headed straight for McLean, Virginia, which is the Central Intelligence Agency suburb. This is not surprising, because Gordon Novel was a CIA employee in the early Sixties.' There is no

With all that protection embracing him, Shaw remained somewhat of a mystery man. According to the press in this country, he was a "gentleman, an outstanding soldier, a playwright, an interior decorator, and a businessman of impeccable reputation." That is what the press was told to write, but when Mr. Clay Shaw's background is taken out of his CIA cocoon a different man with an entirely different character and reputation bursts forth.

What constitutes a "gentleman" is subject to interpretation of the manners and morals of the time when that gentleman lives. Whether Shaw is a gentleman is determined by a person's interpretation of the following items discovered by virtue of a search warrant obtained by District Attorney Garrison in Shaw's home: 5 whips, various lengths of steel chain, three pieces of rope, one black hood and cape, one black net-type hat, one black gown, and one shotgun and case. Mr. Shaw's keepsakes are, to say the least, a little bent toward the Marquis de Sade.

As to his soldiering and business background, Shaw's former occupation was nothing more than a "rear echelon" activity in France, while Mr. Garrison's was flying a Piper Cub directly over the enemy lines for artillery-spotting targets. For business activity in the United States, Mr. Shaw was president of the permanent trade exhibit in New Orleans.

But as to his "business" activity outside the United States, the picture is not so beautiful a scene. After World War II, Mr. Shaw became associated with a mysterious "Centro Mondiale Commerciale" and a company known as "Permindex." Shaw was also associated with a highly classified CIA operation known as "Force III," and with this operation he was given the code name of "Dreyfus" (ironic, for both Oswald and Shaw were to become "patsies," as had Dreyfus).[78]

---

doubt that Gordon Novel was a CIA operative." Jim Garrison, "Jim Garrison: Playboy Interview," *Playboy* magazine, October 1967.

[78] It's likely that Stanley first discovered this information in the March 21, 1969 edition of the *Los Angeles Free Press*, a paper that he regularly read and in which he placed several ads for his books. Accompanying an article on page 8 titled "Jim Garrison's closing

This "Centro Mondiale Commerciale" had within its organization such stalwart believers in democracy as the OAS, which attempted to murder De Gaulle five times and also to overthrow the French Republic; various members and officials of Mussolini's Fascist Party; a few Nazi Hungarians, such as Mr. Nagy, still wanted for war crimes in turning their own people over to the Nazis; and a man whose daughter-in-law was none other than the daughter of Hitler's financial wizard, Hjalmar Schacht. Another associate of Mr. Shaw in this Italian corporation was none other than G. Mantello, who was evicted from Switzerland, with the Nazi Nagy,[79] for "criminal activity."

Mr. Shaw was no mere employee—he was a member of the board of directors, so he could not claim loss of memory as to

---

argument at the Shaw trial," Art Kunkin featured an "Editor's Note": "I find it very difficult to understand why the attempt was not made in court to question Clay Shaw about his known and acknowledged links with Central Intelligence Agency fronts in Europe; his possible involvement, using the name 'Dreyfus,' with the CIA project called Force Three; his possible involvement, according to information in Garrison's files, with other people from New Orleans' Trade Mart in a plot to bomb Cuba in 1947 from a Florida airport rented by a 'Shaw'; or about his job duties at the Trade Mart, which alone make it very probable that he was a government agency operative." I can find no other mention of Clay Shaw as "Dreyfus" or of "Force III" in any JFK research sources. After viewing this information, James DiEugenio wondered if it may have been included in one of the Jim Garrison files that were destroyed or that have since disappeared. The same edition of the *Los Angeles Free Press* features a banner-headline story titled "Is There More Than One James Earl Ray? London publisher's findings point directly to conspiracy." Marks seems to have relied on this article when discussing the Ray case. The *Los Angeles Free Press* often proved to be a rich source of information for his research.

[79] Ferenc Nagy, former prime minister of Hungary who was forced to reign in 1947. After the Second World War, Hjalmar Schacht (né Horace Greeley Hjalmar Schacht) was arrested by the German government and sentenced to eight years imprisonment for war crimes, but he was released in September 1948. Giorgio Mantello, aka George Mandel, made a fortune during the war by trading in the Jewish refugee racket.

the reputations and characters of his fellow members.

A few persons who were involved with this Italian "Centro Mondiale Commerciale" company were to die violent deaths, and after their deaths their personal funds and property mysteriously disappeared. In fact, the rancid activity of this company, supplied with CIA funds, led to that company's expulsion from Italy. No other European nation was interested in permitting that company to settle on its soil, so the all-white nation of South Africa is now its spawning ground—with the "Four Horsemen" riding free as the wind.[80]

Within two days after Shaw was indicted and within one day after Mr. Ramsey Clark was to commence his campaign to save this "persecuted, benign, kindly white-haired paragon of American ingenuity," articles appeared in the foreign press. The "Paesa Sera" and "La Devoir" commenced series of articles outlining the "business" activities of the "Centro Mondiale Commerciale" and "Permindex." It is not a wholesome story to tell the kids at bedtime.

The activities of those two companies, as written by the foreign press, was espionage—with a few murders thrown in to keep the spirits up. When Shaw's telephone book was examined

---

[80] The story of the CIA-sponsored Centro Mondiale Commerciale (CMC), Permindex, and their relationship to Shaw and the JFK assassination was first explored in a series of articles published in 1967 by the *Paesa Sera* newspaper in Rome. Researcher Paris Flammonde, author of *The Kennedy Conspiracy* (1969), conducted an early series of interviews with Jim Garrison and went to considerable personal expense to have the *Paesa Sera* articles translated so that he could devote a section of his book to this subject. Marks was well-aware of Flammonde's work and cites it both here, in *Coup d'État!*, and in his previous JFK title, *Two Days of Infamy*. Conversely, Flammonde includes Marks' *Murder Most Foul!* in a very select, two-page bibliography featured in *The Kennedy Conspiracy*. Jim Garrison was quick to grasp the significance of CMC and Permindex, as revealed in his *On the Trail of the Assassins* (1988). A more recent in-depth investigation of the CMC and Permindex was authored by Michele Metta and privately published under the title *CMC: The Italian Undercover CIA and Mossad Station and the Assassination of JFK* (2018).

under the subpoena legally secured by Mr. Garrison, it was found that among Shaw's friends were several leading present-day Italian Fascists and English neo-Nazis! In spite of this knowledge, Mr. Ramsey Clark, the attorney general of the United States, was to spend two years defending the "patriotism" and "loyalty to American beliefs" of Mr. Shaw. In fact, Mr. Clark became so upset that Mr. Garrison had the gumption to present facts to a grand jury that led to Shaw's indictment for conspiracy to murder that Mr. Clark openly threatened to indict Mr. Garrison for interfering with Mr. Shaw's "civil rights"! Does a person have a "civil right" to conspire to murder?

It is generally considered that when one's country is not at war with another it is rather ungentlemanly to commit murder in the name of "patriotism!" For example, if a clandestine organization is sponsored by a government body, and if that organization determines by itself that the president of the United States lacks "patriotism," can that government body condone the president's murder under the phrase "unpatriotic"? The OAS attempted five times the murder of De Gaulle;[81] the CIA sponsored a Batista group who made one assassination attempt and was successful! And if the reader believes this is a "far out" statement, then the reader is advised to read Mr. J. Edgar Hoover's stunning letter, referring to a CIA "training film," to J. Lee Rankin, general counsel of the Warren Commission, which is published in the illustrated section of this book.

The reader must try and understand criminal law in the United States. The failure to understand is the prime reason why The Establishment has been extremely successful in concealing the conspiracy.

Under the United States Constitution Mr. Garrison, as a district attorney for a state, had no power to subpoena such witnesses as Chief of Police Curry, District Attorney Wade, Lt.

---

[81] In addition, there were thirty-one documented assassination attempts against De Gaulle since his postwar return to Paris. See David Wallechinsky and Irving Wallace, *The People's Almanac* (New York: Doubleday, 1975).

Day, Captain Fritz, Assistant District Attorney Alexander, Justice of the Peace Johnston, Det. Studebaker, Mr. Brennan, Mr. Lovelady, Mr. H. L. Hunt or his sons, who gave some of the money for that infamous advertisement calling the president of the United States a traitor, Mrs. Paine, none of the 26 aides, none of the commissioners, none of the U.S. Secret Service agents, none of the FBI agents stationed in Dallas, New Orleans, or Washington, D.C. He could not compel the archivists of the National Archives to supply him with any of the X-rays, documents, exhibits, or films. None of the CIA or State Department documents. However, every one of those witnesses could have voluntarily appeared—if they so desired and if they were not afraid of death at the hands of the Dallas police. Mr. Ramsey Clark offered them no protection.

In view of this lack of cooperation, Mr. Garrison did prove one vital point in the Shaw trial (January 22, 1969—March 1969). He proved beyond a reasonable doubt that a conspiracy, in fact and in law, murdered President John F. Kennedy in the city of Dallas, Texas on November 22, 1963.

One of the key defense witnesses was none other than Lt. Col. Finck, one of the three military physicians who conducted the autopsy upon the body of President Kennedy. This military doctor, under oath as he was during the testimony he gave to the Warren Commission, testified at the Shaw trial that: (1) NO complete autopsy was performed upon the president's body. (2) The president had been shot in the back near his shoulder, as distinguished from the Commission's allegation that he had been shot near the base of his head. (3) The president's jacket supported the fact that the back wound was at his right shoulder. (4) The reason there was no complete autopsy was due to the fact that there was a constant parade of high military officers in the autopsy room who kept instructing the physicians on what to do and say. (5) And finally, the Autopsy Chart No. 397 is a correct chart locating the president's wound, including two bullets striking him in the head, one in the back, and one in the front of his throat.

But Lt. Col. Finck's testimony was buried on the inside of every major newspaper in the United States—it never made the front page. The same situation occurred when ex-Police Chief

Curry finally admitted on November 5, 1969 that Oswald was never identified as the rifleman.

What Mr. Garrison did not prove was that Mr. Shaw was a member of any conspiracy to murder the president. Under the evidence Mr. Garrison had available for presentation to the jury, the verdict of "not guilty" was proper. Within seven days after the verdict, Mr. Garrison went before the grand jury and presented such facts that the grand jury indicted Shaw for perjury. Again, the press and the Department of Justice rushed to his defense. Again, Mr. Shaw, proclaiming his innocence, has requested delay after delay. If he is so innocent, why ask for repeated delays? However, what is more mystifying is where Mr. Shaw is obtaining the vast sums of money he spent on his defense in the conspiracy trial, and where he is obtaining it for his forthcoming perjury trial. From the CIA, from the "CMC," or "Permindex"? Or have those beautiful friendships with the neo-Nazis, the OAS, the Italian Fascists finally paid off?

B. The Trial of Sirhan B. Sirhan, or .... How an 8-Bullet Gun Can Fire 10 to 14 Bullets without Reloading

As the Warren Commission "whitewashed" the murder of President Kennedy, so the county of Los Angeles played "footloose and fancy free" with the investigation of the conspiracy that murdered Senator Robert F. Kennedy on June 6, 1968 in the kitchen hallway of the Los Angeles Ambassador Hotel.[82]

---

[82] Los Angeles County Chief Medical Examiner Thomas Noguchi's official autopsy report states that RFK's fatal head shot was fired from a gun held within three inches of Kennedy's right ear, and from behind him, even though Sirhan was standing no closer than several feet in front of the RFK. Nonetheless, Noguchi's testimony was ignored. Subsequently, there was a concerted attempt (unsuccessful) to destroy his career. In Noguchi's memoir, *Coroner* (New York: Simon and Schuster, 1983), he writes that tests revealed that the fatal shot had been fired "one inch from the edge of [RFK's] right ear, only three inches behind the head." And it was only because Noguchi instructed one his "investigators to rush to the operating room to see

Again, the lack of understanding of law by the average American permitted the office of the district attorney to conceal the conspiracy. And, again, it was to be a prosecution witness that exposed the fact that more than one person was involved in the murder.

The reason behind the murder was not the Israeli—Arab conflict but one that went back to the murder of President Kennedy. Senator Kennedy, in June 1968, was well on his way to the Democratic nomination for the presidency of the United States. At the time of his murder he had won the delegates from the state of California; and although Vice President Humphrey had many delegates pledged to him, the vital industrial states were waiting to see the results of the California voting. With his victory, Senator Kennedy had more than an even chance to win the nomination. There was a swell toward him, and although it is speculation that he could have beaten Mr. Nixon at the national election, he had an excellent chance. Mr. Humphrey lost by less than 300,000 votes after Mr. Nixon was considered a "shoo-in" by October 15, 1968.

What the conspirators could not do was to wait and see if the senator did triumph in the November election. The senator, three weeks before his death, informed me that it was not the election he feared but whether or not when he won the national election he would be able to live until he was sworn in as the president of the United States.[83] The senator was a fatalist, and I have no doubt that when the bullets struck him he was not surprised. Prior to the day those bullets struck him in the head, the senator had informed several persons—including Jim Garrison, the New Orleans district attorney—that when he

---

if [RFK's] hair shavings were still there" that any of this was discovered. Tests revealed that the hair contained "soot": coroner's jargon for burned grains of gunpowder (carbon particles) that, because of their light mass, travel only a few inches. Noguchi also adds that "Tracks of twelve bullets were found at the scene, and Sirhan's gun contained only eight."

[83] For more on how the author may have been acquainted with Senator Kennedy, see my essay "The Stanley Marks Revival," featured in the 2020 edition of Marks' *Two Days of Infamy*.

became president he would establish a new Commission to investigate the murder of President Kennedy. But, more dangerously, he was dedicated to the philosophy espoused by his brother; he would be threatening the identical forces that commissioned the assassination of President Kennedy.[84] This would eventually involve the FBI and its Director, Mr. Hoover, who knew that the senator now possessed the information that the FBI had twelve days' prior knowledge of the Dallas murder and yet calmly permitted that murder to occur. And Mr. Hoover also knew that, if the senator became president, Mr. Hoover's term of 40 years as director would be finished. The FBI chief, a well-known exponent of power politics, knew that once his power base was destroyed the new director would uncover aspects of the Dallas murder best kept from the populace.

Two vital elements disclosed the existence of a conspiracy that murdered Senator Robert Kennedy, and those elements were revealed by a reading of the transcript of the trial of Sirhan for the murder.

The number of bullets fired at and striking the senator and other members of his entourage exceeded the number of bullets that could be discharged from Sirhan's weapon—a .22 caliber snub-nose Johnson revolver.[85] Mr. D. Wolfer, the Los Angeles police ballistics expert, testified that the senator was "hit three

---

[84] In an interview with Art Kevin published in a *Liberation News Service* dispatch on June 25, 1968 under the heading "Garrison says: 'Any leader who speaks out effectively against the war will be assassinated,'" Jim Garrison said that he met with mutual friends of Senator Kennedy who informed him that "Bobby Kennedy was well aware that there were many guns between him and the White House ... this is why he did not publicly go into the matter of precisely what forces killed his brother until the time came later on."

[85] Sirhan was said to have used a .22-caliber Iver-Johnson Cadet revolver, but according to testimony from several witnesses he may have fired a gun loaded with slugless cartridges or "blanks" (such as those discharged by starter pistols used at track events) to distract from the actual assassins. And if Sirhan was the subject of a hypnotic trance, it might have been that much easier to induce him to fire a gun equipped with harmless blanks. See Lisa Pease, *A Lie Too Big To Fail*, by far the best book on the RFK assassination.

times, while a fourth bullet passed through his jacket." That is four bullets from the murder weapon and four bullets remain.

One of the four remaining bullets strikes a middle-aged woman in the breast, and that bullet is removed in the hospital. Five are gone, leaving three.

One young man is struck by another bullet, and still another youth is also struck by another independent bullet. That is seven, since the physicians testify that an independent bullet has struck each young man: not fragments of a bullet, but each man was struck by a complete bullet.

Now, the mystery in the murder of the senator. Paul Schrade, a CIO Union official is struck in the head, but another bullet grazes his forehead.[86] And during the fray, a TV producer, [William Weisel],[87] is struck by 1, 2, or 3 bullets. From his hospital bed and while on TV camera and after his operation, the TV producer was to state that the physicians removed three bullets from his body. He was fully awake and in command of

---

[86] Paul Schrade, RFK's labor advisor, has long maintained that another assassin shot RFK. On June 4, 2015 he told the *Saratogian* newspaper: "The truth is in the prosecution's own records and the autopsy. It says Sirhan couldn't have shot Robert Kennedy and didn't. He was out of position." In 2016 Schrade appeared at Sirhan Sirhan's parole hearing to argue for Sirhan's release. And in 2018, on the fiftieth anniversary of RFK's death, the ninety-three-year-old Schrade said: "The record ought to be clear in our history that Robert Kennedy gets justice. Justice isn't convicting a man who didn't shoot him. There should be a new investigation. I accuse the prosecution. They're the guilty ones for having evidence of a second gunman and never taking it to a jury; in fact, blocking it." After Robert F. Kennedy Jr. visited Sirhan in prison in December 2017, he also called for a reinvestigation, adding: "The people that were closest to [Sirhan during the assassination], the people that disarmed him all said he never got near my father." See Paul Post, "Spa City native upholds RFK's legacy 50 years later," *Saratogian* (online), June 2, 2018. Marks mistakenly identifies Schrade as a CIO official; actually he was the Western regional director of the United Auto Workers (UAW). In 1965 Schrade also lent his support to Cesar Chavez and Dolores Huerta in the struggle of the farm workers.

[87] The original edition of *Coup d'État!* misidentifies Weisel as a "Mr. Goldberg."

his senses when he made that statement, but, by the end of the day, the three became one.

The mathematics of 4 + 1 +1 + 1 + 2 + 1 equals 10!

Since the authorities of Los Angeles, where one of the best schools of mathematics resides, know that an 8-bullet revolver cannot carry 10 bullets in its chamber, great haste was made to conform the number of bullet holes to the number of bullets, 8, that could be fired from that revolver. Therefore, the police announced that every bullet was accounted for, and the two youths were struck by fragments of bullets that had hit Mr. Schrade and Mr. [Weisel]. The fact that complete bullets were removed from their bodies did not create any degree of queasiness; for the L.A. authorities reasoned, correctly, that the press would back up the 8-bullet theory.

Two days after the murder, a Los Angeles TV station conducted a tour of the kitchen hallway where the senator was murdered by gunfire. As the announcer conducted this historical tour, he calmly pointed out to the viewing audience bullet holes (plural!) in the kitchen wall and on the kitchen's swinging doors! How many holes? Four! The location of those bullet holes was to be photographed and published in the L.A. "Free Press" in May 1969. But the newspapers in Los Angeles, Chicago, New York, and the remaining major areas in the United States did not publish the photographs or the story. Let sleeping dogs lie—the senator could not be brought to life again.

The conspirators were able to evade capture, arrest, and trial for the simple reason the public did not understand the function of the law of their own country. Senator Kennedy was hated by both the Mayor of Los Angeles—Sam Yorty—and his police hierarchy under the direction of Tom Reddin. Yorty was man enough not to hide his hatred of the entire Kennedy clan, and when the senator visited California prior to his murder in June the mayor and the police did everything in their power to harass the senator. He was never given any police protection, and the excuse was that the senator never requested any. That statement has been repeatedly denied by the senator's campaign staff.

The district attorney of Los Angeles County, according to the law, was under no legal compulsion to determine whether a conspiracy did in fact and in law murder Senator Kennedy. His case was determined by the facts given to him by the police department.[88] Of course, he should have been somewhat concerned when he learned that a minimum of twelve (12) bullets had been fired at the senator from a revolver that could only fire eight (8) bullets without being reloaded. But he did nothing except issue statements that confused the public.

Nor did the defense attorneys for Sirhan B. Sirhan have any legal obligation to prove that a conspiracy existed. They were to plead their client insane to save his life, so they did not want any conspiracy involved, since a conspiracy implied sanity. A conspiracy presumes intelligent planning.

Robert F. Kennedy was nominated to be murdered by the same organizations that murdered President Kennedy. This fact can be substantiated by a reading of the Miami, Fla. police tapes which were in the possession of the FBI and U.S. Secret Service on November 10, 1963. The names of the men who paid the assassins are on that tape. Furthermore, on September 1, 1968, Mr. Hall, a man investigated by the FBI as being a possible member of the conspiracy, gave a statement to the "National Enquirer" stating that he had been offered $50,000.00 in October 1963 to murder the president in Dallas. Hall also confirmed the statements on that Miami, Fla. police tape that Robert Kennedy and Martin Luther King were on the assassination list. The government has admitted that Hall was a member of various right-wing paramilitary organizations and an active member of the CIA-sponsored Batista Cuban group.[89]

---

[88] The LA Police Department made sure that, before Sirhan's trial began, 2,400 photographs from the crime scene—taken before, during, and after the assassination—were seized and destroyed.

[89] Loran Eugene Hall was a mercenary who fought alongside Castro but who later broke with the Fidelistas and was imprisoned in Cuba. After his release, he returned to the U.S. and joined the International Anti-Communist Brigade (whose membership included Frank Sturgis and David Ferrie) and the anti-Castro group, Interpen. During his testimony to the Select House Committee on Assassinations, Hall said: "I was a reactionary ... almost every meeting that I ever went to I heard somebody plotting or talking about somebody should blow Kennedy's head off." In the article that he penned for the *National*

Thus, under the law, neither the district attorney nor Sirhan's defense lawyers had any legal obligation to expose the conspiracy. However, in addition to the 12 bullets fired from a gun capable of only firing 8, there existed a woman in a "white polka-dot dress." The only person who saw this "white polka-dot dress" woman was a young lady who was president of a "Kennedy for President" club [at] her university.

According to this young lady, the woman in the polka-dot dress ran from the ballroom accompanied by a young man. As both passed her, the polka-dot-dress woman screamed at her, "We shot him! We shot him!" The university student spoke before a national television audience in a calm rational voice.

With her statement, the police and the district attorney became extremely busy in their efforts to destroy its credibility. Therefore, in the afternoon following the murder, the police, out of the clear sky, produced "the woman in the white polka-dot dress" to the television audience. This woman turned out to be a striptease dancer from a local bar, and she had on the dress she said she wore as she ran past the university student. The dress was not a "white polka-dot," but green.

Enquirer, Hall stated: "When two attempts were made on my life early this year to permanently silence me, I decided that my only safeguard was to take away the reason for these attacks. That is why I have told District Attorney Jim Garrison all I know. And that is why I am talking to the *Enquirer*. There is no point in killing me now. All the information I have is documented in New Orleans, and there is no way it can be hidden." (Loran Hall, "Key Witness in Garrison Probe Says: I Was Offered $50,000 to Kill JFK," *National Enquirer*, September 1, 1968, pp. 4-5.) After conducting numerous interviews with Hall, Garrison released a press statement on May 10, 1968. He said that the inclusion of Hall's name in the Warren Commission Exhibits was part of an intelligence agency's "creation of artificial leads pointing to persons who are not actually involved." Hall subsequently told a journalist: "When President Kennedy started coexisting with these other countries" (Russia, Cuba, "and all of the other communist satellites") and "made the statement that he was doing away with the CIA, he was signing his own death warrant." Paul Eberle, "Hall Deposes to Garrison in New Orleans, is exonerated," *Los Angeles Free Press*, May 24, 1968, pp. 14, 16.

This alleged [witness] was a fake produced by the Los Angeles Police Department. She was never taken before the university student for identification purposes. The proof that the police lied is that, at the trial of Sirhan, this striptease dancer was never placed on the witness stand; for her place was now taken by another "witness." Now, there are two "white polka-dot dress" users. But prior to the introduction of this second woman, the district attorney, with great fanfare, some two months after the murder of the senator (but also two months prior to the Sirhan trial), issued a statement that no such "woman in the white polka-dot dress" existed, and that such a woman was a figment of the student's imagination.

Having successfully branded this student a liar for the rest of her life, the same district attorney then turned 180 degrees and produced a "polka-dot dress" woman at the Sirhan trial! Who was the liar? The student or the district attorney? If the student imagined what she had seen, then it stands to reason that the district attorney could not have produced any "woman in a white polka-dot dress" at the Sirhan trial. QED the district attorney had immorally branded an innocent person—the university student— a liar when he himself was the liar! The district attorney had to produce that fraud, for he had to destroy all proof leading toward a conspiracy.

Four months after the conviction of Sirhan, the "striptease" dancer who cooperated with the police under pressure was found dead in a motel room. The cause of death? Barbiturates—the same weapon used to murder Dorothy Kilgallen and Lisa Howard.[90]

---

[90] Lisa Howard's suspicious death occurred at East Hampton, Long Island, on July 4, 1965. She died after ingesting one hundred phenobarbitals. President Kennedy had tapped Howard to conduct highly secret negotiations with Fidel Castro. Dorothy Kilgallen, a celebrated reporter with the *New York Journal*, had successfully arranged a private interview with Jack Ruby. She later boasted that her scoop would "break the case wide open." Kilgallen subsequently deposited her notes with her friend Margaret Smith, for safe keeping. On November 8, 1965 Kilgallen was found dead in her Manhattan townhouse on East 68 Street. Once again, the official cause of death was attributed to phenobarbitals (this time, mixed with alcohol).

Sweeping aside the machinations of Yorty, the police department, and the district attorney's office, the fact remains that the physical evidence proved Sirhan had an accomplice, for he could not discharge 12 bullets from his revolver. Nor did he explain at his trial how he knew that Robert Kennedy would come through the kitchen, for he admitted that he waited for TWO hours in the kitchen in the event the senator would come through that area. Nor did he explain how he obtained the automobile ignition keys belonging to a kitchen employee whom he did not know.

The fact is that Sirhan was stationed in that area by the conspirators; for there were two other assassins in the main ballroom who guarded those exits in the event the senator used those exits. Sirhan was stationed in the kitchen area so that in the event the senator did use that exit Sirhan, with one other assassin, would gun down the senator—which they did.

One final word: According to the NBC and CBS television tapes, in addition to Sirhan B. Sirhan, a man was arrested within the kitchen area and turned over to the police! What happened to that man, Mr. District Attorney?

C. The James Earl Ray Caper, or....
Always Use the Same Modus Operandi When It Is Successful

"I do not agree with the theory that there was no conspiracy."—James Earl Ray (the "patsy"), after pleading guilty to the murder of Martin Luther King in Memphis, Tennessee.

"The Martin Luther King case is not closed."—J. Edgar Hoover, March 15, 1969, in response to the statement by James Earl Ray in open court when receiving a life sentence for murdering Martin L. King.

The outstanding feature of the James Earl Ray case is the

Margaret Smith died two days later. Needless to say, Kilgallen's interview notes were never recovered.

statement made by the Memphis, Tenn. state attorney that it would not be in the interests of "justice" to have a trial!

The United States of America has now taken the path of dictatorship—Stalin, Hitler, and others of their ilk.

That is a strange set of facts—the murderer and the director of the FBI agreeing that the "murderer" was absolutely correct in informing the court that a conspiracy murdered the Rev. Martin L. King. After all, Mr. Hoover knew that James Earl Ray was a "patsy" from the very moment Dr. King was murdered. In fact, Mr. Hoover also knows that his department knows who the assassins were in (1) the President Kennedy murder; (2) the Dr. King murder; (3) the Senator Kennedy murder; and several future murders in 1970 that will occur in the political arena. He just has to listen to those tapes, and he can keep refreshing his memory.

Who murdered the Rev. Martin Luther King in Memphis, Tenn. in April 1968? The answer can be found in the illustrated section of this book. The official man wanted for that murder was sketched by an FBI illustrator, who obtained the facial features of the murderer from the eyewitnesses who saw the murderer in the house which was used as the ambush site.

With that sketch is a photograph published in "Ramparts" magazine of a man arrested by the Dallas police within ten minutes of the shooting on the grassy knoll.[91] Notice that the policeman is holding a rifle in his right hand as he marches the rifleman down the hill. If the reader will also look at the

---

[91] Marks is referring here to a famous photo of one of the three "tramps," who were arrested at Dealey Plaza and then released. Decades later this figure was identified as a "professional hobo" named Harold Doyle. In 1992 the Dallas Police Department released the identity of all three men: Gus Abrams, John F. Gedney and Harold Doyle. A pair of journalists named Ray and Mary LaFontaine carried out their own research and located Doyle and Gedley, who each later confirmed that they were captured in the photo. While working for the TV program "A Current Affair," the La Fontaines tracked Harold Doyle to Klamath Falls, Oregon and taped an interview with him, during which he denied any involvement in the assassination. The third figure, Gus Abrams, was deceased, but his sister positively identified him as the man in the picture.

reproduction of the front page of the Dallas "Morning News" in the same section, that news story informs the reader that eyewitnesses informed the sheriff's department that the man under arrest had fired shots at the president. This rifleman is mentioned in volume 19, page 526, and another rifleman in volume 20, page 499. Both disappeared from [the] sight of man after being arrested. So did the rifle!

That sketch is not applicable to James Earl Ray. That sketch was used on FBI "wanted" bulletins and then mysteriously withdrawn from public circulation. Why?

James Earl Ray will never write his saga, for a "lifer" does not have that privilege. His story to "Look" leaks worse than a hundred sieves. He was a "patsy" from start to finish, and he is fortunate—if imprisonment for life is considered fortunate—that he is alive. He had a "kangaroo" trial where the truth was forbidden to be spoken; and the money he was supposed to have received for his saga has vanished into the pockets of his various attorneys. The only people who profited from the murder of Martin Luther King are the civil rights haters and Ray's attorneys.

Three essential facts surround James Earl Ray. (1) The woman witness who saw the man shooting Rev. King from the ambush site in her boarding room never identified James Earl Ray to the Memphis police. Her description of that killer never compared to James Earl Ray in any manner, shape, or form. (2) The clothes found in the trunk of the automobile allegedly belonging to and used by Ray did not fit him. (3) In the police chase of that automobile, the police were misdirected by the conspirators [interfering] on the police radio band. That type of interference is not difficult to do.

The parallel between the methods used in the assassination of President Kennedy and Rev. King is amazing. (1) A rifle is conveniently dropped at the ambush site in spite of the fact that the killer had sufficient time to run out of the boarding house and drive away in an automobile after first opening the trunk of the car to throw in some clothes. (2) The rifle is quickly traced to the "killer," an alleged hardened killer who left his fingerprints all over the murder weapon. (3) The "killer" conveniently leaves his clothes, which are traced to him; but, as in the Tippit murder, where the police "found" a jacket belonging to Tippit's killer which they say belonged to Oswald although it contained a laundry mark that could not be traced to him, the clothes did not fit the King murderer. Nor did the jacket fit Oswald. (4) The police radio band wave was used by the conspirators, as in the Oswald case. (5) Furthermore, the police also found a transistor radio and a pair of binoculars. On those two items the FBI located Ray's left thumbprint and a fingerprint on the rifle's telescopic sight. In spite of those prints, the FBI took fifteen days to identify those prints as belonging to James Earl Ray! When the FBI admitted that they had 15 "ID" print cards on Ray, it raised some eyebrows in various police departments around the world.

After fleeing the King murder site, this killer then vanished for many months and, according to FBI statements, committed various holdups and burglaries in the United States, Canada, and London, England. But when captured, all those funds had disappeared, although the "receipts" were in the thousands. Strangely, the FBI stated they had witnesses to those various crimes committed by Ray during his flight, but no witness appeared to support the FBI.

After the arrest of James Earl Ray in London on June 8, 1968, a pattern emerged which revealed that two (2) James Earl Rays were involved—the Oswald "double" modus operandi! The news stories written in London by the Daily "Express" and Daily "Telegraph" conflict regarding the police branch that arrested James Earl Ray; while the N.Y. "Times" carries material that conflicts with the London press. Furthermore, the subsequent stories in the London press give material that directly conflicts with various London police statements issued on the day Ray was taken into custody!

What was happening in London was what had happened in Dallas, Texas on November 22, 1963. The London police were putting out statements that conflicted with each other in such a fashion that the average person could make neither heads nor tails of the arrest or how the London police had known Ray was the man wanted for the King murder.

The time schedule as outlined by the police proved that two Earl Rays were involved. Furthermore, both the London police and the FBI differed in essential facts relating to the discovery and arrest of a "James Earl Ray." In addition, the regular London police or Scotland Yard force was not involved. The branch that did the arresting was none other than the "Special Branch," which has more serious work than dealing with the average criminal but [that] does work with our CIA.

According to the London authorities James Earl Ray was arrested under the name of Raymond George Sneyd[92] and charged with possession of a forged passport and a firearm. The time was 11:15 a.m. on June 8, 1968.

Backtracking this arrest, an investigator found a time schedule relating to two men using the name Raymond George Sneyd.

Sneyd I checked into the New Earl's Hotel in London on May 26, 1968.

Sneyd I checked out on June 5th and flew to Lisbon on that day.

Sneyd II, on June 5, checked into the Pax Hotel, London.

Sneyd II checked out on June 8th at 9 a.m.

Sneyd I flew back to London from Lisbon and arrived at the London airport at 6:10 a.m. on June 8th. He was arrested at the airport and taken to the police station.

Sneyd II, checking out on June 8th at 9 a.m. from the Pax Hotel, arrived at the London airport and, at 11:15 a.m., while waiting for his plane to depart, was arrested by Scotland Yard's

---

[92] As author Philip H. Melanson would later discover, "By all the available evidence and by his own account, Ray had never been in Toronto prior to his arrival on April 8, 1968, after feeling the scene of the King assassination. Yet, four of the five aliases used by Ray in the nine months preceding the crime were real Canadians who lived in close proximity to each other. All four resided in Scarborough, a sprawling mix of suburban neighborhoods and industrial complexes bordering Toronto's eastern boundary.... [Eric Starvo] Galt, [Ramon George] Sneyd, and [Paul E.] Bridgeman lived in a triangular cluster, approximately 1 3/4 miles from each other. [John] Willard lived approximately 3 miles south of this triangle." Philip H. Melanson, *The Martin Luther King Assassination: New Revelations on the Conspiracy and Cover-Up, 1968-1991* (New York: Shapolsky Publishers, 1994), pp. 7-8.

"Special Branch."

Now, the official news releases by both Scotland Yard and the Special Branch become confused. Which man was charged with illegal possession of a forged passport and a firearm? Two men are arrested using the identical name, but which man is James Earl Ray? Both men were charged with the identical criminal violation. Which was Ray?

According to the London press the real James Earl Ray was the one arrested at 6:15 a.m. But the London police slipped on an unseen banana peel, for in the pocket of that James Earl Ray was another ticket for a flight to Brussels at 8:50 a.m. Therefore, the second Earl Ray would not be the first James Earl Ray, since he was arrested at 11:15 a.m. Still, the police had two "Sneyds" in the police station, and not even the press could find out what happened to the one who was not "James Earl Ray" in spite of the fact that both "Sneyds" were arrested and charged with the identical two felonies!

Two days after the arrest of two James Earl Rays, the London "Daily Telegraph" published a story which directly contradicted the original stories put forth by the London police authorities and stated that James Earl Ray had never left London for Lisbon. The new version now had the London Special Branch watching for the name "Sneyd" at all airports and ship docks; and when they saw that name on a passenger manifest that he was flying to Brussels at 11:15 a.m., the police closed in. But then, why did that Earl Ray not use his 8:50 a.m. ticket to fly out on the 8:50 a.m. plane before the police arrived at the airport?

Now, the always-seeking FBI public relations department became involved in salvaging some glory, and the FBI immediately branded the London press a bunch of liars. According to the FBI, James Earl Ray was in London only a day—May 7, 1968—and then he departed to Lisbon, where he stayed until he flew back to London and was arrested at 11:15 a.m.

The FBI, CIA, Scotland Yard, and Special Branch should have checked signals with each other. The man arrested at 11:15 a.m., according to the London Special Branch, was not James Earl Ray. Mr. Hoover said he was. Will the real James Earl Ray stand up? According to the London police, their James Earl Ray was in London from May 17th until the day of his arrest, with the exception of his two-day trip to Lisbon. According to the FBI, their James Earl Ray spent not a single 24-hour day in London. Who is kidding who?

The London authorities stated that their "James Earl Ray" was in London during the time they specified, because he was identified as a robber of several London banks and business firms. Thus, the London police, by arresting "Ray," solved several robberies with their "James Earl Ray!" Why couldn't the FBI help their London counterparts solve a few robberies? "Hands across the sea and all that there!"

Scotland Yard admits that their "Ray" was untraceable between May 17th and May 28th but that they believe he never left London. However, neither the FBI nor the London authorities ever explained how they discovered "James Earl Ray" became "Sneyd" and how they knew "Sneyd" was the James Earl Ray they were seeking. In fact, from the official stories released to the press, both police agencies were seeking totally different men!

Did the London Special Branch have the real James Earl Ray in custody after receiving him from a CIA source, hiding him for a period of time, and then producing him for the benefit of the CIA due to the political situation in the United States?

The fact remains that two "James Earl Ray" persons are involved. The fact remains that both the FBI and Scotland Yard differ as to the man who was arrested. The fact remains that Scotland Yard arrested two men, of the same name, and charged both of them with identical crimes. The fact remains that both men were arrested in the same airport. The fact remains that, within two days after the arrest of both men, the London police authorities were issuing contradictory statements regarding James Earl Ray's arrest and prior conduct to that day of arrest. The fact remains that the FBI official release to the press violently disagreed with the facts issued by their counterpart, the Special Branch. The fact remains that James Earl Ray was, or was not, arrested in London at either 6:15 a.m. or 11:15 a.m., for who can prove otherwise? There is not one single solitary statement given under oath by any Memphis police agent or any

FBI agent that the James Earl Ray sentenced to life imprisonment for murdering Rev. Martin L. King was the same James Earl Ray who was arrested under an alias of "Sneyd" and extradited from London! I claim that James Earl Ray was not the man arrested at either time.

The confusion that surrounds the general public over the method used by the FBI and the British police was confusion created deliberately by those two agencies. An examination of the dates, however, can clear up some small portion of that confusion. Martin Luther King was murdered on April 4, 1968. On April 11th, a white Mustang was found abandoned in Atlanta, Ga., and it was registered to an Eric Starvo Galt.[93]

Laundry marks on clothes found in the Mustang led to Los Angeles, where a man of that name was traced to the International School of Bartending. That school produced a photograph of Galt, and based on that photograph the FBI secured a warrant for the arrest of Galt—not James Earl Ray— on April 17th.

Thus, the FBI "hocus-pokus" commenced. For the FBI admitted that the fingerprints found on the rifle and the binoculars were not used by the FBI[—]but a thumbprint of "Galt" which was found on a map which Galt had left in his rooming house in Atlanta, Ga. This incredible state of affairs was thus used by the FBI to prove that the thumbprint found on a map led them to "Galt." Yet, the FBI stated that those latent fingerprints used by the FBI were not found on the binoculars or the rifle! The only logical answer is that those "fingerprints" were never discovered; nor does the "thumbprint" prove that "Galt" was "Ray" at the time of the King assassination.

When the FBI left the bartending school, they had with them a photograph of "Galt." That photograph was published in the United States, and thus a comparison can be made between that photograph and the photograph used by the Canadian passport bureau, Scotland Yard, and the FBI to identify "Galt" as James Earl Ray. There is no resemblance! Therefore, how did that photograph, rushed to Scotland Yard's Special Branch, lead to James Earl Ray, supposedly traveling under the name of

---

[93] See previous note on Ray's use of aliases.

Raymond George Sneyd?

The movie as played out in the London airport has been described on previous pages. To this day, there has been no explanation of two "Sneyds" being arrested on identical charges, both taken to the same police station, but only one being allegedly "James Earl Ray." As explained, both had forged passports, but only one had a dangerous weapon, and he was the one mysteriously released by the London authorities. Who was he? Three agencies have that answer: the FBI, the CIA, and the Special Branch of Scotland Yard—and all three are not talking.

That "Ray" was improperly extradited under British law was revealed by the additional testimony of Police Inspector Zachary of the Memphis Police Department.[94] The Rev. King was murdered by a rifle firing a "dumdum" bullet into his skull. A "dumdum" explodes into so many pieces that it is impossible for any of those pieces to be reassembled into the original bullet for ballistic examination. A "dumdum" bullet was also used in the murder of President Kennedy. The FBI in that murder admitted to the Warren Commission that the bullets which exploded when striking his head were completely demolished.

In no textbook used in any police department or any university teaching criminology and ballistics is there any record that a "dumdum" can be examined for identification

---

[94] A Black police officer named Jerry Williams was normally assigned to head the security team that guarded Dr. King in Memphis, but on the day of the assassination Williams and all other Black officers were pulled off the assignment by Inspector N. E. Zachary. In an interview with Amy Goodman for Democracy Now conducted in 2007, Williams said: "During the time of Dr. King's assassination, I was working the homicide bureau in the Memphis Police Department. And on two previous occasions when Dr. King would come to Memphis, I was assigned to head his security team. But the last time he came, there were no Black officers assigned for that security." See "Retired Memphis Policeman: No Black Officers Assigned to Martin Luther King on Day of Assassination" (online), democracynow.org. Inspector Zachary, chief of the Memphis Police Department's Homicide Squad, claimed that he was the first to discover the assassin's rifle.

purposes after that bullet has exploded. Therefore, when that inspector testified in the London court that the rifle they found belonged to Ray and that it was the weapon used to murder the Rev. King, he was deceiving the court. The inspector had absolutely no proof that the weapon discharged a "dumdum" bullet on April 8, 1968 into the skull of Dr. King.

As in the Oswald frame-up (now conceded by Dallas ex-Chief of Police Curry on November 5, 1969), there was no evidence that placed James Earl Ray in that rooming house across from the motel when the shot was fired at Dr. King. Ray was never identified as the rifleman by the only person who had a full sight of the killer, and she never identified Ray as the man in her rooming house at the exact time that murder took place. The fact that binoculars and a transistor radio were found with his prints on them does not, in a law court, ipso facto, prove Ray murdered Dr. King. Any more than the fact that Oswald's fingerprints and palm prints proved he was at the 6th-floor window at the exact time the shots were fired. James Earl Ray was a "patsy." So was Oswald.

The proof that Ray was framed can be seen in a reading of the transcript of Ray's trial. There is not a single shred of evidence presented by the Memphis prosecutor that the prints found on the radio and gun were not presented to the court as evidence![95] Furthermore, there is no evidence in the trial record that revealed the legal procedure by which the FBI connected James Earl Ray with an "Eric Galt."

The FBI explanation of how they associated "Galt" with Ray does not hold water, for that explanation was not given under oath but as a statement to the press on April 19, 1968. The reason why the Memphis prosecutor could not use those fingerprints was that those prints do not match those of James Earl Ray—for the FBI, in their statement, admitted that Ray was supposedly traced by his "thumbprint" found on a map.

---

[95] The wording here is ambiguous, but I believe Marks is saying that the fingerprints found on the radio and gun could not have been presented as valid assassination evidence. As Marks reiterates below: "The failure of the state to introduce or produce the fingerprint and thumbprint on the rifle is proof that Ray was framed."

(Remarkable, is it not, how the Dallas police also proclaimed another man's "guilt" by finding a map!)

Thus, an alleged Memphis court, operating under the "basic principles of American justice," sentenced a man to 99 years in jail based upon evidence that could not convict a yellow dog. A law student studying criminal law knows that a "thumbprint" found hundreds of miles from the scene of a crime is no evidence to sentence a man to imprisonment for life when the state prosecutor has presented no evidence found at the crime that links that thumbprint to the crime. The failure of the state to introduce or produce the fingerprint and thumbprint on the rifle is proof that Ray was framed. Assuming the fact that Ray did purchase a rifle, did have binoculars, did have a transistor radio—those facts, standing by and of themselves, cannot, under the "basic principles of American justice," uphold a conviction in a murder case. Those principles are applicable in all criminal cases. They were raped in both the Oswald and Ray cases.

James Earl Ray was betrayed in the same manner as Lee Harvey Oswald. Both men relied upon forces they could not control. They were, in every sense of the word, "patsies." The defense of James Earl Ray was conducted by a notorious legal braggart who was also quoting the fact that he saved men from the chair or hangman's knot. Perhaps he has—but the larger question is whether or not there was sufficient evidence against any of those clients deserving the death penalty. Ray's attorney conducted no defense worthy of the name in spite of the fact that all the evidence quoted above was available for his use. It is one thing to be an incompetent attorney for a person on trial for his life—it is another thing when a competent attorney openly proclaims, as he did in the "Look" article, that he assumed his client's guilt! That is worse than incompetency, for that conduct is a base and deliberate deception in view of the evidence outlined above. And then to cynically brag that he "saved" his client's life is ethical depravity when the evidence would have brought forth a "not guilty" verdict. What this author would like to have answered is: "What did Ray's attorney do with the facts outlined in the letter written by

Joachim Joesten,[96] of which the attorney had full knowledge?"

When a lawyer's client on trial for murder openly confesses that a conspiracy was involved and the lawyer can only weakly confess that, upon his own interrogation of his client, no conspiracy existed, something is "fishy" in that courtroom. Furthermore, when the convicted person and his family engage in a posttrial lawsuit for funds given to the attorney, again something is "fishy."

The client's attorney stated there was no conspiracy involved in the murder of his client's victim; the director of the FBI openly stated that the Dr. King case is not closed. The attorney's client says it was a conspiracy. Who is the public to believe? The convenient death of Judge Battle from "heart failure" the day he was to give his decision regarding Ray's request for a new trial is strange in view of the fact that the judge never had a "heart condition."[97] An autopsy was not conducted by the

---

[96] Joesten's "Open Letter To Judge W. Preston Battle" is dated January 27, 1969 and features a classic Joesten aphorism: "The time has come for thoughtful Americans to start thinking the unthinkable—because it is true." Joesten believed that Ray was paid to serve as a "decoy" in the conspiracy but that he did not himself kill Dr. King. Joesten also did not neglect to point a finger at FBI Director Hoover, lambasting him for his part in knowingly framing Ray: "Because Hoover knows that his false and fraudulent case will not stand up in court, extreme pressure is now being brought on Ray ..." The FBI was already keeping a careful eye on Joesten. Less than a month later, on February 25, Director Hoover received an Airtel that included a copy of the Joesten letter from the Miami Special Agent in Charge. (As of this writing, a copy is available online at jfk.hood.edu.) A prolific writer and former *Newsweek* correspondent who had fled from the Gestapo in Europe, Joesten also authored and privately printed *The James Earl Ray Hoax: The Greatest Police Fraud Ever*, which was published on January 1, 1969.

[97] "The day after the pleading, without Foreman as his attorney, Ray wrote a letter to the judge and told him he would like to change his plea. But Judge Preston Battle died before he could act on the letter, which was lying open on his desk when he had a fatal heart attack. Tennessee law clearly stated that, in such situations, the defendant should be granted a new hearing automatically.... That provision of the law was systematically ignored until it was changed decades later

judge's family physician, nor was it in the case of Lisa Howard or Mrs. Roberts.

Until the FBI can give a satisfactory explanation of the facts outlined on the first page of this concluding chapter, then, by the laws of common sense, a conspiracy in fact and in law murdered Martin Luther King.

The question "Who are the conspirators" can be answered the day the FBI and the U.S. Secret Service release an unedited, fully completed tape recording of the Miami, Fla. police tapes taken on November 7, 1963 in Miami, Florida—and from those tapes all the conspirators will be named.

"SINCE THE DEAD CANNOT SPEAK, SHOULD NOT THE LIVING?"

---

when Judge Joe Brown took up the King case and threatened to break it wide open." James DiEugenio, "*Time-Life* and Political Pornography on the 50th Anniversary," Kennedys and King web site, June 8, 2018. "Shortly after confessing to the assassination, Mr. Ray tried to withdraw his plea, sending a letter to Judge W. Preston Battle of Shelby County Criminal Court. Judge Battle died of a heart attack five days later." See "Death of Judge Is Said to Entitle James Earl Ray to a New Trial," *New York Times* via the Associated Press, Sept. 3, 1997.

CHAPTER XI

A SHORT REPRISE OF THE EVIDENCE

The responsibility for the "success" of the Warren Commission and its "Report" must rest solely upon the mass communication media, which went out of its way to protect the duplicity, deceit, and deception practiced by the Commission upon the American citizen. Why the "lords" of the press decided to uphold such fraud can only be answered by them. It would be fruitless to speculate. Whatever the reason, the "lords" acquiesced in the "Report" and, in the long run, the "lords" and their "peasant" readers will pay the price with the gradual erosion of freedom of the press. The rise of fascism in the United States is proceeding on the same ground, and in the same manner, that the press lords of Germany paved the way for Hitler; those same "lords" in Italy for the Mussolini; those same "lords" who preferred Hitler to Blum; and the same "lords" who exalted at the demise of democracy in Greece in 1967-68.

The author contends that the evidence has proven beyond a reasonable doubt that a conspiracy murdered President Kennedy. Of course, the author relies upon his interpretation of the evidence in the same manner as if he were a member of the jury listening in judgment upon Lee Harvey Oswald.

On the following pages are the volumes which have been used by the author to substantiate his accusation against the Warren Commission that those seven commissioners knowingly, willfully, and deceitfully accused Lee Harvey Oswald of being the "sole and exclusive assassin of President Kennedy."

WITNESSES ACCUSING FBI AGENTS OF PERVERTING THEIR STATEMENTS GIVEN TO THOSE AGENTS

Arnett—12H131; Archer—12H401; Armstrong—13W354;

Brennan—3H154; Beers—13H104; Benton—15H459; Branch—15H477; Clark—8H349; Combest—12H178-80; Crull—15H140-41; Dougherty—6H380; Delgado—8H238, 246, 256, 263-64; Dean—12H429-30; Dow—436-38; Euins—2H208; Eberhardt—13H161; Greer—2H182-85, 185; Frazier—12H57; Fleming—15H161; Hall—15H176; Hansen—15H446-48; Harrison—12H265; Holly—12H265; Hankal—13H[13]; Huffaker—13H117-20; Hodge—15H595-96; Jenkins—15H601. Kellerman—24H93-95; Kravitz—15H235; Knight—15H265; Kaufman—15H515; Lee—18H92; Lowery—12H273; Leavelle—13H18; Maxey—12H290; Miller—12H313, 15H454; McCurdy—15H29-31; Norman—3H196; Oswald—1H425; Paine—3H101-03; Powers—8H267; Pena—11H353; Powell—15H429; Peterson—15H745; Rowland—2H185; Ruby—14H424; Robertson—15H354; Stevenson—12H106; Slack—12H352; Steele—12H356; Senator—14H304, 306, 309, 311; Saunders—15H581; Vaughn—12H371; Worrell—2H201; Williams—3H162, 172-73, 180-81; Watson—12H373; Worley—12H378-81; Wiggins—12H394; Walker—13H293; Waldo—15H587, 594.

The above list comprises SIXTY witnesses, including U.S. Secret Service agents who directly accused, under oath, FBI agents of deliberately perverting the witnesses statements regarding events bearing directly upon the guilt or innocence of Lee Harvey Oswald. Under the "basic principles of American justice," the law states that where a witness testimony given under oath has never been contradicted by other testimony given under oath then the testimony given under oath must be accepted by the court and jury as being the truth.

FBI TESTIMONY & AFFIDAVITS PROVING OSWALD INNOCENT

FBI Reports vols. 1-5 incl. National Archives. Suppressed by Commission. (Nov. 26, Dec. 9, 1963; Jan. 13, 1964.)
Report on code number on all Italian rifles. Com. Dec. 2562.
Rifle sling differences. Com. Exh. 1403, cf. Com. Exh. 139 cf. 3H25, 397; 4H289.

FBI statement: Oswald "owned" rifle; never "used" rifle. FBI Reports 1-5, inc.
Rifle barrel changed. FBI Reports vol. 1-5 incl.
No ammunition clip with rifle, Com. Exh. 2003, 26H449.
No fingerprints on ammunition clip. id.; 4H23.
No Oswald finger or palm prints on rifle. 4H24, 29.
FBI testimony that "found" palm print was flat, not curved. 4H20-29.
Oswald's "flat" palm print taken in police station. 4H218; 7H284.
Rifle repaired by FBI prior to testing. 3H443.
Rifle repaired so it could shoot accurately. 26H104.
Trigger on rifle worthless. 3H447; R193.
Telescopic sight mounted for left-handed person. Com. Exh. 2560.
Oswald was always right-handed. Com. Exh. 1401; 1H293-94.
Telescopic sight "structurally defective." 3H405; 26H104.
White smoke emitted from rifle when discharged. 26H811.
Rust on firing pin; pin worn down, Com. Exh. 26H104: CE 2974.
Shims necessary to hold telescopic sight. None found or used. 3H405; 15H779: 3H444.
Rifle inaccurate when discharged. 26H104.
FBI examination of cartridges from 6th floor, CD 1245; FBI No. DL 100-1046; CE 2968: Com. Exh. 543.
Fake rifle cartridges given to FBI by police. 4H205, 253-55; 26H449.
Deformed cartridge given to FBI by police; no bullet fired from Italian rifle, 26H449.
"Life" and "AP" photographs faked. 4H281, 21H453, 456-58. Illus. section.
Phony Commission rifle tests. Height and time changed. 3H403-07; 441-47.
Rifle received in "well-oiled condition," FBI Reports vol. 1-5; CE 2974.
No oil stains or impressions in or on "brown paper bag." 4H57, 97. FBI finding brown paper bag in Irving, Tex., Post Office. FBI File Dec. 205, p. 148.

No oil stains or telescopic sight indentations on blanket. 9H424-25, 461; FBI Reports vol. 1-5.

Based on the testimony and affidavits of the FBI, Lee Harvey Oswald was proved, by that bureau, to be innocent of being the "sole and exclusive assassin of President Kennedy."

FBI TESTIMONY AND AFFIDAVITS PROVING OSWALD WAS NOT AT 6TH-FLOOR WINDOW WHEN SHOTS WERE FIRED AT PRESIDENT KENNEDY

Edw. Piper saw Oswald near lunch room at 12:15 p.m. FBI File CD 5.

Mrs. Arnold saw Oswald between 12:15 and 12:25 p.m. Id., p. 41.

Oswald saw Jr. Jarman at lunchroom between 12:00 noon and 12:15 p.m. 3H276.

Oswald saw and talked to Mr. Allman. Suppressed. Nat'l Archives, Doc. 354.

Mr. Hoover's letter to Commission. Jan. 20, 1964. Re: Hughes photo. FBI Exh. 29.

Lovelady's affidavit: "Wore red & white striped shirt, buttoned up." Com. Exh. 457.

Shelley's affidavit: "Lovelady seated on steps, not standing." Com. Exh. 1831.

Brennan's affidavit: "Could not identify man in window." Com. Exh. 5323; FBI File CD-5; DL 89-43; 3H147-48; CE R145, 146, 250.

Brennan saw no smoke; FBI disputing his statement. 3H144, cf. 26H811.

Brennan saw no telescopic sight. 3H144.

Brennan saw rifleman standing up and firing last shot. 3H144, cf. Com. Exh. 1311-12; cf. R80, 138.

Cross-examination of Bonnie Ray Williams: Oswald not on 6th floor. 3H169-73.

Mrs. Adams proving Lovelady committed perjury. 6H392.

U.S. SECRET SERVICE PROVING OSWALD INNOCENT

Oswald talked to Mr. Allman at entrance—12:50 p.m., Com. Doc. 354.

Secret Service Official Report—Oswald not at window—CD 5—p. 44.

Secret Service Inspector Sorrels' testimony upholding Oswald—71H732.

Warren Commission accepts Secret Service reports—pp. 95, 101, 111 in "Report"!

DALLAS POLICE TESTIMONY PROVING OSWALD INNOCENT

Lt. Day's official letters to Chief Curry—Jan. 8, 1964.
Lt. Day's admission—No Oswald prints on rifle! 4H260-63.
Oswald's "flat" palm print taken in police station. 4H218.
Capt. Fritz impugning Brennan's "testimony." 4H237.
Police Chief Curry's confessing Oswald innocent! Nov. 5, 1969—"UPI" wire report!

MEDICAL TESTIMONY PROVING OSWALD INNOCENT

Autopsy Chart No. 397; R111; 2H81, 123, 143, cf. 2H82.
Cause of death of President Kennedy. 6H30-35; CE 392.
FBI report: back wound, not wound in back of neck. Nat'l Archives. File 89, R97; CE 886-A; CF 2H103, 127, 143; 5H175.
FBI report: location of back wound. National Archives: File No. 59, 60; CD 7. Sibert—O'Neill Report, suppressed; cf. CE 385-86.
Comdr. Humes' agreement with FBI: 2H365, cf. 2H30.
No proof of Commission's Bullet 399, tracing, 3H428, 497; 6H125-34; 11H468: 18H799; 24H412. Legally, this bullet was a "plant."
Ballistic expert Nicol's testimony that No. 399 was a fake, 3H443, 497.
Physicians "bullet in lung" statement. N.Y. "Times,"

11/23/63; substantiated in 3H9, 361; 5H78; 6H42, 51; 7H4; 17H848.

U.S. Secret Service report and survey proving Oswald innocent. Suppressed. Nat'l Archives. Files 87, 88, 2H127.

The sworn testimony of Lt. Col. Finck, as printed in "Epilogue," stating that the autopsy was a fraud proved not only the innocence of Lee Harvey Oswald but also proved a conspiracy! That Lt. Col. Finck was truthful in his testimony given under oath at the Shaw trial was substantiated by Lt. Comdr. Humes and Dr. Boswell on Nov. 25, 1966 and on the CBS 1967 TV series (see author's Preface).

THE TIPPIT MURDER CASE

Evidence proving Oswald innocent.

Mrs. Markham admits she did not recognize Oswald. 3H310-11, 391. Mr. Benavides admits he did not recognize Oswald. 3H327, 4H452.

Tippit shot by a left-handed person. 17H416.

Time of death of Tippit. 3H304-11; 24H202, 215.

Mr. Bowley supporting time of Tippit's death, 1:06. p.m.—1:08 p.m., Com. Exh. 2003, p. 11.

Oswald's location at 1:04 p.m. 6H440; 7H439.

Police radio description of Tippit's killer. Com. Exh. 1974.

Oswald not a suspect by police. Com. Exh. 1974, pp. 59, 74.

Oswald had no revolver when arrested. 3H300; 7H20-23; Illus. section. A .38 automatic shell found at Tippit murder site. Oswald owned a revolver. 17H417-20; Com. Exh. 1974, pp. 74, 78.

Two guns used to murder Tippit. Com. Exh. 1974, p. 78; 17H417-20.

Oswald never had holster in rooming house. 6H420-22.

Capt. Westbrook never found jacket. 7H30-33, 115-117.

Jacket manufactured evidence by police. 7H30-33; Batchelor and Lawrence Exh. R175, cf. 74, 115, CE 1974, p. 62-77.

McDonald receiving "tip" that Oswald was on first floor, not balcony. 3H298-302.

Police perjury relating to Tippit's whereabouts prior to his murder. 4H443; 26H195; Com. Exh. 705; 1947; 2985.

U.S. Secret Service memorandum; suppressed by Commission. Relates to number of bullet holes and number of bodies involved as "Tippit." File No. 87, 88. Code No. M63-352, November 22, 1963. Signed by Agent Moore.

Police perjury relating to number of bullets. 20H465, 24H253, cf. 3H447-48, Exh. 1974, King Exh. No. 5; 20H465.

Dallas police testifying Tippit shot only 3 times. 20H465; 24H253.

FBI testifying 4 bullets given to them by police. Unidentifiable. 3H473; 24H263.

Dallas policeman failure to find his mark "JMP" on cartridges and shells given to him at murder site. 7H66.

Dallas Police Sgt. Barnes failing to identify Tippit shells. 7H69; 275-76, 24H415.

FBI evidence that one bullet carried button into body. 3H473.

McDonald's perjury. R304, cf. 3H298, 301-02; 7H20-23; R560.

Det. Carroll "jerking" a revolver from "unknown" person. 3H300.

McDonald placed his "mark" on gun in police station. 3H298-302.

FBI statement: "one bullet from two shells." 3H473.

Commission statement that 5 bullets were fired at Tippit. 3H347-48, 3H477-78.

THE EVIDENCE THAT PROVED A CONSPIRACY

The Jarnagin affidavits to the FBI. Com. Exh. No. 2821.
Dallas Police Capt. Martin's Testimony.
Dep. Sheriff Walther's testimony to aide Liebeler.
Ray Krystinik's testimony.
Sen. Russell's admission that a conspiracy existed. 1969.
De Mohrenschildt's son-in-law's accusation.
Dep. Sheriff Mabra's Testimony—Dallas "cycle cop" at fence.
Nix photographs—"Esquire," Dec. 1966; Sept.—Jan., 1967.

The only published map of the president's motorcade route. Dallas "Morning News," November 22, 1963.

The published and selected route had no "double detour." R30-41.

Who planned "double detour?" Ask Police Chief Curry. Dallas "News," 11/23/63.

Miami, Fla., police tape recordings of plot to murder president, Miami "News," 2/2/67.

Deputy Sheriff Craig's testimony and Capt. Fritz's crackup. 6H226, cf. 23H817.

Craig's testimony corroborated by Mr. Robinson. CD 5; 19H524.

Commission's refusal to purchase TV Tapes. Com. Exh. 962.

The bombshell—The FBI's W. S. Walter affidavit in Dist. Att. Garrison's possession, accusing the FBI of being a silent accomplice in Pres. Kennedy's murder! ("Kennedy Conspiracy" by P. Flammonde—1969).

Time of Murder: 12:20 & 12:25 p.m. Dallas "Times-Herald," "News," 11/23/63.

Decker's announcement of time of murder. 12:25 p.m. Dallas police tapes.

Rifleman arrested in Dal-Tex Bldg. Disappears in police station. 19H526-27; 20H499.

Shots also came from Dal-Tex Bldg. Suppressed. Com. Doc. CD 5; 24H385; "Herald," 11/23/63.

Marine Corps cleared Oswald of "treason." Com. Exh. 2718.

FBI approves Oswald as "all right." Dallas police Memo. Feb. 14, 1964; suppressed.

Hudkins' statements, Secret Service: informed by Dallas Chief Sweatt [that] Oswald [was] an FBI informer, paid $200.00 per month. Code 30-030, 767. Cf. "Latitudes"—Feb. 1967.

Man arrested and identified as rifleman on grassy knoll. "Times-Herald." 11/23/63.

Oswald known to Dallas police prior to murder. Com. Exh. 709; 2003; 4H207.

Three (3) spent cartridges found on 3rd floor at 12:45 p.m. Com. Exh. 705, p. 492.

Rifle, with no telescopic sight, carried from Depository.

"Playboy" Oct. 1967.
Phone call to Secret Service: "Oswald not the man." 4H356.
Dallas police knowledge of Tippit murder prior to its happening. Com. Exh. 2003, 79-83, Curry's testimony, vol. 4.
Men impersonating Secret Service agents during Tippit murder. Id.
No brown bag found on 6th floor. 3H288, 6H268, 7H65, 289.
Fingerprints "lost" and "found" on brown paper bag. 3H3-8; 4H266-68; 7H97-98, 104, 143, 288.
Curtain rods found in Paine garage by FBI and aide. 9H425.
"FBI" and "CIA" agents' disturbance in Parkland Hospital. 18H795.
FBI Agent Hosty statement, at 3 p.m., Oswald a "Communist" murderer. 5H34-37.
Police Curry, prior to Tippit murder and prior to arrest of Oswald, that suspect had been captured for both Tippit and President Kennedy murder. 4H.
Oswald never arraigned for murder of President Kennedy. 4H200; 7H289.
Switching of cartridge shells found at Tippit murder site, 7H66, 69, 275-76, 415.
Secret Service report: no gun or person in 6th-floor window. Suppressed. National Archives: File CD 5, p. 44.
Mysterious FBI statements referring to TWO types of reports to the Commission. 5H112.
FBI Testimony proving a conspiracy. File No. 89-30, Nov. 26, 1963: Files 59, 60.
Secret Service testimony proving a conspiracy. 2H93: 127, 143, 368.
Comdr. Humes upholding FBI testimony proving a conspiracy. 2H365.
Governor Connally struck by 2 or more bullets. 4H109, 121.
Physicians' testimony proving a conspiracy. 3H9; 5H78; 6H42, 51; 7H4; 17H848; 2H30; 6H5, 14, 22, 23, 36, 42, 55, 65, 67, 71, 143.
Physician's testimony proving aide Specter wrong. 2H347, 375; 3H340; 4H113; 17H418.
Autopsy chart proving a conspiracy. R95, 105, 111.
Specter's admission proving a conspiracy. "U.S. News," Oct.

1966; "Phil. Mag." Aug. 1966.

Lt. Day's memo referring to description of rifle. Lost! 4H260; Com. Exh. 2003.

Commission referring to Lt. Day's "lost" memo. 4H260.

Impersonation of Secret Service agents. R52, 6H313, 7H107, 535; 18H722; Com. Exh. 2003, N.79.

Policeman informing unknown person at 2 p.m. by telephone that Oswald captured for both murders. 7H12.

Brown paper bag found in Irving, Texas, Post Office by FBI. Suppressed. FBI File 205.

Mr. J. Edgar Hoover's strange statement to Mr. Richard Nixon that by 2:30 p.m. Dallas time the FBI knew a "Communist" killed President Kennedy. "Sat. Eve. Post," 2/27/67.

Finally: The HUGHES photograph, which proved NO person was at the 6th-floor window of the Depository when the shots rang out.

OSWALD'S DEATH AS THE RESULT OF A CONSPIRACY

Ruby's premeditation. 15H491. Lie test. National Archives. Ruby in basement. Perjury by Dallas policemen, 15H682-83; 5H255-56; 12H340; Com. Exh. 2050, 2002. Conspirator impersonating physician, pumping out Oswald's blood. 19H410-13. Hospital prepares autopsy room for Oswald thirty minutes prior to shooting. Ruby in police station, never entered through ramp. Com. Exh. 2050; 15H682-83.

Conclusion: Oswald was innocent, as proven by testimony and photographs, of "being the sole and exclusive assassin of President Kennedy." QED: A CONSPIRACY MURDERED PRESIDENT JOHN F. KENNEDY.

ODDS AND ENDS

FBI surveillance of Oswald prior to murder. Com. Doc. 2718. Suppressed. Mrs. Marina Oswald's statements to Secret Service. Com. Doc. 344. Weitzman affidavit: rifle was a

German Mauser. 24H228; upheld in 7H105-09. Kantor sees and talks to Jack Ruby. Kantor Exh. Nat'l Archives. Kantor's testimony upheld by Mrs. Tice. 15H388; 25H216, 317. Oswald as a CIA agent.[98] 2H84-85, 192, 203; 5H104; 8H260, 297-98; 19H680; CD 320; CD 931; Com. Exh. 2718. Strange U.S. Dept. of Justice statement alleging Shaw and "Clay Bertrand" were "same guy"—Washington "Star" 3/2/67 and "Post" 3/3/67, AP—3/4/67. Pres. Johnson's press statement on Shaw. AP 3/2/67. Lt. Col. Finck's admission as Shaw's defense witness that the Bethesda autopsy was false! Only a partial autopsy was performed! N. Y. "Times," March, 1969. Dr. Perry's press statement—NBC "70 Hours" —Random House—1966.

---

[98] For more on this topic, see John Newman, *Oswald and the CIA* (New York: Skyhorse, 2008).

Epilogue

LT. COL. FINCK ADMITTING A FRAUDULENT AUTOPSY

Testimony of Lt. Col. P. Finck, one of the physicians who performed the autopsy upon the body of President Kennedy at Bethesda [Naval Hospital], Maryland.

This testimony was given by Lt. Col. Finck as a witness under oath at the trial of Clay Shaw, who was indicted as a member of a conspiracy that murdered President Kennedy. Mr. Shaw was found "not guilty" of the accusation, but Jim Garrison proved beyond a reasonable doubt that a conspiracy, in fact and in law, murdered the president.

Portions of this Army officer's testimony is included in this section because of the damaging statements he gave under oath, which completely proves the conspiracy. But far more damaging [are] the physician's statements implicating military members of the Department of Defense as "accessories after the fact."

Portions of Lt. Col. Finck's Sworn Testimony:

"Q—Was Dr. Humes running the show?

A—Well, I heard Dr. Humes stating that—he said, "Who is in charge here?" and I heard an Army general, I don't remember his name, stating, "I am." You must understand that, in those circumstances, there were law enforcement officers, military people in various ranks, and <u>you have to coordinate the operation according to directions.</u>

Q—But you were one of the three qualified pathologists standing at the autopsy table, were you not, doctor?

A—Yes, I was.

Q—Was this Army general a qualified pathologist?

A—No.

Q—Was he a doctor?

A—No, not to my knowledge.

Q—Can you give his name?

A—No, I can't. I don't remember ...

Q—Colonel, did you feel that you had to take orders from this Army general that was there directing the autopsy?

A—No, because there were others, there were admirals.

Q—There were admirals?

A—Oh, yes, there were admirals, and when you are a lieutenant colonel in the Army you just follow orders, and at the end of the autopsy we were specifically told, as I recall it, it was by Admiral Kinney, this surgeon general of the Navy, this is subject to verification—we were specifically told not to discuss the case.

Q—Why did you not trace the track of the wound?

A—I examined the wounds but I didn't remove the organs of the neck.

Q—You said you didn't do this; I am asking you why didn't you do this as a pathologist?

A—From what I recall, I looked at the trachea, <u>there was a tracheotomy wound</u>, but the best I can remember, but I didn't dissect or remove those organs.

Ass't. Dist. Attorney Oser to the court: Your Honor, I would ask the witness to answer my question.

Q—I will ask you (to Lt. Col. Finck) one more time: why did you not dissect the track of the bullet wound you have described today, and [that] you saw at the time of the autopsy [when] you examined the body? Why? I ask you to answer that question.

A—As I recall, <u>I was told not to</u>, but I don't remember by whom.

Q—You were told not to but you don't remember by whom?

A—Right.

Q—But you were told not to go into the area of the neck, is that your testimony?

A—From what I recall, <u>yes</u>, but I don't remember by whom
...

Q—Can you give me the name of the person in charge of the autopsy?

A—Well, there were several people in charge, there were several admirals, and as I recall, the adjutant general of the

Navy.

Q—Do you have a name, Colonel?

A—It was Admiral Kinney, K-i-n-n-e-y, as I recall.[99]

Q—Can you give me the Army general's name?

A—I don't remember it.

Q—How did you know he was an Army general?

A—Because Dr. Humes told me.

Q—Was he in uniform?

A—I don't remember.

Q—Were there any of the admirals or generals or any of the military in uniform in that autopsy room?

A—Yes.

Q—Were there any admirals in uniform in the autopsy room?

A—From what I remember, Admiral Galloway was in uniform, Admiral Kinney was in uniform. I don't remember whether or not Admiral Berkley, the president's physician, was in uniform.

Q—Were there any other generals in uniform?

A—I remember a brigadier general of the Air Force but I don't remember his name ...

Q—Is this in your opinion a complete autopsy under the definition used by the American Board of Pathology? Yes or no, and then you can explain it.

A—On ... NO (!) On the 24th of November, because to my recollection we based our autopsy report on the 24th of November on the <u>information obtained from people on the scene</u>. We based it on our gross autopsy findings pertaining to the wounds as they were described on the body and X-rays taken before and during the course of the autopsy...."

The above questions and answers were taken directly from the transcript of the evidence given by Lt. Col. Finck as a defense witness for Clay Shaw. However, the colonel was lying regarding the last question, for he swore previous to the final question quoted above: "I think I went first to the—I saw those photographs and X-rays to the best of my recollection at the

---

[99] Rear Admiral Edward C. Kenney (corrected spelling), surgeon general of the Navy.

archives of the United States in January 1967, the photographs, for the first time."

Thus, the colonel could not have based an autopsy report on X-rays and photographs he never saw!

As published above, Lt. Col. Finck knew what he was saying when he testified that "when you are a lieutenant colonel in the Army you just follow orders, and at the end of the autopsy we were specifically told ..."

Those three military physicians were told more than not to discuss the case; they were told NOT TO PERFORM A COMPLETE AUTOPSY! BASED ON AN INCOMPLETE AUTOPSY, Comdr. Humes issued a deliberate fraudulent report which CONCEALED NOT ONLY THE CONSPIRACY BUT THE CONDUCT OF MEMBERS OF THE MILITARY OFFICERS IN THE DEPARTMENT OF DEFENSE who were "accessories after the fact."

PHOTOGRAPHS

The following photographs should be carefully studied by the reader, for they substantiate the testimony that a conspiracy murdered President Kennedy, Senator Robert Kennedy, and Martin Luther King, and that Lee Harvey Oswald was not "the sole and exclusive killer of President Kennedy."

1. This is the map published by the Dallas "Morning News" on November 22, 1963, which showed the route to be used by President Kennedy. There is NO detour, and Oswald could NOT have known that the president would drive past the Book Depository.

2. The front page of the Dallas "Times-Herald," evening edition, November 22, 1963. The essential evidence from that paper revealed the astonishing fact that the shots rang out at 12:25 p.m., NOT 12:30 p.m. Also the fact that the police immediately surrounded the railroad tracks. The police broadcast of the "killer" never matched the description of Oswald. The shots also came not from the Book Depository but from the "Dal-Tex" Building! Finally, one of the killers with a rifle in his hands was arrested and taken to the police station. That man was NOT Oswald.

3. This map shows the actual route taken by Police Chief Curry. He was never asked why he, as the leader of the motorcade, drove into a "double detour."

4. The U.S. Secret Service pictograph released by the USIS [United States Information Service] to the foreign press. This was later withdrawn by that government agency under the direct orders of a "higher authority."

5. The TWO different rifles used by the Warren Commission

to "convict" Oswald. The rifle at the top is the one published by the "AP" and labeled authentic by the Commission. The one at the bottom is the one known as Com. Exh. 139.

6. A series of 4 photographs placed side by side that reveal that not less than TWO rifles were used by the Commission to "convict" Oswald. No. 1 and 2 were published by "Life" and the "AP" as the rifle used by the killer. The Commission said both were authentic! No. 2 is the rifle photograph of the "UPI" as held by Capt. Fritz. On the first three photographs there is a white sling; Fritz's has a two-piece cord. By using a magnifier, it can be seen that the trigger guards and the sights are different, and the stock on No. 3 is not the same size.

7. Photograph of Capt. Fritz holding rifle with fingers, but when FBI fingerprint bureau examined the rifle his fingerprints had vanished!

8. This photograph was SUPPRESSED by the Commission, for it proved the entire "Report" was a falsification of the facts surrounding the murder of the president. This photograph was taken between 12:45 p.m. and 1:00 p.m. on the 6th floor of the Book Depository by a photographer of the Dallas "Morning News" on November 22, 1963. This photograph was taken PRIOR to the time the police shifted the cartons from one direction to another and reduced the cartons from 3 to 2. Lieutenant Day, under cross-examination, admitted in his sworn statement that there were three cartons stacked on top of each other. NO rifleman could have shot at the president as seen from this secreted and suppressed authentic photograph.

9. Com. Exh. 1301[100]—a deliberate faked photograph knowingly used by the Commission in an attempt to substantiate its theory that no conspiracy murdered the president. This is the photograph taken by Det. Studebaker at 1:30 p.m., which now showed a carton on the windowsill and only two cartons on top of each other. The position of those two

---

[100] See also CD 81.1 (attorney general of Texas file).

cartons also changed the actual three-carton stance 180 degrees! Studebaker testified that he photographed the area AFTER the cartons had been changed, but he did not identify the police agents who had done the changing.

10. The famous unpublished "Hughes" photograph and unpublished letter by Mr. J. Edgar Hoover, which informed the Commission that Frame 9 of the Hughes pictures revealed that NO person, no rifle, was at the 6th-floor window when the president's automobile was directly under that window as it passed the Depository. That picture also substantiated the Dallas "News" suppressed photograph.

11. Another fraudulent photograph used by the Commission to "convict" Oswald. This supposedly "authentic" reenactment of how the rifleman shot at the president reveals that the rifle is held at a 21-plus-degree "angle of fire," while the Commission said the bullet that theoretically entered the president's neck was at a 12-degree angle! No bullet can change its angle of fire in midair.

12. The famous "shield of cartons" that the Commission said Oswald constructed in TWO minutes! Nor did the Commission take any time to explain how "Oswald" got in and out of that "shield." Both ends are closed, and he could not squeeze in between the cartons. Did he jump a 5-1/2-foot barrier twice?

13. The "casually thrown" rifle found on the 6th floor. A Commission "pipe" dream! Who placed the rifle between the cartons? This photograph is in the Dallas police files.

14. On November 22, 1963 the Commission said Oswald was the world's strongest man! There were NO Oswald prints on the cartons comprising the "shield." Furthermore, as seen in the picture, he lifted a carton with only a left portion of his palm and his right index finger! There were NO prints of his on the carton, or on the windowsill, or on the bottom carton.

15. This suppressed photograph, taken by a Dallas "Times-

Herald" photographer within thirty minutes after the murder of President Kennedy, shows the interior of the 6th floor along the length of the windows. The photograph substantiates the testimony of Bonnie Ray Williams! He was eating his lunch at the windows located in the middle of the photograph. There is no obstruction!

16. Further proof that the alleged cartridges found in No. 18 were planted. Com. Exh. No. 543 is a deformed cartridge, which the FBI and Mr. Hoover testified could not be placed in the rifle chamber! (See letter in affidavit section.)

17. The photograph the Commission should have suppressed. This must be compared to No. 16 above. When Studebaker took No. 16, his camera did NOT take the picture of the "invisible" paper bag, so the Commission drew dotted lines to portray that invisible bag. The reader cannot see it; the camera could not see it; eight Dallas policemen did not see it; but Lt. Day saw it!

18. Another example of how to photograph an invisible object! Taken by Det. Studebaker, which showed three cartridges in positions that defy ballistics, plus the fact that NO ammunition clip was photographed although Lt. Day testified he saw and picked up the clip near the cartridges. The FBI called him a liar.

19. Another suppressed photograph! [Deputy Sheriff Buddy Walthers] picking up a bullet in Dealey Plaza at 12:40 p.m. This is a "UPI" photograph from the Dallas Bureau. Although the Commission knew of the photograph and the bullet they never questioned Walthers, the police sergeant (Dean?), or the plainclothes detective wearing glasses,[101] regarding the disposition of that bullet!

20. Bullet No. 399. A bullet planted in the Parkland Hospital and found "under the rug" on the elevator. A bullet that never

---

[101] Patrolman J. W. Foster is the figure wearing a uniform; Walthers is wearing glasses, and the third man is unidentified.

exploded although it went through the president and smashed into Governor Connally, breaking his wrist and ribs.

21. The famous Altgens "AP" photographs showing Lee Harvey Oswald at the entrance to the Book Depository. This photograph of Oswald was supported by the FBI investigation and the U.S. Secret Service.

22. The clothes worn by Billie Lovelady, which proved that the FBI and Secret Service were correct—not the Warren Commission. Of course, Lovelady was proved to be a perjurer by none other than his immediate superior, Wm. Shelley. (See affidavit section.) As can be seen, Lovelady's shirt does have vertical stripes.

23. The LEGAL autopsy chart, [Commission Exhibit] No. 397, which proved FOUR BULLETS struck the president. THIS PROVED A CONSPIRACY BEYOND A REASONABLE DOUBT.

24. The official FBI reenactment photograph, which shows the bullet hole in the president's BACK—not the back of his neck—substantiating the autopsy chart.

25. [The] suppressed Secret Service survey of the location of the president's automobile proved beyond a reasonable doubt that no bullet struck the president, which was discharged from a rifle held at the 6th-floor Book Depository window.

26. Suppressed Secret Service photographs showing the location of the president's automobile as each bullet was fired. No bullets came from the 6th-floor window.

27. The phony Alexander "affidavit" charging Oswald with the murder of President Kennedy. There is no "affiant" charging Oswald with the murder of President Kennedy. This photograph was taken at the 11:30 p.m. press conference to impress the newspapers. It is and was an outright fake.

28. The official FBI photographs suppressed by the Warren Commission, which revealed the bullet hole in the necktie knot in the front of the president's throat. Also the bullet hole in the back of the president's coat jacket—"six inches below the neck and 2 inches to the right of the seam." Proof that Oswald was innocent and that a conspiracy murdered President Kennedy.

29. Photograph of the "arrest report" of Lee Harvey Oswald. A fake legal document, which was not signed by any policeman, that revealed Oswald was arrested without a revolver; arrested without resisting arrest.

30 & 31. The MYSTERY MAN! This man murdered President Kennedy and also the Rev. Martin Luther King. The photograph is one taken after his arrest on the "grassy knoll" with the murder weapon in the possession of the right hand of the officer. This arrest is mentioned in the testimony of the "Hearings," but the Warren Commission did not ask either the Dallas police or the Dallas Sheriff's Department what happened to the murderer when taken to jail. After the murder of Martin L. King, a sketch of his murderer was made by the FBI [and] circulated; and when this same man was arrested by the Mexican police, FBI agents flew to Mexico and took him into custody. THIS MAN WAS NOT JAMES EARL RAY, the nonkiller of Rev. King.

32 & 33. The TWO James Earl Rays! Both men in these two photographs were alleged to be James Earl Ray by the Memphis Police Department. These are TWO different men. The man on the right was given 99 years. The man with the glasses was photographed as he was taken to the Memphis jail. The woman in London, England, who originally identified "James Earl Ray" as her boarding room tenant said the man with the glasses was NOT her James Earl Ray. NEITHER photographed man is the man in the FBI sketch identified as the murderer of Rev. King.

34 & 35. The TWO letters from Director J. Edgar Hoover of the FBI to Dallas Police Chief Curry were never published in

the Warren "Report." The reason is self-evident, for both letters, introduced in a court of law trying Lee Harvey Oswald for the murders of President Kennedy and officer Tippit, would compel that court if operating under the "basic principles of American justice" to give to Oswald a verdict of "not guilty." The arrows and brackets in the two letters were placed there by the author to emphasize Mr. Hoover's statements.

36. The suppressed "Lt. Revill" letter, which was given under oath on November 22, 1963! Note the time Agent Hosty made the statement: 2:50 p.m. Agent Hosty, under oath, denied making such a statement, but it is slightly incredible that any police officer would make such a statement under oath in view of the admiration Revill's superiors had for the FBI and Mr. Hoover.

THE DALLAS TIMES HERALD

FINAL EDITION

PRESIDENT DEAD

Connally Also Hit By Sniper

By GEORGE CARTER

President Kennedy died of sniper's bullets in Dallas Friday afternoon.

The President and Gov. John Connally were ambushed as they drove in the President's open convertible in a downtown motorcade.

Two priests announced shortly before 1:30 that the President was dead.

Bullets apparently came from a high-powered rifle in a building at Houston and Elm.

A man was arrested and taken in the sheriff's office.

The President immediately clutched his chest and slumped into the arms of his wife. Gov. Connally, apparently shot in the chest, fell to the floor under his wife's feet.

Secret service agents immediately dispatched the motorcade at high speed to Parkland Hospital.

Gov. Connally was reported in critical condition.

Witnesses standing on a balcony of the courthouse gave this account of what they saw:

The motorcade had just turned into Houston Street from Main Street when a shot rang out. Pigeons flew up from the street. Then, two more shots rang out and Mr. Kennedy fell to the floor of the car.

The shots seemed to come from the entrance of Elm Street from just beyond the Texas Textbook Depository building at the corner of Elm and Houston streets.

Police returned into the area toward the railroad tracks and the witnesses could not tell whether he was captured.

The crowds stopped there and there was bedlam.

Deputy Police Chief Ray Lansky, leading the procession through Dallas, said he thought the shots were fired at the President's car entered the Triple Underpass.

Police issued a lookup order for an unknown white man, about 30, slender, 5-10, 165 pounds, armed with a .30 caliber rifle.

Six or seven persons were believed hit by sniper's bullets.

Police reached the building as the stunned crowd of persons watching the downtown parade watched.

The President was rushed to Parkland Hospital.

Sgt. G. D. Henslee, police dispatcher, directed all available police units to the downtown area near the western edge of downtown Dallas.

The Presidential runway cut off its route and sped at high speed immediately toward Parkland Hospital where doctors were ordered to stand by.

The motorcade, originally set to turn off Industrial by the Trade Mart, sped straight down Industrial toward Stemmons Blvd.

The police radio blared that the President had been hit.

Sheriff Decker came on the air around 12:55 p.m.

"I don't know what's happened. Take every available man from the jail and the office and go to the railroad yards off Elm near the triple underpass."

The crowds waiting inside the Trade Mart were not immediately told of the shooting.

A welding report announced told police minutes after the shooting the President appeared to be hit in the head.

President's car roared underneath the triple underpass.

President Kennedy and Gov. Connally were critically wounded by sniper's bullets near the downtown triple underpass shortly afternoon Friday.

Bullets apparently came from a building at Houston and Elm.

But reporters following the President in a motorcade said a man and woman were seen scrambling on a walk over the underpass.

The President and Connally were rushed to Parkland Hospital.

Minutes later they were reported still alive by Rep. Albert Thomas of Houston, who stood outside the emergency surgery door.

Police reports indicated President Kennedy was shot in the head. Connally was apparently shot in the chest.

Mrs. Kennedy apparently was safe. Mrs. Connally also was safe, it appeared. Both women were stunned.

Apparent six or seven shots were fired. The bursts were clearly heard.

Police overturned the area immediately.

Reporters about five or engine behind the chief's car heard what sounded like three bursts of gunfire.

Secret Service agents in a follow-up car quickly unshouldered their automatic rifles.

The bubble top of the President's car was down.

They drew their pistols, but the damage was done.

The President was slumped over in the back seat of the car, face down. Connally lay on the floor of the rear seat.

It was impossible to tell at once where Kennedy was hit, but bullet wounds in Connally's chest were plainly visible indicating the gunfire might possibly have come from an automatic weapon.

Dallas motorcycle officers escorting the President's car, the famous "Bubbletop" from Washington, Mr. was rushed to an emergency room in the hospital.

Other White House officials were in doubt as the survivors of the hospital erupted in pandemonium.

The Secret Service said the President remained in the emergency room at Parkland and the Governor was moved to the general operating room.

One Secret Service man was overheard telling another that there was no need to move the President because emergency facilities were entirely adequate in the emergency room.

Two Roman Catholic priests were summoned to the emergency room where the President lay. One was identified as a Father Huber.

Makolm Kilduff, acting White House press secretary, said that the two priests had been "asked for."

Pandemonium broke loose around the scene.

The Secret Service waved the motorcade on at top speed to the hospital.

Even at high speed it took nearly five minutes to get the car to the ambulance entrance of the hospital.

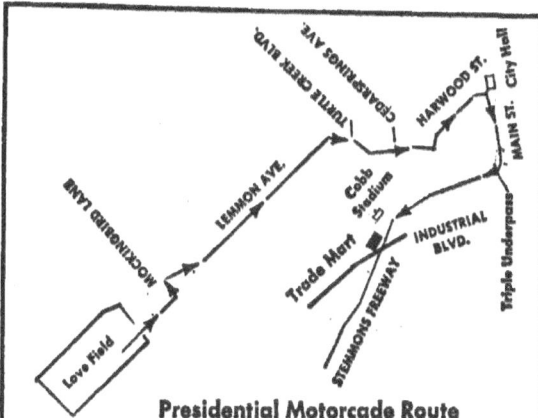

The Dallas Morning News

DALLAS, TEXAS, FRIDAY, NOVEMBER 22, 1963 — 54 PAGES IN 6 SECTIONS

Presidential Motorcade Route

2

1

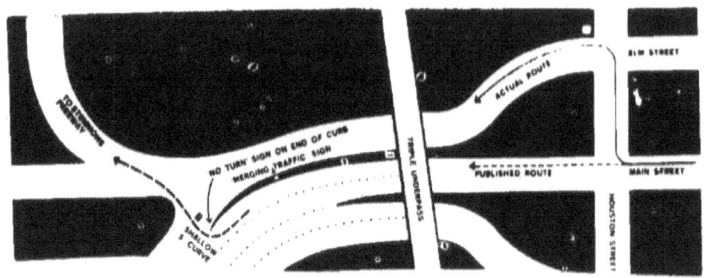

3

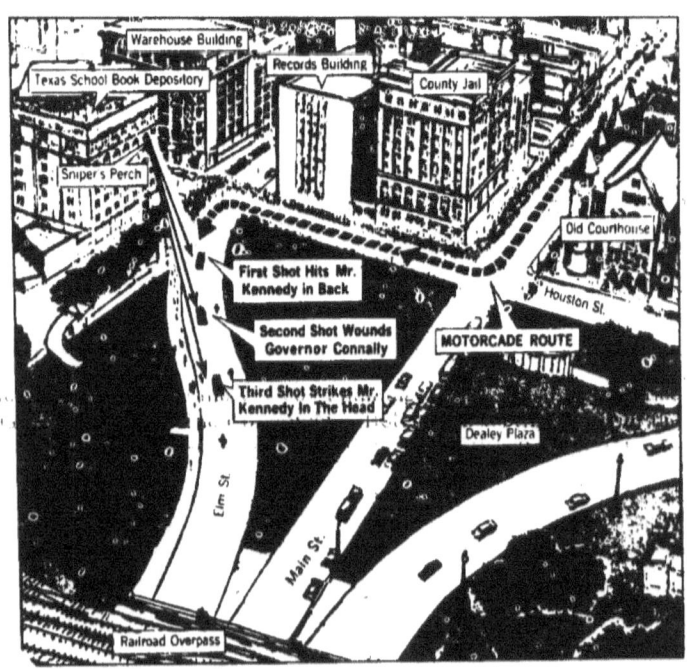

4

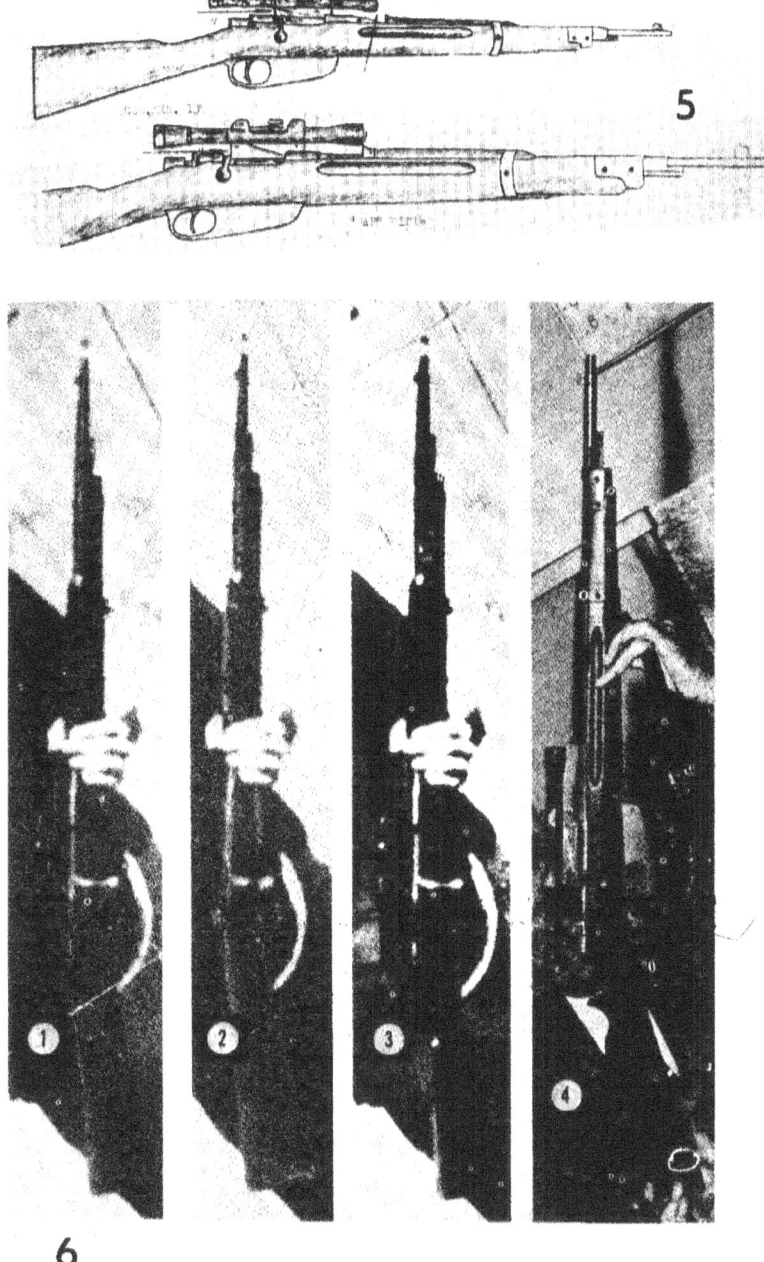

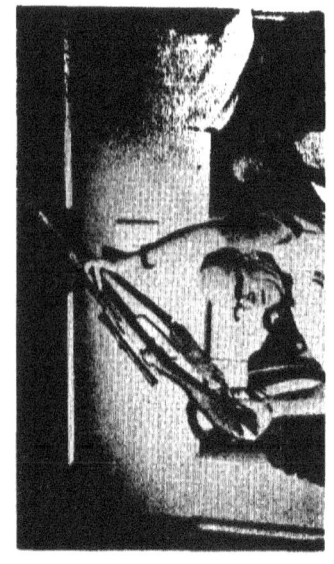

7

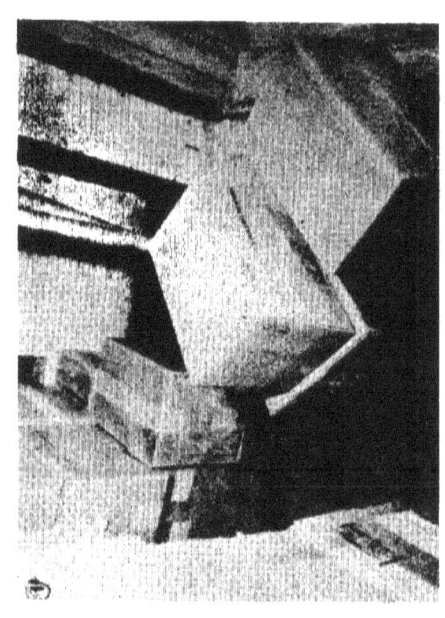

6

8 A photograph which appeared in the *Dallas Morning News* on November 22, 1963 with the caption: "This is the sixth floor window where the killer lay in wait."

10 ENLARGED PRINT FROM 8MM MOVIE FILM OF WINDOW FROM WHICH SHOTS WERE FIRED. PICTURE WAS TAKEN MOMENTS BEFORE ASSASSINATION. TOP FLOOR (7th) NOT SHOWN IN THIS PHOTOGRAPH.

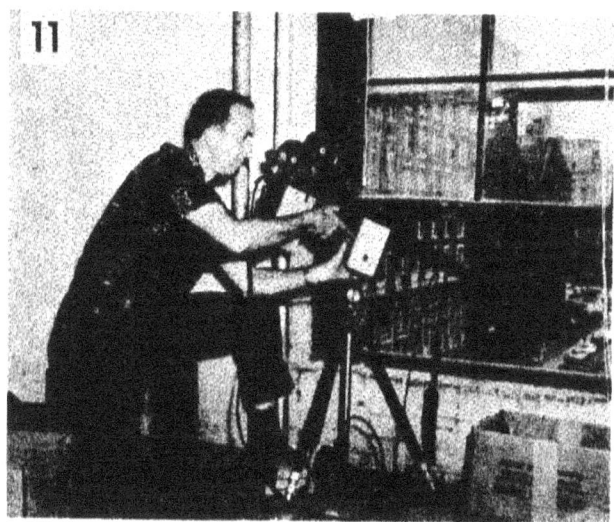

COMMISSION EXHIBIT No. 887

Commission Exhibit No. 723

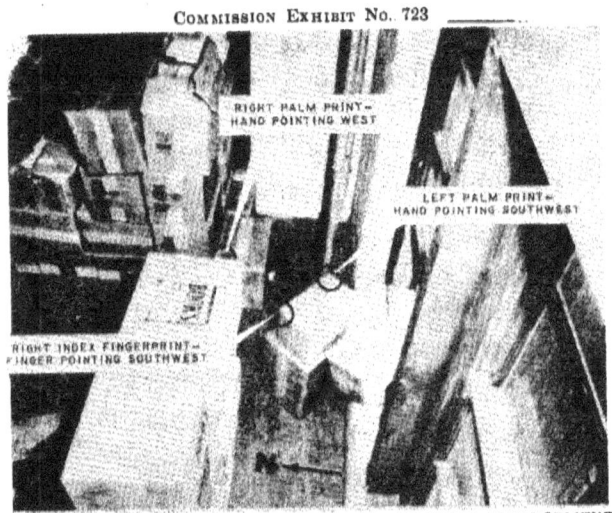

SOUTHEAST CORNER OF SIXTH FLOOR SHOWING ARRANGEMENT OF CARTONS SHORTLY AFTER SHOTS WERE FIRED.

Commission Exhibit No. 1301

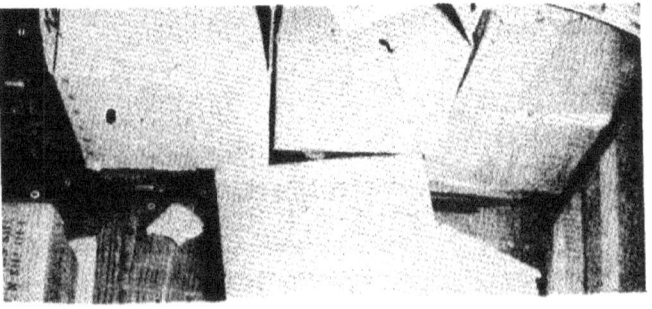

15

Commission Exhibit 543:

16

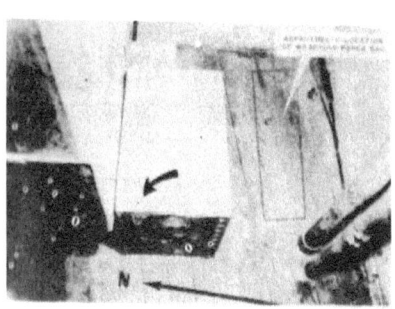

APPROXIMATE LOCATION OF WRAPPING-PAPER BAG AND LOCATION OF PALM PRINT ON CARTON NEAR WINDOW IN SOUTHEAST CORNER. HAND POSITION SHOWN BY DOTTED LINE ON BOX.

Commission Exhibit No. 1302

17

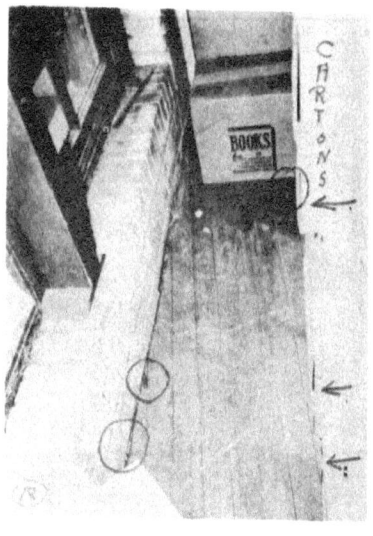

18

19

Commission Exhibit 399: A portion

20

A portion of the AP photo showing the man in the doorway.

21

An actual photograph of Lee Harvey Oswald at a press interview Friday evening November 22, 1963.

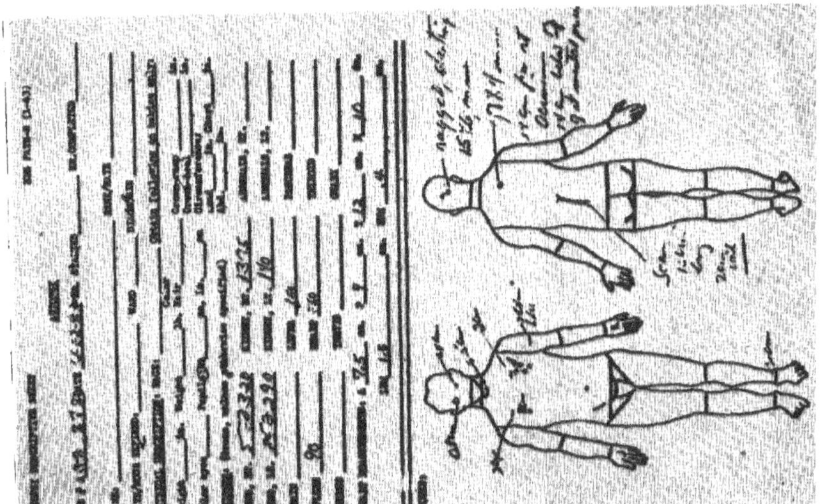

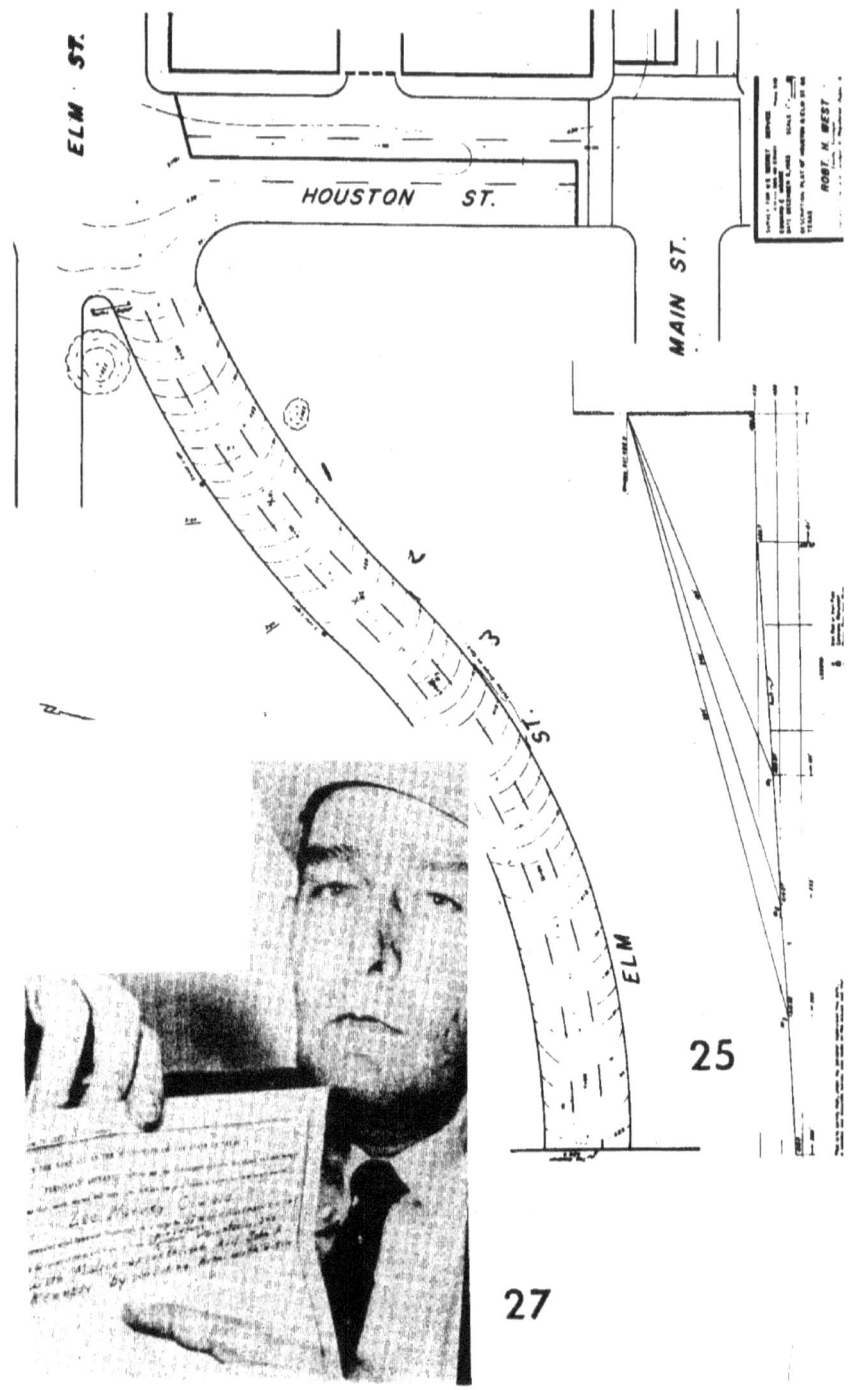

26

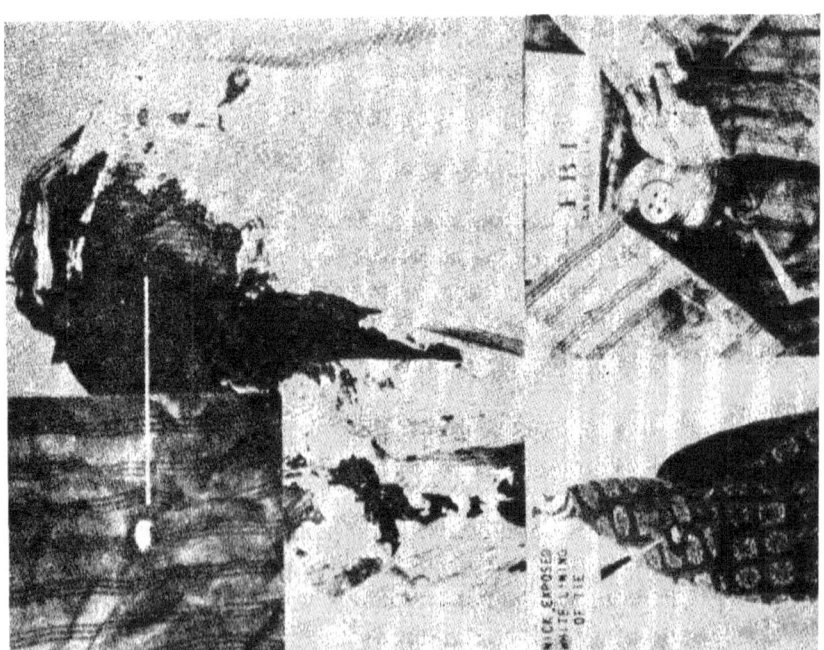

EXHIBIT 28 60 — VIEW OF THE BACK OF PRESIDENT KENNEDY'S SHIRT WITH CLOSE-UP OF BULLET ENTRANCE HOLE. LOWER TWO PHOTOGRAPHS SHOW PROJECTILE EXIT HOLE IN COLLAR AND NICK IN RIGHT SIDE OF TIE.

30-31

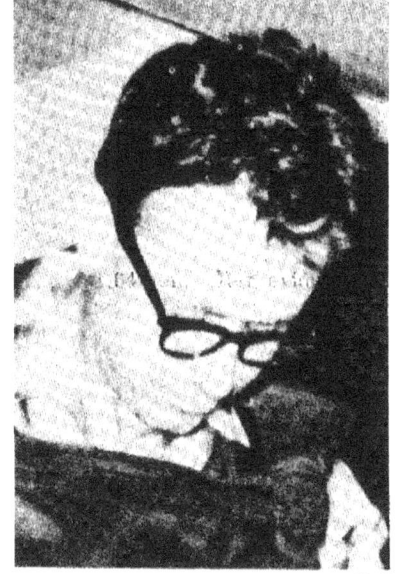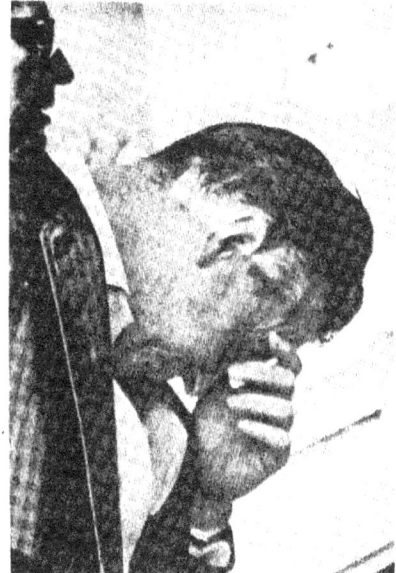
32-33

34   STATEMENTS MADE BY FBI DIRECTOR HOOVER TO CHIEF CURRY, NOV. 23, 1963

Test cartridge cases obtained from the submitted rifle were compared with specimens Q6 and Q7. As a result, specimens Q6 and Q7 were identified as having been fired in this rifle. The bullet, Q13, from Officer Tippett, is a .38 Special copper-coated lead bullet. Q13 weighs 156.6 grains and possesses the physical characteristics of 158 grain Western-Winchester revolver bullets. The surface of Q13 is so badly mutilated that there are not sufficient individual microscopic characteristics present for identification purposes. It was determined, however, that the .38 Special Smith and Wesson revolver, K3, is among those weapons which produce general rifling impressions of the type found on Q13.

A small tuft of textile fibers was found adhering to a jagged area on the left side of the metal butt plate on the K1 gun. Included in this tuft of fibers were gray-black, dark blue and orange-yellow cotton fibers which match in microscopic characteristics the gray-black, dark blue and orange-yellow cotton fibers composing the Q11 shirt of the suspect. These fibers could have originated from this shirt.

No fibers were found on the K1 gun that could be associated with the Q12 blanket and no fibers were found on the Q10 paper bag that could be associated with the Q11 shirt.

The inside surface of specimen Q10 did not disclose markings identifiable with the rifle, K1. A number of indentations, folds and extraneous markings appear on the inner surface of the Q10 wrapping.

The latent prints appearing in the photograph taken of the rifle, K1, by the Dallas Police Department, are too fragmentary and indistinct to be of any value for identification purposes. Photographs of this weapon taken by this Bureau also failed to produce prints of sufficient legibility for comparison purposes.

No latent prints of value were developed on Oswald's revolver, the cartridge cases, the unfired cartridge, the clip in the rifle or the inner parts of the rifle.

35   MARCH 31, 1964 LETTER -FBI DIRECTOR TO CHIEF CURRY

A portion of the surface of each bullet, C251, C252 and C253, is mutilated; however, microscopic marks remain on these bullets for comparison purposes. The C251, C252 and C253 bullets were compared with each other and with test bullets obtained from Oswald's revolver, C15, the .38 Special Smith and Wesson revolver, Serial No. V510210, Assembly No. 65248. No conclusion could be reached as to whether or not C251 through C253 were fired from the same weapon or whether or not they were fired from C15. In addition, it was found that even consecutive .38 Special bullets test fired from the C15 revolver could not be identified with each other. In this connection, it should be noted that the barrel of C15 was designed for .38 S & W bullets and, therefore, it is slightly larger in diameter than barrels designed for .38 Special bullets. Firing of undersized bullets could cause erratic passage of the bullets down the barrel, resulting in individual microscopic characteristics which are not consistent. The barrel of the weapon could also be changing due to the accumulation of lead in the barrel or to wear. That one or both of the above conditions existed is apparent from the fact that consecutive .38 Special test bullets obtained from the C15 revolver could not be identified with each other.

November 22, 1963

Captain W.P. Gannaway
Special Service Bureau

SUBJECT: Lee Harvey Oswald
605 Elsbeth Street

Sir:

On November 22, 1963, at approximately 2:50PM, the undersigned officer met Special Agent James Hosty of the Federal Bureau of Investigation in the basement of the City Hall.

At that time Special Agent Hosty related to this officer that the Subject was a member of the Communist Party, and that he was residing in Dallas.

The Subject was arrested for the murder of Officer J.D. Tippit and is a prime suspect in the assassination of President Kennedy.

The information regarding the Subject's affiliation with the Communist Party is the first information this officer has received from the Federal Bureau of Investigation regarding same.

Agent Hosty further stated that the Federal Bureau of Investigation was aware of the Subject and that they had information that this Subject was capable of committing the assassination of President Kennedy.

Respectfully submitted,

36

Jack Revill, Lieutenant
Criminal Intelligence Section

Sworn to and subscribed before me, this the 7th day of April, 1964.

FRANCES BOCK
Notary, Dallas County, Dallas, Texas

AFFIDAVITS

No. 1. The suppressed memo from Warren Commission aide Willens to J. Lee Rankin, general counsel, implying that the Warren "Report" was being written PRIOR to the examination of the key witnesses. In other words, the Warren "jury" convicted Oswald at the beginning of the trial and then listened to the evidence.

No. 2. The official FBI form letter admitting that the "Report" transposed frames 314 and 315 of the Zapruder film. The FBI was thus admitting that TWO independent bullets struck the victims.

No. 3. The shocking letter of Director J. Edgar Hoover, FBI, to the Commission. Why did the CIA need the Zapruder film? To "retrain" its special squad for its next victim?

No. 4. The official U.S. Secret Service report relating to the assassination.

No. 5. The official U.S. Secret Service report to the Commission that proved that various members of the conspiracy were impersonating agents of that agency.

No. 6. The official FBI report by Agents O'Neill, Jr. and Sibert that also proved a conspiracy murdered President Kennedy. This official FBI report was substantiated by every physician at the Bethesda, Md. hospital where the "autopsy" was performed.

No. 7. The Seymour Weitzman affidavit relating to the finding of a 7.65 German Mauser rifle. This affidavit was supported by the sworn testimony of other police agents who were on the 6th floor when this German Mauser rifle was found.

No. 8. The suppressed FBI report that Oswald "owned" but never "used" the rifle.

No. 9. The suppressed Lt. Day letter of January 8, 1964 admitting that he found no prints of Oswald's on the rifle, nor did he identify the carton palm print as that of one belonging to Oswald.

No. 10. Was Oswald a paid informer of the FBI? The suppressed Hudkins statement to the Secret Service relating to Oswald's FBI number and payment. The Feb. 17, 1964 Dallas Police Intelligence report that the FBI notified a Commission witness that Oswald was "all right." The reader should not forget that at the Chicago "Conspiracy of 7" trial, December 1969—February 1970, the various FBI informers were paid in the identical manner used by the FBI to pay Oswald. However, the FBI used Oswald only after he had received approval from the CIA, who trained Oswald as an agent for espionage for the Soviet Union.

No. 11. Another suppressed Dallas policeman's (Barnett's) official statement to Chief Curry. This statement substantiates the testimony of U.S. Secret Service Inspector Sorrels. This official statement, in addition to the FBI testimony regarding the Hughes' photograph that no person was at the 6th-floor window when the shots were fired, effectively demolished the Warren Commission's accusation against Oswald. Read the final paragraph carefully!

No. 12. Brennan's affidavit given to the sheriff. Every vital statement in this affidavit was admitted to be false by the Commission. Brennan admitted that he also committed perjury. Yet, the Commission used him as the key witness.

No. 13 & 14. Where was Lee Harvey Oswald when the shots were fired at President Kennedy? These two affidavits by Mrs. Arnold revealed that Oswald was on the ground floor of the Book Depository.

No. 15 & 16. The FBI affidavits of Billie Lovelady and his boss, Wm. Shelley, which proved the "man in the doorway" of the famous Altgens photograph was Lee Oswald. Since Oswald was that "man in the doorway," he could not be at the 6th floor Depository window. These TWO affidavits were suppressed by the Commission. The FBI affidavit that proved Lovelady was not wearing the clothes in the photograph.

No. 17. The affidavit of Deputy Sheriff Craig revealing the fact that he saw "Oswald" or an Oswald "double" at 12:45 p.m.

No. 18. Deputy Sheriff Craig's affidavit substantiated by an independent witness.

No. 19. The FBI statement, CD 1245, that the cartridges given to them by the Dallas Police did not prove that they were discharged on November 22, 1963 from the Italian rifle.

No. 20. The suppressed U.S. Secret Service document, Com. Doc. 354, which proved that Lee Oswald [did] see and talk to Mr. Allman of WFAA-TV on the ground floor of the Book Depository immediately following the assassination.[102]

No. 21. The FBI letter, suppressed by the Commission, that stated that the Zapruder camera was operating at 24 f.p.s., not [at] 18.3 [as] alleged by the Commission. The Commission had to fabricate the 18.3 f.p.s. to deceive the public. By increasing the speed, the Commission "proved" that a single bullet struck both victims!

No. 22. FBI Director J. Edgar Hoover's suppressed letter to Police Chief Curry, Com. Exh. 2003, No. 134, stating that the FBI found NO palm or fingerprints of Oswald on the Italian rifle, the ammunition clip, the inner parts of the rifle; nor did

---

[102] As discussed in chapter five of this book, Marks believed that "Mr. Allman was not summoned by the Commission for the reason that Oswald could not have concocted such an incident unless he had been the man involved. Thus, Oswald was seen and spoken to immediately after the shooting."

the FBI find proof that the fibers on the rifle stock came from Oswald's shirt!

UNITED STATES DEPARTMENT OF JUSTICE
FEDERAL BUREAU OF INVESTIGATION

WASHINGTON, D.C. 20535

December 14, 1965

Airmail

Dear Miss

Reference is made to your letter dated December 6, 1965, to Special Agent Lyndal L. Shaneyfelt regarding the labeling of two of the Zapruder frames numbers 314 and 315 of Commission Exhibit 885 in Volume 18 of the "Hearings Before the President's Commission on the Assassination of President Kennedy."

You are correct in the observation that frames labeled 314 and 315 of Commission Exhibit 885 are transposed in Volume 18 as noted in your letter. This is a printing error and does not exist in the actual Commission Exhibit. For your information the slides from which Commission Exhibit 885 was prepared are correctly numbered and are being shown in their correct sequence.

The National Archives is aware of this printing error; however, I do appreciate your interest in this matter.

Sincerely yours,

John Edgar Hoover
Director

GENERAL SERVICES ADMINISTRATION
ROUTING SLIP

TO
1. Mr. Rankin
2.

REMARKS

I discussed the matter of TV tapes and films with Mr. Goldberg and his memorandum of May 25 setting forth his views on this issue was written at my suggestion. I think that we should try to obtain the tapes for viewing by the staff in Washington, D. C., preferably on a weekend day so as not to interfere with their writing schedule. I have prepared the attached letter to Secret Service with the thought that we can get a quicker response from the stations in this manner than by individual letters addressed to them.

FROM: Howard P. Willens

DATE: 5/30/64

OFFICE OF THE DIRECTOR

UNITED STATES DEPARTMENT OF JUSTICE
FEDERAL BUREAU OF INVESTIGATION
WASHINGTON, D.C. 20535

CIA
FBI

December 4, 1964

BY COURIER SERVICE

Honorable J. Lee Rankin
General Counsel
The President's Commission
200 Maryland Avenue, Northeast
Washington, D. C.

Dear Mr. Rankin:

You previously have been informed that this Bureau is in possession of a copy of a film portraying the assassination of President John F. Kennedy. The film being referred to was taken by Adrian Zapruder who, after making a copy available to the FBI, sold the film to "Life" magazine. This Bureau has not permitted the copy of the film to be released outside of this Bureau without the concurrence of the Commission.

The Central Intelligence Agency has inquired if the film copy in possession of this Bureau can be loaned to that Agency solely for training purposes. The showing of the film would be restricted to Agency personnel. We have been informed that the Central Intelligence Agency consulted with Mr. Alfred Goldberg of the Commission who, according to that Agency, has approved the loan of the film.

Unless advised to the contrary, this Bureau will make available a copy of the film to the Central Intelligence Agency on a loan basis and under the arrangement described above.

Sincerely yours,

J. Edgar Hoover

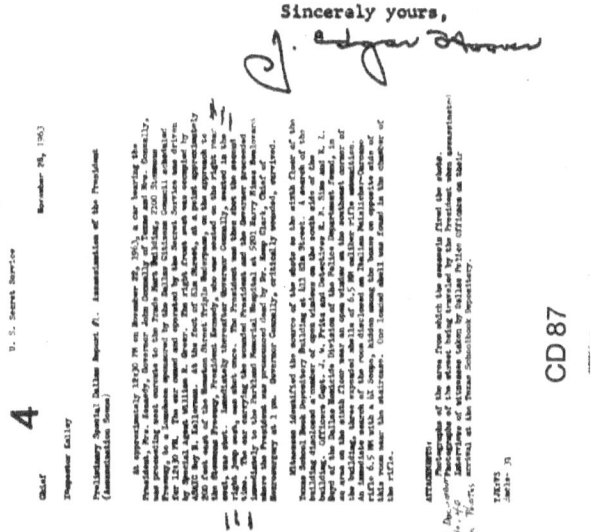

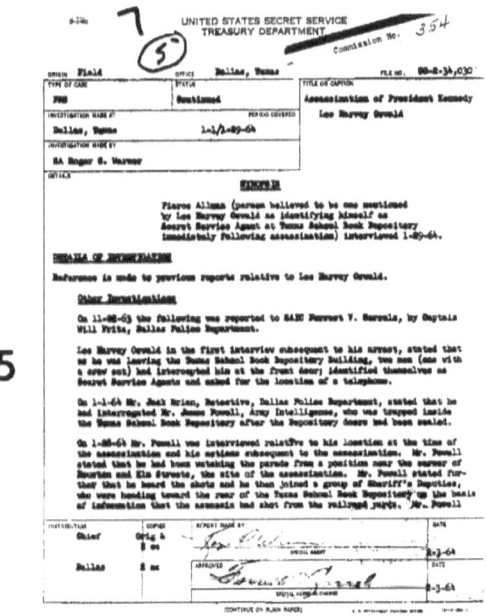

CD 354

During the autopsy inspection of the area of the brain, two fragments of metal were removed by Dr. HUMES, namely, one fragment measuring 7 x 2 millimeters, which was removed from the right side of the brain. An additional fragment of metal measuring 1 x 3 millimeters was also removed from this area, both of which were placed in a glass jar containing a black metal top which were thereafter marked for identification and following the signing of a proper receipt were transported by Bureau agents to the FBI Laboratory.

During the latter stages of this autopsy, Dr. HUMES located an opening which appeared to be a bullet hole which was below the shoulders and two inches to the right of the middle line of the spinal column.

This opening was probed by Dr. HUMES with the finger, at which time it was determined that the trajectory of the missile entering at this point had entered at a downward position of 45 to 60 degrees. Further probing determined that the distance travelled by this missile was a short distance inasmuch as the end of the opening could be felt with the finger.

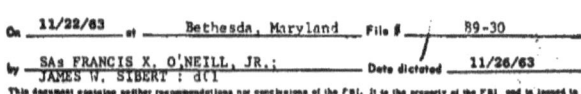

Cartridges Fired in Oswald's Rifle

Three empty cartridge cases were found near the window from which the shots were fired on the sixth floor of the building. These cartridge cases were examined by the FBI Laboratory, and it was determined that all three had been fired in the rifle owned by Oswald. (Exhibit 22)

Immediately after President Kennedy and Governor Connally were admitted to Parkland Memorial Hospital, a bullet was found on one of the stretchers. Medical examination of the President's body revealed that one of the bullets had entered just below his shoulder to the right of the spinal column at an angle of 45 to 60 degrees downward, that there was no point of exit, and that the bullet was not in the body. An examination of this bullet by the FBI Laboratory determined that it had been fired from the rifle owned by Oswald. (Exhibit 23) Bullet fragments found in the automobile in which President Kennedy was riding were examined in the FBI Laboratory. It was definitely established, from markings on two of the fragments, that they had been fired from the rifle owned by Oswald. (Exhibit 24)

Palm Print on Rifle

Dallas police lifted a latent impression off the underside of the gun barrel near the end of the

---

AFFIDAVIT IN ANY FACT

THE STATE OF TEXAS
COUNTY OF DALLAS

BEFORE ME, ____ Mary Rattan ____ a Notary Public in and for said County, State of Texas, on this day personally appeared Seymour Weitzman w/m, 2802 Gatès Drive, DA7 6624. Bus. Rockie Love, RI1 1483

Who, after being by me duly sworn, on oath deposes and says: Yesterday November 22, 1963 I was standing on the corner of Main and Houston, and as the President passed and made his turn going west toward Stemmons, I walked casually around. At this time my partner was behind me and asked me something. I looked back at him and heard 3 shots. I ran in a northwest direction and scaled a fence towards where we thought the shots came from. Some persons said they thought the shots came from the old Texas Building. I immediately ran to the Texas Building and started looking inside. At this time Captain Fritz arrived and ordered all of the sixth floor sealed off and searched. I was working with Deputy S. Boone of the Sheriff's Department and helping in the search. We were in the northwest corner of the sixth floor when Deputy Boone and myself spotted the rifle about the same time. This rifle was a 7.65 Mauser bolt action equipped with a 4/18 scope, a thick leather brownish-black sling on it. The rifle was found between some boxes near the stairway. The time the rifle was found was 1:22 pm. Captain Fritz took charge of the rifle and ejected one live round from the chamber. I then went back to the office after this.

Seymour Weitzman

SUBSCRIBED AND SWORN TO BEFORE ME THIS 23 DAY OF _November_ A.D. 1963

Mary Rattan
Notary Public, Dallas County, Texas

CF-406-410

7

COMMISSION EXHIBIT NO. 2003

8

UNITED STATES SECRET SERVICE
TREASURY DEPARTMENT

FILE NO. CO-2-34,030

ORIGIN: Field	OFFICE: Houston, Tex.
TYPE OF CASE: Protective Research	STATUS: Closed (this matter)
INVESTIGATION MADE AT: Houston, Texas	PERIOD COVERED: 12/16-17/63
INVESTIGATION MADE BY: SAIC Mike Torina	TITLE OR CAPTION: Assassination of President Kennedy, Lee Harvey Oswald

SYNOPSIS

Interview with Houston Post reporter Alonzo M. Hudkins III. He states Oswald reported to be on FBI payroll as an informant, and other information.

DETAILS OF INVESTIGATION

On December 16, Alonzo M. Hudkins, reporter, Houston Post, called the office and advised that he was of the opinion that Jack Rubenstein's roommate, George Senator, could possibly have some connection with the murder of Lee Harvey Oswald. He did not appear to have any particular reason for making this suggestion other than when he interviewed one December 17 he stated that Ruby had a brother and a nephew who formerly worked for Jimmy Hoffa in Detroit, Mich. and he stated it was a "wild guess" that the Hoffa organization could be behind the assassination.

On December 17, Mr. Hudkins advised that he had just returned from a weekend in Dallas, during which time he talked to Allan Sweatt, Chief Criminal Division, Sheriff's Office, Dallas, Chief Sweatt mentioned that it was his opinion that Lee Harvey Oswald was being paid $200 a month by the FBI as an informant in connection with their subversive investigation. He furnished the alleged informant number assigned to Oswald by the FBI as "S172".

Hudkins stated it is significant to him that attorney Milton L. Bell of San Francisco, attorney representing Jack Rubenstein, was listed as an east coast associate on stationery of attorney Eqt who was the first attorney Lee Harvey Oswald asked to represent him.

He states that Chief Deputy Sheriff Allen Sweatt has copies of this stationery. Sweatt censors all of Ruby's mail.

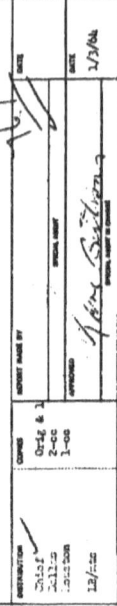

Page 2

January 8, 1964

About fifty photographs were made of the area involved in the shooting and a scale drawing was made of the sixth floor by Detectives J. B. Hicks and R. L. Studebaker.

The cartons in the area where the rifle was found, and also the cartons near the window where the spent hulls were found were dusted for prints. A palm print was found on the top northwest corner of a carton that appeared to have been used by the assassin to sit on while aiming the rifle. This palm print was collected and preserved, along with the carton it came off of, and three cartons stacked by the window apparently to rest the rifle on.

Lieutenant Day returned to the Identification Bureau about 7:00 P.M. and started the examination of the rifle for prints. Two fingerprints were found on the side of the rifle near the trigger and magazine housing and a palm print was found on the underside of the gun barrel near the end of the stock. He exposed probable these prints were made by the palm and fingers of Lee Harvey Oswald. But the rifle was released to the FBI and sent to Washington, D. C. before the examination was completed and before the identification of the prints could be made. The prints were not very good for comparison purposes.

Paraffin casts were made of Oswald's hands and the right side of his face about 9:00 P.M. November 22, 1963, in the Homicide Bureau office by Sergeant W. E. Barnes 593 and Detective J. B. Hicks. These casts were sent to USCRIL November 23, 1963 for nitrate tests.

All other evidence collected by the Crime Scene Search was released at 11:45 P.M. November 22, 1963 to Agent Vince Drain to be delivered to the F.B.I. headquarters at Washington, D.C.

Respectfully submitted,

J.C. Day 391
Lieutenant of Police
Identification Bureau

JCD:ml

COMMISSION EXHIBIT No. 3145.

CITY OF DALLAS
TEXAS
POLICE DEPARTMENT

July 16, 1964

Mr. J. E. Curry
Chief of Police

SUBJECT: Officer W. B. Barnett
Statement

Sir:

I made detail at 9:00 a.m. on November 22, 1963. I received my instructions from Captain Lawrence who instructed us to work traffic; watch the people in the crowd to see they didn't throw anything at the President or his motorcade and that it was lawful for people to carry placards but not throw them. Captain Lawrence told us to stop the cars when the motorcade came through.

I was assigned to Elm and Houston not later than 10:00 a.m. and stayed on my assignment until the motorcade came through. I was on my assignment at 10:00 a.m. I was on the northwest corner of Elm and Houston.

I checked the Texas School Depository Building around 11:00 a.m. and it was raining and all windows were closed. I talked to some people from the building who wanted to know what time the motorcade would come by. They stated that the building was full of people and they wanted to see the President and Mrs. Kennedy. I advised them to come out on the corner at 11:45 a.m. and at that time close to 100 people came out and lined the sidewalks. When the motorcade came through, I helped stop Elm Street and the Southbound traffic on Houston. I also stopped traffic on the small street which runs directly in front of the Depository Building which dead-ends into the railroad track from Elm and Houston.

When the shots were fired, I looked up and could not see anyone or anything extending out of the windows. I thought the shots were coming from top of the building.

Respectfully submitted,

W. E. Barnett
W. B. Barnett
Patrolman, Traffic Division

WEB:nw

11

VOLUNTARY STATE · N. Jader Annex. Form No. 88

SHERIFF'S DEPARTMENT
COUNTY OF DALLAS, TEXAS

Before me, the undersigned authority, on this the 22nd day of November A.D. 1963

personally appeared Howard Leslie Brennan Address 6814 Woodard
Dallas, Texas
Age ___, Phone No. FY 1-2711

Deponent says: I am presently employed by the Wallace and Beard Construction Company as a steam fitter and have been so employed for about two past weeks. I am working on a pipe-line in the Katy Railroad yards at the foot of Pacific Street near the railroad tracks. We had knocked off for lunch and I had dinner at the cafeteria at Record and Main Street and then came back to see the President of the United States. I was sitting on a piece of wall near the intersection of Houston Street and Elm Street near the red light pole. I was facing in a northerly direction looking not only at the street but I could see the large red brick building across across the street from where I was sitting. I take this building, across the street to be about 7 stories anyway, in the east end of this window on the second row of windows from the top I saw a man in this window. He had a brown pair of trousers on and a light shirt. He was just sitting there looking out apparently waiting for the same thing I was to see the President. I did not notice anything unusual about this man a He appeared to be in his early 30's, slender, nice looking, slender and would weigh about 165 to 175 pounds. He had on light colored clothing but definitely not a suit. I proceeded to watch the President's car as it turned left at the corner where I was and about 50 yards from the intersection of Elm and Houston and to a point I would say the President's back was in line with the last window I have previously described. I heard that I thought was a back fire. It run in my mind that it might be someone throwing firecrackers out the window of the red brick building and I looked up at the building. I then saw this man I have described in the window and he was taking aim with a high powered rifle. I could see all of the barrel of the gun. I do not know if it had a scope on it or not. I was looking at the man in this window at the time of the last explosion. Then this man let the gun down to his side and stepped down out of sight. He did not seem to be in any hurry. I could see this man from about his belt up. There was nothing unusual about him at all in appearance. I believe that I could identify this man if I ever saw him again.

H. L. Brennan

Subscribed and sworn to before me on this the 22nd day of November A.D. 19 63

Carl Jones
Notary Public, Dallas County, Texas

13

12 COMMISSION EXHIBIT No. 2003—Continued

Other Individuals and Organizations
Involved or Interviewed

Com #70(4)

1
EJR:vm
DL 100-10461

"Dallas, Texas
March 14, 1964

"I, Mrs. R. E. (Carolyn) Arnold, hereby freely and voluntarily make the following statement to E. J. Robertson who has identified himself as a Special Agent of the F.B.I.

"My name is Carolyn Arnold and I am married to R. E. Arnold. I reside at 3325 South Tyler Street, Dallas, Texas. I am 20 years of age, born June 1, 1943, at Memphis, Tenn. I am a white female, and am employed by the Texas School Book Depository as a Secretary.

"On November 22, 1963, at the time President Kennedy was shot, I was standing in front of the Texas School Book Depository Building. I was with Mr. O. V. Campbell, 7120 Twin Tree Lane, Dallas; Mrs. L. C. (Bonnie) Richey, 220 South Marsalis, Apt. 117, Dallas; Mrs. Barvey (Betty) Dragoo, 2705 West Brooklyn, Dallas; Mrs. Don (Virgie) Baker nee Rackley, 3600½ Live Oak, Dallas; and Miss Judy Johnson, 915 Sunnyside, Dallas, at the time President Kennedy was shot.

"I did not see Lee Harvey Oswald at the time President Kennedy was shot.

"On the morning of November 22, 1963, I do not remember seeing any stranger in the building housing the Texas School Book Depository.

"I left the Texas School Book Depository Building at about 12:25 PM, November 22, 1963, and never returned to this building on that date.

"I have read the above statement consisting of one and one-half pages and it is true and correct to the best of my knowledge.

"/s/ Mrs. R. E. (CAROLYN) ARNOLD

"Witnesses: E. J. ROBERTSON, Special Agent, FBI, Dallas, Texas. 3/18/64
THOMAS T. TRETTIS, Jr., Special Agent, FBI, Dallas, Texas, 3/18/64"

13

FEDERAL BUREAU OF INVESTIGATION

Date 11/26/63

Mrs. R. E. ARNOLD, Secretary, Texas School Book Depository, advised she was in her office on the second floor of the building on November 22, 1963, and just prior to the assassination she went to go to the lunchroom on the first floor to get a drink of coca cola. She stated as she was standing in front of the building, she noticed she thought she caught a fleeting glimpse of LEE HARVEY OSWALD standing in the hallway between the front door and the double doors leading to the warehouse, located on the first floor. She could not be sure that this was OSWALD, but said she felt it was and believed the time to be a few minutes before 12:15 PM.

She stated thereafter, she viewed the Presidential Motorcade and heard the shots that were fired at the President; however, she, which it will be recalled, was among the bystanders concerning OSWALD, did not know and had merely seen him working in the building.

11/26/63 at Dallas, Texas File # DL 89-43
by Special Agent RICHARD E. HARRISON /rmh Date dictated 11/26/63

CD 5

14

FD-302 (Rev. 1-25-60)

FEDERAL BUREAU OF INVESTIGATION

Date 3/2/64

1

BILLY NOLAN LOVELADY appeared at the Dallas FBI Office at which time he permitted to be photographed.

LOVELADY advised that on the day of the assassination of President JOHN F. KENNEDY, November 22, 1963, at the time of the assassination and shortly before, he was standing in the doorway of the front entrance to the Texas School Book Depository (TSBD) Building, 411 Elm Street, Dallas, Texas, where he is employed. He stated he was wearing a red and white vertical striped shirt and blue jeans.

LOVELADY stated his picture has appeared in several publications which picture depicts him on the far left side of the front doorway to the TSBD. LOVELADY was exhibited "Four Dark Days in History," Copyright 1963 by Special Publications, Inc., 6087 Hollywood Blvd., Los Angeles 28, California. He immediately identified the picture of the individual on the far left side of the doorway of the TSBD as being his photograph. He stated this same photograph or one identical to it also appeared in the Dallas Times Herald newspaper of November 23, 1963, and in the Cincinnati Inquirer of December 3, 1963. He stated it also appeared in an edition of the Saturday Evening Post the date of which he does not know.

Mr. LOVELADY stated his close resemblance to LEE HARVEY OSWALD has become apparent to everybody. He stated his step-children, TIMMY MITCHELL, 6, and step-daughter, ANGELA KESTEDT, age 4, when shown LEE HARVEY OSWALD shown while in custody of the Dallas Police Department and both of these children remarked that they thought their daddy was on television referring to his close resemblance to LEE HARVEY OSWALD.

The following physical description and background information was obtained from interrogation and observation of LOVELADY:

Name   BILLY NOLAN LOVELADY
Race   White
Sex   Male
Born   2/19/37, Kyrtle Springs, Texas
Height   5'8"

on 2/29/64 at Dallas, Texas File # DL 100-10461

by Special Agent ROBERT P. GEMBERLING:ga Date dictated 2/29/64
                 EMORY E. HORTON:vm

This document contains neither recommendations nor conclusions of the FBI. It is the property of the FBI and is loaned to your agency; it and its contents are not to be distributed outside your agency.

15

DL 100-10461
ADN/cms

"Dallas, Texas
March 18, 1964

"I, William H. Shelley, make the following voluntary statement to Alfred D. Neeley who has identified himself to me as a Special Agent of the Federal Bureau of Investigation.

"I am of the Caucasian race, thirty-seven years of age and reside at 120 South Tatum St., Dallas 11, Texas.

"On November 22, 1963, I left my office in the Texas School Book Depository and walked just outside the front entrance of the building to watch the Presidential Motorcade pass. This was about 12:15 PM. I recall that as the Presidential Motorcade passed I was standing just outside the glass doors of the entrance. At the time President John F. Kennedy was shot I was standing at this same place. Billy N. Lovelady who works under my supervision at the Texas School Book Depository was seated on the entrance steps just in front of me. I recall that Wesley Frazier, Mrs. Sarah Stanton and Mrs. Carolyn Arnold, all employees of the Texas School Book Depository, were also standing in this entrance way near me at the time Pres. Kennedy was shot. I did not see Lee Harvey Oswald at the time Pres. Kennedy was shot.

"I did not observe any strangers in the building at any time during the morning of November 22, 1963.

"Immediately following the shooting, Billy N. Lovelady and I accompanied some uniformed police officers to the railroad yards just west of the building and returned through the west side door of the building about ten minutes later. I remained in the building until about 1:30 PM when I was asked to go to the Dallas Police Dept. to furnish an affidavit. I returned to the Texas School Book Depository Building about 3:45 PM. I did not leave the building until about 7 PM that day.

"Lee Harvey Oswald worked under my supervision. He was at work when I arrived for work on November 22, 1963 at about 8 AM. I specifically recall seeing Oswald on the first floor about 11:50 AM this day. He was going about his regular duties filling orders at that time. I did not see Oswald again after this until I saw him at the Dallas Police Dept.

"I have read this statement consisting of this and two other pages and it is true.

"/s/William H. Shelley

"Witness: /s/E. J. Robertson, Special Agent, FBI, Dallas, Tex. 3-18-64
         /s/Alfred D. Neeley, Special Agent, FBI, Dallas, Tex. 3-18-64.

16

COUNTY OF DALLAS
SHERIFF'S DEPARTMENT
SUPPLEMENTARY INVESTIGATION REPORT

Name of Complainant

ASSASSINATION OF PRESIDENT KENNEDY

Serial No.

Offense

Officer Roger Craig, Dallas County Deputy Sheriff.

DETAILS OF OFFENSE, PROGRESS OF INVESTIGATION, ETC.
(Investigating Officer must sign)

Date **Nov 23, 1963**

I was standing in front of the Sheriff's Office at 505 Main Street, Dallas, Texas, watching President Kennedy pass in the motorcade. I was watching the rest of the motorcade a few seconds after President Kenney passed where I was standing when I heard a rifle shot and a few seconds later a second and then a third shot. At the retort of the first shot, I started running around the corner and Officer Buddy Walthers and I ran across Houston Street and ran up the terrace on Elm Street and into the railroad yards. We made a round through the railroad yards and I returned to Elm Street by the Turnpike sign at which time Officer Walthers told me that a bullet had struck the curb on the south side of Elm Street. I crossed to Elm with Deputy C. L. Lummie Lewis to search for a spot where a shell might have hit. About this time I heard a shrill whistle and I turned around and saw a white male running down the hill from the direction of the Texas School Book Depository Building and I saw what I think was a light colored Rambler Station wagon with luggage rack on top pull over to the curb and this subject who had come running down the hill get into this car. The man driving this station wagon was a dark complected white male. I tried to get across Elm street to stop the car and talk with subjects, but the traffic was so heavy I could not make it. I reported this incident at once to a secret service officer, whose name I do not know, then I left this area and went at once to the building and assisted in the search of the building.

Later that afternoon, I heard that the City had a suspect in custody and I called and reported the information about the suspect running down the hill and getting into a car to Captain Frits and was requested to come at once to City Hall. I went to City Hall and identified the subject they had in custody as being the same person I saw running down this hill and get into the station wagon and leave the scene.

17

DL 100-10461
RPG/ds

Under date of June 10, 1964, the FBI Laboratory furnished the following information concerning a firearms examination requested by the Dallas Office on May 13, 1964:

Specimens received 11/23/63

Q6   C6   6.5 mm Mannlicher-Carcano cartridge case from Texas School Book Depository
Q7   C7   6.5 mm Mannlicher-Carcano cartridge case from Texas School Book Depository
Q8   C8   6.5 mm Mannlicher-Carcano cartridge from Texas School Book Depository

Evidence received 11/27/63

Q48   C38 6.5 mm Mannlicher-Carcano cartridge case from Texas School Book Depository

Results of examination:

An examination was made of the cartridge cases, C6, C7 and C38 and the cartridge, C8, for loading, chambering, extraction and/or ejection marks for the purpose of determining if these specimens had been loaded into and extracted from Oswald's rifle, C14, more than once.

Marks were found on the C6 cartridge case indicating that it has been loaded into and extracted from a weapon at least three times. One set of marks was identified as having been made by the magazine follower of the C14 rifle. It is pointed out that the extractor and ejector marks on C6 as well as on C7, C8 and C38 did not possess sufficient characteristics for identifying the weapon which produced them. There are also three sets of marks on the base of this cartridge case which were not found on C7, C8, C38 or any of the numerous tests obtained from the C14 rifle. It was not possible to determine what produced these.

Marks were found on the C7 cartridge case indicating that it has been loaded into and extracted from a weapon at least twice. One set of marks was identified as having been produced by the chamber of the C14 rifle and one set of marks was identified as having been produced by contact with the bolt of C14; however, it was not possible to determine whether the two sets of marks which were identified were produced by one or two loading operations in the C14 rifle.

Two sets of marks were found on the C8 cartridge (found in the C14 rifle) which were identified as having been produced by the magazine follower of the C14 rifle. Another set of follower marks was found on C8. The fragmentary nature of this set of marks could possibly account for the fact that these marks were not identified with the C14 rifle.

Marks were found on the C38 cartridge case indicating that it had been loaded into and extracted from a weapon at least twice. One set of marks was identified as having been produced by the magazine follower of the C14 rifle and one set of marks was identified as having been produced by the chamber of C14; however, it was not possible to determine whether the two sets of marks which were identified were produced by one or two loading operations in the C14 rifle.

The results of the above examinations do not preclude the possibility that these items could have been loaded into and extracted from a weapon one or more times when insufficient force was used to produce marks. It is pointed out that if two or more cartridges are loaded into the clip of C14, only the bottom cartridge will be marked by the magazine follower.

DL 100-10461
RPG/ds

Under date of June 10, 1964, the FBI Laboratory furnished the following information concerning a firearms examination requested by the Dallas Office on May 12, 1964:

Specimens received 11/23/63

Q6 C6 6.5 mm Mannlicher-Carcano cartridge case from Texas School Book Depository
Q7 C7 6.5 mm Mannlicher-Carcano cartridge case from Texas School Book Depository
Q8 C8 6.5 mm Mannlicher-Carcano cartridge from Texas School Book Depository

Evidence received 11/27/63

Q48 C38 6.5 mm Mannlicher-Carcano cartridge case from Texas School Book Depository

Results of examination:

An examination was made of the cartridge cases, C6, C7 and C38 and the cartridge, C8, for loading, chambering, extraction and/or ejection marks for the purpose of determining if these specimens had been loaded into and extracted from Oswald's rifle, C14, more than once.

Marks were found on the C6 cartridge case indicating that it has been loaded into and extracted from a weapon at least three times. One set of marks was identified as having been made by the magazine follower of the C14 rifle. It is pointed out that the extractor and ejector marks on C6 as well as on C7, C8 and C38 did not possess sufficient characteristics for identifying the weapon which produced them. There are also three sets of marks on the base of this cartridge case which were not found on C7, C8, C38 or any of the numerous tests obtained from the C14 rifle. It was not possible to determine what produced these marks.

Marks were found on the C7 cartridge case indicating that it has been loaded into and extracted from a weapon at least twice. One set of marks was identified as having been produced by the chamber of the C14 rifle and one set of marks was identified as having been produced by contact with the bolt of C14; however, it was not possible to determine whether the two sets of marks which were identified were produced by one or two loading operations in the C14 rifle.

Two sets of marks were found on the C8 cartridge (found in the C14 rifle) which were identified as having been produced by the magazine follower of the C14 rifle. Another set of follower marks was found on C8. The fragmentary nature of this set of marks could possibly account for the fact that these marks were not identified with the C14 rifle.

Marks were found on the C38 cartridge case indicating that it had been loaded into and extracted from a weapon at least twice. One set of marks was identified as having been produced by the magazine follower of the C14 rifle and one set of marks was identified as having been produced by the chamber of C14; however, it was not possible to determine whether the two sets of marks which were identified were produced by one or two loading operations in the C14 rifle.

The results of the above examinations do not preclude the possibility that these items could have been loaded into and extracted from a weapon one or more times when insufficient force was used to produce marks. It is pointed out that if two or more cartridges are loaded into the clip of C14, only the bottom cartridge will be marked by the magazine follower.

19

(20)

CD 354

20

FEDERAL BUREAU OF INVESTIGATION

Date December 4, 1963

ABRAHAM ZAPRUDER, 3909 Marquette Street, Dallas, advised that on November 22, 1963, he was standing in the park area north of Elm Street and just west of the intersection of Elm and Houston Streets. He had taken this position in order to take 8 millimeter movie film of the President and the Presidential motorcade as it passed by him. He stated he had with him a Bell and Howell 8 millimeter zoom-lens camera, which was either a 1962 or 1963 model. He advised he had loaded this camera previously with a 25-foot roll of 16 millimeter film, which in effect affords 50 feet of 8 millimeter film. He had shot the first 25 feet earlier and had reversed the roll and shot a few feet on November 22, 1963, at the park area of some girls who work in his office, prior to the arrival of the Presidential motorcade. He stated his camera was fully wound, was set, manually, on maximum zoom-lens. The camera was set to take normal speed movie film or 24 frames per second. The control buttons for the zoom-lens were not touched once he started taking photographs of the Presidential motorcade.

on 12/4/63 at Dallas, Texas   File # DL 89-43

by Special Agent ROBERT M. BARRETT /gmf   Date dictated 12/4/63

A single brown viscose fiber and several light green cotton fibers were found adhering to the Q10 paper bag. These fibers match in microscopic characteristics the brown viscose fibers and light green cotton fibers present in the composition of the Q12 blanket and could have originated from this blanket.

It is pointed out, however, that fibers do not exhibit sufficient individual microscopic characteristics to be positively identified as originating from a particular source to the exclusion of all others.

No fibers were found on the K1 gun that could be associated with the Q12 blanket and no fibers were found on the Q10 paper bag that could be associated with the Q11 shirt.

The debris, including foreign textile fibers and hairs, removed from the Q12 blanket and Q11 shirt has been placed in pillboxes for possible future comparisons. These pillboxes and the glass microscope slides containing fibers removed from K1 and Q10 are being temporarily retained in the Laboratory for possible future comparisons with additional items of the suspect's clothing should they be recovered.

The Q12 blanket has been folded double and one corner has been folded in and pinned with a safety pin. A length of white cotton cord has been tied around this corner giving it a triangular-shaped appearance as if it had once contained a long object.

The paper of the wrapping and the tape, Q10, were found to have the same observable physical characteristics as the known wrapping paper and tape, K2, from the Texas Public School Book Depository.

The inside surface of specimen Q10 did not disclose markings identifiable with the rifle, K1. A number of indentations, folds and extraneous markings appear on the inner surface of the Q10 wrapping.

The latent prints appearing in the photograph taken of the rifle, K1, by the Dallas Police Department, are too fragmentary and indistinct to be of any value for identification purposes. Photographs of this weapon taken by this Bureau also failed to produce prints of sufficient legibility for comparison purposes.

A latent fingerprint was developed on the wrapping paper, Q10, which was identified with the left index finger impression of Lee Harvey Oswald. In addition, one latent palm print developed on specimen Q10 was identified with the right palm print of Oswald.

No latent prints of value were developed on Oswald's revolver, the cartridge cases, the unfired cartridge, the clip in the rifle or the inner parts of the rifle.

Specimens Q1 through Q5, Q14 and Q15 are being retained in the Laboratory until called for by a representative of the U. S. Secret Service.

Specimens Q6 through Q13, K1, K2 and K3 are being returned to the Dallas Police Department by Special Agent Vincent E. Drain of the Dallas Field Office of this Bureau. The photograph of the latent print on the rifle is being returned separately. The fingerprints and palm prints of Oswald are being retained.

Selected Books and Periodicals Cited in *Coup d'État!*

Attwood, William. *The Reds and the Blacks: A Personal Adventure*. New York: Harper & Row, 1967.

Epstein, Edward Jay. *Inquest: the Warren Commission and the Establishment of Truth*. New York: The Viking Press, 1966.

Flammonde, Paris. *The Kennedy Conspiracy: An Uncommissioned Report on the Jim Garrison Investigation*. New York: Meredith Press, 1969.

Fonzi, Gaeton. "The Warren Commission, the Truth, and Arlen Specter." *Greater Philadelphia Magazine*, August 1, 1966.

Ford, Gerald R. *Portrait of the Assassin*. New York: Simon and Schuster, 1965.

Garrison, Jim. "Playboy Interview: Jim Garrison. A candid conversation with the embattled district attorney of New Orleans." *Playboy*, 1967.

Jones, Penn. *Forgive My Grief*. Midlothian, TX: The Midlothian Mirror, 1966.

Lane, Mark. *Rush to Judgment*. New York: Holt, Rinehart & Winston, 1966.
— . *A Citizen's Dissent*. New York: Holt, Rinehart and Winston, 1968.

Manchester, William. *The Death of a President*. New York: Harper & Row, 1967.

Meagher, Sylvia. *Accessories After the Fact*. Indianapolis: Bobbs-Merrill, 1967.

Popkin, Richard. *The Second Oswald*. New York: Avon, 1966.

Ramparts, January 1967.

Weisberg, Harold. *Whitewash*. Vols. I-IV. Hyattstown, MD: Harold Weisberg, 1965, 1966, 1967.

BOOKS BY STANLEY J. MARKS

Since the Markses' works on religion contain a powerful political dimension, they have also been included here.

The Bear That Walks Like a Man: A Diplomatic and Military Analysis of Soviet Russia (Dorrance and Company, 1943).

History of the U.S. Army and Military Science. (Circa 1945; most likely extant only in manuscript form in a U.S. military archive.)

Murder Most Foul! The Conspiracy That Murdered President Kennedy: 975 Questions & Answers (Los Angeles: Bureau of International Affairs, September 1967).

A Murder Most Foul! Or, A Time to Die, A Time to Cry, described as "A three-act play that reveals how a chief of state was assassinated." Copyrighted February 19, 1968; publication history unknown. A photocopy of this 81-page manuscript was retrieved from the Copyright Office on April 30, 2021. It was rewritten and expanded under the title *A Time to Die, A Time to Cry* (Los Angeles: Bureau of International Affairs, late 1970) and is described as "A three-act play concerning the three murders that changed the course of history: President Kennedy, Martin Luther King, and Senator Robert F. Kennedy." In October 1979 this work was retitled *A Time to Die, A Time to Cry, or, Murders Most Foul!* and was described as "A three-act play relating to the past, present, and future of the figures and events surrounding the murders of President Kennedy, Martin Luther King, and Senator Robert F. Kennedy." (Retrieved from the Copyright Office on April 30, 2021.) Another version of the play, since lost, was deposited in the Copyright Office in 1988.

Two Days of Infamy: November 22, 1963; September 28, 1964 (Los Angeles: Bureau of International Affairs, March 1969). "A textbook for government agents, lawyers, professors, and students analyzing the methods of the Warren Commission." "An analytical and legal study."

Coup d'État! Three Murders That Changed the Course of History. President Kennedy, Reverend King, Senator R. F. Kennedy (Los Angeles: Bureau of International Affairs, February 1970).

American Dream, American Nightmare (Los Angeles: Bureau of International Affairs, 1971). Little is known about this book. On March 28, 1979, along with four of Marks' other titles, it was included in the Library of Congress's comprehensive JFK assassination index, *The Assassination of President John F. Kennedy: A Chronological Bibliography*. On the same day, the House of Representatives Select Subcommittee on Assassinations issued its report, which cited these same five assassination-related titles authored by Marks. It's possible that *American Dream, American Nightmare* is simply another version of his assassination play that was later retitled, especially since it doesn't appear in the lists of Marks' book titles that are normally featured on his dustjackets.

Watch What We Do ... Not What We Say! (Los Angeles: Bureau of International Affairs, 1971). "An account of the present trend of the Nixon–Agnew–Mitchell–Southern strategy axis to the possibility of Orwell's '1984' being accomplished by 1972" (from the title page). Also described elsewhere as "guidebook" on Watergate.

Through Distorted Mirrors! The Impact of Monotheism–One God–Upon Modern World Civilization, by Stanley and Ethel Marks (Los Angeles: Bureau of International Affairs, 1972). "A brief history of the Jewish people."

A Time to Die: No Time to Cry! or The Four-hour War A.K.A. World War III (Pasadena, CA: Bureau of International Affairs 1980). "A one-act, two-scene play dealing with reasons why nuclear war is inevitable." Relying "heavily" on documents and statements made by Congressional leaders, the drama is largely a critique of the Carter Doctrine (which justified the use of military force in the Persian Gulf). The play is set entirely in the

War Rooms of the Pentagon and Kremlin. The final page of this publication includes a bibliography and a suggestion: "If the world is still 'teetering on the brink,' relax and read something more relaxing." The first book underneath this sentence is Philip Agee's *Inside the Company: CIA Diary*. In the October 1979 version of Marks' play about the assassinations, *A Time to Die, A Time to Cry, or, Murders Most Foul!*, the nucleus of Act III is essentially an earlier rendering of this same play. There it appears under the Act III title: "Armageddon and Apocalypse." Marks must have subsequently realized that Act III worked as a separate, stand-alone dramatic piece.

Three Days of Judgment! by Stanley J. and Ethel Marks (Bureau of International Affairs, March 1981). "A three-act play." "A mystery-detective story, written in the form of a trial, that deals with religion" as well as with the CIA and Vatican politics.

The Two Christs or the Decline and Fall of Christianity, by Stanley J. and Ethel Marks (Los Angeles: Bureau of International Affairs, September 1983). *The Two Christs* is based on secret Vatican documents that became available to the public in 1981, some of which expose the Church's dealings with Mussolini, Franco, and Hitler. The author discusses the establishment of Christianity in the Roman Empire as well as the Reagan–Weinberger doctrine of a preventative nuclear first strike against the USSR. Published in the fall of 1983, Marks also explores the contemporaneous fears of nuclear apocalypse and Armageddon, and the possibility of extermination through the use of nuclear weapons and the widespread use of toxic materials.

Judaism Looks at Christianity, 7 B.C.E.–1986, by Stanley J. and Ethel Marks (San Marino, CA: Bureau of International Affairs, 1986). "A bugle call summoning the American populace to withstand the insidious messages used by the 'reborn' fundamentalist leaders that appeal for a nuclear war against the 'evil empire.'"

A Year in the Lives of the Damned! Reagan, Reaganism, 1986 (San Marino, CA: Bureau of International Affairs, 1988). "The format is written in the form of a diary; each month is a chapter."

Jews Judaism and the United States or the Impact of Judaism upon the American People, by Stanley J. and Ethel M. Marks (San Marino, CA: Bureau of International Affairs, 1990).

Yes, Americans, A Conspiracy Murdered JFK!, by Stanley J. and Ethel M. Marks (San Marino, CA: Bureau of International Affairs, June 1992).

The Defeat, Dishonor, and Disgrace! The Reagan–Bush Regimes: 1981-1993, by Stanley J. Marks (Bureau of International Affairs, 1993).

If This Be Treason…! (San Marino, CA: Bureau of International Affairs, 1996). "The truth of how citizens Reagan, Bush, Casey, and their friends betrayed and destroyed the Carter administration in the 1980 presidential election." "Dedicated to those who seek the spirit of truth and the spirit of freedom."

Justice for Whom? Or, Is Justice for WASPs Only? How the WASP Justice System Worked in Five Trials (Los Angeles: Bureau of International Affairs, 1996). ["Five Americans" (including Oswald) "whose criminal or civil trials engaged the attention of millions of people."]

Judgment Day! A Play in Three Acts (registered for copyright in 1997; publication history unknown). A play about Judaism. A photocopy of this 198-page manuscript was retrieved from the Copyright Office on April 3, 2021.

Beginning in 1974, the Markses also authored at least five guide books on business and financial investment.

ESSAYS PUBLISHED BY SJM

Review of *One World* by Wendell Willkie. *Chicago Defender*, April 24, 1943, p. 15.

"War and Warfare" weekly column. Nine articles published in the *Chicago Defender*, May 1, 1943–July 10, 1943.

Review of *The Thousand Year Conspiracy* by Paul Winkler. *Chicago Defender*, May 1, 1943, p. 15.

Review of *Germany's Master Plan* by Borkin and Welsh; and *The Coming Showdown* by Carl Dreher. *Chicago Defender*, May 8, 1943, p. 15.

Review of *Between Thunder and the Sun* by Vincent Sheean; and *Jake Home* by Ruth McKenney. *Chicago Defender*, May 15, 1943, p. 15.

Review of *Capricornia* by Xavier Herbert; and *A Latin American Speaks* by Luis Quintanilla. *Chicago Defender*, 22 May 1943, p. 15.

Review of *Round Trip to Russia* by Walter Graebner; and *Free Men of America* by Ezequiel Padilla. *Chicago Defender*, May 29, 1943, p. 15.

Review of *Journey Among Warriors* by Eve Curie. *Chicago Defender*, June 5, 1943, p. 15.

Review of *Brothers Under the Skin* by Carey McWilliams; *Combined Operations: The Official Story of the Commandos* by Hilary St. George Saunders; and *We Can Win This War* by W. F. Kernan. *Chicago Defender*, June 12, 1943, p. 15.

Review of *The Autobiography of a Curmudgeon* by Harold Ickes. *Chicago Defender*, June 19, 1943, p. 15.

Review of *Moscow Dateline* by Henry C. Cassidy; *Mother Russia* by Maurice Hindus; and *Pursuit of Freedom* by Chicago Civil Liberties Committee. *Chicago Defender*, June 26, 1943, p. 15.

Review of *Attack Can Win in '43* by Max Werner. *Chicago Defender*, July 3, 1943, p. 15.

"An Ode to the Mothers of the 'Chosen People." *California Jewish Voice*, from his feature newspaper column, "All Things Considered." December 31, 1971, p. 15. (Reproduced on p. 306 of SJM's book, *Through Distorted Mirrors!*)

Diogenes weekly political newsletter (self-published), 1984, 1988, 1990.

INDEX

A

A Lie Too Big To Fail, 91, 224
A Year in the Lives of the Damned!, xv, 302
Accessories After the Fact, 204
Adams, Kenneth, 145
Agnew, Spiro Theodore, xli, xlii, 22, 130, 300
Air Force, 140, 256
Alexander, William F., xlvi, 177, 178, 179, 184, 193, 194, 195, 199, 205, 206, 221, 262
Allman, Pierce, 77, 78, 84, 86, 116, 119, 246, 247, 282
Altgens photograph, xlviii, 83, 86, 262, 282
Altgens, James William, 190
Ambassador Hotel, 18, 222
American Broadcasting Company (ABC), xvi, 21, 136
American Rifle Association, 55, 116
American Rifleman magazine, 49
Ananias, xxiv, xxv, xii
Andrews, Dean, 213
Armstrong, Andy, 155, 243
Army, 134, 140, 151, 153, 203, 254, 255, 256, 257
Arnold, Carolyn, 76, 77, 78, 79, 80, 84, 86, 246, 281
Artime, Manuel (né Manuel Artime Buesa), 128
Asia, 207
Associated Press (AP), 52, 136, 216, 242, 245, 253, 259, 262
Attwood, William, 132, 133, 297
Aynesworth, Hugh Grant, xlvi

B

Baker, Marrion L., 77, 170
Barker, W. E., 173
Barnes, W. E., 111, 249
Barry, Bill, 143
Batchelor, Charles, 171, 248
Batista, Fulgencio, 127, 128, 131
Battle, W. Preston, 241, 242
Bay of Pigs, xxxi, 127, 131, 202, 216
Benavides, Domingo, 94, 95, 96, 111, 209, 248
Berkley, George G., 256
Bertrand, Clay. *See* Shaw, Clay
Bethesda Naval Hospital, xxxvi, xliv, 26, 31, 32, 33, 34, 253, 254, 280
Bismarck, Otto Eduard Leopold von, 205
Bleau, Paul, 146

Blum, André Léon, xxxv, 243
Blunt, Malcolm, xvii, xxxi, 190
Bogard, Albert Guy, 156
Boggs, Thomas hale, 108
Bolden, Abraham W., 139
Boone, Eugene Lawrence, xxvi, 39, 45, 68
Boswell, J. Thornton, xliv, 26, 34, 42, 248
Bouhe, George, xlvii
Bowley, Temple Ford, 100, 113, 163, 175, 248
Breach of Trust, xlvi, 77
Brennan, Howard Leslie, xlviii, l, 84, 85, 86, 98, 169, 177, 221, 244, 246, 247, 281
Brewer, Edwin D., 67, 68, 103
Bridgeman, Paul E., 234
Brown, Joseph Blakeney, 242
Bullet 399, l, 35, 36, 37, 38, 40, 41, 120, 190, 247
Bundy, McGeorge ("Mac"), 132

C

Caesar, Gaius Julius, xxix, 124
Capital ("Das Kapital"), xlvii
Carbo, Sergio, 135, 146
Carlin, Karen Lynn, 152
Carousel Club, 147, 148, 151, 155, 181
Carroll, Bob K., 103, 104, 105, 106, 107, 112, 146, 147, 174, 180, 181, 249
Castro, Fidel, xv
Caulk, Jack, 145
Central Intelligence Agency (CIA), xii, xiv, xv, xvi, xviii, xix, xxix, xxx, xxxi, xxxii,
    xxxiii, 36, 41, 78, 90, 119, 122, 125, 127, 128, 129, 130, 131, 132, 133, 134, 135, 136,
    137, 138, 139, 150, 157, 159, 191, 192, 201, 203, 204, 207, 210, 215, 216, 217, 218,
    219, 220, 221, 222, 227, 228, 234, 235, 236, 238, 251, 253, 280, 281, 301
Centro Mondiale Commerciale (CMC), 219, 222
Chavez, Cesar, 225
Cheramie, Rose, 146
Chicago Tribune, xx
China, xxii, xxiii, xli, 131
Christensen, David, 146
Christianity, 129, 131, 169, 301
civil rights, 143, 144, 220, 232
Clark, Ramsey, xxxiii, 138, 210, 212, 213, 215, 216, 219, 220, 221
CMC: The Italian Undercover CIA and Mossad Station and the Assassination of JFK,
    219
Coleman, Kay ("Kathy Kay") Helen, 181, 182
Columbia Broadcasting System (CBS), xvi, xliv, 21, 131, 136, 180, 230, 248
Communism, 14, 145, 204, 205, 206, 227, 251, 252
Connally, John Bowden, xxv, xlviii, xlix, 16, 17, 20, 28, 29, 35, 38, 41, 42, 43, 88, 114,
    115, 117, 139, 140, 146, 147, 148, 149, 151, 153, 157, 159, 176, 177, 179, 251, 262
Cooper, John Sherman, 104

Coroner, xxxiv, 222
Cosa Nostra (Mafia), 140
coup d'état, xiv, xvii
Crafard, Curtis LaVerne, 153, 154, 155, 156, 157
Craig, Roger Dean, 167, 168, 169, 170, 199, 250, 282
Crowe, William D., 152
Cuba, xv, xxii
Cuban Revolutionary Council, 128
Cudahy, John, xx
Cunningham, Cortlandt, 108, 109, 110, 112, 190
Curry, Jesse Edward, 82, 113, 138, 160, 161, 162, 163, 164, 167, 169, 171, 182, 183, 184, 185, 186, 197, 220, 222, 239, 247, 250, 251, 258, 263, 281, 282
Cutchshaw, Wilbur Jay, 188

D

Daily Express (UK), 233
Daily Telegraph (UK), 233, 235
Dale, Alan, xvii, xxxi, 190
Dallas County Criminal Courts and Jail Building, 119, 173
Dallas County Jail Building, 183, 184, 191, 195, 200
Dallas County Records Building, 173
Dallas Morning News, 158, 165, 173, 193, 232, 250, 258, 259
Dallas Police Department, xxvii, xlvii, li, 36, 46, 49, 51, 55, 59, 90, 110, 113, 159, 166, 179, 184, 191, 192, 202
Dallas Times-Herald, 29, 149, 165, 250, 258, 261
Dal-Tex Building, 118, 120, 161, 173
Davenport, R. A., 89, 119, 188
Davis, Barbara Jeanette, 96, 111, 209
Davis, Floyd Guy, 156
Davis, Virginia, 96, 111, 209
Day, John Carl, xxvi, xlix, 31, 39, 45, 46, 54, 55, 56, 57, 58, 59, 60, 61, 62, 66, 67, 68, 69, 74, 75, 86, 120, 177, 221, 238, 247, 252, 259, 261, 281, 302
de Gaulle, Charles, xxix, xxxi, xxxii, 124, 202, 218, 220
de Mohrenschildt, George Sergius, 130, 192, 193, 200, 249
de Mohrenschildt, Jeanne, 192, 193, 200
de Sade, Donatien Alphonse François, 217
Dean, Patrick, 244, 261
Decker, J. E. ("Bill"), 120, 165, 166, 167, 174, 250
Department of Defense, 127, 254
Department of Justice, xxxiii, 138, 210, 211, 212, 213, 215, 222
Destiny Betrayed, 128
dictatorship, xv
DiEugenio, James, 11, xiii, xiv, xxxvii, 74, 128, 218, 242
Dinkin, Eugene Barry, 146
Dorman, Elsie, 173
Double Chek company, 216
double detour, 119, 153, 158, 159, 160, 161, 166, 250, 258

Dougherty, Jack, 64, 244
Douglass, James W., 137
Drain, Vincent, 36, 119
Dreyfus, Alfred, xxi, xxii, xli, xlv, 43, 217, 218
Dulles, Allen, xviii, xxix, xxx, 35, 36, 41, 78, 79, 122, 128, 129, 150, 174, 202

E

Edisen, Adele, 146
Eisenberg, Melvin Aron, 37, 40
Eisenhower, Dwight David "Ike", 101, 127, 207
Epstein, Edward Jay, xlix, 297
Esquire magazine, 172, 249
Europe, xliv, 94, 218, 219
Executive Council of the Inter-American Press Association, 135

F

Farewell America, 142
fascism, xv, xxiii, 218
Federal Bureau of Investigation (FBI), xxxiv, xxxvii, xlvi
Ferrie, David, 90, 137, 204, 212, 227
Finck, Pierre Antoine, 26, 27, 32, 221, 248, 253, 254, 255, 256, 257
Flammonde, Paris, xiii, 136, 219, 250, 297
Force Three, 217, 218
Ford, Gerald Rudolph, xlvii, 195, 198, 297
Ford, Terrance S., 77
Foreman, Percy, 241
Forgive My Grief, 195, 297
Fortune magazine, 160
Frazier, Buell Wesley, 16, 63, 64, 65, 70, 96
Frazier, Robert A., 37, 40
French Resistance, xxi
Fritz, Will, xxvi, 39, 45, 46, 50, 52, 60, 61, 77, 78, 106, 107, 114, 115, 167, 168, 169, 170, 171, 177, 179, 180, 185, 195, 197, 221, 247, 250, 259

G

Gallagher, John, 37
Galloway, Calvin Burrel, 256
Galt, Eric Starvo, 234, 237, 239
Gannaway, W. P., xlvii
Ganser, Danielle, xxxii
Garrison, Jim, xii, xiii, xiv, xvii, xxxi, xxxii, xxxiii, xlvi, 90, 133, 134, 136, 137, 138, 204, 210, 211, 212, 213, 215, 217, 218, 219, 220, 221, 222, 223, 224, 228, 250, 254, 297
German Mauser rifle, xxvi, 39, 45, 46, 47, 51, 52, 53, 156, 169, 253, 280

Germany, xxxv, 204, 243, 303
Giorgio Mantello (aka George Mandel), 218
Givens, Charles, 76
Goldwater, Barry M., 129
Goodwin, Richard, 128
Gopadze, Leon L., 140
Grant, Eva, 141
Greater Philadelphia Magazine, 252
Green Berets, 134
Gregory, Charles Francis, 42
Griffin, J. T., 96, 97
Guantanamo Naval Base, 130, 207

H

Hall, C. Ray, 142, 186
Hall, Loran Eugene, 227, 228
Halpern, Sam, 128
Hancock, Larry, 128
Harriman, W. Averell, 132
Hellinghausen, F. A., xlvii
Helms, Richard McGarrah, 129, 133, 135, 201
Hepburn, James (alias), 142
Hicks, J. B., 56, 66, 68
Hidell alias, 48, 49, 50, 55, 177
Hill, Clinton J., 34
Hill, Gerald Lynn "Jerry", 68, 101, 105, 106, 180, 181
Hilsman, Roger, xxiii
Himmler, Heinrich, 129
Hitler, Adolf, xxxv, 14, 22, 73, 129, 130, 204, 218, 231, 243, 301
Holmes, Harry D., 48, 116
Hoover, J. Edgar, 33, 48, 83, 84, 110, 120, 123, 131, 134, 136, 137, 138, 145, 147, 149, 150, 161, 183, 190, 220, 224, 230, 231, 235, 241, 246, 252, 260, 261, 263, 264, 280, 282
Hosty, James Patrick, 197, 251, 264
House of Representatives Select Committee on Assassinations (HSCA), 300
House Un-American Activities Committee (HUAC), xx
Houston Post, xlvi
Howard, James F. "Mike", 140, 141
Howard, Lisa, 132, 133, 229, 242
Huber, Oscar L., 33
Hubert, Leon D., 191, 192
Hudkins, Alonzo ("Lonnie"), xlvi, 105, 120, 250, 281
Huerta, Dolores, 225
Hughes film, xlviii, 83, 84, 86, 119, 246, 260, 281
Hughes, Robert, 83
Hull, Cordell, xx
Humes, James J., xliv, 26, 27, 32, 34, 41, 42, 247, 248, 251, 254, 256, 257

Humphrey, Hubert Horatio, 223
Hunt, E. Howard, 216
Hunt, Haroldson Lafayette ("Popsie"), 141, 142, 157, 203, 221
Hutson, T. A., 96, 97

I

Immigration and Naturalization Service, 203
International Trade Mart, 111, 112, 113, 158, 218

J

Jacqueline, Kennedy, 148
Jarman, James (Junior), 78, 84, 116, 246
Jarnagin, Carroll, 146, 147, 148, 149, 150, 151, 154, 157, 249
Jefferson, Thomas, 130
JFK and the Unspeakable, 137
Joesten, Joachim, xvii, 241
John Birch Society, 141, 144, 145, 157, 202, 203
Johnsen, Richard E., 36, 37, 119
Johnson, Lyndon Baines, xvi, xvii, xliv, 22, 129, 133, 135, 136, 138, 141, 149, 162, 171, 203, 206, 207, 210, 212, 253
Johnson, Marvin, 67, 68
Johnston, David L., 50, 177, 178, 179, 221
Jones, Penn, l, 195, 297
Journal of the American Medical Association, 27

K

Kantor, Seth, 142, 147, 152, 181, 193, 253
Kellerman, Roy Herman, 28, 34, 244
Kennedy, John F., 11, xiv, xv, xvi, xvii, xxi, xxiii, xxiv, xxv, xxix, xxx, xxxi, xxxvi, xli, xlii, xliii, xlv, xlviii, xlix, l, xii, 14, 16, 17, 18, 19, 20, 21, 22, 25, 26, 28, 29, 32, 33, 35, 40, 41, 43, 44, 45, 50, 51, 58, 65, 69, 71, 81, 86, 88, 92, 103, 106, 113, 114, 115, 116, 117, 118, 119, 123, 124, 125, 126, 127, 129, 130, 131, 132, 133, 134, 135, 136, 137, 139, 140, 141, 142, 143, 144, 145, 147, 148, 149, 151, 153, 154, 157, 161, 162, 169, 174, 176, 177, 178, 179, 181, 182, 183, 186, 190, 191, 193, 194, 195, 197, 198, 200, 202, 203, 204, 205, 207, 208, 210, 212, 213, 214, 215, 216, 221, 222, 223, 224, 227, 228, 229, 231, 232, 238, 243, 246, 247, 251, 252, 254, 258, 261, 262, 263, 264, 280, 281, 299, 300
Kennedy, Regis, 215
Kennedy, Robert F., xii, xiv, xxxii, 18, 91, 132, 133, 134, 145, 161, 222, 223, 224, 225, 226, 227, 230, 231, 258, 299
Kenney, Edward C., 256
Kilgallen, Dorothy, 215, 229, 230
King, Glen D., 108

King, Martin Luther, xii, xiv, xxxii, xxxv, 113, 123, 134, 145, 227, 230, 231, 232, 233, 237, 238, 241, 242, 258, 263, 299
Klein's Sporting Goods, 47, 48, 49, 50, 51, 55, 177
Krystinik, Raymond Franklin, 198, 249
Ku Klux Klan, 141, 157, 202
Kunkel, Charles Edward, 140
Kunkin, Art, 218

L

La Devoir, 219
Lane, Mark, xiii, xxii, l, 46, 204, 215
Latitudes magazine, 250
Latona, Sebastian F., 59, 60, 61, 74, 75
Leavelle, James R., xxviii, 108, 244
Lechuga, Carlos, 132
Liberation News Service, 224
Library of Congress, 300
Lidice, 129
Liebeler, Wesley J., 190
Life magazine, 51, 52, 53, 62, 116, 245, 259
Litchfield, Wilbyrn Waldon (Robert), 152
Lone Star Steel Company, 203
Look magazine, 122, 232, 240
Los Angeles Free Press, 217, 218, 226, 228
Los Angeles Police Department, 229
Lovelady, Billy, xlix, 82, 83, 84, 86, 120, 221, 246, 262, 282
LSD, xxvii, 72, 90
Lucy, Forest L., 74, 75

M

Mabra, W. W. "Bo", 171, 249
Manchester, William, 205, 206, 297
Mannlicher-Carcano rifle, xxvi, 38, 39, 45, 46, 47, 48, 51, 52, 53, 54, 59, 63, 64, 65, 115, 116
Marcuse, Herbert, xxv
Marine Corps, 116, 191, 250
Markham, Helen L., 93, 94, 95, 98, 99, 100, 109, 209, 248
Martin, Frank M., 191, 192, 199
Martino, John, 146
Marx, Karl, xlvii
Mary Ferrell Foundation, 135
Mauldin, Shirley, 147
Maxey, Billy Joe, 185, 244
Maynard, Harry, 137
McCabe, John A., 54
McCarren Act (Internal Security Act), 130

McClelland, Robert Nelson, 33
McCloud, Lee, 145
McDonald, Maurice N., 19, 103, 104, 105, 106, 107, 114, 115, 116, 120, 174, 180, 181, 248, 249
McGarry, Terrance, 185
McGinley, Michael Conde, 145
McKnight, Gerald D., xlvi, 77
Meagher, Sylvia, xiii, l, 204, 297
Melanson, Philip H., 234
Meller, Anna, xlvii
Memphis Police Department, 238, 263
Metta, Michele, 219
Miami News, 143, 250
Miami Police Department, 157
Mideast, 131
Milteer, Joseph, 139, 145, 146
mind control, 90
Miss Howard, 132
Mitchell, John Newton, xlii, 130, 300
MK-ULTRA, 90
Montgomery, Leslie Dell, 67, 68
Mooney, Luke, xxvi, 39, 45, 68
Mooney, Nancy Jane ("Betty MacDonald"), 192, 195, 200
Moore, Edward E., 89, 249
Moore, Elmer W., 28
Moorman film and photographs, 173
Morley, Jefferson, 201
Mudd, F. Lee, 173
Murder Most Foul!, 11, xiv, xvii, xviii, xxii, xxv, xxvii, 137, 148, 219, 299
Murphy, George Lloyd, 72, 73, 129
Mussolini, Benito, 301

N

Nagell, Richard Case, 146
Nagy, Ferenc, 218
National Archives, xlii, xliii, xlvii, xii, 15, 20, 22, 26, 28, 34, 42, 45, 46, 47, 48, 51, 55, 56, 57, 66, 69, 70, 76, 77, 79, 82, 83, 89, 93, 96, 100, 113, 123, 139, 141, 146, 148, 149, 150, 152, 158, 162, 168, 173, 181, 184, 185, 187, 212, 221, 244, 247, 251, 252
National Broadcasting Company (NBC), xvi, 21, 180, 230, 253
National Enquirer, 227, 228
National Guard, 211
national interests, xiv, xli, 35, 87, 134
national security, xvii, l, 50, 99, 117, 133, 201
National Security Council, xxxi, 133
Navy, 42, 203, 255, 256
Nazis, xx, xxi, 22, 218, 220, 222
New York Herald-Tribune, xxxvi, 32, 83, 206

New York Journal, 229
New York Post, 213
New York Times, 32, 133, 212, 233, 247, 253
New York World-Telegram, 82
Newman, John, xvii, xxxi
Newton, Michael, 146
Nicol, Joseph D., 37, 38, 39, 40, 247
Nix film, 172, 173, 249
Nixon, Richard Milhous, xli, xlii, 14, 22, 130, 140, 208, 223, 252, 300
Noguchi, Thomas, xxxiv, 222, 223
North Atlantic Treaty Organization (NATO), xv, 203
Novel, Gordon, 215, 216, 217

O

O'Donnell, Kenneth P., 149
O'Neill, Francis X., 35, 247
Odio, Silvia, 146
Odum, Bardwell D., 37, 46
Office of Naval Intelligence (ONI), 203
oil depletion allowance, 132, 143
Olsen, Harry, 181, 182
On the Trail of the Assassins, 219
Operation 40, 128
Organisation Armée Secrète (OAS), 218
Oser, Alvin V., 255
Oswald, Lee Harvey, xxi, xxiii, xxiv, xxv, xxvi, xxvii, xxviii, xxix, xxx, xxxiii, xxxiv, xxxv, xlii, xliii, xliv, xlv, xlvi, xlvii, xlviii, xlix, l, xii, 13, 14, 15, 16, 17, 18, 19, 20, 21, 22, 25, 26, 28, 30, 33, 34, 38, 39, 42, 43, 44, 45, 47, 48, 49, 50, 51, 52, 53, 54, 55, 56, 58, 59, 60, 61, 62, 63, 64, 65, 69, 70, 71, 72, 73, 74, 75, 76, 77, 78, 79, 80, 81, 82, 83, 84, 85, 86, 88, 89, 90, 91, 92, 93, 94, 95, 96, 97, 98, 99, 100, 101, 102, 103, 104, 105, 106, 107, 108, 109, 110, 111, 112, 113, 114, 115, 116, 117, 118, 119, 120, 122, 126, 130, 131, 134, 135, 136, 137, 140, 147, 148, 149, 150, 151, 152, 153, 154, 155, 156, 157, 159, 161, 162, 163, 164, 165, 166, 167, 168, 169, 170, 173, 174, 175, 176, 177, 178, 179, 180, 181, 182, 183, 184, 185, 186, 187, 188, 189, 190, 191, 193, 194, 196, 197, 198, 199, 200, 203, 204, 205, 209, 212, 213, 214, 215, 217, 222, 233, 239, 240, 243, 244, 245, 246, 247, 248, 250, 251, 252, 253, 258, 259, 260, 262, 263, 264, 280, 281, 282, 283, 302
Oswald, Marguerite, 140
Oswald, Marina, xlvii, 47, 97, 102, 118, 140, 174, 197, 198, 252

P

Paesa Sera, 219
Paine, Michael, xxx, 198, 199
Paine, Ruth, xxix, xxx, 16, 47, 51, 52, 53, 54, 70, 106, 120, 149, 153, 154, 168, 170, 193, 196, 197, 198, 199, 221, 244, 251
Palamara, Vincent, 140

Parkland Memorial Hospital, xxxv, 26, 30, 31, 33, 34, 38, 39, 113, 119, 120, 162, 164, 169, 170, 171, 187, 193, 251, 261
Parks, P. M., xlvii, 174
Patterson, Robert K., 153
Pearson, Andrew Russell "Drew", 133, 134
Pease, Lisa, 91, 224
Permindex, 217, 219, 222
Perry, Malcolm, xxxvi, xxxvii, 30, 31, 253
Pierce, Rio Sam, 185
Piper, Edward, 78, 84, 217, 246
Playboy magazine, 90, 133, 136, 217, 251, 297
Plotkin, Stephen, 216
Poe, J. M. ("Joe"), 111
Popkin, Richard, 148, 204, 298
Price, Charles Jack, 119, 187
Price, J. C., 172
Price, Malcolm Howard, 156
protective arrest, 130
Prouty, Fletcher, xii
Putman, James A., 185

R

Ramparts magazine, 136, 184, 231, 298
Randle, Linnie Mae, 63, 64, 65, 70
Rankin, James Lee, l, 131, 135, 162, 201, 220, 280
Ray, James Earl, xxxiii, 145, 209, 218, 230, 231, 232, 233, 234, 235, 236, 237, 238, 239, 240, 242, 263
Ray, Manolo, 128
Reagan, Ronald Wilson, 73, 129, 301, 302
Reddin, Thomas, 226
religion, 299, 301
Revill, Jack, xlvii, 264
Rhodes, James Allen, 211
Roberts, Earlene, 50, 98, 99, 107, 167, 194, 210, 242
Robinson, Marvin C., 168, 170, 199, 250
Roosevelt, Theodore, xxv
Rose, Guy, 54, 89, 90, 91
Rowley, J. J., 37
Ruby, Jack, 36, 90, 91, 119, 140, 141, 142, 146, 147, 148, 149, 150, 151, 152, 153, 154, 155, 157, 161, 163, 180, 181, 182, 183, 184, 185, 186, 187, 188, 189, 191, 192, 193, 194, 195, 198, 203, 215, 229, 244, 252, 253
Russell, Bertrand, xxi
Russell, Richard, xliv, li, 249

S

Salandria, Vincent, xiii

Sanjenis, Luis, 128
Saratogian, 225
Saturday Evening Post, 172
Sauvage, Leo, xxv, 18
Schacht, Hjalmar (né Horace Greeley Hjalmar Schacht), 218
Schlesinger, Arthur, 128
Schrade, Paul, 225, 226
Scoggins, William Henry, 102, 109
Scotland Yard, 234, 235, 236, 237, 238
Scott, Peter Dale, xiii
Secret Service, xxiv, xlv, xlvi, xlvii, xlix, li, 26, 28, 34, 35, 36, 37, 40, 42, 43, 47, 49, 55, 56, 68, 70, 77, 78, 81, 83, 84, 86, 89, 90, 91, 94, 97, 105, 108, 110, 112, 113, 115, 117, 118, 119, 120, 125, 126, 138, 140, 143, 144, 149, 158, 159, 160, 161, 162, 167, 169, 171, 172, 183, 186, 200, 203, 208, 221, 227, 242, 244, 247, 248, 249, 250, 251, 252, 258, 262, 280, 281, 282
    Protective Research Section (PRS) and, **138, 143, 144**
Senator, George, 184, 244
Shaw, Clay, xiii, xiv, xxxii, xxxiii, xliv, 21, 27, 136, 137, 138, 210, 211, 212, 213, 214, 215, 216, 217, 218, 219, 220, 221, 222, 248, 253, 254, 256
Shaw, Robert R., xxxv, xxxvi, 30, 32, 41, 42
Shelley, William, 83, 246, 262, 282
Sherman, Mary S., 90
Shires, George Thomas, 41, 42
Sibert, James W., 247, 280
Sims, Richard, 56, 67, 68
Sirhan, Sirhan Bishara, xxxiii, xxxiv, 209, 222, 223, 224, 225, 227, 228, 229, 230
Smith, Joe Marshall, 171, 172
Smith, Margaret, 229, 230
Smith, Matthew, 204
Sneyd, Ramon George, 234, 235, 236, 237, 238
Someone Would Have Talked, 128
Somersett, William, 139, 145
Sorrels, Forrest V., 81, 82, 83, 84, 86, 119, 247, 281
South America, 131
Soviet Union (USSR), xv, xxii, xli, 14, 117, 130, 131, 193, 203, 204, 205, 206, 207, 228, 281, 299, 303, 304
Special Branch (UK), 210, 234, 235, 236, 237, 238
Specter, Arlen, l, 35, 36, 38, 190, 251
Sports Drome Rifle Range, 156
Stalin, Joseph, 29, 231
State Department, xx
States' Rights Party, 139, 143
Steadman, Martin J., xxxv, xxxvi, xxxvii, 30, 31, 32
Stevenson, Adlai Ewing, 132, 160
Studebaker, Robert Lee, 56, 67, 68, 69, 71, 74, 75, 221, 259, 260, 261
Summers, Anthony, xiii, xiv
Summers, H. W., 101, 102, 103
Sweatt, Allan, xlvi, 105, 120, 250

T

Tague, James, 29
Talbot, David, xxxii
Tardieu, Tardieu, xx, xxi, 22
Tasker, Harry, 185
Taylor, Gary E., 192, 193, 200, 249
Taylor, Warren, 174
Terminal Annex Building, 172
Texas School Book Depository, xxv, 13, 16, 17, 25, 28, 43, 63, 65, 70, 76, 77, 78, 81, 82, 83, 84, 86, 103, 111, 112, 113, 116, 118, 161, 165, 167, 168, 169, 172, 173, 175, 181, 196, 258, 259, 262, 281, 282
Texas Theatre, 88, 101, 102, 103, 106, 112, 113, 114, 163, 164, 174, 180, 193, 194
The Ananias Club, xxiv, xxv, 59
The Death of a President, 205
The Devil is in the Details: Alan Dale with Malcolm Blunt, xvii
The Establishment, xiv, xv, 214, 220
The James Earl Ray Hoax: The Greatest Police Fraud Ever, 241
The Kennedy Conspiracy, 136, 219, 297
The Martin Luther King Assassination, 234
The National States Rights Party: A History, 146
The Reds and the Blacks, 132
The Ruby Cover-up, 147, 152, 181
The Second Oswald, 148, 204, 298
The Secret Team, xii
Thompson, Josiah, xiii, xiv
Through Distorted Mirrors!, xxv, 300, 304
Tice, Wilma, 253
Time-Life, 242
Tippit, J. D., xxvi, xxvii, xxviii, xxxiv, l, 17, 19, 20, 21, 44, 47, 88, 89, 90, 91, 92, 93, 94, 95, 96, 97, 98, 99, 100, 101, 102, 103, 105, 106, 107, 108, 109, 110, 111, 112, 113, 114, 115, 116, 117, 118, 120, 138, 141, 154, 162, 163, 164, 167, 172, 174, 175, 176, 177, 178, 182, 188, 191, 193, 194, 198, 200, 209, 233, 248, 249, 251, 264
Todd, Elmer L., 37, 40
Tomlinson, Darrell C., 37, 38, 39, 40, 190
Toynbee, Arnold, xxv
Truly, Roy, 80, 196, 197
Truman, Harry S., 126, 130
Two Days of Infamy, xii, xviii, xx, xxxv, 18, 148, 219, 223, 299

U

U.S. Supreme Court, xliii, 21, 30, 49, 214
U.S. World News, 36
United Auto Workers (UAW), 225
United Press International (UPI), 52, 185, 247, 259, 261
United States, 11, xv, xxii, xxxiv

V

Vallejo, Rene, 132
Varona, Manuel ("Tony"), 128
Vaughn, Roy E., 185, 244
Vietnam, xli, 129, 131, 134, 208

W

Wade, Henry Menasco, 45, 47, 61, 127, 141, 146, 149, 150, 151, 179, 197, 206, 220
Walker, Edwin A., 17, 19, 21, 53, 88, 114, 115, 116, 142, 244
Wall Street Journal, 144
Wallacites, 144
Walter, William, 137, 250
Walthers, Eddy Raymond (Buddy), 105, 106, 120, 197, 199, 261
Warren Commission, 5, xii, xiii, xvii, xviii, xxi, xxiii, xxv, xxvi, xxvii, xxviii, xxxv,
  xxxvi, xxxvii, xli, xlii, xliii, xliv, xlv, xlviii, xlix, l, xii, 13, 14, 15, 19, 20, 21, 24, 25,
  27, 28, 29, 34, 38, 39, 41, 46, 49, 50, 52, 53, 54, 57, 58, 59, 65, 66, 71, 73, 76, 79, 81,
  84, 86, 88, 92, 93, 97, 99, 112, 114, 117, 121, 122, 123, 126, 135, 139, 140, 142, 143,
  144, 146, 147, 148, 149, 150, 152, 154, 155, 156, 157, 158, 159, 160, 164, 169, 173,
  176, 178, 182, 185, 187, 191, 193, 195, 201, 202, 204, 206, 214, 220, 221, 222, 228,
  238, 243, 247, 258, 262, 263, 280, 281, 297, 299
Warren, Earl, xliii, 30, 183, 195
Washington Monument, 134
Washington Post, 203
Washington Star, 253
Washington, George, xxx, 129
Watch What We Do ... Not What We Say!, xlii
Watson, James C., 244
Watson, W. Marvin, 203
Weisberg, Harold, xiii, xiv, xlviii, l, 204, 298
Weisel, William ("Woody"), 225, 226
Weitzman, Seymour, 39, 45, 46, 68, 172, 252, 280
West, Louis Jolyon ("Jolly"), 90, 91
West, Robert, 28
West, Troy Eugene, 64, 65
Westbrook, William R., 96, 190, 248
Westphal, R. W., 174
White Citizens' Council, 141, 144, 157
White, William S., xvi, 135, 136
Whitewash, 204
Willard, John, 234
Willens, Howard P., 201, 280
Williams, Bonnie Ray, 78, 79, 80, 81, 86, 166, 173, 244, 246, 261
Williams, J. Doyle, 37, 119
Williams, Jerry, 238
Willis, Billy Joe, 152
Wolfer, DeWayne, 224

Wood, Homer, 156
Wood, Sterling Charles, 156
Wright, O. P., 37

Y

Yes, Americans, A Conspiracy Murdered JFK!, xix, xxx, 139, 302
Yockey, Ross, 134
Yorty, Samuel William, 226, 230

Z

Zachary, N. E., 238
Zapruder film, 33, 280

www.ingramcontent.com/pod-product-compliance
Lightning Source LLC
Chambersburg PA
CBHW030902080526
44589CB00010B/105